Advanced Perl Programming

The Perl Series

Advanced Perl Programming
Learning Perl
Learning Perl on Win32 Systems
Perl 5 Desktop Reference
Programming Perl

Also by O'Reilly

Mastering Regular Expressions
CGI Programming on the World Wide Web
Web Client Programming with Perl

Advanced Perl Programming

Sriram Srinivasan

O'REILLY™

Cambridge · Köln · Paris · Sebastopol · Tokyo

Advanced Perl Programming
by Sriram Srinivasan

Copyright © 1997 O'Reilly & Associates, Inc. All rights reserved.
Printed in the United States of America.

Published by O'Reilly & Associates, Inc., 101 Morris Street, Sebastopol, CA 95472.

Editors: Andy Oram and Steve Talbott

Production Editor: Jane Ellin

Printing History:

> August 1997:   First Edition

This book is printed on acid-free paper with 85% recycled content, 15% post-consumer waste. O'Reilly & Associates is committed to using paper with the highest recycled content available consistent with high quality.

ISBN: 1-56592-220-4   [12/97]

Table of Contents

Preface

Errors, like straws, upon the surface flow;
He who would search for pearls must dive below.

—John Dryden,
All for Love, Prologue

This book has two goals: to make you a Perl expert, and, at a broader level, to supplement your current arsenal of techniques and tools for crafting applications. It covers advanced features of the Perl language, teaches you how the `perl` interpreter works, and presents areas of modern computing technology such as networking, user interfaces, persistence, and code generation.

You will not merely dabble with language syntax or the APIs of different modules as you read this book. You will spend just as much time dealing with real-world issues such as avoiding deadlocks during remote procedure calls and switching smoothly between data storage using a flat file or a database. Along the way, you'll become comfortable with such Perl techniques as run-time evaluation, nested data structures, objects, and closures.

This book expects you to know the essentials of Perl—a minimal subset, actually; you must be conversant with the basic data types (scalars, arrays, and hashes), regular expressions, subroutines, basic control structures (`if`, `while`, `unless`, `for`, `foreach`), file I/O, and standard variables such as `@ARGV` and `$_`. Should this not be the case, I recommend Randal Schwartz and Tom Christiansen's excellent tutorial, *Learning Perl*, Second Edition.

The book—in particular, this preface—substantiates two convictions of mine.

The first is that a two-language approach is most appropriate for tackling typical large-application projects: a scripting language (such as Perl, Visual Basic, Python, or Tcl) in conjunction with a systems programming language (C, C++, Java). A scripting language has weak compile-time type checking, has high-level data structures (for instance, Perl's hash table is a fundamental type; C has no such thing), and does not typically have a separate compilation-linking phase. A systems programming language is typically closer to the operating system, has fine-grained data types (C has short, int, long, unsigned int, float, double, and so on, whereas Perl has a scalar data type), and is typically faster than interpreted languages. Perl spans the language spectrum to a considerable degree: It performs extremely well as a scripting language, yet gives you low-level access to operating system API, is much faster than Java (as this book goes to press), and can optionally be compiled.

The distinction between scripting and systems programming languages is a contentious one, but it has served me well in practice. This point will be underscored in the last three chapters of the book (on extending Perl, embedding Perl, and Perl internals).

I believe that neither type of language is properly equipped to handle sophisticated application projects satisfactorily on its own, and I hope to make the case for Perl and C/C++ as the two-language combination mentioned earlier. Of course, it would be most gratifying, or *totally tubular*, as the local kids are wont to say, if the design patterns and lessons learned in this book help you even if you were to choose other languages.

The second conviction of mine is that to deploy effective applications, it is not enough just to know the language syntax well. You must know, in addition, the internals of the language's environment, and you must have a solid command of technology areas such as networking, user interfaces, databases, and so forth (specially issues that transcend language-specific libraries).

Let's look at these two points in greater detail.

The Case for Scripting

I started my professional life building entire applications in assembler, on occasion worrying about trying to save 100 bytes of space and optimizing away that one extra instruction. C and PL/M changed my world view. I found myself getting a chance to reflect on the application as a whole, on the life-cycle of the project, and on how it was being used by the end-user. Still, where efficiency was paramount, as was the case for interrupt service routines, I continued with assembler. (Looking back, I suspect that the PL/M compiler could generate far better assembly code than I, but my vanity would have prevented such an admission.)

My applications' requirements continued to increase in complexity; in addition to dealing with graphical user interfaces, transactions, security, network transparency, and heterogeneous platforms, I began to get involved in designing software architectures for problems such as aircraft scheduling and network management. My own efficiency had become a much more limiting factor than that of the applications. While object orientation was making me more effective at the design level, the implementation language, C++, and the libraries and tools available weren't helping me raise my level of programming. I was still dealing with low-level issues such as constructing frameworks for dynamic arrays, meta-data, text manipulation, and memory management. Unfortunately, environments such as Eiffel, Smalltalk, and the NeXT system that dealt with these issues effectively were never a very practical choice for my organization. You might understand why I have now become a raucous cheerleader for Java as the application development language of choice. The story doesn't end there, though.

Lately, the realization has slowly crept up on me that I have been ignoring two big time-sinks at either end of a software life-cycle. At the designing end, sometimes the only way to clearly understand the problem is to create an electronic storyboard (prototype). And later, once the software is implemented, users are always persnickety (er, discerning) about everything they can *see*, which means that even simple form-based interfaces are constantly tweaked and new types of reports are constantly requested. And, of course, the sharper developers wish to move on to the next project as soon as the software is implemented. These are occasions when scripting languages shine. They provide quick turnaround, dynamic user interfaces, terrific facilities for text handling, run-time evaluation, and good connections to databases and networks. Best of all, they don't need prima donna programmers to baby-sit them. You can focus your attention on making the application much more user-centric, instead of trying to figure out how to draw a pie chart using Xlib's* lines and circles.

Clearly, it is not practical to develop complex applications in a scripting language alone; you still want to retain features such as performance, fine-grained data structures, and type safety (crucial when many programmers are working on one problem). This is why I am now an enthusiastic supporter of using scripting languages *along with* C/C++ (or Java when it becomes practical in terms of performance). Many people have been reaping enormous benefits from this *component-based* approach, in which the components are written in C and woven together using a scripting language. Just ask any of the zillions of Visual Basic, Power-Builder, Delphi, Tcl, and Perl programmers—or, for that matter, Microsoft Office and Emacs users.

---

* X Windows Library. Someone once mentioned that programming X Windows is like taking the square root of a number using Roman numerals!

For a much more informed and eloquent (not to mention controversial) testimonial to the scripting approach, please read the paper by Dr. John Ousterhout,* available at *http://www.sunlabs.com/people/john.ousterhout*.

For an even better feel for this argument, play with the Tcl plug-in for Netscape (from the same address), take a look at the sources for Tcl applets ("Tclets"), and notice how compactly you can solve simple problems. A 100-line applet for a calculator, including the UI? I suspect that an equivalent Java applet would not take fewer than 800 lines and would be far less flexible.

Why Perl?

So why Perl, then, and not Visual Basic, Tcl, or Python?

Although Visual Basic is an excellent choice on a Wintel† PC, it's not around on any other platform, so it has not been a practical choice for me.

Tcl forces me to go to C much earlier than I want, primarily because of data and code-structuring reasons. Tcl's performance has never been the critical factor for me because I have always implicitly accounted for the fact and apportioned only the non-performance-critical code to it. I recommend Brian Kernighan's paper "Experience with Tcl/Tk for Scientific and Engineering Visualization," for his comments on Tcl and Visual Basic. It is available at *http://inferno.bell-labs.com/cm/ cs/who/bwk*.

Most Tcl users are basically hooked on the Tk user interface toolkit; count me among them. Tk also works with Perl, so I get the best part of that environment to work with a language of my choice.

I am an unabashed admirer of Python, a scripting language developed by Guido Van Rossum (please see *http://www.python.org/*). It has a clean syntax and a nice object-oriented model, is thread-safe, has tons of libraries, and interfaces extremely well with C. I prefer Perl (to Python) more for practical than for engineering reasons. On the engineering side, Perl is fast and is unbeatable when it comes to text support. It is also highly idiomatic, which means that Perl code tends to be far more compact than any other language. The last one is not necessarily a good thing, depending on your point of view (especially a Pythoner's); however, all these criteria do make it an excellent tool-building language. (See Chapter 17, *Template-Driven Code Generation*, for an example). On the other hand, there are a lot of things going for Python, and I urge you to take a serious

---

* Inventor of Tcl (Tool Command Language, pronounced "tickle").

† Wintel: The Microsoft Windows + Intel combination. I'll henceforth use the term "PC" for this particular combination and explicitly mention Linux and the Mac when I mean those PCs.

look at it. Mark Lutz's book *Programming Python* (O'Reilly, 1996) gives a good treatment of the language and libraries.

On the practical side, your local bookstore and the job listings in the newspaper are good indicators of Perl's popularity. Basically, this means that it is easy to hire Perl programmers or get someone to learn the language in a hurry. I'd wager that more than 95% of the programmers haven't even *heard* of Python. 'Tis unfortunate but true.

It is essential that you play with these languages and draw your own conclusions; after all, the observations in the preceding pages are colored by my experiences and expectations. As Byron Langenfeld observed, "Rare is the person who can weigh the faults of others without putting his thumb on the scales." Where appropriate, this book contrasts Perl with Tcl, Python, C++, and Java on specific features to emphasize that the choice of a language or a tool is never a firm, black-and-white decision and to show that mostly what you can do with one language, you can do with another too.

What Must I Know?

To use Perl effectively in an application, you must be conversant with three aspects:

- The *language syntax* and *idioms* afforded by the language.
- The *Perl interpreter* for writing C extensions for your Perl scripts or embedding the Perl interpreter in your C/C++ applications.
- *Technology issues* such as networking, user interfaces, the Web, and persistence.

Figure 1 shows a map of the topics dealt with in this book. Each major aspect listed above is further classified. The rest of this section presents a small blurb about each topic and the corresponding chapter where the subject is detailed. The discussion is arranged by topic rather than by the sequence in which the chapters appear.

Language Syntax

Pointers or references bring an enormous sophistication to the type of data structures you can create with a language. Perl's support for references and its ability to let you code without having to specify every single step makes it an especially powerful language. For example, you can create something as elaborate as an

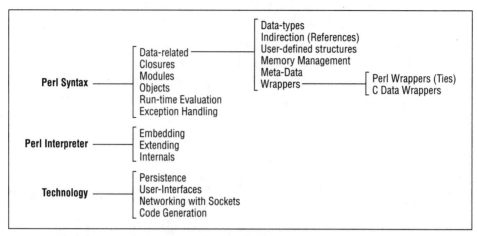

Figure 1. Classification of topics covered in this book

array of hashes of arrays* all in a single line. Chapter 1, *Data References and Anonymous Storage*, introduces you to references and what Perl does internally for memory management. Chapter 2, *Implementing Complex Data Structures*, exercises the syntax introduced in the earlier chapter with a few practical examples.

Perl supports references to subroutines and a powerful construct called closures, which, as LISPers know, is essentially an unnamed subroutine that carries its environment around with it. This facility and its concomitant idioms will be clarified and put to good use in Chapter 4, *Subroutine References and Closures*.

References are only one way of obtaining indirection. Scalars can contain embedded pointers to native C data structures. This subject is covered in Chapter 20, *Perl Internals*. Ties represent an alternative case of indirection: All Perl values can optionally trigger specific Perl subroutines when they are created, accessed, or destroyed. This aspect is discussed in Chapter 9, *Tie*.

Filehandles, directory handles, and formats aren't quite first-class data types; they cannot be assigned to one another or passed as parameters, and you cannot create local versions of them. In Chapter 3, *Typeglobs and Symbol Tables*, we study why we want these facilities in the first place and the work-arounds to achieve them. This chapter focuses on a somewhat hidden data type called a typeglob and its internal representation, the understanding of which is crucial for obtaining information about the state of the interpreter (*meta-data*) and for creating convenient aliases.

Now let's turn to language issues not directly related to Perl data types.

---

* We'll henceforth refer to indexed lists/arrays as "arrays" and associative arrays as "hashes" to avoid confusion.

Perl supports exception handling, including asynchronous exceptions (the ability to raise user-defined exception from signal handlers). As it happens, `eval` is used for trapping exceptions as well as for run-time evaluation, so Chapter 5, *Eval*, does double-duty explaining these distinct, yet related, topics.

Chapter 6, *Modules*, details Perl's support for modular programming, including features such as run-time binding (in which the procedure to be called is known only at run-time), inheritance (Perl's ability to transparently use a subroutine from another class), and autoloading (trapping accesses to functions that don't exist and doing something meaningful). Chapter 7, *Object-Oriented Programming*, takes modules to the next logical step: making modules reusable not only from the viewpoint of a library user, but also from that of a developer adding more facets to the library.

Perl supports run-time evaluation: the ability to treat character strings as little Perl programs and dynamically evaluate them. Chapter 5 introduces the `eval` keyword and some examples of how this facility can be used, but its importance is truly underscored in later chapters, where it is used in such diverse areas as SQL query evaluation (Chapter 11, *Implementing Object Persistence*), code generation (Chapter 17, *Template-Driven Code Generation*), and dynamic generation of accessor functions for object attributes (Chapter 8, *Object Orientation: The Next Few Steps*).

The Perl Interpreter

Three chapters are devoted to working with and understanding the Perl interpreter. There are two main reasons for delving into this internal aspect of Perl. One is to extend Perl, by which I mean adding a C module that can do things for which Perl is not well-suited or is not fast enough. The other is to embed Perl in C, so that a C program can invoke Perl for a specific task such as handling a regular expression substitution, which you may not want to code up in C.

Chapter 18, *Extending Perl: A First Course*, presents two tools (`xsubpp` and `SWIG`) to create custom dynamically loadable C libraries for *extending* the Perl interpreter.

Chapter 19, *Embedding Perl: The Easy Way*, presents an easy API that was developed for this book to enable you to embed the interpreter without having to worry about the internals of Perl.

But if you really want to know what is going on underneath or want to develop powerful extensions, Chapter 20 should quench your thirst (or drown you in detail, depending on your perspective).

Technology Areas

I am of the opinion that an applications developer should master at least the following six major technology areas: user interfaces, persistence, interprocess communication and networking, parsing and code generation, the Web, and the operating system. This book presents detailed explanations of the first four topics (in Chapters 10 through 17). Instead of just presenting the API of publicly available modules, the book starts with real problems and develops useful solutions, including appropriate Perl packages. For example, Chapter 13, *Networking: Implementing RPC*, explains the implementation of an RPC toolkit that avoids deadlocks even if two processes happen to call each other at the same time. As another example, Chapter 11, *Implementing Object Persistence*, develops an "adaptor" to transparently send a collection of objects to a persistent store of your choice (relational database, plain file, or DBM file) and implements querying on all of them.

This book does not deal with operating system specific issues, partly because Perl hides a tremendous number of these differences and partly because these details will distract us from the core themes of the book. Practically all the code in this book is OS-neutral.

I have chosen to ignore web-related issues and, more specifically, CGI. This is primarily because there are numerous books* and tutorials on CGI scripting with Perl that do more justice to this subject than the limited space on this book can afford. In addition, developers of most interesting CGI applications will spend much more time with the concepts presented in this book than with the simple details of the CGI protocol per se.

The Book's Approach

You have not bought this book just to see a set of features. For that, free online documentation would suffice. I want to convey practical problem-solving techniques that use appropriate features, along with the foundations of the technology areas mentioned in the previous section.

A Note to the Expert

This book takes a tutorial approach to explaining bits and pieces of Perl syntax, making the need felt for a particular concept or facility before explaining how Perl fills the void. Experienced people who don't need the justifications for any facilities or verbose examples will likely benefit by first taking a look at Appendix B, *Syntax*

---

* Refer to Shishir Gundavaram's book *CGI Programming on the World Wide Web* (O'Reilly)

Summary, to quickly take in all the syntactic constructs and idioms described in this book and go to the appropriate explanations should the need arise.

It is my earnest hope that the chapters on technology, embedding, extending, and Perl interpreter internals (the non-syntax-related ones) will be useful to the casual user and expert alike.

Systems View

This book tends to take the systems view of things; most chapters have a section explaining what is really going on inside. I believe that you can never be a good programmer if you know only the syntax of the language but not how the compilation or run-time environment is implemented. For example, a C programmer must know that it is a bad idea for a function to return the address of a local variable (and the reason for this restriction), and a Java programmer should know why a thread may never get control in a uniprocessor setup even if it is not blocked.

In addition, knowing how everything works from the ground up results in a *permanent* understanding of the facilities. People who know the etymology of words have much less trouble maintaining an excellent vocabulary.

Examples

Perl is a highly idiomatic language, full of redundant features.* While I'm as enthusiastic as the next person about cool and bizarre ways of exploiting a language,† the book is not a compendium of gee-whiz features; it sticks to the minimal subset of Perl that is required to develop powerful applications.

In presenting the example code, I have also sacrificed efficiency and compactness for readability.

FTP

If you have an Internet connection (permanent or dialup), the easiest way to use FTP is via your web browser or favorite FTP client. To get the examples, simply point your browser to:

ftp://ftp.oreilly.com/published/oreilly/nutshell/advanced_perl/examples.tar.gz

---

* There are hundreds of ways of printing "Just Another Perl Hacker," mostly attributed to Randal Schwartz. See: *http://www.perl.com/CPAN/misc/japh*.

† As a judge for the Obfuscated C Code contest, I see more than my fair share of twisted, cryptic, and spectacular code. See *http://www.reality.sgi.com/~ioccc* if you don't know about this contest. Incidentally, if you think Perl isn't confusing enough already, check out the Obfuscated Perl contest at *http://tpj.com/tpj/tpj/contest*.

If you don't have a web browser, you can use the command-line FTP client included with Windows NT (or Windows 95).

```
% ftp ftp.oreilly.com
Connected to ftp.oreilly.com.
220 ftp.oreilly.com FTP server (Version 6.34 Thu Oct 22 14:32:01 EDT 1992)
ready.
Name (ftp.oreilly.com:username): anonymous
331 Guest login ok, send e-mail address as password.
Password: username@hostname          Use your username and host here
230 Guest login ok, access restrictions apply.
ftp> cd /published/oreilly/nutshell/advanced_perl
250 CWD command successful.
ftp> get README
200 PORT command successful.
150 Opening ASCII mode data connection for README (xxxx bytes).
226 Transfer complete.
local: README remote: README
xxxx bytes received in xxx seconds (xxx Kbytes/s)
ftp> binary
200 Type set to I.
ftp> get examples.tar.gz
200 PORT command successful.
150 Opening BINARY mode data connection for examples.tar.gz (xxxx bytes).
226 Transfer complete. local: examples.tar.gz remote: examples.tar.gz
xxxx bytes received in xxx seconds (xxx Kbytes/s)
ftp> quit
221 Goodbye.
%
```

FTPMAIL

FTPMAIL is a mail server available to anyone who can send electronic mail to and receive electronic mail from Internet sites. Any company or service provider that allows email connections to the Internet can access FTPMAIL, as described in the following paragraph.

You send mail to *ftpmail@online.oreilly.com*. In the message body, give the FTP commands you want to run. The server will run anonymous FTP for you and mail the files back to you. To get a complete help file, send a message with no subject and the single word "help" in the body. The following is an example mail message that gets the examples. This command sends you a listing of the files in the selected directory and the requested example files. The listing is useful if you are interested in a later version of the examples.

```
Subject:
reply-to username@hostname          (Message Body) Where you want files mailed
open
cd /published/oreilly/nutshell/advanced.perl
dir
get README
```

```
mode binary
uuencode
get examples.tar.gz
quit
.
```

A signature at the end of the message is acceptable as long as it appears after "quit."

Conventions

The following typographic conventions are used in this book:

Italic
> is used for filenames and command names. It is also used for electronic mail addresses and URLs.

`Constant Width`
> is used for code examples, as well as names of elements of code.

Bold
> is used in code sections to draw attention to key parts of the program. It also marks user input in examples.

`Courier Italic`
> is used in code sections to draw attention to code generated automatically by tools.

Resources

These are some books that I have found immensely useful in my professional life, in particular in applications development. Perhaps you will too.

1. *Design Patterns. Elements of Reusable Object-Oriented Software.* Erich Gamma, Richard Helm, Ralph Johnson, and John Vlissides. Addison-Wesley (1994)

2. *Programming Pearls.* Jon Bentley. Addison-Wesley (1986)

   Just get it. Read it on the way home!

3. *More Programming Pearls.* Jon Bentley. Addison-Wesley (1990)

4. *Design and Evolution of C++.* Bjarne Stroustrup. Addison-Wesley (1994)

   Fascinating study of the kind of considerations that drive language design.

5. *The Mythical Man-Month.* Frederick P. Brooks. Addison-Wesley (1995)

   One of the most readable sets of essays on software project management and development.

6. *Bringing Design to Software*. Terry Winograd. Addison-Wesley (1996)

   What we typically don't worry about in an application—but should.

7. *BUGS in Writing*. Lyn Dupré. Addison-Wesley (1995)

   Highly recommended for programmers writing technical documentation.

Perl Resources

This is a list of books, magazines, and web sites devoted to Perl:

1. *Programming Perl*, Second Edition. Larry Wall, Tom Christiansen, and Randal Schwartz. O'Reilly (1996)

2. *Learning Perl*. Randal Schwartz. O'Reilly (1993)

3. *The Perl Journal*. Edited by Jon Orwant. At *http://www.tpj.com/*

4. Tom Christiansen's Perl web site, *http://www.perl.com/perl/index.html*

5. Clay Irving's Perl Reference web site, *http://www.panix.com/~clay/perl/*

We'd Like to Hear from You

We have tested and verified all of the information in this book to the best of our ability, but you may find that features have changed (or even that we have made mistakes!). Please let us know about any errors you find, as well as your suggestions for future editions, by writing:

O'Reilly & Associates, Inc.
101 Morris Street
Sebastopol, CA 95472
1-800-998-9938 (in US or Canada)
1-707-829-0515 (international/local)
1-707-829-0104 (FAX)

You can also send us messages electronically. To be put on the mailing list or request a catalog, send email to:

nuts@oreilly.com (via the Internet)

To ask technical questions or comment on the book, send email to:

bookquestions@oreilly.com (via the Internet)

Acknowledgments

To my dear wife, Alka, for insulating me from life's daily demands throughout this project and for maintaining insanely good cheer in all the time I have known her.

To our parents, for everything we have, and are.

To my editors, Andy Oram and Steve Talbott, who patiently endured my writing style through endless revisions and gently taught me how to write a book. To O'Reilly and Associates, for allowing both authors and readers to have fun doing their bit.

To Larry Wall, for Perl, and for maintaining such a gracious and accessible Net presence. To the regular contributors on the Perl 5 Porters list (and to Tom Christiansen in particular), for enhancing, documenting, and tirelessly evangelizing Perl, all in their "spare" time. I envy their energy and dedication.

To this book's reviewers, who combed through this book with almost terrifying thoroughness. Tom Christiansen, Jon Orwant, Mike Stok, and James Lee reviewed the entire book and offered great insight and encouragement. I am also deeply indebted to Graham Barr, David Beazley, Peter Buckner, Tim Bunce, Wayne Caplinger, Rajappa Iyer, Jeff Okamoto, Gurusamy Sarathy, Peter Seibel, and Nathan Torkington for reading sections of the book and making numerous invaluable suggestions. Any errors and omissions remain my own. A heartfelt thanks to Rao Akella, the amazing quotemeister, for finding suitable quotes for this book.

To my colleagues at WebLogic and TCSI, for providing such a terrific work environment. I'm amazed I'm actually paid to have fun. (There goes my raise....)

To all my friends, for the endless cappuccino walks, pool games, and encouraging words and for their patience while I was obsessing with this book. I am truly blessed.

To the crew at O'Reilly who worked on this book, including Jane Ellin, the production editor, Mike Sierra for Tools support, Robert Romano for the figures, Seth Maislin for the index, Nicole Gipson Arigo, David Futato, and Sheryl Avruch for quality control, Nancy Priest and Edie Freedman for design, and Madeleine Newell for production support.

1

Data References and Anonymous Storage

If I were meta-agnostic, I'd be confused over whether I'm agnostic or not—but I'm not quite sure if I feel that way; hence I must be meta-meta-agnostic (I guess).

—Douglas R. Hofstadter,
Gödel, Escher, Bach

There are two aspects (among many) that distinguish toy programming languages from those used to build truly complex systems. The more robust languages have:

- The ability to dynamically allocate data structures without having to associate them with variable names. We refer to these as "anonymous" data structures.

- The ability to point to any data structure, independent of whether it is allocated dynamically or statically.

COBOL is the one true exception to this; it has been a huge commercial success in spite of lacking these features. But it is also why you'd balk at developing flight control systems in COBOL.

Consider the following statements that describe a far simpler problem: a family tree.

> Marge is 23 years old and is married to John, 24.
> Jason, John's brother, is studying computer science at MIT. He is just 19.
> Their parents, Mary and Robert, are both sixty and live in Florida.
> Mary and Marge's mother, Agnes, are childhood friends.

Do you find yourself mentally drawing a network with bubbles representing people and arrows representing relationships between them? Think of how you would conveniently represent this kind of information in your favorite programming language. If you were a C (or Algol, Pascal, or C++) programmer, you would use a dynamically allocated data structure to represent each person's data (name, age, and location) and pointers to represent relationships between people.

A pointer is simply a variable that contains the location of some other piece of data. This location can be a machine address, as it is in C, or a higher-level entity, such as a name or an array offset.

C supports both aspects extremely efficiently: You use `malloc(3)`* to allocate memory dynamically and a pointer to refer to dynamically and statically allocated memory. While this is as efficient as it gets, you tend to spend enormous amounts of time dealing with memory management issues, carefully setting up and modifying complex interrelationships between data, and then debugging fatal errors resulting from "dangling pointers" (pointers referring to pieces of memory that have been freed or are no longer in scope). The program may be efficient; the programmer isn't.

Perl supports both concepts, and quite well, too. It allows you to create anonymous data structures, and supports a fundamental data type called a "reference," loosely equivalent to a C pointer. Just as C pointers can point to data as well as procedures, Perl's references can refer to conventional data types (scalars, arrays, and hashes) and other entities such as subroutines, typeglobs, and filehandles.†
Unlike C, they don't let you peek and poke at raw memory locations.

Perl excels from the standpoint of programmer efficiency. As we saw earlier, you can create complex structures with very few lines of code because, unlike C, Perl doesn't expect you to spell out every thing. A line like this:

```
$line[19] = "hello";
```

does in one line what amounts to quite a number of lines in C—allocating a dynamic array of 20 elements and setting the last element to a (dynamically allocated) string. Equally important, you don't spend any time at all thinking about memory management issues. Perl ensures that a piece of data is deleted when no one is pointing at it any more (that is, it ensures that there are no memory leaks) and, conversely, that it is not deleted when someone is still pointing to it (no dangling pointers).

Of course, just because all this can be done does not mean that Perl is an automatic choice for implementing complex applications such as aircraft scheduling systems. However, there is no dearth of other, less complex applications (not just throwaway scripts) for which Perl can more easily be used than any other language.

---

* The number in parentheses is the Unix convention of referring to the appropriate section of the documentation (man pages). The number 3 represents the section describing the C API.

† We'll study the latter set in Chapter 3, *Typeglobs and Symbol Tables*.

In this chapter, you will learn the following:

- How to create references to scalars, arrays, and hashes and how to access data through them (dereferencing).

- How to create and refer to anonymous data structures.

- What Perl does internally to help you avoid thinking about memory management.

Referring to Existing Variables

If you have a C background (not necessary for understanding this chapter), you know that there are two ways to initialize a pointer in C. You can refer to an existing variable:

```
int a, *p;
p = &a;  /* p now has the "address" of a */
```

The memory is *statically* allocated; that is, it is allocated by the compiler. Alternatively, you can use `malloc(3)` to allocate a piece of memory at run-time and obtain its address:

```
p = malloc(sizeof(int));
```

This dynamically allocated memory doesn't have a name (unlike that associated with a variable); it can be accessed only indirectly through the pointer, which is why we refer to it as "anonymous storage."

Perl provides references to both statically and dynamically allocated storage; in this section, we'll the study the former in some detail. That allows us to deal with the two concepts—references and anonymous storage—separately.

You can create a reference to an existing Perl variable by prefixing it with a backslash, like this:

```
# Create some variables
$a      = "mama mia";
@array  = (10, 20);
%hash   = ("laurel" => "hardy", "nick" =>  "nora");

# Now create references to them
$ra      = \$a;          # $ra now "refers" to (points to) $a
$rarray = \@array;
$rhash  = \%hash;
```

You can create references to constant scalars in a similar fashion:

```
$ra      = \10;
$rs      = \"hello world";
```

That's all there is to it. Since arrays and hashes are collections of scalars, it is possible to take a reference to an individual element the same way: just prefix it with a backslash:

```
$r_array_element = \$array[1];      # Refers to the scalar $array[1]

$r_hash_element  = \$hash{"laurel"}; # Refers to the scalar
                                     # $hash{"laurel"}
```

A Reference Is Just Another Scalar

A reference variable, such as `$ra` or `$rarray`, is an ordinary scalar—hence the prefix '$'. A scalar, in other words, can be a number, a string, or a reference and can be freely reassigned to one or the other of these (sub)types. If you print a scalar while it is a reference, you get something like this:

```
SCALAR(0xb06c0)
```

While a string and a number have direct printed representations, a reference doesn't. So Perl prints out whatever it can: the type of the value pointed to and its memory address. There is rarely a reason to print out a reference, but if you have to, Perl supplies a reasonable default. This is one of the things that makes Perl so productive to use. *Don't just sit there and complain, do something.* Perl takes this motherly advice seriously.

While we are on the subject, it is important that you understand what happens when references are used as keys for hashes. Perl requires hash keys to be strings, so when you use a reference as a key, Perl uses the reference's string representation (which will be unique, because it is a pointer value after all). But when you later retrieve the key from this hash, it will remain a string and will thus be unusable as a reference. It is possible that a future release of Perl may lift the restriction that hash keys have to be strings, but for the moment, the only recourse to this problem is to use the Tie::RefHash module presented in Chapter 9, *Tie*. I must add that this restriction is hardly debilitating in the larger scheme of things. There are few algorithms that require references to be used as hash keys and fewer still that cannot live with this restriction.

Dereferencing

Dereferencing means getting at the value that a reference points to.

In C, if `p` is a pointer, `*p` refers to the value being pointed to. In Perl, if `$r` is a reference, then `$$r`, `@$r`, or `%$r` retrieves the value being referred to, depending on whether `$r` is pointing to a scalar, an array, or a hash. It is essential that you use the correct prefix for the corresponding type; if `$r` is pointing to an array, then you must use `@$r`, and not `%$r` or `$$r`. Using the wrong prefix results in a fatal run-time error.

Think of it this way: Wherever you would ordinarily use a Perl variable ($a, @b, or %c), you can replace the variable's name (a, b, or c) by a reference variable (as long as the reference is of the right type). A reference is usable in all the places where an ordinary data type can be used. The following examples show how references to different data types are dereferenced.

References to Scalars

The following expressions involving a scalar,

```
$a += 2;
print $a;           # Print $a's contents ordinarily
```

can be changed to use a reference by simply replacing the string "a" by the string "$ra":

```
$ra = \$a;          # First take a reference to $a
$$ra  += 2;         # instead of $a += 2;
print $$ra;         # instead of print $a
```

Of course, you must make sure that $ra is a reference pointing to a scalar; otherwise, Perl dies with the run-time error "Not a SCALAR reference".

References to Arrays

You can use ordinary arrays in three ways:

- Access the *array as a whole*, using the @array notation. You can print an entire array or push elements into it, for example.

- Access *single elements* using the $array[$i] notation.

- Access *ranges of elements* (slices), using the notation @array[index1,index2,...].

References to arrays are usable in all three of these situations. The following code shows an example of each, contrasting ordinary array usage to that using references to arrays:

```
$rarray = \@array;

push (@array , "a", 1, 2);   # Using the array as a whole
push (@$rarray, "a", 1, 2);  # Indirectly using the ref. to the array

print $array[$i] ;           # Accessing single elements
print $$rarray[1];           # Indexing indirectly through a
                             # reference: array replaced by $rarray

@sl =  @array[1,2,3];        # Ordinary array slice
@sl =  @$rarray[1,2,3];      # Array slice using a reference
```

Note that in all these cases, we have simply replaced the string **array** with $rarray to get the appropriate indirection.

Beginners often make the mistake of confusing array variables and enumerated (comma-separated) lists. For example, putting a backslash in front of an enumerated list does *not* yield a reference to it:

```
$s = \('a', 'b', 'c');      # WARNING: probably not what you think
```

As it happens, this is identical to

```
$s = (\'a', \'b', \'c');    # List of references to scalars
```

An enumerated list always yields the last element in a scalar context (as in C), which means that $s contains a reference to the constant string c. Anonymous arrays, discussed later in the section "References to Anonymous Storage," provide the correct solution.

References to Hashes

References to hashes are equally straightforward:

```
$rhash = \%hash;
print $hash{"key1"};        # Ordinary hash lookup
print $$rhash{"key1"};      # hash replaced by $rhash
```

Hash slices work the same way too:

```
@slice = @$rhash{'key1', 'key2'}; # instead of @hash{'key1', 'key2'}
```

A word of advice: You must resist the temptation to implement basic data structures such as linked lists and trees just because a pointerlike capability is available. For small numbers of elements, the standard array data type has pretty decent insertion and removal performance characteristics and is far less resource intensive than linked lists built using Perl primitives. (On my machine, a small test shows that inserting up to around 1250 elements at the head of a Perl array is faster than creating an equivalent linked list.) And if you want BTrees, you should look at the Berkeley DB library (described in Chapter 10, *Persistence*) before rolling a Perl equivalent.

Confusion About Precedence

The expressions involving key lookups might cause some confusion. Do you read $$rarray[1] as ${$rarray[1]} or {$$rarray}[1] or ${$rarray}[1]?

(Pause here to give your eyes time to refocus!)

As it happens, the last one is the correct answer. Perl follows these two simple rules while parsing such expressions: (1) Key or index lookups are done at the end, and (2) the prefix closest to a variable name binds most closely. When Perl sees something like $$$rarray[1] or $$$rhash{"browns"}, it leaves index lookups ([1] and {"browns"}) to the very end. That leaves $$$rarray and $$$rhash. It gives preference to the '$' closest to the variable name. So the precedence works out like this: ${$rarray} and ${$rhash}. Another way of visualizing the second rule is that the preference is given to the symbols from right to left (the variable is always to the right of a series of symbols).

Note that we are not really talking about operator precedence, since $, @, and % are not operators; the rules above indicate the way an expression is parsed.

Shortcuts with the Arrow Notation

Perl provides an alternate and easier-to-read syntax for accessing array or hash elements: the ->[ ] notation. For example, given the array's reference, you can obtain the second element of the array like this:

```
$rarray = \@array;
print $rarray->[1] ;     # The "visually clean" way
```

instead of the approaches we have seen earlier:

```
print $$rarray[1];       # Noisy, and have to think about precedence
print ${$rarray}[1];     # The way to get tendinitis!
```

I prefer the arrow notation, because it is less visually noisy. Figure 1-1 shows a way to visualize this notation.

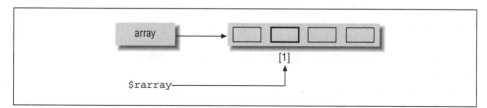

Figure 1-1. Visualizing $rarray->[1]

Similarly, you can use the ->{ } notation to access an element of a hash table:

```
$rhash = \%hash;
print $rhash->{"k1"};

#instead of ........
print $$rhash{"k1"};
# or
print ${$rhash}{"k1"};
```

Caution: This notation works only for single indices, not for slices. Consider the following:

```
print $rarray->[0,2]; # Warning: This is NOT an indirect array slice.
```

Perl treats the stuff within the brackets as a comma-separated expression that yields the last term in the array: 2. Hence, this expression is equivalent to `$rarray->[2]`, which is an index lookup, not a slice. (Recall the rule mentioned earlier: An enumerated or comma-separated list always returns the last element in a scalar context.)

No Automatic Dereferencing

Perl does not do any automatic dereferencing for you.* You must explicitly dereference using the constructs just described. This is similar to C, in which you have to say `*p` to indicate the object pointed to by p. Consider

```
$rarray = \@array;
push ($rarray, 1, 2, 3);    # Error: $rarray is a scalar, not an array
push (@$rarray, 1, 2, 3);   # OK
```

`push` expects an array as the first argument, not a reference to an array (which is a scalar). Similarly, when printing an array, Perl does not automatically dereference any references. Consider

```
print "$rarray, $rhash";
```

This prints

```
ARRAY(0xc70858), HASH(0xb75ce8)
```

This issue may seem benign but has ugly consequences in two cases. The first is when a reference is used in an arithmetic or conditional expression by mistake; for example, if you said `$a += $r` when you really meant to say `$a += $$r`, you'll get only a hard-to-track bug. The second common mistake is assigning an array to a scalar (`$a = @array`) instead of the array reference (`$a = \@array`). Perl does not warn you in either case, and Murphy's law being what it is, you will discover this problem only when you are giving a demo to a customer.

Using References

References are absolutely essential for creating complex data structures. Since the next chapter is devoted solely to this topic, we will not say more here. This section lists the other advantages of Perl's support for indirection and memory management.

Passing Arrays and Hashes to Subroutines

When you pass more than one array or hash to a subroutine, Perl merges all of them into the `@_` array available within the subroutine. The only way to avoid this

---

* Except for filehandles, as we will see in Chapter 3.

merger is to pass references to the input arrays or hashes. Here's an example that adds elements of one array to the corresponding elements of the other:

```
@array1 = (1, 2, 3); @array2 = (4, 5, 6, 7);
AddArrays (\@array1, \@array2); # Passing the arrays by reference.
print "@array1 \n";
    sub AddArrays
{
        my ($rarray1, $rarray2) = @_;
        $len2 = @$rarray2;   # Length of array2
        for ($i = 0 ; $i  < $len2 ;  $i++) {
            $rarray1->[$i] += $rarray2->[$i];
        }
    }
```

In this example, two array references are passed to **AddArrays** which then dereferences the two references, determines the lengths of the arrays, and adds up the individual array elements.

Performance Efficiency

Using references, you can efficiently pass large amounts of data to and from a subroutine.

However, passing references to *scalars* typically turns out not to be an optimization at all. I have often seen code like this, in which the programmer has intended to minimize copying while reading lines from a file:

```
while ($ref_line = GetNextLine()) {
        .....
        .....
}
    sub GetNextLine () {
        my $line = <F> ;
        exit(0) unless defined($line);
        .....
        return \$line;    # Return by reference, to avoid copying
}
```

`GetNextLine` returns the line by reference to avoid copying.

You might be surprised how little an effect this strategy has on the overall performance, because most of the time is taken by reading the file and subsequently working on `$line`. Meanwhile, the user of `GetNextLine` is forced to deal with indirections (`$$ref_line`) instead of the more straightforward buffer `$line`.*

---

* The operative word here is "typically." Most applications deal with lines 60–70 bytes long.

Incidentally, you can use the standard library module called Benchmark to time and compare different code implementations, like this:

```
use Benchmark;
timethis (100, "GetNextLine()"); # Call ProcessFile 100 times, and
                                 # time it
```

The module defines a subroutine called `timethis` that takes a piece of code, runs it as many times as you tell it to, and prints out the elapsed time. We'll cover the `use` statement in Chapter 6, *Modules*.

References to Anonymous Storage

So far, we have created references to previously existing variables. Now we will learn to create references to "anonymous" data structures—that is, values that are not associated with a variable.

To create an anonymous array, use square brackets instead of parentheses:

```
$ra = [ ];            # Creates an empty, anonymous array
                      # and returns a reference to it
$ra = [1,"hello"];    # Creates an initialized anonymous array
                      # and returns a reference to it
```

This notation not only allocates anonymous storage, it also returns a reference to it, much as `malloc(3)` returns a pointer in C.

What happens if you use parentheses instead of square brackets? Recall again that Perl evaluates the right side as a comma-separated expression and returns the value of the last element; `$ra` contains the value "hello", which is likely not what you are looking for.

To create an anonymous hash, use braces instead of square brackets:

```
$rh = { };                        # Creates an empty hash and returns a
                                  # reference to it
$rh = {"k1", "v1", "k2", "v2"};   # A populated anonymous hash
```

Both these notations are easy to remember since they represent the bracketing characters used by the two datatypes—brackets for arrays and braces for hashes. Contrast this to the way you'd normally create a named hash:

```
# An ordinary hash uses the prefix and is initialized with a list
# within parentheses
%hash = ("flock" => "birds", "pride" => "lions");

# An anonymous hash is a list contained within curly braces.
# The result of the expression is a scalar reference to that hash.
$rhash = {"flock" => "birds", "pride" => "lions"};
```

What about dynamically allocated *scalars*? It turns out that Perl doesn't have any notation for doing something like this, presumably because you almost never need it. If you really do, you can use the following trick: Create a reference to an existing variable, and then let the variable pass out of scope.

```
{
    my $a = "hello world";   # 1
    $ra = \$a;               # 2
}
print "$$ra \n";             # 3
```

The my operator tags a variable as private (or *localizes* it, in Perl-speak). You can use the local operator instead, but there is a subtle yet very important difference between the two that we will clarify in Chapter 3. For this example, both work equally well.

Now, $ra is a global variable that refers to the local variable $a (not the keyword local). Normally, $a would be deleted at the end of the block, but since $ra continues to refer to it, the memory allocated for $a is not thrown away. Of course, if you reassign $ra to some other value, this space is deallocated before $ra is prepared to accept the new value.

You can create references to constant scalars like this:

```
$r = \10;   $rs = \"hello";
```

Constants are statically allocated and anonymous.

A reference variable does not care to know or remember whether it points to an anonymous value or to an existing variable's value. This is identical to the way pointers behave in C.

Dereferencing Multiple Levels of Indirection

We have seen how a reference refers to some other entity, including other references (which are just ordinary scalars). This means that we can have multiple levels of references, like this:

```
$a    = 10;
$ra   = \$a;      # reference to $a's value.
$rra  = \$ra;     # reference to a reference to $ra's value
$rrra = \$rra;    # reference to a reference to a reference ...
```

Now we'll dereference these. The following statements all yield the same value (that of $a):

```
print $a;        # prints 10. The following statements print the same.
print $$ra;      # $a seen from one level of indirection.
print $$$rra;    # replace ra with {$rra} : still referring
                 # to $a's value
print $$$$rrra;  # ... and so on.
```

Incidentally, this example illustrates a convention known to Microsoft Windows programmers as "Hungarian notation."* Each variable name is prefixed by its type ("r" for reference, "rh" for reference to a hash, "i" for integer, "d" for double, and so on). Something like the following would immediately trigger some suspicion:

```
$$rh_collections[0] = 10;     # RED FLAG : 'rh' being used as an array?
```

You have a variable called `$rh_collections`, which is presumably a reference to a hash because of its naming convention (the prefix `rh`), but you are using it instead as a reference to an array. Sure, Perl will alert you to this by raising a run-time exception ("Not an ARRAY reference at—line 2."). But it is easier to check the code while you are writing it than to painstakingly exercise all the code paths during the testing phase to rule out the possibility of run-time errors.

A More General Rule

Earlier, while discussing precedence, we showed that `$$rarray[1]` is actually the same as `${$rarray}[1]`. It wasn't entirely by accident that we chose braces to denote the grouping. It so happens that there is a more general rule.

The braces signify a block of code, and Perl doesn't care what you put in there as long as it yields a reference of the required type. Something like `{$rarray}` is a straightforward expression that yields a reference readily. By contrast, the following example calls a subroutine within the block, which in turn returns a reference:

```
sub test {
    return \$a;      # returns a reference to a scalar variable
}
$a = 10;
$b = ${test()};      # Calls a subroutine test within the block, which
                     # yields a reference to $a
                     # This reference is dereferenced
print $b;            # prints "10"
```

To summarize, a block that yields a reference can occur wherever the name of a variable can occur. Instead of `$a`, you can have `${$ra}` or `${$array[1]}` (assuming `$array[1]` has a reference to `$a`), for example.

Recall that a block can have any number of statements inside it, and the last expression evaluated inside that block represents its result value. Unless you want to be a serious contender for the Obfuscated Perl contest, avoid using blocks containing more than two expressions while using the general dereferencing rule stated above.

---

* After Charles Simonyi who started this convention at Microsoft. This convention is a topic of raging debates on the Internet; people either love it or hate it. Apparently, even at Microsoft, the systems folks use it, while the application folks don't. In a language without enforced type checking such as Perl, I recommend using it where convenient.

Trojan horses

While we are talking about obfuscation, it is worth talking about a very insidious way of including executable code within strings. Normally, when Perl sees a string such as "$a", it does variable interpolation. But you now know that "a" can be replaced by a block as long as it returns a reference to a scalar, so something like this is completely acceptable, even within a string:

```
print "${foo()}";
```

Replace `foo()` by `system ('/bin/rm *')` and you have an unpleasant Trojan horse:

```
print "${system('/bin/rm *')}"
```

Perl treats it like any other function and trusts `system` to return a reference to a scalar. The parameters given to `system` do their damage before Perl has a chance to figure out that `system` doesn't return a scalar reference.

Moral of the story: Be very careful of strings that you get from untrusted sources. Use the taint-mode option (invoke Perl as `perl -T`) or the Safe module that comes with the Perl distribution. Please see the Perl documentation for taint checking, and see the index for some pointers to the Safe module.

Nested Data Structures

Recall that arrays and hashes contain only scalars; they cannot directly contain another array or hash as such. But considering that references can refer to an array or a hash and that references are scalars, you can see how one or more elements in an array or hash can point to other arrays or hashes. In this section, we will study how to build nested, heterogeneous data structures.

Let us say we would like to track a person's details and that of their dependents. One approach is to create separate *named* hash tables for each person:

```
%sue = (              # Parent
    'name' => 'Sue',
    'age'  => '45');
%john = (             # Child
    'name' => 'John',
    'age'  => '20');
%peggy = (            # Child
    'name' => 'Peggy',
    'age'  => '16');
```

The structures for John and Peggy can now be related to Sue like this:

```
@children = (\%john, \%peggy);
$sue{'children'} = \@children;
```

```
# Or
$sue{'children'} = [\%john, \%peggy];
```

Figure 1-2 shows this structure after it has been built.

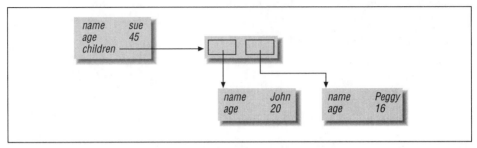

Figure 1-2. Mixing scalars with arrays and hashes.

This is how you can print Peggy's age, given **%sue**:

```
print $sue{children}->[1]->{age};
```

Implicit Creation of Complex Structures

Suppose the first line in your program is this:

```
$sue{children}->[1]->{age} = 10;
```

Perl automatically creates the hash **%sue**, gives it a hash element indexed by the string `children`, points that entry to a newly allocated array, whose second element is made to refer to a freshly allocated hash, which gets an entry indexed by the string `age`. Talk about programmer efficiency.

Final Shortcut: Omit Arrows Between Subscripts

While on the subject of programmer efficiency, let us discuss one more optimization for typing. You can omit -> if (and only if) it is between subscripts. That is, the following expressions are identical:

```
print $sue{children}->[1]->{age};
print $sue{children}[1]{age};
```

This is similar to the way C implements multidimensional arrays, in which every index except the last one behaves like a pointer to the next level (or dimension) and the final index corresponds to the actual data. The difference—which doesn't really matter at a usage level—between C's and Perl's approaches is that C treats an *n*-dimensional array as a contiguous stream of bytes and does not allocate space for pointers to subarrays, whereas Perl allocates space for references to intermediate single-dimension arrays.

Continuing from where we left off, you will find that even such a simple example benefits from using *anonymous* arrays and hashes, rather than named ones, as shown in the following snippet:

```
%sue = (                                        # Parent
    'name'     => 'Sue',
    'age'      => '45',
    'children' => [                             # Anon array of two hashes
                    {                           # Anon hash 1
                        'name' => 'John',
                        'age'  => '20'
                    },
                    {                           # Anon hash 2
                        'name' => 'Peggy',
                        'age'  => '16'
                    }
                  ]
);
```

This snippet of code contains only one named variable. The "children" attribute is a reference to an anonymous array, which itself contains references to anonymous hashes containing the children's details. This nesting can be as deep as you want; for example, you might represent John's educational qualifications as a reference to an anonymous array of hash records (each of which contain details of school attended, grade points, and so on). None of these arrays or hashes actually embed the next level hash or array; recall that the anonymous array and hash syntax yields references, which is what the containing structures see. In other words, such a nesting does not reflect a *containment* hierarchy. Try `print values(%sue)` to convince yourself.

It is comforting to know that Perl automatically deletes all nested structures as soon as the top-level structure (`%sue`) is deleted or reassigned to something else. Internal structures or elements that are are still referred to elsewhere aren't deleted.

Querying a Reference

The `ref` function queries a scalar to see whether it contains a reference and, if so, what type of data it is pointing to. `ref` returns false (a Boolean value, not a string) if its argument contains a number or a string; and if it's a reference, `ref` returns one of these strings to describe the data being referred to: "SCALAR", "HASH", "ARRAY", "REF" (referring to another reference variable), "GLOB" (referring to a typeglob), "CODE" (referring to a subroutine), or *"package name"* (an object belonging to this package—we'll see more of it later).

```
$a = 10;
$ra = \$a;
```

`ref($a)` yields FALSE, since `$a` is not a reference.

`ref($ra)` returns the string "SCALAR", since `$ra` is pointing to a scalar value.

Symbolic References

Normally, a construct such as `$$var` indicates that `$var` is a reference variable, and the programmer expects this expression to return the value that was pointed to by `$var` when the references were taken.

What if `$var` is not a reference variable at all? Instead of complaining loudly, Perl checks to see whether `$var` contains a string. If so, it uses that string as a regular variable name and messes around with this variable! Consider the following:

```
$x = 10;
$var = "x";
$$var = 30;    # Modifies $x to 30 , because $var is a symbolic
               # reference !
```

When evaluating `$$var`, Perl first checks to see whether `$var` is a reference, which it is not; it's a string. Perl then decides to give the expression one more chance: it treats `$var`'s contents as a variable identifier (`$x`). The example hence ends up modifying `$x` to 30.

It is important to note that symbolic references work only for global variables, not for those marked private using `my`.

Symbolic references work equally well for arrays and hashes also:

```
$var = "x";
@$var = (1, 2, 3);    # Sets @x to the enumerated list on the right
```

Note that the symbol used before `$var` dictates the type of variable to access: `$$var` is equivalent to `$x`, and `@$var` is equivalent to saying `@x`.

This facility is immensely useful, and, for those who have done this kind of thing before with earlier versions of Perl, is much more efficient than using `eval`. Let us say you want your script to process a command-line option such as "-Ddebug_level=3" and set the `$debug_level` variable. This is one way of doing it:

```
while ($arg = shift @ARGV){
    if ($arg =~ /-D(\w+)=(\w+)/) {
        $var_name = $1; $value = $2;
        $$var_name = $value;      # Or more compactly, $$1 = $2;
    }
}
```

On the other hand, Perl's eagerness to try its damnedest to get an expression to work sometimes doesn't help. In the preceding examples, if you expected the program logic to have a real reference instead of a string, then you would have wanted Perl to point it out instead of making assumptions about your usage. Fortunately, there's a way to switch this eagerness off. Perl has a number of compile-time directives, or pragmas. The `strict` pragma tells Perl to do strict error checking. You can even enumerate specific aspects to be strict about, one of which is 'refs':

```
use strict 'refs';   # Tell Perl not to allow symbolic references
$var = "x";
$$var = 30;
```

This results in a run-time error whenever you try to use a symbolic reference:

```
Can't use string ("x") as a SCALAR ref while "strict refs" in use at
try.pl line 3
```

The `strict` directive remains in effect until the end of the block. It can be turned off by saying `no strict` or, more specifically, `no strict 'refs'`.

A View of the Internals

Let us now take a look inside Perl to understand how it manages memory. You can safely skip this section without loss of continuity.

A variable logically represents a binding between a *name* and a *value*, as Figure 1-3 illustrates.*

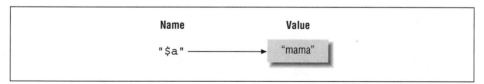

Name   **Value**

`"$a"` ⟶ "mama"

Figure 1-3. A variable is a name and value pair

An array or a hash is not just a collection of numbers or strings. It is a collection of *scalar values,* and this distinction is important, as Figure 1-4 illustrates.

Each box in Figure 1-4 represents a distinct value. An array has one value that represents *the collection* of scalar values. Each element of the array is a distinct scalar value. This is analogous to a pride of lions being treated as a single entity (which is why we refer to it in the singular) that has properties distinct from those of the individual lion.

---

* This is true whether the variable is global, dynamically scoped (using `local()`), or lexically scoped (using `my()`). More details are given in Chapter 3.

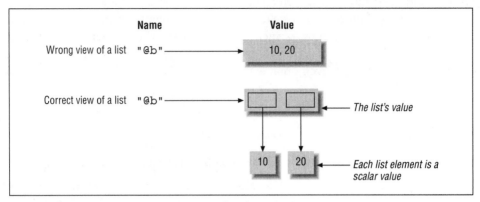

Figure 1-4. An array value is a collection of scalar values

Notice also that while a name always points to a value, a value doesn't always have to be pointed to by a name, as the array elements in Figure 1-4 or anonymous arrays and hashes exemplify.

Reference Counts

To support painless and transparent memory management, Perl maintains a reference count for every *value*, whether it is directly pointed to by a name or not. Let's add this piece of information to our earlier view. Refer to Figure 1-5.

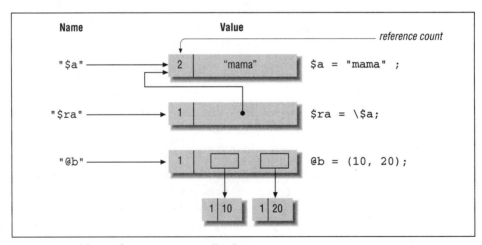

Figure 1-5. Adding reference counts to all values

As you can see, the reference count represents the number of arrows pointing to the value part of a variable. Because there is always an arrow from the name to its value, the variable's reference count is at least 1. When you obtain a reference to a variable, the corresponding value's reference count is incremented.

It is important to stress the point that even though we would like to think of $ra as pointing to $a, it really points to $a's *value*. In fact, $ra does not even know whether the value it is pointing to has a corresponding entry in the symbol table. The value of the reference variable is the *address* of another scalar value, which does not change even if $a's value changes.

Perl automatically deletes a value when its reference count drops to zero. When variables (named values) go out of scope, the binding between the name and the value is removed, resulting in the value's reference count being decremented. In the typical case in which this count is 1, the value is deleted (or *garbage collected*).*

The reference counting technique is sometimes referred to as "poor man's garbage collection," in contrast to much more sophisticated techniques used by environments such as LISP, Java, and Smalltalk (though the early versions of Smalltalk used reference counting). The problem is that reference counts take up space, which adds up if you consider that every piece of data in your application has an extra integer associated with it.

Then there is also the problem of circular references. The simplest case is this:

```
$a = \$a;
```

This is a classic case of narcissism. $a's reference count indicates that something is pointing to it, so it will never get freed. A more practical case of circular references is that of network graphs (each node keeps track of each of its neighbors) or ring buffers (where the last element points to the first one). Modern garbage collection algorithms implemented in Java and Smalltalk can detect circular references and deallocate the entire circular structure if none of the elements are reachable from other variables.

On the other hand, reference counting is simple to understand and implement and makes it easy to integrate Perl with C or C++ code. Please refer to item 2 in the "Resources" section at the end of the chapter for a comprehensive treatment of garbage collection techniques.

Note that while symbolic references allow you to access variables in an indirect way, no actual reference variables are created. In other words, the reference count of a symbolically accessed variable is not modified. Hence symbolic references are also called *soft* references, in contrast to *hard* references, which actually allocate storage to keep track of the indirection.

---

* For efficiency, Perl doesn't actually delete it; it just sends it to its own free pool and reuses it when you need a new value. It is *logically* deleted, nevertheless.

This is similar to the concept of soft versus hard links in the Unix filesystem. The i-node of a file has its reference count incremented every time someone creates a hard link to that file, so you can't really delete the file's *contents* until its reference count goes down to zero. A symbolic link, on the other hand, stores only the name of the file and can point to a nonexistent file; you'll never know until you try to open the file using the symbolic link.

Array/Hash References Versus Element References

Recall that there is a distinction between the array as a whole and each of its constituent scalar values. The array's value maintains its own reference count, and each of its elements has its own. When you take a reference to an array, its own reference count is incremented without its elements getting affected, as shown in Figure 1-6.

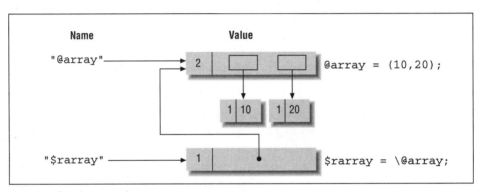

Figure 1-6. Taking a reference to an array

In contrast, Figure 1-7 shows the picture when you create a reference to an *element* of an array or a hash.

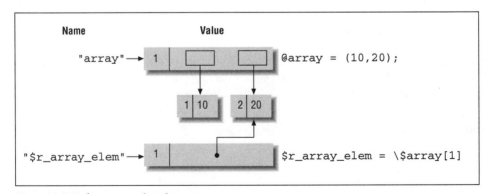

Figure 1-7. Referring to a list element

When you take a reference to an element of an array (or a hash), Perl increments that scalar value's reference count. If, say, you now **pop** it from the array, its reference count goes down by 1 because the array is no longer interested in the scalar value. But since there is an outstanding reference to the array element (and its reference count is still 1), it is not destroyed. Figure 1-8 shows the picture after **@array** has been popped once.

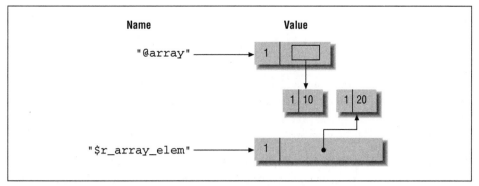

Figure 1-8. @array popped once; $r_array_elem holds on to the popped scalar

References in Other Languages

Tcl

Tcl does not have a way of dynamically allocating anonymous data structures but, being a dynamic language, supports creation of new variables (names assigned automatically) at run-time. This approach is not only slow, but also highly error prone. In addition, the only way to pass a variable by reference is to pass the actual name of a variable, such as Perl's symbolic references. All this makes it very difficult to create complex data structures (and very unmaintainable if you do so). But, in all fairness, it must be stressed that Tcl is meant to be a glue language between applications and toolkits, and it is expected that most complex processing happens in the C-based application itself, rather than within the script. Tcl was not designed to be used as a full-fledged scripting or development language (though I have heard that its limited scope hasn't stopped people from writing 50,000-line scripts to drive oil rigs!).

Python

Python is similar to Java in that, except for fundamental types, all objects are passed around by reference. This means that assigning a list-valued variable to another simply results in the second list variable being an alias of the first; if you want a copy, you have to explicitly do so and pay the corresponding price in performance. I much prefer this style to Perl's because you typically refer to structures much more than making a copy, and it is nice to have a default that is efficient and eases typing.

Like Perl, Python reference counts each of its data types, including user-defined types defined in C/C++ extensions.

C/C++

C and C++ support pointers whose type safety can be checked at compile time. Since a pointer contains the raw address of the data, a reference to a piece of data is as efficient and compact as it gets. On the other hand, this puts all the responsibility of memory management on the programmer. It is worth examining the implementation of interpreters such as Tcl, Perl, and Python (all having been implemented in C) to learn about memory management strategies.

C++ supports the notion of references, which allows you to create aliases to existing variables. This facility is reminiscent of the typeglob aliasing facility (which we'll study in Chapter 3) but bears no resemblance to Perl references.

Java

In Java, everything is passed by reference except for fundamental types such as *int* and *float*. There are no issues of memory management, since the Java framework supports garbage collection (which runs in a separate thread so as not to freeze up the application threads). Being as rich as C++ in data types and with no memory management hassles, it holds immense promise for programming-in-the-large.

Resources

1. *perlref* (Perl documentation)

2. *Uniprocessor Garbage Collection Techniques.* Paul Wilson. International Workshop on Memory Management, 1992.

   This paper gives a comprehensive treatment of GC issues. Available from *ftp://ftp.cs.utexas.edu/pub/garbage/gcsurvey.ps*

2

Implementing Complex Data Structures

> *Don't worry, spiders,*
> *I keep house*
> *casually.*
> —Kobayashi Issa

The success of Perl is a tribute to the fact that many problems can be solved by using just its fundamental data types. Jon Bentley's books *Programming Pearls* and *More Programming Pearls* are further testament to how much can be achieved if the basic data structures are dynamic and memory management is automatic. But as programs become more complex, moving from the domain of the script to that of the application, there is an increasing need for representing data in much more complex ways than can sometimes be achieved with the basic data types alone.

In this chapter, we will apply the syntax and concepts learned in Chapter 1 to a few "real" examples. We will write bits of code that build complex structures from file-based data and use sequences of $'s and @'s without batting an eyelid. For each problem, we will examine different ways of representing the same data and study the trade-offs in program versus programmer efficiency. In the interest of clarity, we will not worry too much about error handling.

Tom Christiansen has written an excellent series of tutorials called FMTEYEWTK (Far More Than Everything You've Ever Wanted to Know!) [1]. This series contains a motley collection of topics that crop up on the Perl Usenet groups. I admire them for their lucid, patient, and detailed explanations and recommend that you read them at some point. (Now is better!) Some of them are now packaged with the Perl distribution; in particular, the *perldsc* (data structures cookbook) document is a tutorial for building and manipulating complex structures.

Before we start the examples, we will study what it takes to create structures *à la* C or C++.

User-Defined Structures

The *struct* declaration in C provides a notion of user-defined types (though it doesn't quite have first-class status, like an *int*), and a *typedef* statement is then used to alias it to a new type name. Java and C++ have the *class* declaration to compose new data types out of fundamental data types. These constructs allow you to combine a bunch of named attributes under a single banner but still provide access to each individual attribute.

Perl has no such built-in template feature.* One commonly used *convention* is to simulate structures using a hash table, as shown in 2-1.

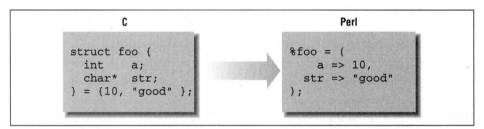

Figure 2-1. Simulating C structures with Perl hashes

Perl's implementation of hash tables is actually quite efficient in terms of both performance and space. Since hash keys are immutable strings, Perl keeps only one systemwide copy of a hash key. This prevents a hundred **foo** structures from creating a hundred copies of the strings **a** and **str**.

Another way to create a user-defined collection of attributes is to use an array **@foo** instead, which is slightly more efficient, yet a tad more cumbersome:

```
$a = 0; $str = 1;      # Indices
$foo[$a]    = 10;      # Equivalent to foo.a = 10 in C.
$foo[$str] = "hello"; # equivalent to foo.str = "hello" in C.
```

Remember, if a certain data structure is represented far more easily in C than in Perl and requires a considerable amount of manipulation, you could consider keeping it in C/C++ itself and not bother duplicating it in Perl. You will need to provide a set of C procedures that can manipulate this data. A very simple tool called SWIG (discussed in Chapter 18, *Extending Perl: A First Course*) allows you to do this painlessly.

---

* We'll discuss a module called ObjectTemplate in Chapter 7, *Object-Oriented Programming*, that provides this.

You can also use `pack` or `sprintf` to encode a set of values to get one composite entity, but accessing individual data elements is neither convenient nor efficient (in time). `pack` is a good option when you need to be frugal about space, because it converts a list of values into one scalar value without necessarily changing each individual item's machine representation; `sprintf` is less efficient in this regard, because it converts everything to a printable representation.

Example: Matrices

Before we embark on this example, you must know that if you really want a good efficient implementation of matrices, you should check out the PDL module (Perl Data Language) from CPAN.

To gain a better understanding of different matrix representations, we will write routines to construct these structures from a data file and to multiply two matrices. The file is formatted as follows:

```
MAT1
1   2   4
10  30  0

MAT2
5   6
1   10
```

Each matrix has a label and some data. We use these labels to create global variables with the corresponding names (`@MAT1` and `@MAT2`).

An array of arrays is the most intuitive representation for a matrix in Perl, since there is no direct support for two-dimensional arrays:

```
@matrix = (
    [1, 2, 3],
    [4, 5, 6],
    [7, 8, 9]
);
# Change 6, the element at row  1, column 2 to 100
$matrix[1][2] = 100;
```

Note that `@matrix` is a simple array whose elements happen to be references to anonymous arrays. Further, recall that `$matrix[1][2]` is a simpler way of saying `$matrix[1]->[2]`.

Example 2-1 reads the file and creates the array of arrays structure for each matrix. Pay particular attention to the **push** statement (highlighted); it uses the symbolic reference facility to create variables (`@{$matrix_name}`) and appends a reference to a new row in every iteration. We are assured of newly allocated rows in every iteration because `@row` is local to that block, and when the **if** statement is done, its contents live on because we squirrel away a reference to the array's value. (Recall that it is the value that is reference counted, not the name.)

Example 2-1. Reading a Matrix from a File

```
sub matrix_read_file {
    my ($filename) = @_;
    open (F, $filename) || die "Could not open $filename: $!";
    while ($line = <F>) {
        chomp($line);
        next if $line =~ /^\s*$/; # skip blank lines
        if ($line =~ /^([A-Za-z]\w*)/) {
            $matrix_name = $1;
        } else {
            my (@row) = split (/\s+/, $line);
            push (@{$matrix_name}, \@row;) # insert the row-array into
                                           # the outer matrix array
        }
    }
    close(F);
}
```

Now let us use this array-of-arrays structure to multiply two matrices. In case you have forgotten how matrix multiplication works, the product of two matrices A_{mn} (*m* rows, *n* columns) and B_{np} is defined as

$$X_{ij} = \sum_{\kappa=1}^{n} A_{ik} \cdot B_{kj} \quad \text{where } i = 1 \ .. \ m, \ \ j = 1 \ .. \ p$$

The element (i, j) of the matrix product is the sum of successive pairs of elements taken from the i_{th} row of **A** and the j_{th} column of **B**. Translated into Perl, it looks like Example 2-2.

Example 2-2. Matrix Multiply

```
sub matrix_multiply {
    my ($r_mat1, $r_mat2) = @_;        # Taking matrices by reference
    my ($r_product);                   # Returing product by reference
    my ($r1, $c1) = matrix_count_rows_cols ($r_mat1);
    my ($r2, $c2) = matrix_count_rows_cols ($r_mat2);
    die "Matrix 1 has $c1 columns and matrix 2 has $r2 rows."
        . " Cannot multiply\n" unless ($c1 == $r2);
    for ($i = 0; $i < $r1; $i++) {
        for ($j = 0; $j < $c2; $j++) {
            $sum = 0;
            for ($k = 0; $k < $c1; $k++) {
                $sum += $r_mat1->[$i][$k] * $r_mat2->[$k][$j];
            }
            $r_product->[$i][$j] = $sum;
        }
    }
    $r_product;
}

sub matrix_count_rows_cols {  # return number of rows and columns
    my ($r_mat)  = @_;
```

Example 2-2. Matrix Multiply (continued)

```
    my $num_rows = @$r_mat;
    my $num_cols = @{$r_mat->[0]}; # Assume all rows have an equal no.
                                   # of columns.

    ($num_rows, $num_cols);
}
```

`matrix_multiply` takes two matrices by reference. A single element is obtained as `$r_mat->[$i][$j]`, and a single row is obtained as `$r_mat->[0]`.

Hash of Hashes Representation

If the matrix is large and sparse (only a few elements have nonzero values), a hash of hashes is likely a more space-efficient representation. For example, the matrix

$$\begin{bmatrix} 0 & 0 & 100 \\ 200 & 0 & 0 \\ 0 & 300 & 0 \end{bmatrix}$$

can be built like this:

```
    $matrix{0}{2} = 100;
    $matrix{1}{0} = 200;
    $matrix{2}{1} = 300;
```

The code above creates a hash table, **%matrix**, which maps a row number to a nested hash. Only rows with nonzero elements are represented. Each nested hash maps a column number to the actual value of the element at that row and column. Again, only columns with nonzero values in that row are represented. Of course, we have to store the total number of rows and columns separately, since unlike the array representation, these numbers are not implicit. Since **%matrix** is a hash, they can be stored as `$matrix{rows}` and `$matrix{cols}`. Because hash indices are strings, this approach is efficient only if the matrix is large and sparse.

To make the matrix routines developed in the previous section work for this new representation, it might seem a simple matter to convert all square brackets to braces. True, it'll work, but there's a subtle problem. Let's say that the entire third row of a matrix is zero-valued (so there's no entry for `$r_mat->{2}`). Now, if you do this:

```
    $element = $r_mat->{2}{3};
```

Perl automatically creates an entry for `$r_mat->{2}`, and hangs a hash reference off this entry. (The nested hash table is not created.) Thus the very act of examining an element gobbles up space, which is what we had hoped to avoid in the first place when we chose the hash of hashes representation. To prevent this, we have to check for the presence of a hash element with **exists** before retrieving it, as shown next:

```
if ((exists $r_mat->{$row}) && (exists $r_mat->{$row}{$col})) {
    ....
```

Other Matrix Representations

If the columns are sparse but the rows are well represented, you could choose an array of hashes structure. It is possible to store a matrix even more economically in terms of space, using a single hash table, at the expense of more complex code. If you imagine the matrix as a grid and number each cell of the grid consecutively, any cell can then be identified with exactly one unique number. So in a matrix with 10 rows and 5 columns, the element (8, 4) will have the number 38 (7 * 5 + 3) and hence can be referred to as **$r_mat->{38}**. We actually use this scheme in Chapter 15, *GUI Example: Tetris* (though that usage is more for convenience than for saving space). The choice of data structure depends on the size of the matrices, performance, and coding convenience.

Changing the data structure of a program clearly ends up changing all code that depends on it. To contain the amount of changes required (should the structure change), it is always a good idea to have only a small set of procedures that know the structure. For example, if you had procedures such as **create_matrix()**, **get_element(mat,i,j)**, and **set_element(mat,i,j)**, other procedures do not have to know the internal representation. Coding for change is often better than coding for run-time efficiency. We'll discuss this approach a great deal more in Chapter 7.

Professors, Students, Courses

This example shows how you might represent professor, student, and course data as hierarchical records and how to link them up. Assume that the data files look like this:

```
#file: professor.dat
id         : 42343                  #Employee Id
Name       : E.F.Schumacher
Office Hours: Mon 3-4, Wed 8-9
Courses    : HS201, SS343           #Course taught
...


#file: student.dat
id         : 52003                  # Registration id
Name       : Garibaldi
Courses    : H301, H302, M201       # Courses taken
...
```

```
#file: courses.dat
id          : HS201
Description : Small is beautiful
Class Hours : Mon 2-4, Wed 9-10, Thu 4-5
...
```

Each "id:" line starts a new record.

Among other tasks, let us say we are required to find out whether there is a scheduling conflict on professors' and students' hours. Because our focus is on data representation and getting a feel for Perl's reference syntax, we will look at implementing only some parts of the problem.

Representation

A hash table is a good representation for a heterogeneous record, as we mentioned earlier, so a student structure may be implemented like this:

```
$student{42343} = {
    'Name'    => 'Garibaldi',
    'Courses' => [ ]};
```

A number of subtle design choices have been made here.

We could have replaced "foreign keys" (to use the database term) such as "HS201" with references to the corresponding course data structures. We didn't, because it is then tempting to directly dereference these references, in which case the student code is aware of how the course data is structured.

We maintain separate global hash tables for students, courses, and professors— yet another effort to keep mostly unrelated data completely separate and to make it possible to change a part of the system without affecting everyone.

There is one piece of data we haven't discussed before: time ranges. Both professors and courses have certain "busy" or "active" hours. What is a good representation for this? You might choose to represent the line "Mon 2-3, Tue 4-6" as follows:

```
$time_range = {
    'Mon' => [2,3],
    'Tue' => [4,6]
};
```

There is a much simpler representation, in case you haven't already guessed it. The key insight is that since we are concerned only with clashes in time, the system should be able to quickly tell us whether a professor or a course is "active" in a given hour of the week or not. Considering that there are only 24 * 7 = 168 hours in a week, the entire week's schedule can be represented by a bitmap vector of 21 bytes (168/8). If a bit is set, we know that the professor is teaching something in that hour. In fact we can reduce the storage requirements further if we only account for the *effective* hours in a week (say, 7:00 A.M. to 7:00 P.M., Monday to Friday). That brings it down to 8 bytes (12 hours * 5 days / 8). The nice thing here is that an entire sequence of time ranges boils down to one scalar containing a bitmap vector. The other cool thing is that you can obtain time conflicts by logically AND-ing two bitmaps.

Having settled the representation, let us write some code to read the *professor.dat* file, and construct the data structures.

Example 2-3. Read professor.dat and Create Hierarchical Records in Memory

```perl
my (%profs);  # prof_read_file() populates this data structure from file

sub prof_read_file {
    my ($filename) = @_;
    my ($line, $curr_prof);
    open (F, $filename) || die "Could not open $filename";
    while ($line = <F>) {
        chomp($line);
        next if $line =~ /^\s*$/;        # skip blank lines
        if ($line =~ /^id.*:\s*(.*)/) {
            # Use an anonymous hash to store a professor's data
            $profs{$1} = $curr_prof = {};
        } elsif ($line =~ /^Office Hours.*:\s*(.*)/) {
            # $1 contains a string like 'Mon 2-3, Tue 4-6'
            $curr_prof->{Office Hours} = interval_parse($1);
        } elsif ($line =~ /^Courses.*:\s*(.*)/) {
            # $1 contains something like 'HS201, MA101'
            my (@courses_taught) = split(/[\s,]+/, $1);
            $curr_prof->{Courses} = \@courses_taught;
        }
    }
}
```

Notice that the **courses_taught** array is local to the block. When the block ends, $curr_prof->{Courses} continues to hang on to this array. You can omit one step like this:

```perl
    $curr_prof->{Courses} = [split(/[\s,]+/, $1)];
```

I prefer the earlier approach because it is more readable.

The **interval_parse** method parses a string such as "Mon 3-5, Wed 2-6" into a bit string, as was mentioned earlier. The code looks like this:

```perl
    # Each hour in a week (with days from 7am to 7pm) gets its own
    # unique bit in an 8-byte string.
    # Mon 7-8 is the 0th bit, Mon 6-7pm is 11, ... Fri 6-7 (pm) is 60th.
    my %base_hours = (
        mon => 0, tue => 12, wed => 24 , thu => 36, fri => 48
    );
    sub interval_parse {
        my ($interval_sequence) = @_; #contains "Mon 3-5, Tue 2-6"
        my ($time_range) = "";
```

```
    foreach $day_hours (split /,/, $interval_sequence) {
        # $day_hours contains "Mon 3-5" etc.
        my ($day, $from, $to) =
            ($day_hours =~ /([A-Za-z]+).*(\d+)-(\d+)/);
        # if $from or $to is less than 7, it must be afternoon. Normalize
        # it by adding 12. Then reduce it to a zero base by subtracting 7
        # (that is, 7 hrs to 19 hrs becomes 0 - 12. Finally,
        # normalize each hour in a day with respect to weekly hours,
        # by adding in the day's "base hour"
        $to = 19 if $to == 7;
        $from += 12 if $from < 7 ; $to += 12  if $to <= 7;
        my $base = $base_hours{lc $day};
        $from += $base - 7; $to += $base - 7;
        # At this point Tue 7a.m ==> 12 and Tue 4 p.m => 21
        for ($i = $from; $i < $to;  $i++) {
            # Set the corresponding bit
            vec($time_range, $i, 1) = 1;
        }
    }
    $time_range;
}
```

To check for scheduling constraints on a professor's time, we have to calculate overlapping hours between the professor's office hours and each course he or she teaches and between the courses themselves, as shown in Example 2-4.

Example 2-4. Checking Constraints on a Professor's Time

```
sub prof_check_constraints {
    my ($prof) = @_;
    my $r_prof = $profs{$prof};  # %profs created by prof_read_file
    my $office_hours = $r_prof->{Office Hours};
    my $rl_courses = $r_prof->{Courses};
    for $i (0 .. $#{$rl_courses}) {
        $course_hours = course_get_hours($rl_courses->[$i]);
        if (interval_conflicts($office_hours, $course_hours)) {
            print "Prof. ", $r_prof->{name},
                " Office hours conflict with course $course_taught\n";
        }
        for $j ($i .. $#{$rl_courses}) {
            my ($other_course_hours) = course_get_hours($rl_courses->[$j]);
            if (interval_conflicts ($course_hours, $other_course_hours)) {
                print "Prof. ", $r_prof->{name},
                    ": Course conflict: ", $rl_courses->[$i], " "
                                            $rl_courses->[$j], "\n";
            }
        }
    }
}
```

The subroutine `interval_conflicts` simply compares the two bitmaps, as shown below:

```
sub interval_conflicts {
    my ($t1, $t2) = @_;
```

```
    my ($combined) = $t1 & $t2;
    # $combined will have at least one bit set if there's a conflict
    my $offset = length($combined) * 8;
    # start counting down from last bit, and see if any is set
    while (--$offset >= 0) {
        return 1 if vec($combined,$offset,1);
    }
    return 0;
}
```

Note that all knowledge of the internal representation of a time interval is encapsulated in functions with the prefix `interval_`. These functions thus encapsulate an *abstract data type* called "interval." When we study modules and objects in later chapters, we will learn ways of organizing such pieces of code into reusable entities.

Pass the Envelope

Let us say we are given a text file containing Academy Award (Oscar) winners by year and category, formatted as follows:

```
1995:Actor:Nicholas Cage
1995:Picture:Braveheart
1995:Supporting Actor:Kevin Spacey
1994:Actor:Tom Hanks
1994:Picture:Forrest Gump
1928:Picture:WINGS
```

We would like to provide the following services:[*]

- Given a year and category, print the corresponding entry.

- Given a year, print all entries for that year.

- Given a category, print the year and title of all entries for that category.

- Print all entries sorted by category or by year.

Data Representation

Since we would like to retrieve entries by category or by year, we use a double indexing scheme, as shown in Figure 2-2.

Each entry includes a category, a year, and the name of the corresponding winner. We choose to keep this information in an anonymous array (an anonymous hash would do just as well). The two indices **%year_index** and

---

[*] To see real historical databases for the Oscars, look at *http://oscars.guide.com/*. (Illustra, an object-oriented database from Informix, is used for the grunge work.)

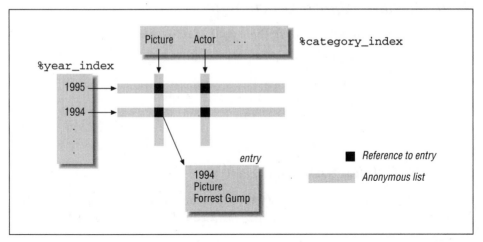

Figure 2-2. Data structure to represent Oscar winners

`%category_index` map the year and category to anonymous arrays containing references to the entries. Here is one way to build this structure:

```
open (F, "oscar.txt") || die "Could not open database: $:";
%category_index = (); %year_index = ();
while ($line = <F>) {
    chomp $line;
    ($year, $category, $name) = split (/:/, $line);
    create_entry($year, $category, $name) if $name;
}

sub create_entry {              # create_entry (year, category, name)
    my($year, $category, $name) = @_;
    # Create an anonymous array for each entry
    $rlEntry = [$year, $category, $name];
    # Add this to the two indices
    push (@{$year_index {$year}}, $rlEntry);         # By Year
    push (@{$category_index{$category}}, $rlEntry);  # By Category
}
```

Notice that each **push** statement does a fair bit of work. It creates an entry in the index (if required), hangs an anonymous array off that entry (if required), and pushes the reference to the entry into that array.

Another important thing to notice is how braces have been used to specify the correct precedence in the expression **@{$year_index{$year}}**. If we had omitted the braces, the expression **@$year_index** would be evaluated first and then indexed as a hash, according to the rules explained in the section "Confusion About Precedence" in Chapter 1, *Data References and Anonymous Storage.*

Print All Entries for a Given Year

This is a simple matter of traversing the `%year_index` hash:

```
sub print_entries_for_year {
    my($year) = @_;
    print ("Year : $year \n");
    foreach $rlEntry (@{$year_index{$year}}) {
        print ("\t",$rlEntry->[1], "  : ",$rlEntry->[2], "\n");
    }
}
```

Print All Entries Sorted by Year

We already know how to print entries for a given year. Find out all years for which we have data, sort them, and call `print_entries_for_year` for each year:

```
sub print_all_entries_for_year {
    foreach $year (sort keys %year_index) {
        print_entries_for_year($year);
    }
}
```

Print a Specific Entry, Given a Year and Category

We can traverse either index, and we choose to traverse the `%year_index` index, since there are substantially fewer categories per year than the number of years for which a category is valid:

```
sub print_entry {
    my($year, $category) = @_;
    foreach $rlEntry (@{$year_index{$year}}) {
        if ($rlEntry->[1] eq $category) {
            print "$category ($year), ", $rlEntry->[2], "\n";
            return;
        }
    }
    print "No entry for $category ($year) \n";
}
```

Pretty-Printing

In building complicated data structures, it is always nice to have a pretty-printer handy for debugging. There are at least two options for pretty-printing data structures. The first is the Perl debugger itself. It uses a function called `dumpValue` in a file called *dumpvar.pl*, which can be found in the standard library directory. We can help ourselves to it, with the caveat that it is an unadvertised function and could change someday. To pretty-print this structure, for example:

```
@sample = (11.233,{3 => 4, "hello" => [6,7]});
```

we write the following:

```
require 'dumpvar.pl';
dumpValue(\@sample); # always pass by reference
```

This prints something like this:

```
0   11.233
1   HASH(0xb75dc0)
    3 => 4
    'hello' => ARRAY(0xc70858)
        0  6
        1  7
```

We will cover the `require` statement in Chapter 6, *Modules*. Meanwhile, just think of it as a fancy `#include` (which doesn't load the file if it is already loaded).

The Data::Dumper module available from CPAN is another viable alternative for pretty-printing. Chapter 10, *Persistence*, covers this module in some detail, so we will not say any more about it here. Both modules detect circular references and handle subroutine and glob references.

It is fun and instructive to write a pretty-printer ourselves. Example 2-5 illustrates a simple effort, which accounts for circular references but doesn't follow type-globs or subroutine references. This example is used as follows:

```
pretty_print(@sample); # Doesn't need a reference
```

This prints

```
11.233
{ # HASH(0xb78b00)
: 3 => 4
: hello =>
:  :  [ # ARRAY(0xc70858)
:  :  :  6
:  :  :  7
:  :  ]
}
```

The following code contains specialized procedures (`print_array`, `print_hash`, or `print_scalar`) that know how to print specific data types. `print_ref`, charged with the task of pretty-printing a reference, simply dispatches control to one of the above procedures depending upon the type of argument given to it. In turn, these procedures may call `print_ref` recursively if the data types that they handle contain one or more references.

Whenever a reference is encountered, it is also checked with a hash `%already_seen` to determine whether the reference has been printed before. This prevents the routine from going into an infinite loop in the presence of circular references. All functions manipulate the global variable `$level` and call `print_indented`, which appropriately indents and prints the string given to it.

Example 2-5. Pretty-Printing

```perl
$level = -1; # Level of indentation

sub pretty_print {
    my $var;
    foreach $var (@_) {
        if (ref ($var)) {
            print_ref($var);
        } else {
            print_scalar($var);
        }
    }
}

sub print_scalar {
    ++$level;
    my $var = shift;
    print_indented ($var);
    --$level;
}

sub print_ref {
    my $r = shift;
    if (exists ($already_seen{$r})) {
        print_indented ("$r (Seen earlier)");
        return;
    } else {
        $already_seen{$r}=1;
    }
    my $ref_type = ref($r);
    if ($ref_type eq "ARRAY") {
        print_array($r);
    } elsif ($ref_type eq "SCALAR") {
        print "Ref -> $r";
        print_scalar($$r);
    } elsif ($ref_type eq "HASH") {
        print_hash($r);
    } elsif ($ref_type eq "REF") {
        ++$level;
        print_indented("Ref -> ($r)");
        print_ref($$r);
        --$level;
    } else {
        print_indented ("$ref_type (not supported)");
    }
}

sub print_array {
    my ($r_array) = @_;
    ++$level;
    print_indented ("[ # $r_array");
    foreach $var (@$r_array) {
        if (ref ($var)) {
            print_ref($var);
        } else {
```

Example 2-5. Pretty-Printing (continued)

```
            print_scalar($var);
        }
    }
    print_indented ("]");
    --$level;
}

sub print_hash {
    my($r_hash) = @_;
    my($key, $val);
    ++$level;
    print_indented ("{ # $r_hash");
    while (($key, $val) = each %$r_hash) {
        $val = ($val ? $val : '""');
        ++$level;
        if (ref ($val)) {
            print_indented ("$key => ");
            print_ref($val);
        } else {
            print_indented ("$key => $val");
        }
        --$level;
    }
    print_indented ("}");
    --$level;
}

sub print_indented {
    $spaces = ":  " x $level;
    print "${spaces}$_[0]\n";
}
```

`print_ref` simply prints its argument (a reference) and returns if it has already seen this reference. If you were to read the output produced by this code, you would find it hard to imagine which reference points to which structure. As an exercise, you might try producing a better pretty-printer, which identifies appropriate structures by easily identifiable numeric labels like this:

```
:  hello =>
:  :  [          # 10
:  :  :  6
:  :  :  7
:  :  ]
:  foobar => array-ref # 10
}
```

The number 10 is an automatically generated label, which is more easily identifiable than something like `ARRAY(0xc70858)`.

Resources

1. The FMTYEWTK series (Far More Than You Ever Wanted To Know). Tom Christiansen. Available at *http://www.perl.com/perl/everything_to_know*.

3

Typeglobs and Symbol Tables

> *We are symbols, and inhabit symbols.*
> —Ralph Waldo Emerson

This chapter discusses typeglobs, the symbol table, filehandles, formats, and the differences between dynamic and lexical scoping. At first sight, these topics may seem to lack a common theme, but as it happens, they are intimately tied to typeglobs and symbol tables.

Typeglobs are immensely useful. They allow us to efficiently create aliases of symbols, which is the basis for a very important module called Exporter that is used in a large number of freely available modules. Typeglobs can also be aliased to ordinary references in such a way that you don't have to use the dereferencing syntax; this is not only easier on the eye, it is faster too. At the same time, using typeglobs without understanding how they work can lead to a particularly painful problem called *variable suicide*. This might explain why most Perl literature gives typeglobs very little attention.

Closely related to typeglobs and symbol tables is the subject of dynamic versus lexical scoping (using `local` versus `my`). There are a couple of useful idioms that arise from these differences.

This is the only chapter that starts off by giving a picture of what is going on inside, rather than first presenting examples that you can use directly. The hope is that you will find the subsequent discussions really easy to follow.

Perl Variables, Symbol Table, and Scoping

Variables are either global or *lexical* (those tagged with my). In this section we briefly study how these two are represented internally. Let us start with global variables.

Perl has a curious feature that is typically not seen in other languages: you can use the same name for both data and nondata types. For example, the scalar $spud, the array @spud, the hash %spud, the subroutine &spud, the filehandle spud, and the format name spud are all simultaneously valid and completely independent of each other. In other words, Perl provides distinct namespaces for each type of entity. I do not have an explanation for why this feature is present. In fact, I consider it a rather dubious facility and recommend that you use a distinct name for each logical entity in your program; you owe it to the poor fellow who's going to maintain your code (which might be you!).

Perl uses a symbol table (implemented internally as a hash table)[*] to map identifier names (the string "spud" without the prefix) to the appropriate values. But you know that a hash table does not tolerate duplicate keys, so you can't really have two entries in the hash table with the same name pointing to two different values. For this reason, Perl interposes a structure called a typeglob between the symbol table entry and the other data types, as shown in Figure 3-1; it is just a bunch of pointers to values that can be accessed by the same name, with one pointer for each value type. In the typical case, in which you have unique identifier names, all but one of these pointers are null.

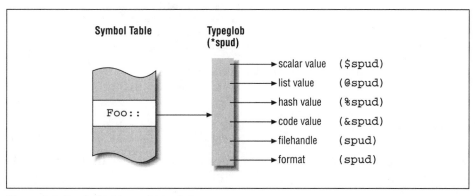

Figure 3-1. Symbol table and typeglobs

---

[*] Actually, it is one symbol table per package, where each package is a distinct namespace. For now, this distinction does not matter. We'll revisit this issue in Chapter 6, *Modules*.

A typeglob is a real data type accessible from script space and has the prefix "*"; while you can think of it as a wildcard representing all values sharing the identifier name, there's no pattern matching going on. You can assign typeglobs, store them in arrays, create local versions of them, or print them out, just as you can for any fundamental type. More on this in a moment.

Lexical Variables

Lexical variables (those tagged with my) aren't listed in the symbol table at all. Every block and subroutine gets a list of one or more arrays of variables called *scratchpads* (typically one, but more if the subroutine recurses). Each lexical variable is assigned one slot from a scratchpad; in fact, different types of variables with the same name—$spud and %spud, say—occupy different slots. Since a subroutine's lexical variables are independent of any other's, we get truly local variables. We will have more to say on this subject in Chapter 20, *Perl Internals*.

Lexical Versus Dynamic Scoping

There are two ways of getting private values inside a subroutine or block. One is to use the local operator, which operates on global variables only; it saves their values and arranges to have them restored at the end of the block. The other option is to use my, which not only creates a new variable, it marks it as private to the block.

On the surface, both local and my behave identically:

```
$a = 20;                          # global variable
{
      local ($a);                 # save $a's old value;
                                  # new value is undef
      my (@b);                    # Lexical variable
      $a = 10;                    # Modify $a's new value
      @b = ("wallace", "grommit");
      print $a;                   # prints "10"
      print "@b";                 # prints "wallace grommit"
}
# Block ended. Back to global scope where only $a is valid
print $a;                         # prints "20", the old value
print @b;                         # prints a warning, because no global @b
```

A global variable created because of a local statement gets deallocated at the end of the block.

While their usage is identical, there's one important difference between local and my. The my declaration creates truly local variables, such as auto variables in C. This is called *lexical* binding. The variable is private to the block in which it is declared and is available only to that block (what you can *see lexically* defines the bounds). It is not available to subroutines that are called from the block.

In contrast, the `local` operator does *not* create new variable. When applied to global variables, it squirrels their values away and restores them at the end of the block. Because the variables themselves are global, their new value is available not only to the block in which the `local` operator is used, but also to *all called subroutines*. Consider

```
$x = 10;
first();

sub first {
    local ($x) = "zen";      # $x is still global, and has a new value
    second();
}
sub second {
    print $x;   # Prints "zen", the current value of the global $x
}
```

From global scope, we call `first`, which *localizes* the global $x, sets it to a new value (the string "zen"), and calls `second`. `second` sees the last value of $x, as set by `first`. This process is called *dynamic scoping*, because the value of $x seen by `second` depends on the particular call stack. This feature can be quite confusing in practice, because if you wrote another subroutine that declared a `local $x` and called `second`, it would pick up that version of $x.

In other words, `local` makes a global variable's new value temporary; it does not change the essential nature of the variable itself (it still remains global). `my` creates a truly local variable. Which is why you can say

```
local $x{foo}; # Squirrel away $x{foo}'s value.
```

but not

```
my $x{foo};    # Error. $x{foo} is not a variable
```

It is recommended that you use `my` wherever possible, because you almost always want lexical scoping. In addition, as we shall see in Chapter 20, lexically scoped variables are faster than dynamically scoped variables.

When would you ever need to use local?

The fact that `local` saves a variable's value and arranges to have that value restored at the end of the block results in a very neat idiom: localizing built-in variables. Consider a local version of the built-in array representing the program's arguments, @ARGV:

```
{ # Start of a new block
    local(@ARGV) = ("/home/alone", "/vassily/kandinski");
    while (<>) {
        # Iterate through each file and process each line
        print;  # print, for example
    }
} # Block ends. The original @ARGV restored after this.
```

The diamond operator (<>) needs a globally defined @ARGV to work, so it looks at the typeglob corresponding to the ARGV entry in the symbol table.* What it doesn't know, however, is that local has temporarily replaced @ARGV's value with a different array. The diamond operator treats each element of this array as a filename, opens it, reads a line in every iteration, and moves on to the first line of the next file when necessary. When the block is over, the original @ARGV is restored. This example does not work with my, because this operator creates a wholly new variable.

This technique works for other built-in variables too. Consider the variable $/, which contains the input record separator ("\n" by default). The diamond input operator uses this separator to return the next chunk (by default, the next line). If you undef it, the whole file is slurped in, in one fell swoop. To avoid having to save the original value of $/ and restore it later, you can use local instead, like this:

```
{
    local $/ = undef; # Saves previous value of $/, and substitutes
                      # it with undef
    $a = <STDIN>;     # Slurp all of STDIN into $a
}
```

local is also used for localizing typeglobs, which, as it turns out, is the only way of getting local filehandles, formats, and directory handles.

Typeglobs

Typeglobs, we mentioned earlier, can be localized (with local only) and assigned to one another. Assigning a typeglob has the effect of aliasing one identifier name to another. Consider

```
$spud   = "Wow!";
@spud   = ("idaho", "russet");
*potato = *spud;   # Alias potato to spud using typeglob assignment
print "$potato\n"; # prints "Wow!"
print @potato, "\n"; # prints "idaho russet"
```

Once the typeglob assignment is made, all entities that were called "spud" can now also be referred to as "potato"—the names are freely interchangeable. That is, $spud and $potato are the same thing, and so are the subroutines &spud and &potato. Figure 3-2 shows the picture after a typeglob assignment; both entries in the symbol table end up pointing to the same typeglob value.†

---

* For efficiency, Perl doesn't do a symbol table lookup at run-time. The compilation phase ensures that the corresponding opcodes know which typeglob to pick up. More on this in Chapter 20.

† There is a wee bit of simplification here, which we will clarify in Chapter 20.

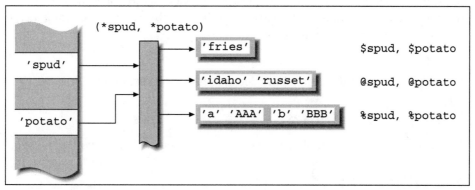

Figure 3-2. Assigning *spud to *potato: both symbol table entries point to the same typeglob

The alias holds true until the typeglob is reassigned or removed. (We will shortly see how to remove a typeglob.) In the example, there is no subroutine called spud, but if we define it *after* the typeglobs have been assigned, that subroutine can also be invoked as potato. It turns out that the alias works the other way too. If you assign a new list to @potato, it will also be automatically accessible as @spud.

Temporary Aliases

For now, there is no easy, intuitive way to get rid of an alias created by a typeglob assignment (you may reassign it, of course). You can, however, get temporary aliases using local, because it restores the typeglob's values at the end of the block.

Consider

```
$b = 10;
{
    local *b;      # Save *b's values
    *b = *a;       # Alias b to a
    $b = 20;       # Same as modifying $a instead
}                  # *b restored at end of block
print $a;          # prints "20"
print $b;          # prints "10"
```

local *b localizes all changes to variables named "b"; that is, it puts all of *b's value pointers into safekeeping and substitutes an undef value for all of them. This lasts until the end of the block, whereupon the previous values of everything named "b" are restored ($b becomes 10 again). Now, because of the alias (*b = *a), the assignment $b = 20 has the effect of modifying both $a and $b. But at the end of the block, only $b is restored, and $a is left with the new value.

While we are on the subject, it is important to recall that lexical variables and the symbol table have nothing to do with each other; for this reason, localizing a typeglob with my is a compile-time error:

```
my(*F);
```

The script dies with this error: "Can't declare ref-to-glob cast in my."

Using Typeglob Aliases

This section discusses a number of places where typeglob aliases work very well.

Efficient parameter passing

Aliases happen to be quite a bit faster than references, because they don't need to do any dereferencing. Consider

```
$a = 10;
*b = *a ; $b++ ;  # 1. Increment $a indirectly through the typeglob
$r = \$a; $$r++;  # 2. Increment $a indirectly through the reference
```

Case 1 is around one and a half times faster than case 2 on my PC.

The example code below uses typeglobs to efficiently pass an array by reference to a subroutine, DoubleEachEntry, which doubles each element of the array:

```
@array = (10,20);
DoubleEachEntry(*array); # @array and @copy are identical.
print "@array \n"; # prints 20 40

sub DoubleEachEntry {
    # $_[0] contains *array
    local *copy = shift;  # Create a local alias
    foreach $element (@copy) {
        $element *= 2;
    }
}
```

Note that only one parameter is passed to the subroutine. The typeglob *copy springs into existence when it is first encountered, but because it didn't exist prior to the local statement, it and the corresponding entry in the symbol table are removed at the end of the block.

Incidentally, the code also takes advantage of the fact that the foreach statement internally aliases each successive element of @copy to $element, so modifying $element affects the elements of @copy (and therefore @array as well).

You cannot use a lexically scoped array as a parameter to DoubleEachEntry, because lexical variables don't have typeglobs associated with them. The restriction is easily circumvented, however. Typeglobs and references are strangely equivalent, as it turns out. You can pass in an ordinary reference to a subroutine expecting a typeglob, and it'll work well. (We'll have a little more to say about this in the section "Typeglobs and References.") That is, you can pass lexically scoped arrays to `DoubleEachEntry` like this:

```
my @array = (1, 2, 3);
DoubleEachEntry(\@array); # Instead of *array, which wouldn't work
```

Aliasing on command lines

I often embed the Perl interpreter in my C/C++ programs to provide a powerful shell-like frontend. While I like to use long and descriptive subroutine names in Perl scripts, it is painful to keep typing them on the frontend's prompt. Aliases are very useful here:

```
sub a_long_drawn_out_sub_name {
    print "A sub by any other name is still a sub \n";
}
*f = *a_long_drawn_out_sub_name; # create an alias
```

Now typing `f()` on the command line is the same as calling the original subroutine but much easier on the carpals!

Friendly predefined variables with aliases

Consider the opposite case. Perl has a number of cryptic built-in variables such as `$!`, `$/`, and `$@`, and many people would much rather work with longer descriptive names. The module *English.pm* in the standard Perl library comes to the rescue; it provides nice big, long aliased names, such as `$ERRNO`, `$INPUT_RECORD_SEPARATOR`, and `$EVAL_ERROR` (respectively). Try this:

```
use English;    # Import the module file called English.pm
# Try deleting a non-existent file
unlink ('/tmp/foo');
if ($ERRNO) {   # Use $ERRNO instead of $!
    print $ERRNO, "\n"; # Prints "No such file or directory"
}
```

(We'll cover packages and the `use` statement in Chapter 6, *Modules*.) I think these well-known names should have been in there from the very beginning, instead of having to memorize funny-looking variables and an accompanying list of mnemonics. Some argue that you can use the same scheme for other languages ("`use Dutch;`"), but considering that the other system calls are in English anyway, I think that there's no point providing specific aliases for a small subset of the things you have to remember.

Aliasing Problem: Variable Suicide

Aliases, combined with the fact that `local` doesn't really create new variables (it temporarily slaps a new value onto a global variable), often leads to weird values of variables that presumably haven't even been touched. Consider the following simple case:

```
$x = 10;
foo(*x);
sub foo {
    local(*y) = @_;
    print "Before value of y : $y \n";
    local($x) = 100;
    print "After value of y : $y \n";
}
```

This prints the following:

```
Before value of y : 10
After value of y : 100
```

Can you resolve the mystery? Clearly, $y has not been touched between the two **print** statements, but its value seems to have changed. Hint: it reflects that of $x.

Let's trace the events in sequence:

```
$x = 10;                   # Assign a value to global $x
                           # function called
local *y = *x;             # Save global *y's values. Alias it to *x
print "before value"       # Because of the alias, $y is the same as $x,
                           # hence this prints 10
local $x = 100;            # IMPORTANT: local saves $x's value (10)
                           # and substitutes 100. Note that it does not
                           # create a new $x variable
                           # replaced by 100
print "after value";       # But *y is still aliased to *x. Therefore,
                           # $y now contains 100
```

The interaction of aliases and **local** can be even more subtle. Consider

```
foreach $f (10, 20, 30) {
    foo (*f);
}
sub foo {
    local (*g) = @_;
    $g++;
}
```

This prints the error: "Modification of a read-only value attempted at *try.pl* line 6."

The sequence is as follows: For efficiency, the **foreach** operator aliases $f to the next element of the list in every iteration, each of which is a constant. The subroutine **foo** aliases *g to *f, which means that $g is aliased to a constant. For this reason, the operation $g++ causes a problem.

Moral of the story: if you want truly local variables, use **my**. Use typeglob aliasing and **local** sparingly.

Typeglobs and References

You might have noticed that both typeglobs and references point to *values*. A variable `$a` can be seen simply as a dereference of a typeglob `${*a}`. For this reason, Perl makes the two expressions `${\$a}` and `${*a}` refer to the same scalar value. This equivalence of typeglobs and ordinary references has some interesting properties and results in three useful idioms, described here.

Selective Aliasing

Earlier, we saw how a statement like `*b = *a` makes everything named "a" be referred to as "b" also. There is a way to create selective aliases, using the reference syntax:

```
*b = \$a;     # Assigning a scalar reference to a typeglob
```

Perl arranges it such that `$b` and `$a` are aliases, but `@b` and `@a` (or `&b` and `&a`, and so on) are not.

Constants

We get read-only variables by creating references to constants, like this:

```
*PI = \3.1415927;
# Now try to modify it.
$PI = 10;
```

Perl complains: "Modification of a read-only value attempted at *try.pl* line 3."

Naming Anonymous Subroutines

We will cover anonymous subroutines in the next chapter, so you might want to come back to this example later.

If you find it painful to call a subroutine indirectly through a reference (`&$rs()`), you can assign a name to it for convenience:

```
sub generate_greeting {
    my ($greeting) = @_;
        sub { print "$greeting world\n";}
}
$rs = generate_greeting("hello");
# Instead of invoking it as $&rs(), give it your own name.
*greet = $rs;
greet();    # Equivalent to calling $&rs(). Prints "hello world\n"
```

Of course, you can also similarly give a name to other types of references.

References to Typeglobs

We have seen how references and typeglobs are equivalent (in the sense that references can be assigned to typeglobs). Perl also allows you to take references *to* typeglobs by prefixing it with a backslash as usual:

```
$ra = \*a;
```

References to typeglobs are not used much in practice, because it is very efficient to pass typeglobs around directly. This is similar to the case of ordinary scalars, which don't need references to pass them around for efficiency.

Filehandles, Directory Handles, and Formats

The built-in functions `open` and `opendir` initialize a filehandle and a directory handle, respectively:

```
open(F, "/home/calvin");
opendir (D, "/usr");
```

The symbols `F` and `D` are user-defined identifiers, but without a prefix symbol. Unfortunately, these handles don't have some basic facilities enjoyed by the important data types such as scalars, arrays, and hashes—you cannot assign handles, and you cannot create local handles:[*]

```
local (G);    # invalid
G = F;        # also invalid
```

Before we go further, it is important to know that the standard Perl distribution comes with a module called FileHandle that provides an object-oriented version of filehandles. This allows you to create filehandle "objects," to assign one to the other, and to create them local to the block. Similarly, directory handles are handled by DirHandle. Developers are now encouraged to use these facilities instead of the techniques described next. But you still need to wade through the next discussion because there is a large amount of freeware code in which you will see these constructs; in fact, the standard modules FileHandle, DirHandle, and Symbol, as well as the entire IO hierarchy of modules, are built on this foundation.

Why is it so important to be able to assign handles and create local filehandles? Without assignment, you cannot pass filehandles as parameters to subroutines or maintain them in data structures. Without local filehandles, you cannot create recursive subroutines that open files (for processing included files, which themselves might include more, for example).

---

[*] I don't know why filehandles didn't get a standard prefix symbol and the other features enjoyed by the other data types.

The simple answer to this solution is to use typeglob assignment. That is, if you feel the urge to say,

```
G = F;
# or,
local(F);
```

you can write it instead in terms of typeglobs:

```
*G = *F;
# or,
local (*F);
```

Similarly, if you want to store filehandles in data structures or create references to them, you use the corresponding typeglob. All I/O operators that require filehandles also accept typeglob references. Let us take a look at what we can do with assigning filehandles and localizing them (using typeglobs, of course).

I/O Redirection

The following example shows how I/O can be simply redirected:

```
open(F, '>/tmp/x') || die;
*STDOUT = *F;
print "hello world\n";
```

The **print** function thinks it is sending the output to **STDOUT** but ends up sending it to the open file instead, because the typeglob associated with **STDOUT** has been aliased to **F**. If you want this redirection to be temporary, you can localize ***STDOUT**.

Passing Filehandles to Subroutines

The following piece of code passes a filehandle to a subroutine:

```
open (F, "/tmp/sesame") || die $!;
read_and_print(*F);
sub read_and_print {
    local (*G) = @_;  # Filehandle G is the same as filehandle F
    while (<G>) { print; }
}
```

You might wonder why you don't need to do the same with **open**; after all it is a subroutine too and takes a filehandle as a parameter. Well, for built-in functions such as **open**, **read**, **write**, and **readdir**, Perl automatically passes the typeglob of that symbol (instead of a string called "F", for example).

Localizing Filehandles

Let us look at a subroutine that traverses include declarations in C header files. The subroutine shown next, **ProcessFile**, looks at each line of a file and, if it matches a *#include* declaration, extracts the filename and calls itself recursively. Since it has more lines to process in the original file, it cannot `close` the file-handle `F`. If `F` is global, it cannot be reused to open another file, so we use `local(*F)` to localize it. That way, each recursive invocation of `ProcessFile` gets its own unique filehandle value.

```perl
sub ProcessFile {
    my ($filename) = @_;
    my ($line);
    local (*F);              # Save old value of typeglob, (which means
                             # its filehandles, among other things)
    open (F, $filename) || return;
    while ($line = <F>) {
      # same as before
      ........
    }
    close(F);
}
```

Although we have not studied packages, it might be worth it to see how we could have used the FileHandle module in this case:

```perl
use FileHandle;
sub ProcessFile {
    my ($filename) = @_;
    my ($line);
    my $fh = new FileHandle; # Create local filehandle
    open ($fh, $filename) || return;
    while ($line = <$fh>) {
        ........
    }
    close($fh);
}
```

Strings as Handles

It so happens that typeglobs and objects of the FileHandle module are not the only solution. All Perl I/O functions that accept a handle also happen to accept a string instead. Consider

```perl
$fh = "foo";
open ($fh, "< /home/snoopy") ;
read ($fh, $buf, 1000);
```

When `open` examines its parameters, it finds a string where a typeglob should have been. In this case, it automatically creates a typeglob of that name and then proceeds as before. Similarly, when `read` gets a string instead of a typeglob, it looks up the corresponding typeglob from the symbol table, and then the internal filehandle, and proceeds to read the appropriate file. This extra lookup is slightly slower than using a bareword symbol, but the time taken is insignificant if you do the I/O in reasonably large chunks (the optimal size varies from system to system).

4

Subroutine References and Closures

> *Many are called, but few are called back.*
> —Sister Mary Tricky

As with ordinary variables, subroutines can be named or anonymous, and Perl has a syntax for taking a reference to either type. Such references work rather like pointers to functions in C, and they can be used to create such sophisticated structures as the following:

- *Dispatch tables.* Or data structures that map events to subroutine references. When an event comes in, a dispatch table is used to look up the corresponding subroutine. This is useful in creating large and efficient switch statements, finite state machines, signal handlers, and GUI toolkits.

- *Higher-order procedures.* A higher-order procedure takes other procedures as arguments (like the C library procedure `qsort`) or returns new procedures. The latter feature is available only in interpreted languages such as Perl, Python, and LISP (hey, LISPers, you have lambda functions!).

- *Closures.* A closure is a subroutine that, when created, packages its containing subroutine's environment (all the variables it requires and that are not local to itself).

In the following sections, we look at the syntax for taking and managing subroutine references and subsequently use them in the applications listed.

Subroutine References

There's nothing particularly fancy or magical about subroutine references. In this section, we'll study how to create references to named and anonymous subroutines and how to dereference them.

References to Named Subroutines

We saw earlier that to take a reference to an existing variable, we prefix it with a backslash. It is much the same with subroutines. `\&mysub` is a reference to `&mysub`. For example:

```
sub greet {
    print "hello \n";
}
$rs = \&greet; # Create a reference to subroutine greet
```

It is important to note that we are not *calling* the `greet` subroutine here, in the same way that we don't evaluate the value of a scalar when we take a reference to it.

Contrast this to the following code, which uses parentheses:

```
$rs = \&greet();
```

This expression likely doesn't do what you expect. It calls `greet` and produces a reference to its *return value*, which is the value of the last expression evaluated inside that subroutine. Since `print` executed last and returned a 1 or a 0 (indicating whether or not it was successful in printing the value), the result of this expression is a reference to a scalar containing 1 or 0! These are the kind of mistakes that make you wish for type-safety once in a while!

To summarize, do not use parentheses when taking a subroutine reference.

References to Anonymous Subroutines

You can create an anonymous subroutine simply by omitting the name in a subroutine declaration. In every other respect, the declaration is identical to a named one.

```
$rs = sub {
        print "hello \n";
    };
```

This expression returns a reference to the newly declared subroutine. Notice that because it is an expression, it requires the semicolon at the end, unlike the declaration of a named subroutine.

Dereferencing Subroutine References

Dereferencing a subroutine reference calls the subroutine indirectly. As with data references, Perl does not care whether `$rs` is pointing to a named or an anonymous subroutine; dereferencing works the same way in either case.

It should come as no surprise that prepending `$rs` with the appropriate prefix—"&", in this case—dereferences it:

```
&$rs(10, 20);  # Call the subroutine indirectly
```

That's all there is to it.

Just as you can use the `->` syntax with arrays or hashes (`$ra->[10]` or `$rh->{'k2'}`), you can call subroutines indirectly through references, like this:

```
$rsub->(10);
```

In fact, subroutine calls can be chained if the intermediate calls return subroutine references. For example:

```
$rs = \&test1;
$rs->("Batman")->("Robin"); # Prints "Batman and Robin"

sub test1 {
    my $arg = shift;
    print "$arg";
    return \&test2;
}
sub test2 {
    my $arg = shift;
    print " and $arg\n";
}
```

Symbolic References

Recall that symbolic references contain names (strings), not real references. There is no difference in syntax between real and symbolic references. Consider

```
sub foo { print "foo called\n" }
$rs = "foo";
&$rs();  # prints "foo called"
```

Using symbolic references is a mite slower than using real references.

Using Subroutine References

Let's look at some common examples of using subroutine references: callback functions and higher-order procedures.

A callback function is an ordinary subroutine whose reference is passed around. The caller (who uses that reference) doesn't necessarily have an idea of which subroutine is getting invoked. Let's examine three simple examples involving callback functions: dispatch tables, signal handlers, and plotting functions.

Dispatch Table

A typical dispatch table is an array of subroutine references. The following example shows %options as a dispatch table that maps a set of command-line options to different subroutines:

```
%options = (        # For each option, call appropriate subroutine.
    "-h"        => \&help,
    "-f"        => sub {$askNoQuestions = 1},
    "-r"        => sub {$recursive = 1},
    "_default_" => \&default,
);

ProcessArgs (\@ARGV, \%options); # Pass both as references
```

Some of these references in this code are to named subroutines. Others don't do much, so it is just simpler to code them as inline, anonymous subroutines. ProcessArgs can now be written in a very generic way. It takes two arguments: a reference to an array that it parses and a mapping of options that it refers to while processing the array. For each option, it calls the appropriate "mapped" function, and if an invalid flag is supplied in @ARGV, it calls the function corresponding to the string _default_.

ProcessArgs is shown in Example 4-1.

Example 4-1. ProcessArgs

```
ProcessArgs (\@ARGV, \%options); # Pass both as references
sub ProcessArgs {
    # Notice the notation: rl = ref. to array, rh = ref. to hash
    my ($rlArgs, $rhOptions) = @_;
    foreach $arg (@$rlArgs) {
        if (exists $rhOptions->{$arg}) {
            # The value must be a reference to a subroutine
            $rsub = $rhOptions->{$arg};
            &$rsub();   # Call it.
        } else {            #option does not exist.
            if (exists $rhOptions->{"_default_"}) {
                &{$rhOptions{"_default_"}};
            }
        }
    }
}
```

You can omit one step by using the block form of dereferencing (hark back to "A More General Rule" in Chapter 1, *Data References and Anonymous Storage*), like this:

```
if (exists $rhOptions->{$arg}) {
    &{$rhOptions->{$arg}}(); # Dereference and call sub in one shot
}
```

I prefer the more verbose version for its readability.

Signal Handlers

Usually, a program works by calling functions implemented by the operating system, not vice versa. An exception to this rule is when the operating system has an urgent message to deliver to the program. In many operating systems, the delivery is accomplished by means of signals. A signal might be issued, for example, when a user presses Ctrl-C, when a floating-point exception is trapped by the hardware, or when a child process dies. You can specify a function to be called whenever a signal is delivered to your program. This allows you to take appropriate action. A Ctrl-C handler, for example, might perform clean-up before exiting. A floating-point exception handler might set an error flag and resume normal operation.

Perl provides a convenient way to specify signal handlers for each type of signal. There's a special variable called %SIG whose keys are the names of signals, and its values correspond to subroutine names or references, which are called for the corresponding signal.

```
sub ctrl_c_handler  {
        print "Ctrl C pressed \n";
}
$SIG {"INT"} = \&ctrl_c_handler;  # "INT" indicates  "Interrupt"
                                  # signal.
```

Here, the word INT is a reserved string and signifies keyboard interrupts with Ctrl-C. Your operating system's documentation for signals will tell you the names of signals that might be sent to your program or script. In fact, you can get this information from Perl also by asking it to print out some of its configuration information:

```
use Config; # Load the Config module
print $Config{sig_name};
```

When you assign values to %SIG, Perl also allows you to give the *name* of the subroutine, so you don't *have* to give it a subroutine reference:

```
$SIG {"INT"} = 'ctrl_c_handler';  # Name of the subroutine passed.
```

Incidentally, signal handlers are fraught with peril. Perl internally uses C library functions such as malloc, which are not *reentrant*. If a signal handler is triggered just when such a function is being called and the signal handler also happens to call the same function, the function gets totally confused and is likely to crash the system. This behavior is even more insidious at the script level, because you have no idea when Perl might call malloc. (Chapter 20, *Perl Internals*, should give you a very good idea.) The moral of the story is that you should attempt to do the least possible work in a signal handler, such as set a previously defined global variable to true, and check this variable's value in the code outside.

Expression plotting

Suppose we want to plot a variety of functions, of the general type:

```
y = f(x)
```

where `f(x)` is a function that takes a number as an argument and returns another number. Examples include `sin(x)`, `cos(x)`, and `sqrt(x)`. But in addition to such simple examples, we would like to be able to plot arbitrarily complex expressions such as

```
y = sin(2x) + cos²(x);
```

It is easy to develop a subroutine `plot` that can plot this expression in the range 0 to 2π:

```
$PI = 3.1415927;
$rs = sub {                              # Anonymous subroutine
    my($x) = @_;
    return sin (2*$x) + cos($x) ** 2; # Function to be plotted
};
plot ($rs, 0, 2 * $PI, 0.01);
```

This is an example of a higher-order procedure that takes (a reference to) another user-defined subroutine as an input parameter and calls it one or more times. `sort` is an example of a built-in higher-order procedures; the difference is that it takes subroutine *names*, not references.

Closures

Instead of returning *data*, a Perl subroutine can return a reference to a *subroutine*. This is really no different from any other ways of passing subroutine references around, except for a somewhat hidden feature involving anonymous subroutines and lexical (**my**) variables. Consider

```
$greeting = "hello world";
$rs = sub {
    print $greeting;
};
&$rs();   #prints "hello world"
```

In this example, the anonymous subroutine makes use of the global variable `$greeting`. No surprises here, right? Now, let's modify this innocuous example slightly:

```
sub generate_greeting {
    my($greeting) = "hello world";
    return sub {print $greeting};
}
$rs = generate_greeting();
&$rs(); # Prints "hello world"
```

The `generate_greeting` subroutine returns the reference to an anonymous subroutine, which in turn prints `$greeting`. The curious thing is that `$greeting` is a `my` variable that belongs to `generate_greeting`. Once `generate_greeting` finishes executing, you would expect all its local variables to be destroyed. But when you invoke the anonymous subroutine later on, using `&$rs()`, it manages to still print `$greeting`. How does it work?

Any other expression in place of the anonymous subroutine definition would have used `$greeting` right away. A subroutine block, on the other hand, is a package of code to be invoked at a *later* time, so it keeps track of all the variables it is going to need later on (taking them "to go," in a manner of speaking). When this subroutine is called subsequently and invokes `print "$greeting"`, the subroutine remembers the value that `$greeting` had when that subroutine was *created*.

Let's modify this a bit more to really understand what this idiom is capable of:

```
sub generate_greeting {
    my($greeting) = @_;      # $greeting primed by arguments
    return sub {
                my($subject)= @_;
                print "$greeting $subject \n";
            };
}
$rs1 = generate_greeting("hello");
$rs2 = generate_greeting("my fair");

# $rs1 and $rs2 are two subroutines holding on to different $greeting's
&$rs1 ("world") ;  # prints "hello world"
&$rs2 ("lady") ;   # prints "my fair lady"
```

Instead of hardcoding `$greeting`, we get it from `generate_greeting`'s arguments. When `generate_greeting` is called the first time, the anonymous subroutine that it returns holds onto `$greeting`'s value. Hence the subroutine referred to by `$rs1` behaves somewhat like this:

```
$rs1 = sub {
    my ($subject) = @_;
    my $greeting = "hello";
    print "$greeting $subject\n";   # $greeting's value is "hello"
}
```

The subroutine is known as a *closure* (the term comes from the LISP world). As you can see, it captures `$greeting`'s value, and when it is invoked later on, it needs only one parameter.

Like some immigrants to a country who retain the culture and customs of the place in which they are born, closures are subroutines that package all the variables they need from the scope in which they are created.

As it happens, Perl creates closures only over lexical (my) variables and not over global or localized (tagged with local) variables. Let's take a peek under the covers to understand why this is so.

Closures, Behind the Scenes

If you are not interested in the details of how closures work, you can safely go on to the next section without loss of continuity.

Recall that the name of a variable and its value are separate entities. When it first sees $greeting, Perl binds the name "greeting" to a freshly allocated scalar value, setting the value's reference count to 1 (there's now an arrow pointing to the value). At the end of the block, Perl disassociates the name from the scalar value and decrements the value's reference count. In a typical block where you don't squirrel away references to that value, the value would be deallocated, since the reference count comes down to zero. In this example, however, the anonymous subroutine happens to use $greeting, so it increments that scalar value's reference count, thus preventing its automatic deallocation when generate_ greeting finishes. When generate_greeting is called a second time, the name "greeting" is bound to a whole new scalar value, and so the second closure gets to hang on to *its own* scalar value.

Why don't closures work with local variables? Recall from Chapter 3, *Typeglobs and Symbol Tables*, that variables marked local are dynamically scoped (or "temporarily global"). A local variable's value depends on the call stack at the moment at which it is *used*. For this reason, if $greeting were declared local, Perl would look up its value when the anonymous subroutine is *called* (actually when print is called inside it), not when it is *defined*. You can verify this with a simple test:

```
sub generate_greeting {
    local ($greeting) = @_;
    return sub {
        print "$greeting \n" ;
    }
}
$rs = generate_greeting("hello");
$greeting = "Goodbye";
&$rs();        # Prints "Goodbye", not "hello"
```

The anonymous subroutine is *not* a closure in this case, because it doesn't hang onto the local value of $greeting ("hello") at the time of its creation. Once generate_greeting has finished executing, $greeting is back to its old global value, which is what is seen by the anonymous subroutine while executing.

It might appear that every time generate_greeting returns an anonymous subroutine, it creates a whole new packet of code internally. That isn't so. The code for the anonymous subroutine is generated once during compile time. `$rs` is internally a reference to a "code value," which in turn keeps track not only of the byte-codes themselves (which it shares with all other subroutine references pointing to the same piece of code), but also all the variables it requires from its environment (each subroutine reference packs its own private context for later use). Chapter 20 does less hand-waving and supplies exact details.

To summarize, a closure is the special case of an anonymous subroutine holding onto data that used to belong to its scope at the time of its creation.

Using Closures

Closures are used in two somewhat distinct ways. The most common usage is as "smart" callback procedures. The other idiom is that of "iterators" (or "streams," as they are known in the LISP world).

Using Closures as "Smart" Callbacks

Since closures are subroutine references with a bit of private data thrown in, they are very convenient to use as callback procedures in graphical user interfaces.

Let's say you create a button using the Tk toolkit and give it a subroutine reference. When the button is pressed, it calls this subroutine back. Now if the same subroutine is given to two different buttons on the screen, there's a problem: How does the subroutine know which button is calling it? Simple. Instead of giving the button a reference to an ordinary subroutine, you give it a "smart" callback subroutine—a closure. This closure stores away some data specific to a button (such as its name), and when the subroutine is called, it magically has access to that data, as shown in Example 4-2.

This example creates two buttons that when clicked, print out their title strings. Though the discussion about packages and, specifically, the Tk module is slated for chapters to come, you might still understand the gist of the code in Example 4-2. For the moment, pay attention only to the part that uses closures (highlighted in boldface) and not to the mechanics of using the Tk module.

`CreateButton` creates a GUI button and feeds it a reference to an anonymous subroutine reference (`$callback_proc`), which holds on to `$title`, a `my` variable in its enclosing environment. When the user clicks on the button, the callback is invoked, whereupon it uses its stored value of `$title`.

Example 4-2. Passing Closures Instead of Ordinary Subroutines

```
use Tk;
# Creates a top level window
$topwindow = MainWindow->new();
```

Example 4-2. Passing Closures Instead of Ordinary Subroutines (continued)

```
# Create two buttons. The buttons print their names when clicked on.
CreateButton($topwindow, "hello");
CreateButton($topwindow, "world");
Tk::MainLoop();  # Dispatch events.
#-----------------------------------------------------------------
sub CreateButton {
    my ($parent, $title) = @_;
    my($b);
    $callback_proc = sub {
                            print "Button $title pressed\n";
                        };
    $b = $parent->Button(
        '-text'    => "$title",      # Button title
        '-fg'      => 'red',         # foreground color
        '-command' => $callback_proc   # sub to call when the button
                                     # is pressed
    );
    $b->pack();
}
```

Note that the buttons couldn't care less whether they get references to ordinary subroutines or closures.

Iterators and Streams

An iterator keeps track of where it currently is in a "stream" of entities and returns the next logical entity every time it is called. It is like a database cursor, which returns the next record from a stream of records (the list of records that match the given query). A stream can be bounded (a set of records from a database) or unbounded (a stream of even numbers).

Let's take a look at how closures can be used to represent streams and iterators. The first example is a stream of even numbers and an iterator on this stream that returns the next even number whenever it is called. Clearly, we cannot generate all possible even numbers (as in the bounded case), but we can always compute the next even number if we remember the previous number generated. The iterator remembers this crucial piece of information.

Subroutine `even_number_printer_gen` takes an integer and returns a subroutine that prints even numbers starting from the given integer.[*] This program is shown in Example 4-3.

---

[*] This example and explanation are based on Robert Wilensky's excellent book *LISPcraft* (W.W. Norton and Co.).

Example 4-3. An Even Number Stream Generator

```
sub even_number_printer_gen {
    # This function returns a reference to an anon. subroutine.
    # This anon. subroutine prints even numbers starting from $input.
    my($input) = @_;
    if ($input % 2) { $input++};   # Next even number, if the given
                                   # number is odd
    $rs = sub {
                print "$input ";   # Using $input,which is a my variable
                                   # declared in an outside scope
                $input += 2;
          };
    return $rs;   # Return a reference to the subroutine above
}
```

And now for its usage:

```
# We want even numbers starting from 30. Ask even_number_printer_gen
# for a customized iterator that can do such a thing.

$iterator = even_number_printer_gen(30);
# $iterator now points to a closure.
# Every time you call it, it prints the next successive even number.
for ($i = 0; $i < 10; $i++) {
    &$iterator();
}
print "\n";
```

This prints

```
30 32 34 36 38 40 42 44 46 48
```

`$iterator` holds on to `$input` and uses it as private storage subsequently, storing the last even number. Of course, you can create as many iterators as you want, each primed with its own starting number:

```
$iterator1 = even_number_print_gen (102);
$iterator2 = even_number_print_gen (22);

&$iterator1(); # Prints 102
&$iterator2(); # Prints 22
&$iterator1(); # Prints 104
&$iterator2(); # Prints 24
```

Notice how each subroutine reference is using its own private value for `$input`.

Can two closures share the same variables? Sure, as long as they are created in the same environment. Example 4-4 produces two anonymous functions, one that prints even numbers and another that prints odd numbers. Each of these functions prints out the even (or odd) number after the number last printed (by either function), regardless of how many times either of them is called in succession.

Example 4-4. Closures Sharing Variables

```
sub even_odd_print_gen {
    # $last is shared between the two procedures
    my ($rs1, $rs2);
    my ($last) = shift;  # Shared by the two closures below
    $rs1 = sub { # Even number printer
        if ($last % 2) {$last ++;}
        else { $last += 2};
        print "$last \n";
    };
    $rs2 = sub { # Odd number printer
        if ($last % 2) {$last += 2 }
        else { $last++};
        print "$last \n";
    };
    return ($rs1, $rs2);   # Returning two anon sub references
}

($even_iter,$odd_iter) = even_odd_print_gen(10);
&$even_iter ();   # prints 12
&$odd_iter ();    # prints 13
&$odd_iter  ();   # prints 15
&$even_iter ();   # prints 16
&$odd_iter  ();   # prints 17
```

This example takes advantage of the fact that Perl can return multiple values from one subroutine, so there is no problem returning references to two anonymous subroutines, both of which happen to be referring to $last. You can call even_ odd_print_gen as many times as you want with different seeds, and it keeps returning pairs of subroutine closures. The important point is that to share the same data, the anonymous subroutines must have been created in the same scope. This example also highlights the fact that a closure truly hangs onto the my variables it needs instead of copying or interpolating the variable's values.

Random number generation

Let's turn our attention to a more useful example of an unbounded stream, that of a stream of random numbers. The strategy is identical to that used in the previous example: the iterator keeps track of the last generated pseudo-random number.

You might argue that the rand() function represents an iterator primed with a seed (using srand). You are right. But let's say you want to write a simulation program that depends on two *independent* sources of random number generation. Using rand in both these sources does not make them independent; the reason is that rand happens to calculate a new random number based on the last number it generated (it stores it in a global variable), and calling rand for one stream affects the next number retrieved by the other stream.

Closures provide a nice solution, because they are a combination of code and *private* data. Instead of using `srand`, we'll use the function `my_srand`, which returns a random-number-generating subroutine, seeded with an appropriate initial value. In other words, `my_srand` is a "generator of random number generators" that returns a custom anonymous subroutine, primed with an initial value for `$rand`.

In the implementation in Example 4-5, please don't pay too much attention to the algorithm itself (the linear congruential method), because the randomness due to the particular constants chosen has not been tested (it also repeats every 1,000 numbers). Besides, there are much better algorithms.

Example 4-5. A Random-Number-Generating Stream

```
sub my_srand {
    my ($seed) = @_;
    # Returns a random number generator function
    # Being predictive, the algorithm requires you to supply a
    # random initial value.

    my $rand = $seed;
        return sub {
            # Compute a new pseudo-random number based on its old value
            # This number is constrained between 0 and 1000.
            $rand = ($rand*21+1)%1000;
    };
}
```

We can now use `my_srand` as many times as we want and get back completely independent closures, each capable of generating random numbers from its own starting point:

```
$random_iter1 = my_srand  (100);
$random_iter2 = my_srand (1099);
for ($i = 0; $i < 100; $i++) {
    print $random_iter1(), " ", $random_iter2(), "\n";
}
```

Closures Versus Objects

If you don't have a background in object orientation, you might be able to understand this section better after you have read Chapter 7, *Object-Oriented Programming*.

An object, to give the street definition, is a package of data and functions. The data provides the context for the object's functions to work properly. When you say, for example, `$button->setForeground("yellow")`, the `setForeground` function automatically knows which button you are talking about.

In a sense, the facility for closures attempts the same feature—it is also a binding between a subroutine and some private data that is available only to that subroutine. As we saw earlier, in the `even_odd_print_gen` example, there can be any number of subroutines that can refer to the same basic data, as long as they were all created in exactly the same scope. Abelson, Sussman, and Sussman's delightful *Structure and Interpretation of Computer Programs* [2] illustrates how to create and use such objects in Scheme (a LISP dialect).

Perl supports a number of features for object orientation (such as inheritance and virtual functions *à la* C++) that make it easier to create iterators and streams in an object-oriented style than by using closures (the object's attributes reflect the "state" of the iterator). Closures are also *much* more space-intensive than objects but a trifle faster; we will study the reason for this in Chapter 20.

I prefer objects to closures in all cases except one: callback procedures. I find it easier to implement callbacks with simple closures than to create "callback objects," as you might typically do in C++ (and *have* to, in Java). In the `Create-Button` example above, you could create a callback object with exactly one "method," say, `execute()`. The button would call the method `$callback_object->execute()` when it was clicked upon, and the `execute` method of that object would know exactly what to do. The callback object can store all the context for `execute` to work. Instead of all this work, it is simpler and more direct to use closures, because they automatically squirrel away the required context.

Tom Christiansen's *perltoot* document (*toot* stands for Tom's Object-Oriented Tutorial [1]) implements objects *using* closures to represent the objects' state. It is an interesting approach, but I don't use it because there are simpler approaches for obtaining privacy; besides, they are faster too. More on this in Chapter 7.

Comparisons to Other Languages

Tcl

Tcl programmers rely heavily on dynamic evaluation (using `eval`) to pass around bits and pieces of code. While you can do this in Perl also, Perl's anonymous subroutines are packets of precompiled code, which definitely work faster than dynamic evaluation. Perl closures give you other advantages that are not available in Tcl: the ability to share private variables between different closures (in Tcl, they have to be *global* variables for them to be sharable) and not worry about variable interpolation rules (in Tcl, you have to take care to completely expand all the variables yourself using interpolation before you pass a piece of code along to somebody else).

Python

Python offers a weak form of closures: a subroutine can pick up variables only from its immediate containing environment. This is called "shallow binding," while Perl offers "deep binding." Mark Lutz's *Programming Python* (O'Reilly, 1996) shows a workaround to achieve deep binding, by setting default arguments to values in the immediately enclosing scope.

I prefer the environment to handle this stuff automatically for me, as Perl does.

C++

C++ supports pointers to subroutines but does not support closures. You have to use the callback object idiom wherever a callback subroutine needs some contextual data to operate. If you don't want a separate callback object, you can inherit your object from a standard callback class and override a method called, say, "execute," so that the caller can simply say `callback_object->execute()`.

Java

Java offers neither closures nor pointers to subroutines (methods). Interfaces can be used to provide a standardized callback interface so that the caller doesn't have to care about the specific class of the object (as long as it implements that interface).

Resources

1. *perlref, perlmod, perlsub, perltoot* (Perl documentation).

2. *Structure and Interpretation of Computer Programs.* Harold Abelson, Gerald Jay Sussman, Julie Sussman. MIT Press, 1996.

   Uses LISP to explain higher-order procedures and closures. A pleasure to read.

5

Eval

> *One person's data is another person's program.*
> —Programming Pearls
> *Communications of the ACM, Sept. 1985*

Years ago, a friend of mine showed me an elegant program running on a tiny 48K machine, the BBC Micro, that accepted any mathematical expression such as `sin(x) + cos (x**2)` and graphed it. Fresh from a study of parsers, I'd wondered how many hundreds of lines it took him to write it. He showed me the code; the entire program fit on the small screen. He had used the `eval` statement provided by BASIC.

Most self-respecting scripting languages such as BASIC (some versions, anyway), Perl, Tcl, LISP, and Python have a feature that clearly sets them apart from systems programming languages like C: the ability to treat character strings as little programs.*

For me, Perl's run-time evaluation capability is one of the biggest reasons for using the language. (The other is its terrific support for regular expressions.) I use run-time evaluation for creating little snippets of code on the fly, which then execute at typical Perl speeds (i.e., fast!), for writing sophisticated interpreters for little languages.† The `eval` function is the gateway to this power. We will use this

---

* On a related note, see the section "Dynamic Behavior" in Appendix B for other Perl constructs that set Perl apart from systems programming languages.

† For a delightful discussion of little languages, do have a look at Jon Bentley's *More Programming Pearls* [1].

feature in Chapter 7, *Object-Oriented Programming*, for creating object accessor functions, and in Chapter 11, *Implementing Object Persistence*, for building an SQL query evaluator, among other things.

As it turns out, Perl's `eval` function works in two somewhat distinct ways, depending on the type of its argument. If given a *string*, `eval` treats the string as a little program and compiles and executes it (as mentioned above); this is called dynamic expression evaluation. The contents of the string may or may not be known at compile time. Alternatively, if given a *block* of code—that is, the code is known at compile time—`eval` traps run-time exceptions.

Dynamic expression evaluation and exception handling are very different topics and one would expect them to be performed by different keywords. Larry Wall once mentioned that he had toyed with the idea of using a different keyword, `try`, for the exception-handling version, but he was into keyword conservation at that point. I find that a single keyword actually works well because expressions evaluated on the fly have a greater chance of generating run-time exceptions as code known at compile-time.

In this chapter, you will gain an in-depth understanding of how the two forms of `eval` work and add an important dimension to your toolkit of idioms.

The String Form: Expression Evaluation

When Perl is given a file to execute or a string as a command line option (using -*e*), it needs to parse the contents, check it for syntax errors, and, if all is fine, execute it. Perl makes this feature available to the programmer through the `eval` *string* form. This contrasts powerfully with languages such as C, C++, or Java, where the compiler itself is a separate beast from your program, not available to it at run-time. In other words, the Perl interpreter itself works *somewhat* like this:

```
# Slurp in the entire file
while ($line = <>) {
    $str .= $line;   # Accumulate the entire file.
}

# $str now contains the entire file. Execute it !
eval $str;
```

As you can see, `eval` handles any Perl script handed to it. The beauty of this thing is that this facility is available not just to Larry, but to mortals like you and me. Try this:

```
# put some code inside $str
$str = '$c = $a + $b'; # Perl doesn't care what's inside $str
$a = 10; $b = 20;
eval $str;             # Treat $str as code, and execute it.
print $c;              # prints 30
```

In this snippet, `$str` is treated as an ordinary string at first, because that is what it is. But `eval` thinks of it as a program and executes it. The important point is that it doesn't think of it as a *separate* program, but as if it belonged right there in the original code *instead* of the `eval` statement, as shown in Figure 5-1.

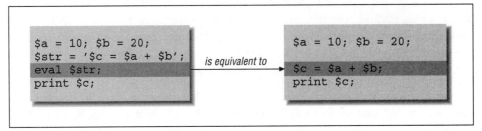

Figure 5-1. eval compiles and executes the string in its own context

For this reason, the string that is given to `eval` can use variables and subroutines available to it at that point, including `my` and `local` variables, and optionally produce new ones in the same environment. In the preceding example, the string given to `eval` adds two initialized variables (`$a` and `$b`) and produces a new variable, `$c`.

If you have more than one statement inside the string (remember that the string can be as big a program as you want), `eval` evaluates all of them and returns the result of the last evaluation:

```
$str = '$a++; $a + $b'; # Contains two expressions
$a = 10; $b = 20;
$c = eval $str; # $c gets 31 (result of the 2nd expression, $a+$b)
```

Of course, it's quite pointless to `eval` a piece of code that you know at compile time, as in the example above. Things get interesting if `$str` comes from else-where—standard input, a file, or over the network. We will shortly look at some examples that make use of this.

NOTE   The string form of `eval` is a security risk. If the string argument comes from an untrusted source and contains, say,

```
system('rm *')
```

the code would be merrily executed—and result in a distinct lack of merriment on your part. In situations in which you cannot trust input, you can use the taint-checking option provided by Perl, which prevents you from using data derived from outside the program to affect files or things outside the program [3]. You can also use the Safe module bundled with the Perl distribution, which provides safe compartments in which to `eval` strings, similar to the environment that a web browser provides for Java or Tcl/Tk applets.

What if `$str` doesn't contain a valid Perl expression? Perl then puts an error message in a special variable called `$@` (or `$EVAL_ERROR`, if you use the English module). Since `eval` compiles the string before actually executing it, this can be either a compilation or a run-time error. `$@` is guaranteed to be `undef` if `$str` contains error-free code (well, I should say free of syntax errors, because it can't really protect you against flawed logic).

Since `eval` is used by the Perl interpreter itself to parse and execute a given script, the error strings (in `$@`) are exactly those you see on the standard error output when processing a flawed script.

There is one subtle, yet important, point that needs to be mentioned. `eval` treats the string as a block, which is why it is able to process a number of statements (not just expressions) and return the value of the last statement. This also means that you don't see the changes to localized or lexical variables present in the `eval`'ed string.

The Block Form: Exception Handling

In this form, `eval` is followed by a block of code, not a scalar containing a string. It is used for handling run-time errors, or *exceptions*. Errors can be internal built-in ones (out-of-memory, divide-by-zero) or user-defined ones produced by `die`.

The following example shows how you can use the block form `eval` to trap a run-time divide-by-zero error:

```
eval {
    $a = 10; $b = 0;
    $c = $a / $b;      # Causes a run-time error,
                       # which is trapped by eval
};
print $@;   # Prints  "Illegal division by 0 at try.pl line 3
```

When the script is compiled, Perl syntax-checks the block of code and generates code. If it encounters a run-time error, Perl skips the rest of the `eval` block and sets `$@` to the corresponding error text.

To signal your own errors, you use `die`. Perl knows whether a piece of code is currently executing inside an `eval`, and so, when `die` is called, Perl simply gives the error string—`die`'s argument—to the global `$@`, and jumps to the statement following the `eval` block. In the following example, `open_file` invokes `die` if it has trouble opening a file. To use this function, wrap it inside an eval.

```
sub open_file {
    open (F, $_[0]) || die "Could not open file: $!";
}

$f = 'test.dat';
while (1) {
```

```
eval {
      open_file($f);    # if open_file dies, the program doesn't quit
};
last unless $@;     # no error: break out of the loop.
print "$f is not present. Please enter new file name $f";
chomp($f = <STDIN>);
}
```

Java/C++ programmers would of course recognize the parallel to the *throw, try,* and *catch* statements, where *try* corresponds to the **eval** block, *catch* to the checking of $@, and *throw* to **die**. (Essentially, the caller says to the run-time environment, "Here, *try* this code, and *catch* whatever errors are *thrown* by the callee.")

One thing I like a lot about the Java environment is that both the interpreter and the standard libraries make extensive and *consistent* use of *try, throw,* and *catch* for error handling. In some ways, using these constructs is better than simply returning an error code, because it *requires* the programmer to pay attention to errors (if you ignore the error, the program dies).

In C++ and Java, a function can rethrow an exception if it doesn't want to handle it itself. In Perl, you can do so by calling **die** without arguments:

```
eval {
   ...
};
if ($@ =~ /sorry, bucko/) {
   ....
} else {
   # hmm .. don't know what to do with it.
   die;  # Identical to die $@
}
```

If there is an enclosing **eval** block, this exception will be caught; otherwise, the program terminates.

Standard Modules

Since C++ and Java contain special constructs for trapping and handling errors, some Perl programmers would like them too. Here are a couple of options.

Exception.pm

As this book goes to press, a new module, Exception, built over **eval** and **die**, is just being announced to CPAN. You need to understand Perl's support for object orientation to understand the following small example, so you might want to revisit this example on a subsequent reading.

This snippet throws exceptions if you attempt to withdraw more than $300 or exceed the current balance:

```
use Exception;
package AmountExceededException; # User-defined exception
@ISA = ('Exception');

package OverdraftException;        # User-defined exception
@ISA = ('Exception');

package BankAccount;
sub withdraw_money {
    my $amount = shift;
    if ($amount > 300) {
        throw new AmountExceededException;
    }
    if ($amount > $balance) {
        throw new OverdraftException;
    }
    ...    # Change balance
}

try {
    print "How much do you need?"; chomp($amount = <STDIN>);
    withdraw_money ($amount);
}
catch AmountExceededException =>
            sub {print 'Cannot withdraw more than $300'},
        OverdraftException        =>
            sub {print $_[0]->message},
        Default =>
            sub {print "Internal error. Try later"};
```

exceptions.pl

The standard Perl library currently has a module called *exceptions.pl,* which is also a thin wrapper over eval and die and provides subroutines called catch and throw. catch takes a piece of code as a *string* (instead of as a block, as the previous example) and a list of regular expressions to match against the error string when it eval's the code.

This module has one serious problem, which is actually solved by the newer module, *Exception.pm:* because catch is a subroutine, lexical variables in the current scope (localized with my) are not available to it.

I suspect that programmers disdain making a language look like another;[*] in the final analysis, using eval and die in the raw is probably the easiest option.

---

[*] That excludes Larry Wall, considering that he designed Perl to look like C, sh, and awk!

Watch Your Quotes

There are some subtleties associated with the way quotes or blocks are interpreted by Perl. Consider the differences between the following statements:

```
$str = '$c = 10';
#
eval  $str;      # 1
eval  "$str";    # 2
eval  '$str';    # 3
eval  { $str }; # 4
```

Cases 1 and 2 have identical results, and cases 3 and 4 behave identically. Can you see why? The trick is to know what the interpreter does *before* handing it over to eval.

In case 1, Perl gives the *contents* of $str to eval, just as it would for any other function. Hence eval sees the string '$c = 10', treats it like a little program, and executes it.

In case 2, Perl does variable interpolation on the double-quoted string before handing it over to eval. Again, eval sees the contents of $str, compiles it, and executes it, assigning 10 to $c.

In case 3, the argument to eval is a single-quoted string, which is not expanded during the variable interpolation stage. For this reason, eval sees a hardcoded string (with the characters "$", "s", "t", "r") and treats it like a little program as before. As a standalone program, it is quite useless, of course. Since eval returns the result of the last expression, it returns the value of $str (the string $c = 10). That is, if you say,

```
$s = eval '$str';
```

$s will contain $c = 10.

Case 4 is identical to case 3, except that the code inside the block is checked for syntax errors at compile-time (at the same time as the rest of the script).

That's all there is to know about eval. Now, let us see how to use it for expression evaluation, exception handling, and efficiency.

Using Eval for Expression Evaluation

There are a number of tasks, such as parsing and expression evaluation, in which you can make Perl do all the dirty work. Assuming, of course, that your parsing requirements are similar to Perl's own. Perl, after all, knows a thing or two about parsing and evaluating Perlish statements!

Let's assume that your input data is a bunch of quoted strings and you would like to verify that the quotes are balanced:

```
'He said, "come on over"'
'There are times when "Peter" doesn\'t work at all'
```

Instead of fretting over backslash escapes and writing code to check whether the quotes are correctly paired (balanced), you can simply `eval` the strings, as shown in Example 5-1. Remember that a string is a correct Perl expression too. If Perl puts an error in `$@`, you can be sure you have faulty input.

Example 5-1. eval.pl

```
while (defined($s = <>)) {         # Read a line into $s
    $result = eval $s;             # Evaluate that line
    if ($@) {                      # Check for compile or run-time errors.
        print "Invalid string:\n $s";
    } else {
        print $result, "\n";
    }
}
```

The neat thing about this code is that it works equally well as a fancy calculator, because `$s` can be *any* valid Perl statement, with arithmetic operators, loops, variable assignments, subroutines, and so on. Here's how you might use the program:

```
% perl eval.pl
2 * log (10);
4.60517018598809
$a = 10; $a += $a ** 2;
110
for (1..10) {print $_ , " " }
1 2 3 4 5 6 7 8 9 10
```

For each line you enter, Perl computes and prints out the result (shown in non-bold type). How much simpler a shell can you possibly ask for? Note that the code requires each input line to be a fully formed expression, so you cannot write multiline expressions, but you can always change the program to start evaluating only when the user enters a blank line.

It is worth contrasting these few lines with the effort of learning *lex* and *yacc*—see, for example, the *yacc*, *lex*, and C-based calculator ("hoc") developed by Kernighan and Pike in their classic, *The Unix Programming Environment*. Other static languages such as Java and C++ present similar challenges: you are forced to reinvent the wheel, since you don't have access to the power of the compiler itself.

Expression Evaluation in Substitutions

The Perl substitution operator is ordinarily of the form *s/regex/replacement/* and substitutes the replacement string wherever the input string matches the regular expression pattern. The /e flag adds a twist to this: it tells the substitution operator that the second part is a *Perl expression*, not an ordinary replacement string; the *result* of the expression is used as the replacement instead. Consider

```
$line = 'Expression Evaluation';
$line =~ s/(\w+)/ scalar (reverse($1)) /eg;
print $line; # prints "noisserpxE noitaulavE"
```

The second parameter to the substitute operator is an expression: `reverse` is used in a scalar context to reverse the string given to it. The /g flag ensures that every word is matched and reversed.

This topic is somewhat tangential to the `eval` keyword, but it is still germane to our discussion about run-time expression evaluation; in fact, /e stands for "expression," not for "eval." This expression is checked for syntax at compile-time, so if you need to watch for run-time errors, you still need to put the entire statement within an `eval` block. Consider another example, which replaces any string containing the pattern "number/number" with an equivalent fraction:

```
$l = 'His chances of winning are between 2/5 and 1/3';
eval {
    $l =~ s|(\d+)/(\d+)| $1 / $2 |eg;
};
print $l unless $@;
```

This prints "His chances of winning are between 0.4 and 0.333333333333333." The `eval` block traps divide-by-zero errors.

Using Eval for Efficiency

Here are some examples where run-time evaluation can greatly speed up execution.

A Fast Multipattern grep

Consider a *grep*-like Perl script that can search for any number of patterns and print out only those lines that match *all* the given patterns (the order of the patterns being unimportant). You might structure the code like this:

```
while ($s = <>) {
    $all_matched = 1;      # start by assuming all patterns match $s
    foreach $pat (@patterns) {
        if ($s !~ /$pat/) {
            $all_matched = 0; # No, our assumption was wrong
            last;
        }
    }
    print $s if $all_matched;
}
```

The problem with this code is that the regular expression (/$pat/) is compiled afresh for every line and for every pattern. That is, if you have, say, 10,000 lines in the text to be searched, and three patterns to search for, a.*b, [0-9], and [^def], the patterns will be compiled 30,000 times. The /o flag, which tells Perl to compile the regular expression, cannot be used here because $pat can vary as the program executes.

The fastest approach would be to hardcode the patterns as shown next. Unfortunately, it is also the least reusable approach.

```
while ($s = <> ) {
    if (  ($s =~ /a.*b/) &&
          ($s =~ /[0-9]$/) &&
          ($s =~ /[^def]/)) {
        print $s;
    }
}
```

The good news is that it is possible to get this level of efficiency without losing generality. The idea is to hand-craft the "hard-wired" code above at run-time and then to eval it.

The strings constituting the code to be generated are shown in bold in Example 5-2.

Example 5-2. Compiling Regular Expression Strings for Blazing Speed

```
$code = 'while (<>) {';
$code .= 'if (/';
$code .= join ('/ && /', @patterns);
$code .= '/) {print $_;}}';
print $code, "\n";
eval $code;    # Ahh, finally !
# Check if faulty regular expressions given as input patterns
die "Error ---: $@\n Code:\n$code\n"    if ($@);
```

If @patterns contains the three strings "^abc", "ghi", "efg$", for example, the code supplied to eval looks like this:

```
while (<>) {if (/^foo/ && /bar$/ && /ghi/) {print $_;}}
```

One way to make this example even more efficient is to sort the patterns such that those patterns with beginning- or end-of-line markers (^ and $) are evaluated first. It is much faster to check for a pattern anchored to the beginning or end of the line than to search all over the string. Another enhancement to make is for the user to supply the Boolean operator instead of hardcoding &&. See the *perlfaq6* document (FAQ on regular expressions) that is bundled with the Perl distribution.

Extracting Columns from a File

Let us look at another example that builds and evaluates Perl code dynamically, for efficiency. We build a program called `col`, which extracts columns from a file, similar to the Unix `cut(1)` command. It is invoked as shown below:

```
% col -s80 8-14 20+8 test.dat
```

This invocation treats *test.dat* as a fixed-format file with 80-column records and extracts two columns from each record, one starting at character position 8 and ending at 14 (the index of the leftmost column is 1, not 0) and the other going from 20 through 28, as shown in Figure 5-2. If the *-s* option is not given, the script treats newlines as record terminators and reads the file line by line. `col` allows column ranges to overlap.

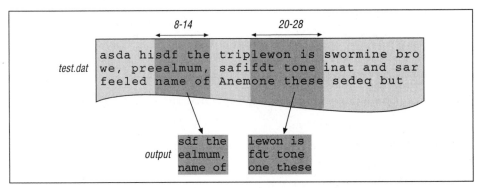

Figure 5-2. Using col for extracting columns

You already know that **substr** extracts substrings given a starting location and the substring length. Writing `col` is a simple matter of calling **substr** in a loop, once for each range given on the command line:

```
for each line in the file {
    for each column range in the command line arguments {
        print substr (line, range);
    }
}
```

As an aside, we don't use **unpack** instead of **substr** because we would like the input ranges to overlap.

A more efficient alternative to the preceding solution is to "flatten the loop" and use constants wherever possible, as shown in the following code snippet (for the specific command-line invocation above). For each record read from a file, this code extracts the substring indicated by input range and pads it with spaces as necessary. It also appends a delimiter ("|") to each extracted column.

```
#PART 1 ----------------------------------------------------------
sub col {
    my $tmp;
    while (1) {
        $s = get_next_line();
        $col = "";

#PART 2 ----------------------------------------------------------
        $s .= ' ' x (14 - length($s))  if (length($s) < 14);
        $tmp = substr($s, 7, 7);
        $tmp .= " " x (7 - length($tmp));
        $col .= '|' . $tmp;
        $s .= ' ' x (28 - length($s))    if (length($s) < (28));
        $tmp = substr($s, 19, 9);
        $tmp .= " " x (9 - length($tmp));
        $col .= '|' . $tmp;

#PART 3 ----------------------------------------------------------
        print $col, "\n";
    }
}
```

$tmp contains one column at any time, and $col accumulates each such column to be output and is finally printed.

Given the command line as shown, let's compose this subroutine at run-time. Notice that parts 1 and 3 are independent of the command-line arguments. Part 2, which extracts all the columns in each line, is the only one that is shaped by command-line arguments.

As was mentioned earlier, you must watch your quotes carefully. Assume that $col1 and $offset hold 7 and 6, respectively, so that we need to insert this line of code into our executable string:

```
$tmp = substr($s, 7, 6);
```

Here is how we can generate this line:

```
$code = '$tmp = substr($s, ' . "$col1, $offset)";
```

Note how we use single and double quotes to carefully control variable interpolation. Example 5-3 shows the three parts being generated by generate_part1, generate_part2, and generate_part3. The subroutine get_next_line converts tabs to equivalent spaces to preserve the visual effect of a tab. generate_part3 also evals this generated code and introduces the new subroutine col. As before, the strings representing the code are shown in bold lettering.

Example 5-3. col: A Script to Extract Columns from a File

```
# Extracts columns of text from a file
# Usage : col [-s<n>] col-range1, col-range2, files ...
# where col-range is specified as col1-col2 (column 1 through column2)
```

Example 5-3. col: A Script to Extract Columns from a File (continued)

```perl
#           or col1+n, where n is the number of columns.
$size = 0;              # 0 => line-oriented input, else fixed format.
@files = ();            # List of files
$open_new_file = 1;     # force get_next_line() to open the first file
$debugging = 0;         # Enable with -d commmand line flag
$col = "";
$code = "";
generate_part1();
generate_part2();
generate_part3();
col();              # sub col has now been generated. Call it !
exit(0);


#----------------------------------------------------------------
sub generate_part1 {
    # Generate the initial invariant code of sub col()
    $code  = 'sub col { my $tmp;';             # Note the single quotes
    $code .= 'while (1) {$s = get_next_line(); $col = "";';
    $delimiter = '|';
}


#----------------------------------------------------------------
sub generate_part2 {
    # Process arguments
    my ($col1, $col2);
    foreach $arg (@ARGV) {
        if (($col1, $col2) = ($arg =~ /^(\d+)-(\d+)/)) {
            $col1--;# Make it 0 based
            $offset = $col2 - $col1;
            add_range($col1, $offset);
        } elsif (($col1, $offset) = ($arg =~ /^(\d+)\+(\d+)/)) {
            $col1--;
            add_range($col1, $offset);
        } elsif ($size = ($arg =~ /-s(\d+)/)) {
            # noop
        } elsif ($arg =~ /^-d/) {
            $debugging = 1;
        } else {
            # Must be a file name
            push (@files, $arg);
        }
    }
}


#----------------------------------------------------------------
sub generate_part3 {
    $code .= 'print $col, "\n";}}';

    print $code if $debugging; # -d flag enables debugging.
    eval $code;
    if ($@) {
```

Example 5-3. col: A Script to Extract Columns from a File (continued)

```perl
        die "Error ..........\n $@\n $code \n";
    }
}

#------------------------------------------------------------------
sub add_range {
    my ($col1, $numChars) = @_;
    # substr complains (under -w) if we look past the end of a string
    # To prevent this, pad the string with spaces if necessary.
    $code .= "\$s .= ' ' x ($col1 + $numChars - length(\$s))";
    $code .= "     if (length(\$s) < ($col1+$numChars));";
    $code .= "\$tmp = substr(\$s, $col1, $numChars);";
    $code .= '$tmp .= " " x (' . $numChars .  ' - length($tmp));';
    $code .= "\$col .= '$delimiter' . \$tmp; ";
}

#------------------------------------------------------------------
sub get_next_line {
    my($buf);

  NEXTFILE:
    if ($open_new_file) {
        $file = shift @files || exit(0);
        open (F, $file) || die "$@ \n";
        $open_new_file = 0;
    }
    if ($size) {
        read(F, $buf, $size);
    } else {
        $buf = <F>;
    }
    if (! $buf) {
        close(F);
        $open_new_file = 1;
        goto NEXTFILE;
    }
    chomp($buf);
    # Convert tabs to spaces (assume tab stop width == 8)

    # expand leading tabs first—the common case
    $buf =~ s/^(\t+)/' ' x (8 * length($1))/e;

    # Now look for nested tabs. Have to expand them one at a time - hence
    # the while loop. In each iteration, a tab is replaced by the number of
    # spaces left till the next tab-stop. The loop exits when there are
    # no more tabs left
    1 while ($buf =~ s/\t/' ' x (8 - length($`)%8)/e);

    $buf;
}
```

`get_next_line` uses the substitute operator's `/e` option to remove tabs. Can you guess why we have to use the `while` loop instead of the `/g` option? The reason is that to expand a tab to the correct number of spaces, we have to know where the tab and the next tab stop are located. This means we have to know the number of characters from the beginning of the line to the tab, which is obtained by computing `length($`)`. In the next iteration, this length needs to account for the previously expanded tab. While `/g` does a global replace, it never revisits a substituted portion (that is, it always moves forward), with the result that by using this option, you can never find out how long the partially substituted string is at any point. Instead, we use the `while` loop to traverse the string from the beginning for each tab found.

Using Eval for Time-Outs

When you call `eval`, Perl makes a note of the next statement to start executing just in case a `die` is invoked somewhere within. Internally, `die` happens to invoke a `longjmp`, so Perl wastes no time at all transferring control back up to the statement following `eval`, regardless of how deep the stack is. (All temporary and local variables created in the `eval`'ed code are automatically garbage collected.)

The use of `setjmp` and `longjmp` internally gives us one new technique: aborting blocked system calls and infinite loops. Let's say you want to wait at most 10 seconds for the user to type something.* If you say `$buf = <>`, the program is blocked until the user deigns to hit a carriage return, but we would like Perl to abort it after waiting 10 seconds. Generating a time-out is not really a problem; the built-in function `alarm()` can be used to generate an `ALRM` signal after a given number of seconds, like this:

```
$SIG{ALRM} = \&timed_out;
alarm(10);      # Tells the OS to issue an ALRM signal after 10 seconds
$buf = <>;      # Go into a blocking read
```

The procedure `timed_out` is called (after 10 seconds) regardless of what Perl happens to be executing at that time, be it a blocked `read` or an infinite loop. The problem is, how does `timed_out` force Perl to abandon what Perl happened to be doing at the time it was called? That's where `eval/die` come in. Put an `eval` around `$buf = <>` and a `die` inside `timed_out()`, and control will be restored to the statement following `eval` (the `if` statement), as shown here:

```
$SIG{ALRM} = \&timed_out;
eval {
    alarm (10);
```

---

* Thanks to Tom Christiansen for this example.

```
        $buf = <>;
        alarm(0);              # Cancel the pending alarm if user responds.
    };
    if ($@ =~ /GOT TIRED OF WAITING/) {
        print "Timed out. Proceeding with default\n";
        ....
    }

    sub timed_out {
        die "GOT TIRED OF WAITING";
    }
```

If the user doesn't hit a return within 10 seconds, `timed_out` is called from the signal handler, which calls `die`, which internally `longjmps` over to the statement following the innermost `eval`. If the user does hit a return within the allotted time, `alarm(0)` is called to reset the alarm.

Note that if the alarm goes off, `$@` contains something like "GOT TIRED OF WAITING at *foo.pl* line 100," so you cannot use `eq`; you must use a regular expression match (or the `index` operator).

Tom Christiansen pointed out a subtle and interesting point. It is essential that you set `alarm` inside the `eval` block, because on a heavily loaded machine (and for small time-out periods), it is possible to lose the time-slice after the call to `alarm` and before it has a chance to enter the protected section (the `eval` block). Later on, when the program regains the time-slice, it is possible that the time-out interval has expired, and the program will abort.

Eval in Other Languages

Let's find out what other languages have by way of run-time evaluation and exception handling.

Tcl (Tool Command Language)

The Tcl interpreter follows the typical shell syntax: each statement is a command followed by a bunch of arguments. If the command is known at compile-time, it generates byte-codes and executes it subsequently, but if it is a variable, the interpreter waits until run-time to compile and execute that statement. (Earlier versions of Tcl always treated the program as strings and parsed a statement every time it was hit, even if it was within a loop. As this book goes to press, the Tcl interpreter has just recently taken some steps toward becoming a byte-code interpreter.) Tcl supports a user-level `eval` call, which recursively calls the parser and interprets the contents of the string as a command followed by a bunch of parameters.

For error handling, Tcl provides the `error` and `catch` statements, equivalent to `die` and `eval` in Perl.

Python

Python's `eval` function allows a string to be evaluated and executed, but the string cannot contain newlines. An `exec` statement allows newlines, but since Python relies on leading whitespace instead of an explicit block structure, it is important that you get the whitespace correct in a dynamically constructed string to be given to `exec`. This is quite a bit more painful than getting the block scoping right in Perl.

Python goes through a compilation and execution stage similar to Perl, and for every module called *module.py*, it stores the intermediate byte codes in a file called *module.pyc*. The next time the module is used, the intermediate byte code file is automatically picked up. Perl is likely to see this kind of facility in the near future, considering that Malcolm Beattie's Perl compiler is in the alpha stage as of this writing.

For exception handling, Python supports the notion of exception classes as part of the language, like Java and C++. You raise exceptions with `raise` and trap them with a `try`/`except`/`finally` syntax. (`try` and `except` are equivalent to the `eval BLOCK` form. The `finally` keyword indicates a default `except` block that is invoked if none of the other `except` statements is able to trap the exception.) I especially like how the interpreter and the Python library make consistent use of this facility.

C / C++

There is no run-time evaluation, but there are a number of public domain and commercial interpreters that can be linked in with your C application to support C or C++-like interpreted languages. Look for C-Interp or XCoral in the free compilers list available from *http://www.idiom.com/free-compilers*.

C has no keywords for exception handling. C++ has a `try`/`catch`/`throw` syntax identical to Java's. Exceptions can be user-defined objects and can have their own private data as well as behavior.

Java

Java goes through the same two phases as Perl: (1) compilation to an intermediate byte-code form, and (2) execution of this intermediate code. What it doesn't allow, however, is the production and evaluation of *new* code on the fly. There is really no reason why this isn't technically feasible, because the `javac` compiler itself is written in Java, and it should be possible to package it as a library instead of a standalone program without violating new security constraints.

For error handling, Java has a `try/catch` syntax that is equivalent to the `eval BLOCK` approach in Perl, in that all the code is known at compile-time. Exceptions are true first-class objects in Java, so you can discriminate between them much better than the string comparison required in Perl. Java has the `throw` keyword to raise a user-defined exception, similar to Perl's `die`.

Java does strict type-checking and requires that a function enumerate the exceptions it might throw (this is considered part of the signature of the function). So if you call a function that throws an exception, Java either requires your function to either not rethrow it or, if you want to pass it on, you have to include that exception as part of your function's signature. This way, when you see a function, you know the exact list of exceptions you have to deal with, which is very important for big applications written by a team of people. Depending on your viewpoint, Perl doesn't have any such feature or restriction.

Resources

1. *More Programming Pearls*. Jon Bentley. Addison-Wesley, 1990.

   Especially relevant to this chapter is Column 9, *Little Languages*.

2. *Run-time code generation*. Collection of WWW links and papers by Don Pardo, at *http://www.cs.washington.edu/homes/pardo/rtcg.d/index.html*.

3. *perlsec*. Perl documentation on security-related issues.

6

Modules

> Life is a struggle with things to maintain itself among them. Concepts are the strategic plan we form in answer to the attack.
>
> —Jose Ortega y Gasset
> The Revolt of the Masses

One of the chief reasons why languages such as *awk* and the various Unix shells don't get used for building even moderately complex systems is their lack of support for modular programming. There are no bodies of code that you can just pick up and plug into your application; instead, you end up cutting and pasting from other standalone scripts. In contrast, languages such as Perl have been highly successful because of the wide availability of third-party modules (libraries). When comparing languages, I consider the availability of libraries to be more important than pure language features.

Perl allows you to partition your code into one or more reusable modules. In this chapter, we will study how to:

- Define modules using the **package** keyword.

- Load predefined modules with **use** and **require**; we have already seen a few examples of **use** in the earlier chapters.

- Access package specific variables and subroutines using the "::" notation.

- Load functions at run-time.

Basic Package

The `package` keyword signifies the beginning of a new namespace. All global identifiers (names of variables, subroutines, filehandles, formats, and directory handles) mentioned after this statement "belong" to that package. For example:

```
package BankAccount;
$total = 0;
sub deposit {
    my ($amount)= @_;
    $total += $amount;
    print "You now have $total dollars \n";
}
sub withdraw {
    my ($amount)= @_;
    $total -= $amount;
    $total = 0   if $total < 0;
    print "You now have $total dollars \n";
}
```

The user-defined global identifiers `$total`, `deposit`, and `withdraw` belong to the BankAccount package. The scope of a package lasts until the end of the innermost enclosing block (if it is declared inside that block) or until another `package` statement is encountered. In the absence of an explicit package declaration, Perl assumes a package name called `main`.

This is how you use the global symbols from another package:

```
package ATM;              # Start a different name-space now
BankAccount::deposit(10); # Call a foreign subroutine
print $BankAccount::total; # Access a foreign variable
```

To access an identifier in a different namespace, you need to put the package name before the variable name; this is called *fully qualifying* the name. Note that you must say `$BankAccount::total`, not `BankAccount::$total`; the `$` sign is followed by the fully qualified name. If an identifier is not fully qualified, Perl looks for it in the currently active package.

Since the `package` statement simply dictates the effective namespace, you can switch between different namespaces at will:

```
package A;
$a = 10;      # This $a is in package A
package B;
$a = 20;      # This $a is in package B, and is completely independent
              # of the other $a
package A;     # Make A the current package.
print $a;     # prints 10;
```

C++ programmers will recognize the resemblance to that language's namespace facility.

Packages and Variables

In Chapter 3, *Typeglobs and Symbol Tables*, I mentioned that all global names go into a symbol table. That was a bit of a white lie. Each package actually gets its *own* symbol table, distinct from all others. (We will have more to say on this subject in the section "Accessing the Symbol Table" later in this chapter). User-defined identifiers in package **main** are not treated specially in any way except that you can also refer to a variable, say $x, in that package as "$::x".

The built-in variables such as $|, $_, @ARGV, and %ENV always belong to package **main**, and Perl allows you to refer to these variables in any package without having to prefix them with **main::**. These are the only truly global variables in Perl.

You may also recall that lexical (**my**) variables are not associated with symbols and typeglobs and therefore have nothing to do with packages. It is a compile-time error to say something like

```
my $BankAccount::total; # Error
```

This also means that you can have two variables of the same type and the same name, if one is a package global and one is a lexical. The following piece of code is legal, but definitely not recommended:

```
$x = 10 ;   # global to package main
my $x = 20; # lexical at file scope
print $x;   # prints 20. Lexical variables are given priority.
```

Symbolic References

Symbolic references work as we have seen earlier, for variables as well as functions. Consider

```
package A;
$x = 10;

package B;
# Access $A::x symbolically
print ${"A::x"};

# or even more indirectly
$pkg      = "A";
$var_name = "x";
print ${"${pkg}::$var_name"};

# Call a subroutine indirectly
&{"A::foo"}(10, 20); # Identical to A::foo(10,20);
```

We will make extensive use of this facility in Chapter 8, *Object Orientation: The Next Few Steps.*

Packages and Files

The same package declaration can be present in multiple files. Or multiple packages can be declared in one file. By convention, a package is usually assigned its own file and named *package.pm* or *package.pl*. Files with the suffix *.pm* are called Perl *modules*, and packages inside files with the suffix *.pl* are usually referred to as *libraries*. The former naming convention is preferred now because the use statement requires it, as we will soon see.

The require keyword simply loads a file into your program (*sources* it, in shell parlance). This is identical in spirit to #include in C, except that Perl does not bother about a file that has already been loaded:[*]

```
require "test.pl"; # load test.pl if it hasn't already been loaded
```

If you omit the suffix and the quotes, a *.pm* suffix is assumed. The use statement is similar in that respect, but is more restrictive in that it accepts only module names, not filenames. So, while there is no necessary relation between module names and filenames in general, use does force you to adopt a standard naming convention, which is a very good thing indeed, in my opinion. But there is more to use than just syntactic sugar.

The big difference between use and require is that the use statement is executed as soon as it is *parsed*. For this reason, the following attempt to load a module dynamically won't work, because the assignment statement is executed only after everything has been parsed and compiled:

```
$pkg_name = "Account";   # executes at run-time
use $pkg_name;           # executes at compile-time
```

It is, in fact, a syntax error; you have to use require in this case. The advantage of use is that when a program starts executing, there's a guarantee that all required modules have been successfully loaded, and there won't be any surprises at run-time.

Another important difference between use and require is described later, in the section "Importing Symbols."

When a file is require'd or use'd, it is expected to return a Boolean success value (zero for failure, nonzero for success). That is, the last executing statement at global scope must be a statement such as "return 1;" or just "1;". Note that this is not necessarily the last statement in the file; it is just the last executing statement.

---

[*] Another important distinction from C or C++ is that modules are not split up into separate declaration and implementation files (header files versus ".c" files) and it is not necessary to go through a linker to bring modules together.

Load Path

Perl first looks for the file given to **use** or **require** in the current directory and then looks up the @INC built-in array to search the include paths. By default, @INC contains a few standard directory names specified when the interpreter was installed and built. On my machine, @INC looks like this:

```
% perl -e 'print "@INC \n";'
/opt/lib/perl5/sun4-solaris/5.004 /opt/lib/perl5 /opt/lib/perl5/site_
perl/sun4-solaris /opt/lib/perl5/site_perl .
```

You can also use **perl -V** to get this and other configuration information.

If you want to specify additional directories of your own, you have these choices:

1. Use the **-I** command-line option as you would with the C preprocessor:

   ```
   % perl -I/home/sriram/perl -I/local/mylib script.pl
   ```

   I sometimes have instrumented or development versions of my modules in a separate directory. This option makes it easy to use these modules without having to change any of the code that uses them.

2. Set the **PERL5LIB** environment variable as a set of paths, separated by colons.

3. Modify @INC before calling **require**:

   ```
   unshift (@INC, "/usr/perl/include"); # Prepend a directory name
   require 'foo.pl';
   ```

Package Initialization and Destruction

There are times when you want to do some initialization before any other code is executed. Perl goes further: it gives you a chance to execute code while it is still in the *compilation* stage.

Normally, while parsing a file, Perl compiles the entire code, and when this process is successfully completed, it starts executing from the first global statement onward. However, if it encounters a subroutine or a block called BEGIN while parsing, it not only compiles it, but also *executes* it right away, before resuming the compilation of the rest of the file. A small experiment underscores this point:

```
sub BEGIN {   # can also just say BEGIN { }; the word "sub" is optional
    print "Washington was here \n";
}
foo*** ;      # Intentional error
```

This prints the following:

```
Washington was here
syntax error at x.pl line 4, near "** ;"
Execution of x.pl aborted due to compilation errors.
```

Whereas a program with a syntax error normally does not get executed at all, a BEGIN subroutine occurring before the error will be executed.

Because a BEGIN block gets executed even before the compilation phase is over, it can influence the rest of the compilation. If you want to hardcode an include path in your program, here is how to do it:

```
BEGIN {
    unshift (@INC, "../include");
}
use Foo;  # Looks for Foo.pm in "../include" first
```

An easier approach is to use the lib module that is packaged with the Perl distribution:

```
use lib qw(../include); # prepends the directory to @INC
```

Just as you want to do initialization before any other code executes, there are times when you want to do some clean-up *after* all the code has executed. The END block is called just before the program is due to exit, independent of whether it was a successful exit or not. That is, even if the program dies because of, say, an arithmetic exception, the END block is called anyway. The block is not invoked if the program dies because of an uncaught signal.

BEGIN and END are borrowed from *awk*. And as in *awk*, Perl supports multiple BEGIN and END statements. BEGIN statements are executed in the order in which they are seen, while END statements are executed in *reverse* order of appearance (last in, first out). If there are multiple packages with many BEGIN or END blocks, the order in which the packages were loaded is taken into account.

Privacy

Symbols in Perl are freely accessible; privacy is not enforced. The online documentation says, rather colorfully, "Perl does not enforce private and public parts of its modules as you may have been used to in other languages like C++, Ada, or Modula-17. Perl doesn't have an infatuation with enforced privacy. It would prefer that you stayed out of its living room because you weren't invited, not because it has a shotgun."[*]

In addition to accessing a foreign package's existing variables or subroutines, a package can easily create new names in another package's namespace, as we saw earlier. Consider

```
package Test;
# Create a variable subroutine and subroutine in another package
```

---

[*] I once saw this gem in a piece of C++ code: "#define private public", just before including a header file. Someone who wants data that badly will find a means to get at it!

```
$main::foo = 10;
sub main::myFunc {
    print "Hello \n";
}

package main;
myFunc();   #  prints "Hello"
```

Although this is not a very kosher thing to do in a normal application, this facility can be put to good use if applied in a controlled manner. You can use it to import foreign package symbol names into your own namespace; we will study this in the next section.

Enforcing Privacy

You can use the my operator at file scope to get unassailably private variables. Because they are not associated in any way with a package, they cannot be accessed from a different scope (in this case, file scope). But because they don't have anything to do with packages, they are restricted at most to file boundaries. Consider

```
package A;
my $a = 10;    # A lexical variable

package B;
print $A::a;   # No such variable in package A
print $a;      # prints 10, because it can see the lexical variable
               # (even though package B is in effect)
```

What if you want to make a subroutine name private? You cannot use my to declare a private subroutine, but you can use anonymous subroutines and hold references to them in lexical variables:

```
my $rs_func = sub {
                ....
             };
```

Now, `$rs_func` can be dereferenced from within that scope (if it is a global variable anywhere within that file), but it cannot be accessed in another file. Whenever you want to call this function, you can either say `&$rs_func` or, if you intend to call it a number of times, use typeglob aliasing for convenience and efficiency:

```
{
    local (*func) = $rs_func;
    for (1..100) {func()};
}
```

While you can hide your own global identifiers, there's nothing you can do to prevent another module from installing new names into your namespace. In fact, older Perl libraries took this liberty a lot more. (Look at the *bigint.pl* package in the standard Perl library, for example.)

Importing Symbols

Sometimes, you may want to selectively import symbols into your namespace, just for typing efficiency. For example, you might want to say `sqrt` instead of `math::sqrt` or `deposit` instead of `BankAccount::deposit`. The `use` statement allows you to specify an optional list of function names to be imported:

```
use BankAccount ('withdraw', 'deposit');
withdraw();  # Can now call function without fully qualifying it.
```

For its part, the module has to be ready to export these names (and only them) to whoever `uses` it. It should also have a policy for what it should do if the user does not specify a list at all. Both these tasks are handled for you by a standard module called Exporter. The BankAccount class can be implemented as shown next:

```
package BankAccount;
use Exporter;
@ISA = ('Exporter');     # Inherit from Exporter
@EXPORT_OK = ('withdraw', 'deposit');

sub deposit { .... }
sub withdraw { .... }
```

This code loads the Exporter module and arranges to inherit from that module, using the `@ISA` array. For now, take it on faith that this works; we will study inheritance shortly. The `@EXPORT_OK` array states which symbols are fine to export. The user of this module can in turn specify a list of one or more symbols specified in `@EXPORT_OK` to the `use` statement. If the user says,

```
use BankAccount ('deposit');
```

the `deposit` function can be called without fully qualifying the name, in contrast to `withdraw()`. To tell the Exporter module not to export any symbols into your namespace, leave the list blank.

If the module uses `@EXPORT` instead of `@EXPORT_OK`, the user gets all the exported symbols, regardless of whether they were mentioned in the import list or not. I recommend that as a module writer, you use the more polite `@EXPORT_OK`.

Please see the Exporter documentation for numerous other features, which, among other things, allow the user of the module to import groups of functions using tag names, or to specify the group using one or more regular expressions.

How Do use and Exporter Work?

If you are not interested in the details of how `use` and Exporter work, you can easily skip this section without loss of continuity. This is one of those "knowledge for knowledge's sake" kind of sections.

The statement

```
use BankAccount ('withdraw', 'deposit');
```

behaves exactly as if you had said

```
BEGIN { require BankAccount;
        BankAccount::import('withdraw', 'deposit');}
```

BEGIN ensures that this statement is parsed and executed as soon as it is seen. require loads the file *BankAccount.pm* if it has not been loaded already. Finally, the import subroutine is called on that module.[*]

import is not a Perl keyword. It is simply a call to a user-defined subroutine known as import, and the module can define it any way it wishes and do what it wants with its argument list. If BankAccount does not define import and doesn't inherit it, there is no difference between use BankAccount and require BankAccount. By using Exporter, a module can simply inherit an import method without having to implement it.

To understand how Exporter works, let us build an import subroutine ourselves. We develop a simple module called Environment that lets us quickly access environment variables. This is how we want to use it:

```
use Environment;
print $USER, $PATH;
```

Instead of saying $ENV{'USER'}, we can now simply say $USER. In other words, the Environment module (and specifically a function called import in that module) installs variables like $USER and $PATH in its caller's namespace.

Example 6-1 shows one way to do write this subroutine.

Example 6-1. Environment.pm: Create Variables Corresponding to Environment Variables

```
package Environment;
sub import {
    # Get some caller details; its package name, and the current file name
    # and line number
    my ($caller_package) = caller;
    foreach $envt_var_name (keys %ENV) {
        *{"${caller_package}::${envt_var_name}"} = \$ENV{$envt_var_name};
    }
}
1;  # To signify successful initialization
```

---

[*] A bit of a white lie here. It actually does BankAccount->import (uses an arrow instead of the ::), a slightly different way of calling a subroutine. We'll study this notation in detail in Chapter 7, *Object-Oriented Programming*. For now, this explanation is adequate.

To keep the example small, `import` ignores its parameter list. It uses the `caller` built-in function to find out the calling package's name and creates aliases in that package. For an environment variable `USER`, the statement inside the `foreach` line is translated to this:

```
*{"main::USER"} = \$ENV{USER};
```

assuming that `main` is the calling package.

This small nugget encapsulates most of the knowledge of Chapter 3. The right-hand side returns a reference to the scalar containing the value of the environment variable, which is assigned to a typeglob. (Remember our discussion of selective aliasing?) The typeglob expression on the left creates a symbol table entry in `main`'s symbol table, whose scalar component is made to point to the value from the right-hand side. Exporter works exactly the same way, except that it aliases only function names.

Incidentally, the standard Perl distribution contains a module called Env that looks quite similar to our Environment package. The only distinction is that instead of creating an alias of the environment variables, Env uses the `tie` mechanism,[*] a much more inefficient way of doing things than the approach just shown.

Nesting Packages

Since all packages are global in scope, nesting of packages is not supported. However, you can have two packages, one called `A` and another called `A::B`, to give an illusion of nesting. This is a naming convention only and implies no necessary relation between the two packages; however, this convention is typically applied to groups of related packages, and the term "nested packages" does not seem wrong in such cases. For example, you could have a module called Math::Matrix for matrix manipulation and another called Math::Poisson that supports an infrastructure for simulating queuing models. The only relation between the two modules is that they both are mathematical in nature; they don't share any implementation characteristics.

The `::` notation is used as before to access variables and subroutines of nested packages:

```
$p = Math::Poisson::calculate_probability($lambda, $t);
print $Math::Constants::PI;
```

When you say `use File`, recall that Perl looks for a file called *File.pm*. If you say, `use Math::Poisson`, Perl looks for a file called *Math/Poisson.pm* (directory *Math*, file *Poisson.pm*). The double colon gets translated to a filename

---

[*] We'll discuss the `tie` approach in Chapter 9, *Tie*.

separator, because the colon has a special significance for DOS filenames. Perl imposes no limits on the level of nesting.

Autoloading

If you invoke a function called `Test::func()`, for example, and if `func()` has not been defined in module Test, Perl automatically looks for a subroutine called `Test::AUTOLOAD()`. If such a subroutine exists, Perl calls it with the arguments that were passed to `func()`. In addition, a variable called `$AUTOLOAD` is set to the full name of the function that was called (`"Test::func"`). Objective-C programmers will recognize this as being similar to the ":forward" declaration, in which an object uses this statement to trap all procedure calls it doesn't handle, in order to forward it to a "delegate."

The `AUTOLOAD` subroutine can do just about anything it wants. For example, it can do one of the following:

- Handle the call itself. The caller of Test::func does not know that `AUTOLOAD` really handled the call.

- Automatically create a subroutine on the fly (using **eval**) to do the right thing, and then call that new subroutine. In fact, instead of *calling* that subroutine, you can simply go to it, like this:

    ```
    sub AUTOLOAD {
        ... create subroutine ...
        goto &$AUTOLOAD;  # jump to it
    }
    ```

    This is a special form of **goto** that erases the stack-frame of the `AUTOLOAD` routine so that Test::func will not know it has been being called from AUTO-LOAD.

- Dynamically load an object file (or a DLL in Microsoft Windows), using the standard Dynaloader module, and then execute the appropriate call. This is one of the more popular uses of `AUTOLOAD`.

- Use the **system** function to launch another program by the same name. *Shell.pm* in your Perl library is the really fancy version of this facility. Here is a simplified version:

    ```
    #-----------------------------------------------------------------
    package Shell;
    #-----------------------------------------------------------------
    sub AUTOLOAD {
        my($program) = $AUTOLOAD;
        # We are just interested in the command name, not in
        # the package name
        $program =~ s/^.*:://;
    ```

```
        system ("$program @_");
    }
    #-----------------------------------------------------------------
    use Shell;
    ls ('-lR'); # Triggers a call to AUTOLOAD since sub ls() doesn't exist
    mail ('-s "This is a test" joe@foo.com < letter.txt');
```

Autoloading can also be used to delay the loading of subroutines until they are absolutely necessary. A module called Autosplit (in the standard distribution) is used to split a module into multiple modules, each with one subroutine from the original, and the Autoloader module can subsequently be used to subsequently load only the file corresponding to the called subroutine.

Accessing the Symbol Table

Perl has a number of features that permit introspection, chief among them the ability to get information about the contents of the symbol table. This property is sometimes called *reflection* or *introspection*.

Reflection makes it easy to write system-level tools such as debuggers and profilers. We will also use this property in Chapter 11, *Implementing Object Persistence*, to develop a module that can transparently dump an object's data to a file or a database (and subsequently restore it) without having to write any application-specific code.

We saw earlier in this chapter that each package gets its own symbol table (also called *stash*, short for "symbol table hash"). Perl makes these stashes available as regular associative arrays. The stash for a package named Foo can be accessed by using the hash called %Foo::. The **main** package is available as %main::, or simply as %::. In fact, all other packages' hash tables are available from the **main** stash (%main:: hence points to itself), as illustrated in Figure 6-1.

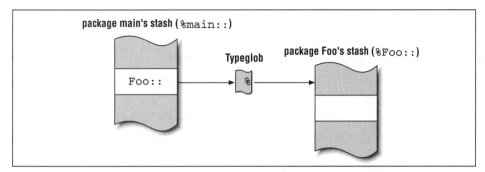

Figure 6-1. Packages' stashes are available in main's namespace

Iterating through the all the symbolic names inside a package is simple:

```
foreach $name (keys %main::) {
    print "$name, \n";
}
```

As we saw earlier, each of these symbolic names maps to a typeglob, which itself points to one or more values (one or more of each type: scalar, array, hash, subroutine, filehandle, format name, or directory handle). Unfortunately, there's no direct way to find out which values actually exist. Example 6-2 shows a way to dump all the variables in a given package and also demonstrates a way to find out which values exist for a given typeglob.

Example 6-2. Dumping All Symbols in a Package

```
package DUMPVAR;
sub dumpvar {
    my ($packageName) = @_;
    local (*alias);                  # a local typeglob
    # We want to get access to the stash corresponding to the package
    # name
    *stash = *{"${packageName}::"};  # Now %stash is the symbol table
    $, = " ";                        # Output separator for print
    # Iterate through the symbol table, which contains glob values
    # indexed by symbol names.
    while (($varName, $globValue) = each %stash) {
        print "$varName ============================ \n";
        *alias = $globValue;
        if (defined ($alias)) {
            print "\t \$$varName $alias \n";
        }
        if (defined (@alias)) {
            print "\t \@$varName @alias \n";
        }
        if (defined (%alias)) {
            print "\t \%$varName ",%alias," \n";
        }
    }
}
```

This snippet of a code illustrates how to use **DUMPVAR**:

```
package XX;
$x = 10;
@y = (1,3,4);
%z = (1,2,3,4, 5, 6);
$z = 300;
DUMPVAR::dumpvar("XX");
```

This prints:

```
x ============================
        $x 10
y ============================
```

```
        @y 1 3 4
  z ============================
        $z 300
        %z  1 2 3 4 5 6
```

`dumpvar()` works by creating an alias to each typeglob successively and then enumerating each type to see whether that value is defined. It is important to realize that it merely dumps the global data at the topmost level, because anonymous data structures hanging off various references are not dumped at all.

Language Comparisons

In this chapter, we have seen that Perl offers namespace partitioning, limited access protection, reflection, run-time subroutine loading (autoloading), package initialization and destruction constructs, and exportation of names to different namespaces. Let's look at some other languages with these features in mind.

Tcl

Tcl's "package" feature basically provides a way to annotate a set of code with a version number and for the user of that code to explicitly state the version it requires. Tcl flags an error if there's a mismatch. Perl supports version numbers also (more on this in the next chapter).

Packages don't act like global namespaces as they do in Perl. Instead, Tcl supports the concept of multiple interpreters coexisting in the same program to provide completely distinct namespaces. This facility is used to create `SafeTcl`, which offers secure and insecure compartments in which to evaluate code. Perl's `Safe` package uses a completely different mechanism internally (neither packages nor multiple interpreters), as we shall see in Chapter 20, *Perl Internals.*

For reflection, Tcl has an "info" command for finding out about global symbols. It has no inheritance feature, but several free extensions such as [*incr Tcl*] and *stoop* attempt to fill the gap by providing an object orientation layer over the basic language.

Dynamic function calls are common and trivial to implement; just specify the name of a command as a variable, and it will get interpolated and executed at run time.

Python

Python offers packaging facilities very similar to Perl's. Each Python module is a namespace (a dictionary or hash table keyed by name), and Python allows you to traverse and query this dictionary. Like Perl, it does not enforce privacy of namespaces and leaves it to the programmer's judgment to respect module boundaries. As a module's user, you can import specific symbols into your namespace. (There is no mechanism equivalent to @EXPORT, which I think is a good thing.) Python does not provide anything like Perl's file-scope lexicals, which means that, unlike Perl, Python cannot give you true privacy if you need it.

C/C++

Of all the languages mentioned here, C and C++ are the least dynamic; their focus is on getting everything nailed down at compile-time so at run-time the code can just whistle along.

Virtual functions in C++ provide run-time binding of functions. While compile-time type checking ensures that this is a safe binding, it also tends to make the code verbose in comparison to more dynamic languages such as Objective C or even Java.

C++ supports RTTI (Run Time Type Identification), but this feature is limited to finding the actual type of a pointer and to dynamically cast it. (The run-time environment throws an exception if a pointer is wrongly cast.) The facility does not tell you what a variable is really pointing to.

Java

Java offers two levels of modularity: *packages* and *classes*, where a package is a collection of classes. (We'll learn about the notion of classes in the next chapter.) Perl's package is equivalent to both. Java does not allow one package to mess around with another package's namespace (no export) but allows a package to selectively import the classes it requires. It focuses a considerable amount of attention on security, which hasn't really stopped determined crackers. The Perl world has third-party packages called Safe and Penguin (which depends on Safe) that attempt to provide similar isolation characteristics (and don't offer any security guarantees either).

Since the arrival of the Java Beans and the 1.1 version of the Java Development Kit (JDK), Java has gained significant reflection capabilities, though nowhere near the amount of publicly available information Perl gives you. There are reasonably good arguments to be made both for providing this information and for not providing it; everything comes down to different models of programming. Men were sent to the moon while FORTRAN and COBOL ruled the roost, which proves that you can get a whole lot done if you don't indulge in language wars.

Java allows you to dynamically "dispatch" a function call, by giving the function's name as a string, and to trap an exception if the function doesn't exist; this is like using Perl's symbolic references.

7

Object-Oriented Programming

There was a child went forth every day,
And the first object he look'd upon,
that object he became.

—Walt Whitman
There Was a Child Went Forth

Object orientation (OO) is the latest software methodology to occupy the airwaves, hyped to a point where the term "object-oriented design" seems to automatically imply a good design. In this chapter, we will study what the noise is all about and build objects using Perl. I will leave it to the plethora of OO literature to convince you that there is a respectable middle-ground and that the object revolution is indeed a good thing.

If you are already conversant with OO, you could simply read the "Objects" section in Appendix B, *Syntax Summary*. Among other things, it supplies a C++ example and translates it to equivalent Perl code.

OO: An Introduction

Fred Brooks, in his classic *The Mythical Man-Month* [6], says:

> The programmer at wit's end for lack of space can often do best by disentangling himself from his code, rearing back, and contemplating his data. Representation *is* the essence of programming.

He was talking about space reduction, but it is nevertheless sage advice.

Complex systems are inherently hierarchical, and many abstractions and methodologies have been invented to take advantage of this aspect. Until the late seventies, functional decomposition (top-down design) held sway as the definitive method to understand and implement complex systems. A developer would begin by writing high-level pseudo-code and continue refining each part of it until it was detailed enough to be translated into an implementation language. Nicklaus Wirth called this approach stepwise refinement. Then came structured methodologies, SA/SD (structured analysis/structured design) chief among them, which employed many tools and notations such as data-flow diagrams, process specifications, data dictionaries, state transition diagrams, and entity-relationship diagrams to design, document, and develop a system. The accent continued to be on the *procedural* side of systems development rather than on the *dynamic* (state transitions) or *structural* (data) facets.

The key realization in the last 15 years or so has been that a system's functionality tends to change a lot more than the data on which it acts. A personnel information system keeping track of employee details soon knows as much about an employee as it ever will. On the other hand, its functionality tends to track management reshuffles, tax laws, medical insurance changes, and the noisy arrivals and silent departures of Directors of Human Resources.

This realization has completely inverted the way a problem is tackled now. Data and ways of structuring it are now given primary importance, and code is organized in modules around important pieces of data. The benefits are immense and immediate.

First, the database and the code are in sync, since the code is organized along lines of data. There are those who cry about the "impedance mismatch" between object-oriented programs and relational databases (RDBMSs), but that is because RDBMSs have been limited to simple data types; there is no fundamental mismatch between the relational and object models. Vendors such as Informix/ Illustra and Oracle have recently begun to offer abstract data types also in their RDBMS offerings.

Focusing on data has another important advantage: Data structures tend to be something you can identify with. For example, an airline company has airplanes, routes, and flight legs as prominent entities. In designing a flight-planning system, these entities provide a good focus on which to center your discussions, analysis, and design. Anybody who has had writer's block when starting a brand-new design document would surely appreciate this approach! The final design and implementation are also more comprehensible (and hence maintainable) because it is easier to explain. Fred Brooks remarks in *The Mythical Man-Month*, "Show me your flowcharts and conceal your tables, and I'll continue to be mystified. Show me your tables, and I won't usually need your flowcharts; they'll be obvious."

Finally, a system divided into data-centric modules can be easily apportioned among a team of programmers. All changes to a given piece of data or a set of related data are done only by its "owner"; that developer becomes a component supplier for other people in the project.

Object orientation is the latest step along this course. Not only is the code data-centric, it also strives to *encapsulate* (hide) the actual data structures, preferring instead to expose a limited, well-documented interface: a set of functions that know how to manipulate these data structures. These data structures are called *objects.* VCRs, watches, cars, and other real-world objects are excellent examples of the kind of objects we wish to emulate, because they successfully hide all the myriad complexities behind really simple interfaces. (Of course, the fact that most VCRs show a blinking "12:00" indicates that there is still a considerable amount of interface simplification to be done.) While you can surely implement well-encapsulated data-centric designs using conventional languages such as C or COBOL or even assembler, object-oriented languages provide two features that are more than just syntactic conveniences: *polymorphism* and *inheritance.* We will see how these features facilitate the construction of reusable modules.

It must be stressed that OO methodologies are similar to SA/SD in that both account for the functional, dynamic, and structural aspects of a system. But they differ significantly in style and emphasis; OO design methodologies pay attention to data abstractions first and procedural abstractions last.

Objects in Perl

Let us define a few preliminary terms before we start implementing objects in Perl.

An *object* (also called an *instance*), like a given car, has the following:

- *Attributes* or properties (color: red; seating capacity: 4; power: 180 HP)
- *Identity* (my car is different from your car)
- *Behavior* (it can be steered and moved forward and backward)

Objects of a certain type are said to belong to a *class.* My car and your car belong to the class called Car or, if you are not too worried about specific details, to a class called Vehicle. All objects of a class have the same functionality.

In this section, we study how to create objects and how to enrich basic designs using inheritance and polymorphism.

Attributes

An object is a collection of attributes. An array or a hash can be used to represents this set, as we discussed in Chapter 2, *Implementing Complex Data*

Structures. For example, if you need to keep track of an employee's particulars, you might choose one of these approaches:

```
# Use a hash table to store Employee attributes
%employee = ("name"     => "John Doe",
             "age"      => 32,
             "position" => "Software Engineer");
print "Name: ", $employee{name};


# Or use an array
$name_field = 0; $age_field = 1; $position_field = 2;
@employee = ("John Doe", 32, "Software Engineer");
print "Name: ", $employee[$name_field];
```

The section "Efficient Attribute Storage" in Chapter 8, *Object Orientation: The Next Few Steps* describes a more efficient approach for storing attributes. Meanwhile, we will use a hash table for all our examples.

Unique Identity

Clearly, one %employee won't suffice. Each employee requires a unique identity and his or her own collection of attributes. You can either allocate this structure dynamically or return a reference to a local data structure, as shown below:

```
# Using an anonymous hash
sub new_employee {
    my ($name, $age, $starting_position) = @_;
    my $r_employee = {                    # Create a unique object
        "name"     => $name,              # using an anonymous hash
        "age"      => $age,
        "position" => $starting_position
    };
    return $r_employee;                   # Return "object"
}


# OR, returning a reference to a local variable
sub new_employee {
    my ($name, $age, $starting_position) = @_;
    my %employee = (
        "name"     => $name,
        "age"      => $age,
        "position" => $starting_position
    );
    return \%employee;  # return a reference to a local object
}
# Use it to create two employees
$emp1 = new_employee("John Doe",   32, "Software Engineer");
$emp2 = new_employee("Norma Jean", 25, "Vice President");
```

new_employee() returns a reference to a unique data structure in both cases.

As a *user* of this subroutine, you are not expected to know whether this scalar contains a reference to a Perl data structure or whether it contains a string (for example, it could just contain a database primary key, while the rest of the details are in a corporate database). The employee details are hence well encapsulated. Not that encapsulation should not be confused with enforced privacy.

In the preceding example, the hash table is the object, and the reference to the hash table is termed the *object reference*. Keep in mind that we have not introduced any new syntax since the last chapter.

Behavior

All functions that access or update one or more attributes of the object constitute the behavior of the object.

Consider

```
sub promote_employee {
    my $r_employee = shift;
    $r_employee->{"position"} =
        lookup_next_position($r_employee->{"position"});
}

# To use it
promote_employee($emp1);
```

Such functions are also called *instance methods* in OO circles because they require a specific *instance* of the an object; an employee, in this case.

To avoid having to suffix every method with the suffix "_employee," we put all these functions in a package of their own, called Employee:

```
package Employee;
sub new {    # No need for the suffix.
    ....
}
sub promote {
    ....
}
```

To use this module, you need to say:

```
$emp = Employee::new("John Doe", 32, "Software Engineer");
Employee::promote($emp);
```

As you can see, this code is beginning to encapsulate a class called **Employee**: the user of this code invokes only the *interface functions* **new** and **promote** and does not know or care about the type of data structure used to store employee details, or, as we mentioned earlier, whether a database is being used behind the scenes.

The Need for Polymorphism

What we have seen thus far is the kind of stuff that a C programmer would do, except that he or she would likely use a *struct* to keep track of the attributes. This is precisely the way the `stdio` library works, for example. `fopen()` is a constructor that returns a pointer to a unique `FILE` structure, allocated dynamically. The pointer (the object reference) is supplied to other methods like `fgets()` and `fprintf()`.

Unfortunately, complications arise when the problem gets more involved. Let us say we have to keep information about hourly and regular employees. Hourly employees get paid by the hour and are eligible for overtime pay, while regular employees get a monthly salary. One way to approach it is to create a **new** function per type of employee:

```perl
package Employee;
# Creating Regular Employees
sub new_regular {
    my ($name, $age, $starting_position, $monthly_salary) = @_;
    my $employee = {
        "name"           => $name,
        "age"            => $age,
        "position"       => $starting_position,
        "monthly_salary" => $monthly_salary,
    };
    return $employee;  # return the object reference
}
# Hourly Employees
sub new_hourly {
    my ($name, $age, $starting_position,
        $hourly_rate, $overtime_rate) = @_;
    my $employee = {
        "name"          => $name,
        "age"           => $age,
        "position"      => $starting_position,
        "hourly_rate"   => $hourly_rate,
        "overtime_rate" => $overtime_rate
    };
    return $employee;  # return the object reference
}
```

Now, if we want to get an employee's year-to-date salary, we have to make a distinction between the two types of employees. We could provide the two subroutines `compute_hourly_ytd_income()` and `compute_regular_ytd_income()`, but of course the story doesn't end there. Other differences between hourly and regular employees (such as allowed vacation, medical benefits, and so on) or the introduction of other *types* of employees (such as temporary employees) results in a combinatorial explosion of functions. Worse, the interface requires the *user* of this package to make a distinction between types of employees to be able to call the right function.

To get us out of this bind, we put different types of employees in different packages. Then we use the **bless** keyword to tag objects internally with a pointer to the packages they belong to. The boldface lines in the following example show the changes from the code presented above (explanations follow):

```perl
#-------------------------------------------------------------
package RegularEmployee;
sub new {
    my ($name, $age, $starting_position, $monthly_salary) = @_;
    my $r_employee = {
        "name"           => $name,
        "age"            => $age,
        "position"       => $starting_position,
        "monthly_salary" => $monthly_salary,
        "months_worked"  => 0,
    };
    bless $r_employee, 'RegularEmployee';     # Tag object with pkg name
    return $r_employee;                       # Return object
}
sub promote {
    #...
}
sub compute_ytd_income{
    my $r_emp = shift;
    # Assume the months_worked attribute got modified at some point
    return $r_emp->{'monthly_salary'} * $r_emp->{'months_worked'};
}


#-------------------------------------------------------------
package HourlyEmployee;
sub new {
    my ($name, $age, $starting_position,
        $hourly_rate, $overtime_rate) = @_;
    my $r_employee = {
        "name"          => $name,
        "age"           => $age,
        "position"      => $starting_position,
        "hourly_rate"   => $hourly_rate,
        "overtime_rate" => $overtime_rate
    };
    bless $r_employee, 'HourlyEmployee';
    return $r_employee;
}
sub promote {
    #...
}
sub compute_ytd_income {
    my ($r_emp) = $_[0];
    return $r_emp->{'hourly_rate'} * $r_emp->{'hours_worked'}
        + $r_emp->{'overtime_rate'} * $r_emp->{'overtime_hours_worked'};
}
```

`bless` is given an ordinary reference to a data structure. It tags that data structure (note: not the *reference*[*]) as belonging to a specific package and thus bestows on it some more powers, as we shall soon see. `bless` is to our hash table what baptism is to a child. It doesn't change the data structure in any way (which still remains a hash table), just as baptism doesn't really alter a person except to give them an additional identity.

The nice thing about `bless` is that it gives us a direct way of using this object. Here's how:

```
# First create two objects as before.
$emp1 = RegularEmployee::new('John Doe', 32,    # Polymorphism
                             'Software Engineer', 5000);
$emp2 = HourlyEmployee::new('Jane Smith', 35,   # Polymorphism
                            'Auditor', 65, 90);
```

Now use the *arrow notation* to directly invoke instance methods, or, as they say in OO-land, invoke methods *on the object*:

```
# Direct invocation
$emp1->promote();
$emp2->compute_ytd_income();
```

When Perl sees `$emp1->promote()`, it determines the class to which `$emp1` belongs (the one under which it has been blessed). In this case, it is the `Regular-Employee`. Perl then calls this function as follows: `RegularEmployee::promote($emp1)`. In other words, the object on the left side of the arrow is simply given as the first parameter of the appropriate subroutine.

Both the `::` and `->` notations are in fact permissible, unlike in C++. The first one is more flexible because Perl figures out the class at run time, while the latter is faster because the function to be called is known at compile time. There is nothing magical about an instance method in Perl. It is an ordinary subroutine whose first parameter simply happens to be an object reference. (You might have noticed that the `promote` method did not change from the previous section.)

So is this mere syntactic sugar? Finally, all we seem to have achieved is the ability to call an instance method of an object through an alternate notation.

No, we have gained an important advantage. The module user doesn't have to discriminate between types of objects using an `if` statement but instead lets Perl take care of routing a call to the appropriate function. That is, instead of saying something like

```
if (ref($emp) eq "HourlyEmployee") {
    $income = HourlyEmployee::compute_ytd_income($emp);
```

---

[*] The reference is like a `void *` in C. The object is typed, not the C pointer or Perl reference.

```
    } else {
        $income = RegularEmployee::compute_ytd_income($emp);
    }
```

we can simply say,

```
    $income = $emp->compute_ytd_income();
```

This ability of Perl to call the appropriate module's function is called *run-time binding*. Incidentally, recall from Chapter 1, *Data References and Anonymous Storage*, that the `ref` function returns a string indicating the type of the entity pointed to by the reference; in the case of a blessed object reference, it returns the name of the corresponding class.

Note that while processing payroll records, `$emp` can be a regular employee in one iteration and an hourly employee in another. This feature is called *polymorphism* (poly + morph = the ability of an object to take on many forms).

Polymorphism and run-time binding are the chief contributions of object-oriented languages. They give a system an enormous amount of flexibility because you can now add a new type of employee (with the same *interface* as the other types) without having to change the payroll-processing code. This is possible because each object "knows" how to compute its own year-to-date income. It pays to remember this cardinal rule:

> *It is indicative of inflexible procedural design if you find yourself using conditional statements to distinguish between object types.*

The design is flexible also because you can add new methods to any of the packages without hurting what is already present.

Class Methods and Attributes

Class attributes are properties that pertain to all instances of a class, but don't vary on a per-employee basis. For example, one insurance company might provide health coverage for all employees, so it doesn't make sense to store the name of this company in each and every employee.

Class methods (also known as *static methods*) are functions that are relevant to that class but don't need a specific object instance to work with. For example, a subroutine called `get_employee_names()` doesn't require an employee object as input to figure out what it has to do.

Perl has no specific syntax for class attributes and methods, unlike C++ or Java. Class attributes are simply package global variables, and class methods are ordinary subroutines that don't work on any specific instance. Perl supports polymorphism and run-time binding for these ordinary subroutines (not just instance methods), which can be leveraged to produce a truly flexible design. Consider

```
$record = <STDIN>; # Tab delimited record containing employee details
($type, $name, $age, $position) = split(/\t/, $details);

# Create an employee object of the appropriate class
$emp = $type->new($name, $age, $position);

# Now use the object as before
$emp->compute_ytd_income();
```

In this example, `$type` can contain either of these two strings: "HourlyEmployee" or "RegularEmployee." Note that this variable is not an object; it is simply the name of a class. This approach improves on the example in the previous section by avoiding having to hardcode the name of the package. Why is that an improvement? Well, if you *didn't* have this facility, you would have had to say something like this to create an appropriately typed object:

```
if ($type eq "HourlyEmployee") {
    $emp = HourlyEmployee->new(....);
} else {
    $emp = RegularEmployee->new(....);
}
```

Any piece of code that explicitly depends upon checking the class or type of an object requires too much maintenance. If you introduce a new type of employee tomorrow, you'll have to go back and add the new type to all such pieces of code.

Recall that in the case of an instance method, the object to the left of the arrow is passed as the first parameter to the subroutine. It is no different here. The procedure `HourlyEmployee::new` must be rewritten to expect this:

```
package HourlyEmployee;
sub new {
    my ($pkg, $name, $age, $starting_position,
        $hourly_rate, $overtime_rate) = @_;
```

Given that both instance and class methods are ordinary subroutines, you can always write a subroutine that can function as either, by checking the type of the first parameter supplied to it. Consider the following constructor, which creates a new object or a clone of an existing one, depending on how it is invoked:

```
package Employee;
sub new {
    $arg = shift;
    if (ref($arg)) {
        # Called as $emp->new(): Clone the Employee given to it
        #....
    } else {
        # Called as Employee->new():  Create a new employee
        #...
    }
}
```

You can now use this method as follows:

```
# Using new() as a class method
$emp1 = Employee->new("John Doe", 20, "Vice President");

# Using new() as an instance method to clone the employee details
$emp2 = $emp1->new();
```

I'll leave it up to you to answer why you might want to clone an employee!

What have we learned in this section? If we write all our class methods to expect the name of the module as the first parameter, we make it possible for the module's user to employ run-time binding and polymorphism. We will follow this practice from now on.

You might be curious why a class method needs to be supplied the name of its own module. We'll answer this shortly when we deal with inheritance.

Detour: The indirect notation

Perl wouldn't be Perl if there weren't a couple of alternatives to suit everyone's fancy. It supports an alternative to the arrow notation, called the *indirect notation*, in which the function name precedes the object or class name. An example should make this clear:

```
$emp = new Employee ("John Doe", 20, "Vice President");
```

C++ folks will identify with this notation. This approach can be used for objects too:

```
promote $emp "Chairman", 100000; # Give him a promotion and a raise
```

Notice that there is no comma between $emp and the first argument ("Chairman"). This is how Perl knows that you are calling a method using the indirect notation and not calling a subroutine in the current package. Perhaps you will identify more with the following example:

```
use FileHandle;
$fh = new FileHandle("> foo.txt");
print $fh "foo bar\n";
```

print is a method on the FileHandle module.

While the indirect notation has the same effect as the arrow notation, it cannot be used in a chain of calls. The following is possible only with the arrow notation:

```
use FileHandle;
$fh = FileHandle->new("> foo.txt")->autoflush(1); # Chain of calls
```

The Need for Inheritance

Perl allows a module to specify a list of other module names, in a special array called @ISA. When it does not find a particular class or instance method in a module, it looks to see if that module's @ISA has been initialized. If so, it checks to see if any of those modules support the missing function, picks the first one it can find, and passes control to it. This feature is called *inheritance*. Consider

```
package Man;
@ISA = qw(Mammal Social_Animal);
```

This allows us to specify that **Man** is-a **Mammal** and is-a **Social_Animal**. All traits (read: methods) common to mammals are supported in the **Mammal** class and don't have to be implemented in **Man** too. Let us look at a more practical example.

In our attempts to distinguish between hourly and regular employees, we have gone to the other extreme and made them completely independent. Clearly, there are a number of common attributes (name, age, and position) and behavior (**promote**, say) that they all share as employees. We can thus use inheritance to "pull out" the common aspects into a *superclass* (or *base class*) called **Employee**:

```
#--------------------------------------------------------
package Employee; #Base class
#--------------------------------------------------------
sub allocate{
    my ($pkg, $name, $age, $starting_position) = @_;
    my $r_employee = bless {
        "name"              => $name,
        "age"               => $age,
        "position"          => $starting_position
    }, $pkg;
    return $r_employee;
}
sub promote {
    my $r_employee           = shift;
    my $current_position     = $r_employee->{"position"};
    my $next_position        = lookup_next_position($current_position);
    $r_employee->{"position"} = $next_position;
}
#--------------------------------------------------------
package HourlyEmployee;
#--------------------------------------------------------
@ISA = ("Employee"); # Inherits from Employee
sub new {
    my ($pkg, $name, $age, $starting_position,
        $hourly_rate, $overtime_rate) = @_;
    # Let the Employee package create and bless the object
    my $r_employee = $pkg->allocate($name, $age,
                                    $starting_position);
    # Add HourlyEmployee-specific attributes and we are done.
```

```
        $r_employee->{"hourly_rate"}   = $hourly_rate;
        $r_employee->{"overtime_rate"} = $overtime_rate;
        return $r_employee; # return the object reference
    }
    sub compute_ytd_income {
        ....
    }
    # ... And similarly for package RegularEmployee
```

Whatever is common to all employees is implemented in the base class. Since both **HourlyEmployee** and **RegularEmployee** need a class method called **new()** to allocate a hash table, to bless it, and to insert common attributes into this table, we factor this functionality out into a inheritable subroutine called **allocate** in module Employee.

Notice how **allocate** avoids hardcoding the name of a class, thus ensuring maximum reusability. **HourlyEmployee::new()** calls **$pkg->allocate**, which means that the first parameter to **allocate**, $pkg, has the value Hourly-Employee. **allocate** uses this to bless the object directly into the inherited class. **HourlyEmployee::new** doesn't need to create the object anymore; it just has to insert its own specific attributes.

Nothing has changed from the user's point of view. You still say,

```
    $emp = HourlyEmployee->new(....);
```

But we have now managed to eliminate redundant code in the modules and left them open for future enhancements.

Overriding base classes

Let us say we wanted to ensure that hourly employees should never rise above the level of a manager. The example shows how to *override* the base class's **promote()** method to do this check. Here's how:

```
    package HourlyEmployee;
    sub promote {
        my $obj = shift;
        die "Hourly Employees cannot be promoted beyond 'Manager'"
            if ($obj->{position} eq 'Manager');
        # call base class's promote
        $obj->Employee::promote(); #Specify the package explicitly
    }
```

This syntax tells Perl to start the search for **promote()** in the **@ISA** hierarchy, starting from **Employee**. A small problem here is that by hardcoding the name of a class (**Employee**), we make it difficult for us to change our mind about the inheritance hierarchy. To avoid this, Perl provides a pseudoclass called **SUPER**, like Smalltalk, so that you can say,

```
    $obj->SUPER::promote();
```

This searches the @ISA hierarchy for the appropriate **promote** subroutine. Now, if we interpose another package between **Employee** and **HourlyEmployee** in the inheritance hierarchy, we just need to update **HourlyEmployee**'s @ISA array.

NOTE   We have now gradually eliminated the need for the `::` notation to call a module's subroutines. A subroutine either is imported directly into your namespace, in which case you don't need to fully qualify its name, or is invoked by using the `->` notation. You still need to use "`::`" to access a foreign package's *variables*.

Object Destruction

Perl automatically garbage collects a data structure when its reference count drops to zero. If a data structure has been blessed into a module, Perl allows that module to perform some clean-up before it destroys the object, by calling a special procedure in that module called **DESTROY** and passing it the reference to the object to be destroyed:

```
package Employee;
sub DESTROY {
    my ($emp) = @_;
    print "Alas, ", $emp->{"name"}, " is now no longer with us \n";
}
```

This is similar to C++'s destructor or the **finalize()** method in Java in that Perl does the memory management automatically, but you get a chance to do something before the object is reclaimed. (Unlike Java's **finalize**, Perl's garbage collection is deterministic; **DESTROY** is called as soon as the object is not being referred to any more.)

Note that you are not compelled to declare this subroutine; you do so only if you have some clean-up work to be done. In a module such as Socket, you would close the corresponding connection, but in something like Employee, where no external system resources are being held up, you don't have to provide a **DESTROY** method. But recall that **AUTOLOAD** is called if a function is not found. In the case in which you supply **AUTOLOAD** but not the **DESTROY** method, you might want to ensure that **AUTOLOAD** checks for this possibility:

```
sub AUTOLOAD {
    my $obj = $_[0];
    # $AUTOLOAD contains the name of the missing method

    # Never propagate DESTROY methods
    return if $AUTOLOAD =~ /::DESTROY$/;
    # ....
}
```

Accessor Methods

According to Rumbaugh et al. [3]:

> Encapsulation can be violated when code associated with one class directly accesses the attributes of another class. Direct access makes assumptions about storage format and location of the data. These details must be hidden within the class....The proper way to access an attribute of another object is to "ask for it" by invoking an operation on the object, rather than simply "taking it."

This is as true for classes related by inheritance as for unrelated classes.

To discourage direct access to an object's attributes, we provide "accessor methods." These two methods read and update the "position" attribute of an employee:

```
$pos = $emp->get_position();                  # read attribute
$emp->set_position("Software Engineer");       # write attribute
```

The more popular convention is to have one method to handle both read and write access:

```
$pos = $emp->position();                       # read attribute
$emp->position("Software Engineer");           # write attribute
```

This is how the module might implement it:

```
package Employee;
sub position {
    my $obj = shift;
    @_ ? $obj->{position} = shift       # modify attribute
       : $obj->{position};              # retrieve attribute
}
```

Note that the method returns the latest value of the position attribute in both cases, because in both cases (get and set), the expression `$obj->{position}` is the last to be evaluated.

It might seem a complete waste of time to call a method every time you need to touch an attribute. But, as it happens, accessor methods are absolutely necessary in *designing for change*. Consider the following advantages:

Encapsulation

Accessor methods hide how object attributes are stored. If you change the way this layout is done, only these methods need to be modified; the rest of the code, including derived classes, remain untouched. In Perl, as in other OO scripting languages, in which reengineering may be necessary for performance or space efficiency, accessor methods are a good thing. Smalltalk, CORBA (Common Object Request Broker Architecture), and ActiveX are other well-known cases in which the only way to an attribute is through an accessor.

Side effects

Accessor methods are sometimes used for triggering actions in addition to retrieving or updating the attribute. GUI toolkits use this idiom routinely. For example:

```
$button->foreground_color('yellow');
```

This not only changes the value of the foreground color attribute, but updates the screen too.

Access checking

Accessor methods can be made to disallow updates. For example, primary key attributes such as an employee's name should not be updatable once created; an accessor can easily enforce this.

Computed attributes

An employee's income can be seen as an attribute, though internally it needs to be computed. Instead of writing a method like `compute_ytd_ income()`, you simply call it `income()`. This makes it look like an attribute accessor, and it can disallow updates to this attribute.

Moral of the story: Get in the habit of writing accessor methods. In the next chapter, we will study a module called ObjectTemplate, a standard library called Class::Template, and a module on CPAN called MethodMaker, all of which automatically create accessor methods for you, so there is really no reason not to use such methods.

Caveat: Even if your attributes are wrapped in accessor methods, you should be wary of unrelated classes using these methods. When reviewing a piece of code, always look for the real intention behind these accesses; sometimes it may be better to provide other methods that make this access unnecessary. For example, a user should always use `$emp->promote()` instead of directly updating the `position` attribute.

UNIVERSAL

All modules implicitly inherit from a built-in module called UNIVERSAL and inherit the following three methods:

`isa` (*package name*)

For example, `Rectangle->isa('Shape')` returns true if the Rectangle module inherits (however indirectly) from the Shape module.

`can` (*function name*)

`Rectangle->can('draw')` returns true if the Rectangle or any of its base packages contain a function called `draw`.

VERSION (*need version*)

> If you say,
>
> ```
> package Bank;
> $VERSION = 5.1;
> ```
>
> and the user of this module says,
>
> ```
> use Bank 5.2;
> ```
>
> Perl automatically calls `Bank->VERSION(5.2)`, which can, for instance, make sure that all libraries required for version 5.2 are loaded. The default `VERSION` method provided by UNIVERSAL simply dies if the `Bank`'s `$VERSION` variable has a lower value than that needed by the user of the module.

Because Perl allows a package to shamelessly trample on other namespaces, some packages use the UNIVERSAL module as a holding area for some global subroutines that they wish to export to everyone. I recommend that you do not use this "feature" yourself (or at least not in those that you contribute to CPAN!).

Searching for Methods

We have mentioned two places that Perl searches when it cannot find a method in the target module: the inheritance hierarchy (`@ISA`) and `AUTOLOAD`. While checking the inheritance hierarchy, Perl checks the base classes' `@ISA` arrays too: a depth-first search is conducted, and the first available one is used. Let us examine the precise order in which all these subroutines are searched. Given:

```
package Man;
@ISA = qw(Mammal Social_Animal);
```

a call to `Man->schmooze` results in the following search sequence. First the normal inheritance hierarchy is checked:

1. `Man::schmooze`

2. `Mammal::schmooze`

3. (`Mammal`'s base classes, recursively)`::schmooze`

4. `Social_Animal::schmooze`

5. (`Social_Animal`'s base classes, recursively)`::schmooze`

6. `UNIVERSAL::schmooze` (because UNIVERSAL is implicitly at the end of every module's `@ISA` array)

Then `AUTOLOAD` is looked up in the same order:

7. `Man::AUTOLOAD`

8. `Mammal::AUTOLOAD`

9. (`Mammal`'s base classes, recursively)::AUTOLOAD

10. `Social_Animal::AUTOLOAD`

11. (`Social_Animal`'s base classes, recursively)::AUTOLOAD

12. `UNIVERSAL::AUTOLOAD`

The first available subroutine is given the control and the search is stopped. If all fails, Perl throws a run-time exception.

Recap of Conventions

While Perl allows us infinite flexibility in how we organize our modules, we choose to stick to the particular set of conventions introduced in this chapter so that everyone deals with modules in a consistent fashion. Let us quickly summarize these conventions:

- A module must be present in its own file called *<module>.pm*. (Remember that the last executing global statement must return 1 to signify successful loading.)

- All subroutines in a module should be designed as methods. That is, they should expect either the name of a class or an object reference as their first parameter. For added convenience, they should be able to deal with either.

- Package names should never be hardcoded. You must always use the package name obtained as the first argument to supply to **bless**. This enables a constructor to be inherited.

- Always provide accessor methods for class and instance attributes.

The following example puts all these techniques and conventions into practice.

Example

Consider a store that sells computers and individual components. Each component has a model number, a price, and a rebate. A customer can buy individual components, but can also put together a custom computer with specific components. The store adds a sales tax to the final price. The objective of this example is to provide the net price on any item you can buy from the store.

We need to account for the facts that a part may consist of other parts, that the sales tax may depend on the type of part and the customer's location, and that we may have to charge for labor to assemble a computer

One useful technique for jump-starting a design is to use *case analysis*, as propounded by Ivar Jacobson [7]. You look at the interface from the point of view of the user, without worrying about specific objects' attributes. That way, we can understand the objects' interface without worrying about implementation details. Let's say this is how we want to use the system:

```
$cdrom   = new CDROM   ("Toshiba 5602");

$monitor = new Monitor ("Viewsonic 15GS");
print $monitor->net_price();

$computer = new Computer($monitor, $cdrom);
print $computer->net_price();
```

Figure 7-1 shows one way of designing the object model. I have used Rumbaugh's OMT (Object Modeling Technique) notation to depict classes, inheritance hierarchies, and associations between classes. The triangle indicates an is-a relationship, and the line with the 1+ indicates a one-to-many relationship. The computer *is-a* store item and contains other components (has-a relationship). A CD-ROM or monitor is a component, which in turn is a store item.

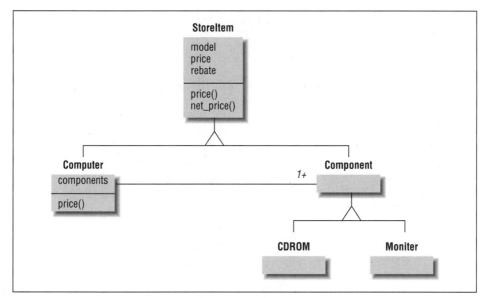

Figure 7-1. Object model for computer store example

All attributes common to all store items are captured in the StoreItem class. To compute the net price of any component, we have to take rebate and sales tax into account. But when assembling components to build a computer, we have to add sales tax only at the end; we can't simply add up all the components' net prices. For this reason, we split the calculation into two: price, which subtracts the rebate from the price, and net_price, which adds on the sales tax. At present, the component classes are empty classes, because their entire functionality is captured by StoreItem. Clearly, if the problem stopped here, this design would be unnecessarily complex; we could have simply had one lookup table for prices and rebates and one function to calculate the prices. But we are designing for change here. We expect it to get fleshed out when we start accounting for taxes by location, dealing with components containing other components, and charging for labor. It is best to adopt a generalized mentality from the very beginning.

The `Computer` class does not use its price attribute; instead, it adds up the prices of its constituent components. It doesn't need to override the `net_price` functionality, because that function simply adds the sales tax onto an object's price, regardless of the type of the object.

Example 7-1 gives a translation of the object model into code.

Example 7-1. Sample Object Implementation

```
package StoreItem;

my $_sales_tax = 8.5;  # 8.5% added to all components's post rebate price

sub new {
    my ($pkg, $name, $price, $rebate) = @_;
    bless {
        # Attributes are marked with a leading underscore, to signify that
        # they are private (just a convention)
        _name => $name, _price => $price, _rebate => $rebate
    }, $pkg;
}

# Accessor methods
sub sales_tax {shift; @_ ? $_sales_tax = shift : $_sales_tax}
sub name {my $obj = shift; @_ ? $obj->{_name} = shift : $obj->{_name}}
sub rebate {my $obj = shift; @_ ? $obj->{_rebate} = shift
                                : $obj->{_rebate}}
sub price  {my $obj = shift; @_ ? $obj->{_price} = shift
                                    : $obj->{_price} - $obj->_rebate}
}

sub net_price {
    my $obj = shift;
    return $obj->price * (1 + $obj->sales_tax / 100);
}
#------------------------------------------------------------------------
package Component;
@ISA = qw(StoreItem);


#------------------------------------------------------------------------
package Monitor;
@ISA = qw(Component);
# Hard-code prices and rebates for now
sub new { $pkg = shift; $pkg->SUPER::new("Monitor", 400, 15)}
```

Example 7-1. Sample Object Implementation (continued)

```perl
#--------------------------------------------------------------------------
package CDROM;
@ISA = qw(Component);
sub new { $pkg = shift; $pkg->SUPER::new("CDROM", 200, 5)}


#--------------------------------------------------------------------------
package Computer;
@ISA = qw(StoreItem);

sub new {
    my $pkg = shift;
    my $obj = $pkg->SUPER::new("Computer", 0, 0);   # Dummy value for price
    $obj->{_components} = [];                        # list of components
    $obj->components(@_);
    $obj;
}

# Accessors
sub components {
    my $obj = shift;
    @_ ? push (@{$obj->{_components}}, @_)
        : @{$obj->{_components}};
}
sub price {
    my $obj = shift;
    my $price = 0;
    my $component;
    foreach $component ($obj->components()) {
        $price += $component->price();
    }
    $price;
}
```

The design for change philosophy is in evidence here. All instance variables get accessor methods, which makes it possible for us to override price() in the Computer class. The Computer::components accessor method can now be changed at a later date to check for compatibility of different components. Even the package global variable $sales_tax is retrieved through an accessor method, because we expect that different components may later on get different sales taxes, so we ask the object for the sales tax.

Notice also that the constructors use SUPER to access their super classes' new routines. This way, if you create a Component::new tomorrow, none of the other packages need to be changed. StoreItem::new blesses the object into a package given to it; it does not hardcode its own package name.

If you put these packages into different files, recall from Chapter 6, *Modules*, that the files should have the *<package name>.pm* naming convention. In addition, they should have a 1; or return 1; as the last executing statement.

Comparison with Other OO Languages

Tcl

The base Tcl library does not have any object-oriented features. It has recently acquired a package construct that provides a namespace for subroutines and global variables (there is no relationship between packages). Tcl is a very malleable language, and several freely available libraries strive to impose an object-oriented structure on the language. A package called `stoop` provides a pure Tcl solution featuring single and multiple inheritance, dynamic binding, runtime type identification, and so on. Another, called [`incr Tcl`], is a slightly more ambitious effort and provides a C++-like set of keywords and facilities. `incr Tcl` requires a patch to Tcl, though.

Python

Python is an excellent language for learning object orientation. (It also happens to be my favorite OO scripting language.) All facilities, including internal data structures such as lists and dictionaries (hash tables) and external libraries have consistent object-oriented interfaces. Python provides a number of hooks for class developers to write different types of accessor methods and supports multiple inheritance. All objects in Python are implemented as hash tables, unlike in Perl, in which you have to choose a representation (or looking at it more optimistically, where you are free to choose the optimal representation).

C++ and Java

There are a number of significant differences between Perl and C++ in their approach to object-orientation.

- *Object structure.* C++ requires you to declare your object's structure using the **class** keyword, unlike Perl, which doesn't care how you keep your object's state—as a hash, array, or scalar. The only thing Perl really asks is that you return a blessed reference to that data.

- *Privacy.* C++ has keywords to enforce various shades of privacy (**private**, **protected**, **public**). Perl does not enforce privacy; if you need privacy you can use lexical variables.

- *Constructors/destructors.* C++ requires that the constructing subroutine of an object have the same name as the class. Perl doesn't have any such strictures—any subroutine can be a constructor (the name **new** is just a convention). On the other hand, when an object is going to be destroyed, both Perl and C++ require well-known destructor names. A C++ constructor is really an initializer; the memory is allocated before the constructor is given control. In Perl, it is the programmer's responsibility to do both allocation and initialization.

- *Static versus instance methods.* C++ provides the `static` keyword to distinguish between static functions and object methods. Perl doesn't make that distinction—subroutines are indistinguishable from each other. A Perl subroutine can examine its arguments and can act as either.

- *Declaration and definition.* C++, unlike Perl, requires that declaration of a class be independent of its implementation (unless the implementation is inline). The typical C++ convention is to put the declarations in a header file and the implementation in a separate file.

- *Compile-time versus run-time features.* C++ requires that all class information, such as the inheritance hierarchy, the number and type of attributes and methods, and so on, be known at compile-time. Perl allows a run-time redefinition of everything; you can add, delete, or update methods or change the inheritance hierarchy by changing `@ISA`. I recommend that you not take advantage of this ability.

- *Run-time binding.* Since C++ does strict type-checking, run-time binding works only if the objects inherit from a common base class. Perl doesn't have this restriction.

Much of what has been said of C++ in the above comparison is true of Java too.

Resources

1. *perltoot* (Perl documentation). Tom Christiansen.

   "Tom's object-oriented tutorial" gives an excellent treatment of object orientation and, specifically, OO with Perl. A must-read.

2. *comp.object FAQ*

   From *ftp://rtfm.mit.edu/pub/usenet/comp.object*. One of the best FAQ compilations around.

3. *Object-Oriented Modeling and Design.* J. Rumbaugh, M. Blaha, W. Premerlani, F. Eddy, and W. Lorensen. Prentice-Hall, 1991.

   An excellent treatment of object orientation, especially as translated to a programming language. Also contains good comparisons of OO with other software methodologies.

4. *Design Patterns: Elements of Reusable Object-Oriented Software.* Erich Gamma, Richard Helm, Ralph Johnson, and John Vlissides. Addison-Wesley, 1994.

This book is a catalog of commonly used patterns of interacting objects (independent of language). Even if the patterns themselves are sometimes intuitive, the very act of giving them a name enriches an object practitioner's vocabulary.

5. *Bringing Design to Software.* Terry Winograd. Addison-Wesley, 1996.

   Among other things, this book examines several highly successful software products and argues that user-oriented design is the best software methodology. (None of the products that have really sold have worried particularly about object-oriented programming.) Interesting and persuasive.

6. *The Mythical Man-Month.* Frederick P. Brooks. Addison-Wesley, 1995.

7. *Object-Oriented Software Engineering: A Use Case Driven Approach.* Ivar Jacobson. Addison-Wesley, 1994.

8

Object Orientation: The Next Few Steps

No ties bind so strongly as the links of inheritance.
—Stephen Jay Gould

This chapter is essentially a motley collection of ideas, techniques, and opinions related to Perl objects. I have not attempted to weave these threads too closely. The topics are as follows:

Efficient attribute storage

Search for an alternative way of representing object attributes, instead of hash tables. The two strategies examined in this chapter occupy less space and are faster.

Delegation

How to use **AUTOLOAD** to automatically forward method calls.

Inheritance and composition

What I find objectionable about inheritance, along with alternative ways of structuring classes.

Efficient Attribute Storage

Hash tables have traditionally been used for storing object attributes. There are good reasons for doing this:

- Each attribute is self-describing (that is, the name and type of each attribute are easily obtained from the object), which makes it easy to write readable code. It also helps modules that do automatic object persistence or visualization of objects, without the object's explicit cooperation.

- Each class in an inheritance hierarchy can add attributes freely and independently.

- In fact, each *instance* (not just the class) can possess a unique set of attributes and can change this set at run time. The artificial intelligence community often uses this *slot-* or *frame*-based approach because it adapts itself very well to new pieces of information.

Of course, not every problem requires this degree of generality. In addition, while Perl's hash tables are fast (within 15% of the speed of arrays) and reasonably compact (key strings are not duplicated), they are not exactly inexpensive. Creating 100 objects means that you have 100 hash tables, each of which tends to optimistically allocate extra space to accommodate future insertions.

This section illustrates two alternate approaches, one using arrays and another using typeglobs. Both approaches are less general than the hash table approach but are faster and leaner. The first is a module called ObjectTemplate developed for this book.* The other uses typeglobs and has seen limited application in some standard CPAN modules, most notably IO and Net. I hesitate to suggest this as an alternative approach because it is way too "hackish," but I present it here to enable you to understand these standard modules.

ObjectTemplate: Attribute Storage Using Arrays

The module presented in this section uses arrays to store attributes (but not the array per object approach). Let us briefly see its usage before moving on to the implementation.

To implement the **Employee** class, with the attributes "name," "age," and "position," you simply inherit from ObjectTemplate, and supply a list of attribute names to a static method called *attributes* (exported by **ObjectTemplate**), as follows:

```
package Employee;
use ObjectTemplate;                 # Import ObjectTemplate
@ISA = qw(ObjectTemplate);          # Inherit from it.
attributes qw(name age position);   # Declare your attributes
```

That's all. A user of this module can now create **Employee** objects using a dynamically generated method called **new** and retrieve and modify attributes using accessor methods (also created automagically):

```
use Employee;
$obj = Employee->new(
                "name" => "Norma Jean",
                "age"  => 25
              );  # new() created by ObjectTemplate
```

---

* I originally posted a trial version of this approach to *comp.lang.perl.misc* as a module called ClassTemplate. The version presented here is a significant improvement.

```
$obj->position("Actress");
print $obj->name, ":", $obj->age, "\n";
```

Note that Perl permits you to omit the trailing parentheses for any method call in which there is no ambiguity about its usage. Any word following an arrow is automatically treated as a method, as in the preceding case.

ObjectTemplate provides the following features for an inherited class:

1. An allocator function called **new**. This allocates an object blessed into the inherited class. **new** calls `initialize`, which in turn can be overridden in the inherited class, as explained earlier.

2. Accessor methods with the same name as the attributes. These methods are created in the inherited module, and everyone, *including the object's own methods*, gains access to the attributes only through these methods. This is because ObjectTemplate is the only module that knows how the attributes are stored. For example,

```
package Employee;
sub promote {
    my $emp = shift;                          # $emp is the object
    my $current_position = $emp->position();  # Get attribute
    my $next_position    = lookup_next_position($current_position);
    $r_employee->position($next_position);    # Set attribute
}
```

3. The user package can create its own custom accessor methods with the same naming convention as above; in this case, ObjectTemplate does not generate one automatically. If a custom accessor method wants access to the attribute managed by ObjectTemplate, it can use the `get_attribute` and `set_attribute` methods.

4. **new()** takes an initializer list, a sequence of attribute name-value pairs.

5. ObjectTemplate takes attribute inheritance (**@ISA**) into account, for both the memory layout, and the accessors. Consider

```
package Employee;
use ObjectTemplate;
@ISA = qw(ObjectTemplate);
attributes qw(name age);

package HourlyEmployee;
@ISA = qw(Employee);
attributes qw(hourly_wage);
```

In this example, an object of the **HourlyEmployee** class contains two inherited attributes, **name** and **age**, that all employees possess, and **hourly_wage**, that only hourly employees possess.

6. All attributes are scalar-valued, so a multivalued attribute such as `friends` has to be stored as a reference:

```
attributes qw(friends);
$obj->friends([J'Joe']); # an array reference to the accessor
```

This is of course true of the hash table representation also.

ObjectTemplate internals overview

Figure 8-1 shows how ObjectTemplate organizes object attributes.

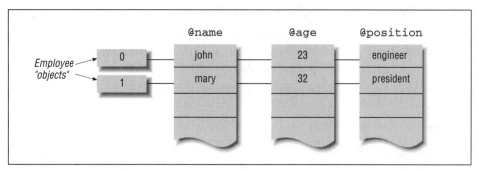

Figure 8-1. ObjectTemplate's attribute storage scheme

The data structure is quite simple. Instead of allocating one array or hash per object, ObjectTemplate creates only as many arrays as there are attributes (the columns shown in the figure). Each object is merely a "horizontal slice" across these attribute columns. When `new()` is called, it allocates a new logical row and inserts each element of the initializer array in the corresponding attribute column at the new row offset. The "object," therefore, is merely a blessed scalar containing that row index. This scheme is more space-efficient than the hash approach, because it creates so few container arrays (only as many as there are attributes), and it is faster because array accesses are always a little faster than hash accesses.

There's a slight hitch when an object is deleted. Although the corresponding row is logically free, we can't really move up the rest of the rows below, because the other object references (which are indices) and their data will get out of sync. ObjectTemplate therefore reuses deallocated (free) rows by maintaining a per-package "free list" called `@_free`. This is a linked list of all free rows with a scalar `$_free` pointing to the head of this list. Each element of this list contains the row index of the next free row. When an object is deleted, `$_free` points to that row, and the corresponding index in the free list points to the previous entry pointed to by `$_free`.

Since the freed and active rows do not overlap, we take the liberty of using one of the attribute columns (the first one) to hold `@_free`. This is done using typeglob aliasing. Figure 8-2 shows a snapshot of this structure.

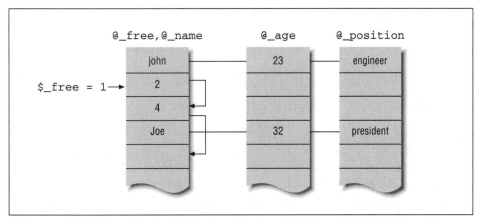

Figure 8-2. ObjectTemplate's scheme for managing holes created by deleted objects

You might have noticed that I'm using the same identifier name, `_free`, for two variables, `$_free` and `@free`. Although I frown on this idea in general, I have used it here for two reasons. First, both are required for the same task; second, one typeglob alias gives us access to both variables in one shot. This is important for performance, as we shall see soon.

ObjectTemplate implementation

ObjectTemplate uses objects, typeglob aliasing, symbolic references, and **eval** liberally, so if you understand the code below, you can consider yourself a Perl hacker! One way to pore through this code is to read the descriptions supplied in this section while using the debugger to step through a small example that uses this module. Of course, you don't *have* to understand the code to use it.

```
package ObjectTemplate;
require Exporter;
@ObjectTemplate::ISA = qw(Exporter);
@ObjectTemplate::EXPORT = qw(attributes);

my $debugging = 0; # assign 1 to it to see code generated on the fly

# Create accessor methods, and new()
sub attributes {
    my ($pkg) = caller;
    @{"${pkg}::_ATTRIBUTES_"} = @_;
    my $code = "";
    foreach my $attr (get_attribute_names($pkg)) {
        # If a field name is "color", create a global array in the
        # calling package called @color
        @{"${pkg}::_$attr"} = ();
```

```
        # Define accessor only if it is not already present
        unless ($pkg->can("$attr")) {
            $code .= _define_accessor ($pkg, $attr);
        }
    }
    $code .= _define_constructor($pkg);
    eval $code;
    if ($@) {
        die  "ERROR defining constructor and attributes for '$pkg':"
           . "\n\t$@\n"
           . "-------------------------------------------------"
           . $code;
    }
}
```

attributes uses symbolic references to create a global array called @_ ATTRIBUTES that remembers the attribute names. This array is then used by get_attribute_names to access all attributes defined in the current package and all its super classes. For each such attribute, **attributes** creates a global array in the current package, as we saw in Figure 8-1. If an accessor has not been defined for that attribute, it calls **_define_accessor** to generate the method dynamically. Finally, it calls **_define_constructor** to create the subroutine **new** directly into the calling package.

```
    sub _define_accessor {
        my ($pkg, $attr) = @_;

        # This code creates an accessor method for a given
        # attribute name. This method  returns the attribute value
        # if given no args, and modifies it if given one arg.
        # Either way, it returns the latest value of that attribute

        # qq makes this block behave like a double-quoted string
        my $code = qq{
            package $pkg;
            sub $attr {                                  # Accessor ...
                \@_ > 1 ? \$_${attr} \[\${\$_[0]}] = \$_[1]  # set
                        : \$_${attr} \[\${\$_[0]}];          # get
            }
            if (!defined \$_free) {
                # Alias the first attribute column to _free
                \*_free = \*_$attr;
                \$_free = 0;
            };
        };
        $code;
    }
```

_define_accessor is called for every field name given to **attributes** and for every attribute found in the module's superclasses. For an attribute called **age** in the Employee module, for example, it generates the following code:

```
    package Employee;
    sub age {                                      # Accessor
```

```
            @_ ? $_age[$$_[0]] = $_[1];                      # set
               : $_age[$$_[0]];                              # get
    }
    if (!defined $_free) {
        *_free = *_age; # Alias the first attribute column
                        #to _free
        $_free = 0;
    };
```

$_[0] contains the object, and $_[1] contains the attribute value. Therefore $$_
[0] contains the row index, and $_age[$$_[0]] contains the value of the age
attribute of that object. In addition, **_define_accessor** aliases **_free** to **_age**
if the aliases don't already exist.

```
    sub _define_constructor {
        my $pkg = shift;
        my $code = qq{
            package $pkg;
            sub new {
                my \$class = shift;
                my \$inst_id;
                if (defined(\$_free[\$_free])) {
                    \$inst_id = \$_free;
                    \$_free = \$_free[\$_free];
                    undef \$_free[\$inst_id];
                } else {
                    \$inst_id = \$_free++;
                }
                my \$obj = bless \\\$inst_id, \$class;
                \$obj->set_attributes(\@_) if \@_;
                \$obj->initialize;
                \$obj;
            }
        };
        $code;
    }
```

_define_constructor generates code for a constructor called **new** to be
installed in the calling package. **new** checks the free list, and if it contains rows to
spare, it uses the row number from the top of that list. It then **undef**'s the head
of the list, because the free list is aliased to the first attribute column, and we
don't want that attribute's assessor picking up garbage values. If the free list does
not contain any spare rows, the object is assigned the next logical index.

```
    sub get_attribute_names {
        my $pkg = shift;
        $pkg = ref($pkg) if ref($pkg);
        my @result = @{"${pkg}::_ATTRIBUTES_"};
        if (defined (@{"${pkg}::ISA"})) {
            foreach my $base_pkg (@{"${pkg}::ISA"}) {
                push (@result, get_attribute_names($base_pkg));
            }
        }
        @result;
    }
```

get_attribute_names recurses through the package's **@ISA** array to fetch all attribute names. This can be used by anyone requiring object meta-data (such as object persistence modules).

```
# $obj->set_attributes (name => 'John', age => 23);
# Or, $obj->set_attributes (['age'], [# sub set_attributes {
    my $obj = shift;
    my $attr_name;
    if (ref($_[0])) {
        my ($attr_name_list, $attr_value_list) = @_;
        my $i = 0;
        foreach $attr_name (@$attr_name_list) {
            $obj->$attr_name($attr_value_list->[$i++]);
        }
    } else {
        my ($attr_name, $attr_value);
        while (@_) {
            $attr_name = shift;
            $attr_value = shift;
            $obj->$attr_name($attr_value);
        }
    }
}
```

set_attributes is given a list of attribute name-value pairs and simply calls the accessor method for each attribute. It can also be called with two parameters; an array of names and an array of values.

```
# @attrs = $obj->get_attributes (qw(name age));
sub get_attributes {
    my $obj = shift;
    my (@retval);
    map $obj->${_}(), @_;
}
```

get_attributes uses **map** to iterate through all attribute names, setting **$_** to each name in every iteration. The first part of **map** simply calls the corresponding accessor method using a symbolic reference. Because of some weird precedence issues, you cannot omit the curly braces in **${_}**.

```
sub set_attribute {
    my ($obj, $attr_name, $attr_value) = @_;
    my ($pkg) = ref($obj);
    ${"${pkg}::_$attr_name"}[$$obj] = $attr_value;
}

sub get_attribute {
    my ($obj, $attr_name, $attr_value) = @_;
    my ($pkg) = ref($obj);
    return ${"${pkg}::_$attr_name"}[$$obj];
}
```

The `get`/`set_attribute` pair updates a single attribute. Unlike the earlier pair of methods, this pair does not call an accessor; it updates the attribute directly. We saw earlier that `attributes` does not attempt to create accessor methods for those that already exist. But if the custom accessors still want to use the storage scheme provided by ObjectTemplate, they can use the `get`/`set_attribute` pair. The expression `${pkg}::_$attr_name` represents the appropriate column attribute, and `$$obj` represents the logical row. (Recall that the object is simply a reference to an array index.) These methods are clearly not as fast as the generated accessor methods, because they use symbolic references (which involve variable interpolation in a string and an extra hash lookup).

```
sub DESTROY {
    # release id back to free list
    my $obj = $_[0];
    my $pkg = ref($obj);
    local *_free = *{"${pkg}::_free"};
    my $inst_id = $$obj;
    # Release all the attributes in that row
    local(*attributes) = *{"${pkg}::_ATTRIBUTES_"};
    foreach my $attr (@attributes) {
        undef ${"${pkg}::_$attr"}[$inst_id];
    }
    $_free[$inst_id] = $_free;
    $_free = $inst_id;
}
```

DESTROY releases all attribute values corresponding to that object. This is necessary because the object is merely a reference to an array index, which, when freed, won't touch the reference counts of any of the attributes. A module defining its own `DESTROY` method must make sure that it always calls `ObjectTemplate::DESTROY`.

```
sub initialize { }; # dummy method, if subclass doesn't define one.
```

Modules are expected to override this method if they want to do specific initialization, in addition to what the automatically generated `new()` does.

Suggested changes to ObjectTemplate

There are (at least) two areas that could use considerable improvement. One is that `get_attributes` and `set_attributes` are slow because they always call accessor methods, even if they know which accessors are artificially provided. Because `set_attributes` is called by the automatically generated `new`, it slows down object construction dramatically. (Using this `new` without arguments is twice as fast as allocating an anonymous hash, but after invoking `set_attributes`, it is around three times slower.)

Second, custom accessor methods suffer in speed because they are forced to invoke the other slow pair, `get_attribute` and `set_attribute`. Possibly a better alternative is to dynamically generate accessor methods prefixed with an

"_", so that the developer can write normal accessor methods (without the prefix), and also call these private methods.

You might also want to check out the MethodMaker module available on CPAN, and the Class::Template module that is bundled with the standard distribution. These modules also create accessor methods automatically but assume that the object representation is a hash table. If you like the interface these modules provide, you can attempt to merge their interface with the attribute storage scheme of ObjectTemplate.

Attribute Storage Using Typeglobs

This approach, as we mentioned earlier, is not exactly a paragon of readability and is presented here only because it is used in some freely available libraries on CPAN, like the IO and Net distributions. If you don't wish to understand how these modules work, you can easily skip this section without loss of continuity.

We learned from Chapter 3, *Typeglobs and Symbol Tables*, that a typeglob contains pointers to different types of values. If we somehow make a typeglob into an object reference, we can treat these value pointers as attributes and access them very quickly. Consider the following `foo` typeglob:

```
${*foo} = "Oh, my!!" ;   # Use the scalar part to store a string
@{*foo} = (10, 20);      # Use the array part to store an array
open (foo, "foo.txt");   # Use it as a filehandle
```

We are able to hang different types of values (at most one of each type) from just one identifier, `foo`. If we want many such objects, we can use the Symbol module in the Perl library to create references to dynamically created typeglobs:

```
use Symbol;
$obj = Symbol::gensym(); # ref to typeglob
```

`$obj` contains a reference to a typeglob. The different parts of a typeglob can be individually accessed (by replacing `foo` with `$obj`):

```
${*$obj} = "Oh, my!!" ;   # Use the scalar part to store a string
@{*$obj} = (10, 20);      # Use the array part to store an array
open ($obj, "foo");       # Use it as a filehandle
```

Clearly, this is a hideous approach for most general objects; if you need another scalar-valued attribute, for example, you have no option but to put it in the hash part of this typeglob. The reason why the IO group of modules uses this hack is that an instance of any of these modules can be treated as a filehandle and passed directly (without dereferencing) to the built-in I/O functions such as **read** and **write**. For example:

```
$sock = new IO::Socket( ... various parameters ...) ;
print $sock "Hello, are you there";
$message = <$sock>;
```

We'll use IO::Socket module extensively in the chapters on networking with sockets.*

Let us build a small module called File to examine this technique in greater detail. This module allows you to open a file and read the next line; in addition, it allows you to put back a line so that the next attempt to read the file returns that line:

```
package main;
$obj = File->open("File.pm");
print $obj->next_line();
$obj->put_back("----------------------\n");
print $obj->next_line(); # Should print the string put back above
print $obj->next_line();
```

Since this code opens the File module itself, it should print the following:

```
package File;
----------------------
use Symbol;
```

This module uses the scalar part of the typeglob object as a "putback" buffer, the array part of the typeglob to store all the lines read from the file, and the file-handle part of the typeglob to store the filehandle. The implementation of the File module is shown in Example 8-1.

Example 8-1. File Module, Built Using a Typeglob Representation

```
package File;
use Symbol;
sub open {
    my ($pkg, $filename) = @_;
    $obj = gensym();                       # Allocate a typeglob
    open ($obj, $filename) || return undef; # Use it as a filehandle
    bless $obj, $pkg;                      # Upgrade to a File "object"
}

sub put_back {
    my ($r_obj, $line) = @_;
    ${*$r_obj} = $line;                    # The scalar part holds the
}                                          # current line

sub next_line {
    my $r_obj = $_[0];
    my $retval;
    if (${*$r_obj}) {                      # Check putback buffer
        $retval = ${*$r_obj};              #   yep, it's got stuff
        ${*$r_obj} = "";                   #   empty it.
    } else {
        $retval = <$r_obj>;                #   no. read from file
```

---

* You don't have to know the following technique, or how the IO::Socket module is built, to use it.

Example 8-1. File Module, Built Using a Typeglob Representation (continued)

```
        push(@{*$r_obj}, $retval);               #    add to history list.
    }
    $retval;
}
1;
```

Delegation

Delegation is a technique whereby an object forwards method calls to an appointed *delegate* object. In the following example, an `Employee` class simply delegates all tax-related functionality to the `$acccounting_dept` object:

```
package Employee;
sub compute_after_tax_income {
    $me = $_[0];
    return $accounting_dept->compute_after_tax_income($me);
}
```

There are cases in which you want all method calls that are not handled by a class to be automatically forwarded to a delegate. This is a cinch in Perl, since the `AUTOLOAD` function is called when a procedure is not found within that package or its base classes:

```
package Employee;
sub AUTOLOAD {
    my $obj = $_[0];
    # $AUTOLOAD contains the name of the missing method

    # Never propagate DESTROY methods
    return if $AUTOLOAD =~ /::DESTROY$/;

    # Strip it off its leading package name (such as Employee::)
    $AUTOLOAD =~ s/^.*:://;
    $obj->{delegate}->$AUTOLOAD(@_);  # Note, $obj is still part of @_,
                                      # so the delegated function knows
                                      # the original target
}
```

Notice that `AUTOLOAD` is called if `DESTROY` is not defined, and it is important that you not forward that message, or the delegate will think Perl is about to destroy it and release its resources prematurely.

This technique is often employed in the guts of client/server libraries. In a typical client/server system, the server has the "real" objects. But the system is written in such a way that a client can remotely invoke a method of the object, with familiar OO syntax. For example, if a client program wants to invoke a method on a remote bank account, it should be able to say something like this:

```
$account->deposit(100); # Deposit 100 bucks.
```

On the surface, it seems like an ordinary method call. What the library hides from you is that the `deposit()` functionality is actually sitting on a different machine. How is this accomplished? Well, the `$account` object reference is actually a reference to a lightweight *proxy* object on the client side. Its sole purpose is to forward calls to the remote machine (by sending messages over a socket, for example) and to wait for the response to come back. In other words, the `account` object is not the real account. It is only a message forwarder. It delegates its functionality to the remote object with the help of the messaging system underneath.

On Inheritance

I have never been quite comfortable with using inheritance liberally, and I don't subscribe to the theory that this feature is essential for software reuse. There are three related but distinct flavors of inheritance, and in this section, I'll list what I like or dislike about these aspects. The three types of inheritance are as follows:

- Attribute inheritance

- Implementation inheritance

- Interface inheritance

Attribute Inheritance

The facility provided by a language for a subclass to inherit attributes from a base class or a structure is called attribute inheritance. While C++ and Java provide this facility, Perl doesn't. The onus is on the Perl programmer to figure out a way for a superclass and a subclass to agree on a common inheritable representation. For this reason, a hash table is a frequent choice, but not necessarily an economical one, as has been pointed out earlier.

My problem with attribute inheritance is that it introduces a tremendous amount of coupling between an inherited class and a derived class. A change in the way a base class is laid out has drastic consequences for the derived class. This is clearly a violation of encapsulation. C++ treats all attributes as private by default but then provides a keyword called "protected," whereby it makes them freely available to derived classes, while still hiding them from the general public. Bjarne Stroustrup, the creator of C++, regrets this in his excellent book *The Design and Evolution of C++* [2]:

> One of my concerns about `protected` is exactly that it makes it too easy to use a common base the way one might sloppily have used global data....In retrospect, I think that `protected` is a case where "good arguments" and fashion overcame my better judgement and my rules of thumb for accepting new features.

A better option is to provide accessor methods and rely on interface inheritance. More on this soon.

Implementation Inheritance

Perl supports only this flavor of inheritance. Implementation inheritance, like attribute inheritance, forces base and inherited classes to have a common understanding of the layout of the object's attributes; attribute inheritance is almost always required in using implementation inheritance.

Subclassing is not easy, as Erich Gamma et al. say in *Design Patterns* [1]:

> Designing a subclass also requires an in-depth understanding of the parent class. For example, overriding one operation might require overriding another. An overridden operation might be required to call an inherited operation. And subclassing can lead to an explosion of classes, because you might have to introduce many new subclasses for even a simple extension.

They suggest using composition instead, a topic we will touch on shortly.

Interface Inheritance

Attribute and implementation inheritance are for the convenience of the object implementor. Interface inheritance is for the user of a package. Perl supports only implementation inheritance.

The set of publicly available methods defines an object's interface. A derived class can add to this interface by adding new methods. But whether it actually overrides a base class implementation is strictly a matter of implementation detail; from the user's point of view, it still offers the same methods.

The important thing about an interface is that it represents the contract between the user and the object. If two objects have identical interfaces, they can be interchangeably used. This substitutability aspect represents the most important feature a language or a set of components can provide.

Using Composition Instead

I was once convinced about the need for implementation inheritance when I was writing some widgets for Xt/Motif (GUI frameworks for the X Windows platform). This framework goes to a great extent to provide single inheritance in C (both attribute and implementation), but the result isn't easy to work with. When C++ came along, I quickly became enthusiastic about a language that supported inheritance, and attempted to implement the widget set in C++. Then when John Ousterhout's Tk came along, I marveled at the ease of creating widgets, even though it was in C and provided all the features that Motif provides (and much more). The Tk architecture used composition, not inheritance. I have been suitably chastened.

The idea of composition is for an object to be composed out of other objects. That is, it forms a *has-a* or *uses-a* relationship with other classes, instead of an *is-a* relationship. Many examples in published literature glorify implementation inheritance, but these turn out to be far better (simpler and more readable) candidates for composition. Take this commonly illustrated example of a class called `Vice-President`, inheriting from a class called `Manager`, inheriting from a class called `Employee`. It is true that a V.P. *is-a* Manager, who in turn is an Employee, so the case is made for attribute and implementation inheritance. But what happens when an employee is promoted? The object is forced to change its class—clearly, a terrible design. The better way to approach this issue is to realize that an employee plays one or more roles in a company (that of a manager, vice-president, or lead technical engineer), and when the employee is promoted, this role is merely updated. In other words, the `Employee` object *uses* the `Role` class, which for its part, captures everything to be known about that role, such as the job description, salary range, and prerequisites.

Composition is also called component-driven programming. The key to developing reusable software is to develop completely encapsulated components with well-defined and documented interfaces. Designing for inheritance has, in my experience, rarely yielded the benefit that the hype would suggest.

Perl provides the most crucial features required to create plug and play components: polymorphism and run-time binding. You can say `$obj->draw()`, and Perl calls the appropriate `draw()` method, depending on `$obj`'s class. Since Perl is an untyped language, it makes this statement work for graphic shapes, guns, and lotteries. I value this feature much more than its support for implementation inheritance.

Resources

1. *Design Patterns: Elements of Reusable Object-Oriented Software.* Erich Gamma, Richard Helm, Ralph Johnson and John Vlissides. Addison-Wesley, 1994.

2. *The Design and Evolution of C++.* Bjarne Stroustrup. Addison-Wesley, 1994.

9

Tie

> *Give me a wild tie brother,*
> *One with a cosmic urge,*
> *A tie that will swear and rip and tear,*
> *When it sees my old blue serge.*
>
> —Stoddard King
> *The Ties That Bind*

Normally, when you read or update a scalar, array, hash, or filehandle, Perl performs the appropriate operation on the corresponding internal data structure. Alternatively, you can use the `tie` keyword to bind the value (or variable) to a user-defined object, so that when you read from or write to that variable, Perl simply calls a specific method of the object it is tied to. In other words, while it provides the implementation for a "normal" variable, Perl expects a user-defined module to do so for a tied variable. Once a variable is tied, even accesses from the C API of the Perl library are delegated to the corresponding tied object.

This approach may seem like syntactic sugar, but as you'll see from the examples in this chapter, it is the *syntax* that gives it its power: an ordinary variable can be made to invoke a user-defined function whenever a variable is manipulated, without the user's code changing or being necessarily aware of the subterfuge. The most common use of this technique is to tie a hash variable to a module that can manipulate DBM files, which are typically disk-based hash tables (they can also be BTrees). This technique allows you to make a hash value persistent and is capable of storing much more information than can fit into available memory, while giving the impression that you are manipulating an ordinary associative array.

In the following pages, we will study how `tie` works with the various data types, and look at a few useful examples of this feature.

Tying Scalars

At the most basic level, there are only four things you can do with a scalar. You can create it, get or set its value, and destroy it (by ending the scope or undef'ing it). tie allows you to supply a subroutine to be called back for each of these operations.

The syntax of tie is as follows:

```
tie variable, classname, list;
```

The first parameter should be one of the four supported types described above. The second parameter is the name of a user-defined class. You are expected to have invoked use *classname* or require *classname* before calling tie.

When this statement is executed, Perl checks the type of the variable (the first parameter). It then calls the method *classname*–>TIESCALAR(*list*), or TIEARRAY, TIEHASH, or TIEHANDLE, depending on whether the tied variable is a scalar, array, hash, or filehandle. It is a run-time error if this method is not present in the class. TIESCALAR() is expected to return an object, which is then internally associated with (or *tied* to) the given variable. Now, when you read and write to the variable, Perl internally calls *object*–>FETCH() and *object*–> STORE(*new value*), respectively. Finally, when the tied variable goes out of scope, Perl calls *object*–>DESTROY(). Simple, isn't it?

The names FETCH, STORE, and TIESCALAR are similar to AUTOLOAD and DESTROY in that they have a special significance for Perl only under appropriate circumstances. That is, a module can have a method called FETCH, which can be used normally like any other user-defined subroutine. But if you use tie, this method assumes a special meaning.

Perl does not care about the exact data structure used for the object (whether you used a hash or ObjectTemplate). Table 9-1 shows a variable "$temperature" tied to an automatic temperature control system, which is represented by a Perl module called *AC.pm*.* An attempt to read $temperature's value is translated to a call to the temperature sensor, and an attempt to set its value translates to a command to the heating system to do what is needed.

---

* Air conditioning, not alternating current!

Table 9-1. Flow of Control in a Tie Scalar Operation

When you say:	Perl translates it to the method call:	The method looks like this:
`tie $temperature, 'AC';`	`$obj = AC->TIESCALAR()` Perl now "ties" `$temperature` and `$obj`	```package AC; sub TIESCALAR { ... $ac = bless {...}, $pkg; return $ac; }```
`$x = $temperature;`	`$x = $obj->FETCH();`	```sub FETCH { $ac->get_temp(); }```
`$temperature = 20;`	`$obj->STORE(20);`	```sub STORE { ($obj, $t) = @_; $ac->set_temp($t); }```
`untie $temperature;` `#or` `undef $temperature;` or when `$temperature` goes out of scope	`$obj->DESTROY()`	```sub DESTROY { }```

As you can see, the AC module is an ordinary class with a constructor and three object methods (whose names happen to be special). Perl interacts with this module behind the scenes, providing the user with a much simpler interaction model. You can get the tied object as the return value of `tie` or invoke the `tied` function to get to it at any other time. Therefore the statement

```
$temperature = 20;
```

is identical to

```
(tied $temperature)->STORE(20);
```

The `untie` function restores the original value of the variable and also calls the object's `DESTROY` method.

Perl does not constrain the object's module in any way other than to expect it to provide the methods we saw earlier. It can store whatever data it wants, can have other methods, and is perfectly usable even in a non-tie context.

Example: Stopwatch

Let us look at a simple example of a stopwatch using a tied scalar. When you store any value into it, it notes the current time (that is, it ignores the value).

When you retrieve a value from it, it returns the amount of time elapsed since the last time a store was attempted on it. This is how it is used:

```
use Stopwatch;
tie $s, 'Stopwatch';

# $s is scalar transparently tied to a Stopwatch object.
$s = 0;                  # Writing to it forces a reset
sleep(10);               # Sleep 10 seconds
print "$s\n";            # Should print 10
```

The example might sometimes print 9 because of **sleep**'s resolution.

Example 9-1 shows how Stopwatch is implemented.

Example 9-1. Stopwatch Implemented Using tie

```
package Stopwatch;

sub TIESCALAR {
    my ($pkg) = @_;
    my $obj = time();  # $obj stores the time at last reset.
    return (bless \$obj, $pkg);
}

sub FETCH {
    my ($r_obj) = @_;
    # Return the time elapsed since it was last reset
    return (time() - $$r_obj);
}

sub STORE {
    my ($r_obj, $val) = @_;
    # Ignore the value. Any write to it is seen as a reset
    return ($$r_obj = time());
}

1;
```

TIESCALAR notes the current time and returns a reference to a blessed scalar (with the current time in it). As was mentioned earlier, you are under no obligation to provide a blessed *scalar* reference; Perl does not care whether the object is a scalar or an array or a complex data structure. The only requirement is that it be blessed into a module that supports the **FETCH** and **STORE** methods. In this case, **FETCH** computes the interval between the current time (as reported by time) and the last reset time.

Incidentally, the time calculations in this module work at the granularity of only a second. If you want a finer granularity, you can use the Time::HiRes module available from CPAN, which gives microsecond resolution on Unix systems (gives access to the usleep and ualarm system calls). On Microsoft Windows systems, you can use the **Win32::Timer** call for millisecond-level timing.

tie works with anonymous values

The first argument to `tie` must boil down to a scalar, array, hash, or filehandle *value*; it does not *have* to be a variable. The following code shows two valid examples of scalar ties:

```
$r = \$s;
tie $$r, 'Stopwatch';  # Indirect tie to $s

@foo = (1, 2);
tie $foo[1], 'Stopwatch';
```

As you can see, this facility works with the underlying values and is not associated with a variable name (unlike the *trace* facility in TCL).

Tying Arrays

Tying an array to a module runs along very similar lines, as shown in Table 9-2. There are two levels at which you can work with a normal array. At one level, you can get and set the value of the entire array and the last element's index (using `$#array`). At another level, you can get or set individual elements and create or destroy its elements using `splice`, `push`, `pop`, and so on. As this book goes to print, `tie` handles reads and writes only to array elements and does not allow the array itself to be modified in any way. This situation is expected to be remedied in the not-too-distant future.

Table 9-2. tie and Array Access

When you say:	Perl translates it to:
`tie @array, 'Foo',1,2`	`$obj = Foo->TIEARRAY (1,2);`
`$a = $array[5];`	`$obj->FETCH(5);`
`$array[5] = "aa"`	`$obj->STORE(5, "aa");`
`untie @array;`	`$obj->DESTROY();`

One useful example of tied arrays is to emulate a bitset. If you set the 200th element to 1, the module can set the 200th bit in a bit array, using `vec()`.

The next section shows an example of tied arrays to wrap a text file.

TIEARRAY Example: File as an Array

This example builds a facility called TieFile to make a text file appear as an array. If you want to examine the 20th line of *foo.txt*, for example, you write:

```
tie @lines, 'TieFile', 'foo.txt';
print $lines[20];
```

For simplicity, this module does not accept updates to any element.

When asked to fetch the *n*th line, the TieFile module shown in Example 9-2 reads the file until it reaches that line and returns it. Since it is wasteful to keep traversing the entire file every time a line is requested, TieFile keeps track of the file offsets of the beginning of each line so that when you ask it for a line that it has already visited, it knows the precise offset to **seek** to before reading. The object created by **TIEARRAY** has two fields: one to store this array of offsets and another to store the filehandle of the open file. These two fields are stored in an anonymous array. (Alternatively, you can use a hash or the ObjectTemplate module.)

Example 9-2. TieFile.pm: Mapping a File to an Array

```
package TieFile;
use Symbol;
use strict;
# The object constructed in TIEARRAY is an array, and these are the
# fields
my $F_OFFSETS    = 0;  # List of file seek offsets (for each line)
my $F_FILEHANDLE = 1;  # Open filehandle

sub TIEARRAY {
    my ($pkg, $filename) = @_;
    my $fh = gensym();
    open ($fh, $filename) || die "Could not open file: $!\n";
    bless [  [0],  # 0th line is at offset 0
             $fh
         ], $pkg;
}

sub FETCH {
    my ($obj, $index) = @_;
    # Have we already read this line?
    my $rl_offsets = $obj->[$F_OFFSETS];
    my $fh = $obj->[$F_FILEHANDLE];
    if ($index > @$rl_offsets) {
        $obj->read_until ($index);
    } else {
        # seek to the appropriate file offset
        seek ($fh, $rl_offsets->[$index], 0);
    }
    return (scalar <$fh>);  # Return a single line, by evaluating <$fh>
                            # in a scalar context
}

sub STORE {
    die "Sorry. Cannot update file using package TieFile\n";
}

sub DESTROY {
    my ($obj) = @_;
    # close the filehandle
    close($obj->[$F_FILEHANDLE]);
}
```

Example 9-2. TieFile.pm: Mapping a File to an Array (continued)

```perl
sub read_until {
    my ($obj, $index) = @_;
    my $rl_offsets = $obj->[$F_OFFSETS];
    my $last_index = @$rl_offsets - 1;
    my $last_offset = $rl_offsets->[$last_index];
    my $fh = $obj->[$F_FILEHANDLE];
    seek ($fh, $last_offset, 0);
    my $buf;
    while (defined($buf = <$fh>)) {
        $last_offset += length($buf);
        $last_index++;
        push (@$rl_offsets, $last_offset);
        last if $last_index > $index;
    }
}

1;
```

You may have noticed that this module works only if you assign strings or numbers to the tied array's elements. If you assign it a reference, it simply converts it into a string and stores it into the file, which is patently useless when the data is read back from the file. In other words, this module should ideally "serialize" the data structure pointed to by the reference before storing it into the file, and recreate it when requested. We'll have more to say on this subject in Chapter 10, *Persistence*.

Tying Hashes

Accesses to tied hash tables are fully supported, unlike arrays. The tie-hash facility allows you to trap operations on the entire hash table (%h = ()), accesses to individual elements, and queries (**exists**, **defined**, **each**, **keys**, and **values**). Table 9-3 shows how these actions are mapped to method invocations on the tied object.

Table 9-3. tie and Hash Access

When you say:	Perl translates it to:
`tie %h, 'Foo', 'a' => 1`	`$obj = Foo->TIEHASH('a',1);`
`$h{a}`	`$obj->FETCH ('a')`
`$h{a} = 1`	`$obj->STORE ('a', 1)`
`delete $h{a}`	`$obj->DELETE('a')`
`exists $h{a}`	`$obj->EXISTS('a')`

`keys (%h),values(%h)`
`each (%h)`
	`$lk = $obj->FIRSTKEY ();`
	`do {`
	`    $val = $obj->FETCH{$lk};`
	`} while ($lk = $obj->NEXTKEY($lk));`

Table 9-3. tie and Hash Access (continued)

When you say:	Perl translates it to:
%h = ()	$obj–>CLEAR()
%h = (a=> 1)	$obj–>CLEAR() $obj–>STORE('a',1)
untie %h	$obj–>DESTROY()

FIRSTKEY and NEXTKEY are expected to return the next key in the sequence. This suffices if keys is invoked by the calling code; but if values or each is called, it calls FETCH for each key.

The most common (and natural-looking) use of tie is as a frontend for DBM files, which, as we mentioned earlier, are disk-based hash tables. Perl comes enabled with various flavors of DBM support. The following example uses the SDBM module, which comes with the standard Perl distribution:

```
use Fcntl;
use SDBM_File;
tie (%h, 'SDBM_File', 'foo.dbm', O_RDWR|O_CREAT, 0640)
      || die $!;                     # Open dbm file
$h{a} = 10;                          # Write to file transparently
while (($k, $v) = each %h) {         # Iterate over all keys in file
    print "$k,$v\n"
}
untie %h;                            # Flush and close the dbm file
```

Perl old-timers may recognize the similarity to the **dbm_open** function. tie just happens to be a more general facility.

Tied hashes have the same problem outlined in the last section: You cannot store references unless you explicitly serialize the structures referred to into one stream (from which you can recreate the data structure later). The MLDBM module, which we will explore further in Chapter 10, attempts to tie multilevel hashes to a DBM file.

Two other modules in the standard Perl distribution use tie internally. Config makes all information known to the build environment (that is, to **configure**) as a hash (%Config) in the caller's namespace, like this:

```
use Config;
while (($k, $v) = each %Config) {
    print "$k => $v \n";
}
```

Env is another standard library that uses tie to make environment variables appear as ordinary variables. We saw a non-tie variant of Env in the section "Importing Symbols" in Chapter 6, *Modules*.

Tying Filehandles

Tied filehandles call a user-defined object whenever you read from or write to a filehandle, as shown in Table 9-4. Note that the `tie` statement takes a typeglob, not a bareword.

Table 9-4. tie and Filehandles

When you say:	Perl translates it to:
`tie *FH, 'Foo', 'a','b'`	`$obj = Foo->TIEHANDLE('a','b');`
`<FH>`	`$obj->READLINE();`
`read (FH, $buf, $len, $offset)` `sysread (FH, $buf, $len, $offset)`	`$obj->READ($buf, $len, $offset)`
`getc(FH)`	`$obj->GETC()`
`print FH "I do"; #No comma after FH`	`$obj->PRINT("I do");`
`untie *FH;`	`$obj->DESTROY();`

This method can be used to simulate a file or process with a test driver or to monitor access to a filehandle for silently logging a conversation (like the `tee(1)` command). Tk, which we will study in detail in Chapter 14, *User Interfaces with Tk*, supports ties to let you redirect I/O to its text widget. We will look at a small example of this feature when we study that widget.

Example: Monitoring Variables

`tie` makes it really convenient to monitor a variable. In this section, we will develop a module called *Monitor.pm* that prints out a message on STDERR whenever a variable of your choice is accessed. [*]

```
use Monitor;
monitor(\$x, 'x');
monitor(\%y, 'y');
```

Whenever `$x` or `%y` is changed, this module prints out something like this on STDERR:

```
Wrote   : $x ... 10
Read    : $x ... 10
Died    : $x
Wrote   : $y{a} ... 1
Cleared : %y
```

---

[*] This is a lightweight version of a CPAN module called Tie::Watch, written by Stephen Lidie. Tie::Watch is used to invoke user-defined callbacks when certain variables are accessed.

This module is useful while debugging, where it is not clear at what point a certain variable is changing, especially when it changes indirectly through a reference. This module can be enhanced to support watch expressions such as `print 'ahhh' when $array[5] > 10`. Given Perl's support for `eval`, this is a reasonably simple task.

`monitor` takes a variable by reference and a name to be used when it prints out its messages. The first parameter is used to do a `tie` on the variable. `tie` has the unfortunate property that it hides the original value held by the variable. (The value is restored upon `untie`.) Clearly, we don't want Heisenberg's Uncertainty Principle to creep in here—our act of monitoring should not affect the user's view of that variable. For this reason, we store away the original value as an attribute of the tied object and have `FETCH` and `STORE` use this copy. Finally, when we are not interested in the variable any more, we use `unmonitor`, which calls `untie` internally.

Monitor, shown in Example 9-3, delegates responsibility to a nested module dedicated to each type of value (scalar, array, hash). The `tie` constructors in these modules return a blessed anonymous array (the tied object), which stores the name supplied by the user (the second parameter of `monitor`) and the current value of the variable.

Example 9-3. Monitor.pm

```
#---------------------------------------------------------------------
package Monitor;
require Exporter;
@ISA = ("Exporter");
@EXPORT = qw(monitor unmonitor);
use strict;

sub monitor {
    my ($r_var, $name) = @_;
    my ($type) = ref($r_var);
    if ($type =~ /SCALAR/) {
        return tie $$r_var, 'Monitor::Scalar', $r_var, $name;
    } elsif ($type =~ /ARRAY/) {
        return tie @$r_var, 'Monitor::Array', $r_var, $name;
    } elsif ($type =~ /HASH/) {
        return tie %$r_var, 'Monitor::Hash', $r_var, $name;
    } else {
        print STDERR "require ref. to scalar, array or hash" unless $type;
    }
}
sub unmonitor {
    my ($r_var) = @_;
    my ($type) = ref($r_var);
    my $obj;
    if ($type =~ /SCALAR/) {
        Monitor::Scalar->unmonitor($r_var);
```

Example 9-3. Monitor.pm (continued)

```perl
    } elsif ($type =~ /ARRAY/) {
        Monitor::Array->unmonitor($r_var);
    } elsif ($type =~ /HASH/) {
        Monitor::Hash->unmonitor($r_var);
    } else {
        print STDERR "require ref. to scalar, array or hash" unless $type;
    }
}
#---------------------------------------------------------------------
package Monitor::Scalar;

sub TIESCALAR {
    my ($pkg, $rval, $name) = @_;
    my $obj = [$name, $$rval];
    bless $obj, $pkg;
    return $obj;
}

sub FETCH {
    my ($obj) = @_;
    my $val = $obj->[1];
    print STDERR 'Read    $', $obj->[0], " ... $val \n";
    return $val;
}
sub STORE {
    my ($obj, $val) = @_;
    print STDERR 'Wrote   $', $obj->[0], " ... $val \n";
    $obj->[1] = $val;
    return $val;
}

sub unmonitor {
    my ($pkg, $r_var) = @_;
    my $val;
    {
        my $obj = tied $$r_var;
        $val = $obj->[1];
        $obj->[0] = "_UNMONITORED_";
    }
    untie $$r_var;
    $$r_var = $val;
}

sub DESTROY {
    my ($obj) = @_;
    if ($obj->[0] ne '_UNMONITORED_') {
        print STDERR 'Died    $', $obj->[0];
    }
}
```

Example 9-3. Monitor.pm (continued)

```perl
#-------------------------------------------------------------------------
package Monitor::Array;

sub TIEARRAY {
    my ($pkg, $rarray, $name) = @_;
    my $obj = [$name, [@$rarray]];
    bless $obj, $pkg;
    return $obj;
}

sub FETCH {
    my ($obj, $index) = @_;
    my $val = $obj->[1]->[$index];
    print STDERR 'Read     $', $obj->[0], "[$index] ... $val\n";
    return $val;
}

sub STORE {
    my ($obj, $index, $val) = @_;
    print STDERR 'Wrote    $', $obj->[0], "[$index] ... $val\n";
    $obj->[1]->[$index] = $val;
    return $val;
}


sub DESTROY {
    my ($obj) = @_;
    if ($obj->[0] ne '_UNMONITORED_') {
        print STDERR 'Died     %', $obj->[0];
    }
}

sub unmonitor {
    my ($pkg, $r_var) = @_;
    my $r_array;
    {
        my $obj = tied @$r_var;
        $r_array = $obj->[1];
        $obj->[0] = "_UNMONITORED_";
    }
    untie @$r_var;
    @$r_var = @$r_array;
}
#-------------------------------------------------------------------------
package Monitor::Hash;
sub TIEHASH {
    my ($pkg, $rhash, $name) = @_;
    my $obj = [$name, {%$rhash}];
    return (bless $obj, $pkg);
}

sub CLEAR {
    my ($obj) = @_;
```

Example 9-3. Monitor.pm (continued)

```
      print STDERR 'Cleared %', $obj->[0], "\n";
}

sub FETCH {
    my ($obj, $index) = @_;
    my $val = $obj->[1]->{$index};
    print STDERR 'Read    $', $obj->[0], "{$index} ... $val\n";
    return $val;
}

sub STORE {
    my ($obj, $index, $val) = @_;
    print STDERR 'Wrote   $', $obj->[0], "{$index} ... $val\n";
    $obj->[1]->{$index} = $val;
    return $val;
}

sub DESTROY {
    my ($obj) = @_;
    if ($obj->[0] ne '_UNMONITORED_') {
        print STDERR 'Died    %', $obj->[0];
    }
}
sub unmonitor {
    my ($pkg, $r_var) = @_;
    my $r_hash;
    {
        my $obj = tied %$r_var;
        $r_hash = $obj->[1];
        $obj->[0] = "_UNMONITORED_";
    }
    untie %$r_var;
    %$r_var = %$r_hash;
}
1;
```

unmonitor is slightly tricky. We want to do an untie, but Perl restores the variable's value to that held by it just before tie was invoked. Clearly, this is undesirable. We want this operation to go on without the variable's user being affected in any way. Since we have the variable's current value as an attribute of the tied object, we can attempt to restore the value after the untie. Unfortunately, the following code doesn't quite work:

```
    # For a tied scalar
    my $obj = tied $$r_var;        # Get the object tied to the variable
    $latest_value = $obj->[1];     # Extract the latest value
    untie $$r_var;                 # untie
    $$r_var = $latest_value;       # Restore the variable to the latest
                                   # value
```

Perl complains, "Can't untie: 1 inner references still exist ..." if the *-w* flag is turned on. The problem is that the local variable $obj bumps up the reference count of the tied object, so an untie is not able to DESTROY the tied object. The solution is fairly straightforward: extract the value in an inner block and let $obj go out of scope, like this:

```
my $latest_value;
{
    my $obj = tied $$r_var;
    $latest_value = $obj->[1]; # Extract the latest value.
                               # Note that $latest_value is defined
                               # outside this inner block
}
# $obj is no longer in scope, so we can peacefully untie.
untie $$r_var;
$$r_var = $latest_value;
```

Comparisons with Other Languages

We have used the tie facility in two ways. One is to give an existing package an easy frontend (as Perl does for DBM files); another is to monitor an existing variable. Let us examine what the other languages have to offer in these contexts.

Tcl

Tcl provides a command called **trace** to trap read and write accesses to scalars and associative arrays. (Scalars and lists are interchangeable, so there's no separate facility for the latter.) The Tk toolkit puts tracing to good use, as we shall soon see in Chapter 14. **trace** doesn't occlude the previous value, so writing a monitoring package is simpler.

Tcl's C API allows you to create traces much more easily than is possible with Perl. (Actually, this ease of use factor is true of the rest of the Tcl API also, as we shall see in Chapter 20, *Perl Internals.*)

While an existing Tcl package can use this facility to provide an easy frontend for a package, I'm not aware of any that take advantage of it, as Perl does for DBM files.

Python

Python allows you to write special functions per class called __getattr__ and __setattr__ that allow you to trap accesses to member attributes (or simulate new attributes). Similarly, you can make a class simulate an array by providing special methods called __getitem__ and __setitem__. There are 40 such methods to overload all kinds of behavior.

C++

C++ does not allow dynamic traces to be put on a variable. On the other hand, it does provide an extensive set of operators and operator-overloading syntactic structures to allow you to substitute an object where fundamental data types or other objects are used.

Commercial tools and libraries such as Purify are capable of setting a dynamic trace on any region of memory. They also provide a C API to write your own callbacks on such an event.

Java

Java does not allow you to arbitrarily trap accesses. Some commercial transaction-processing systems go to the extent of looking at the byte-code to recognize accesses to member attributes and insert traces where necessary. This allows them to make any object transactional without the explicit cooperation of the object. This approach is clearly not for the faint of heart!

Java does not have any way to implement the other aspect either: making a class appear as an ordinary variable.

10

Persistence

There must be at least 500,000,000 rats in the United States. Of course, I'm speaking only from memory.

—Edgar Wilson Nye

It would be an ideal world indeed if we never had to worry about fatal bugs or power failures.[*] For now, we have to contend with the fact that the attention span of a computer is only as long as its cord and that our data is too precious to be left within the confines of electronic memory. The ability of a system or module to make an application's data live longer than its application is called *persistence.*[†]

Considering that databases amount to a multi-billion-dollar industry and that DBI (Database Interface) and associated Perl modules are next only to CGI in CPAN's download statistics, it would not be a stretch to say that persistence is the most important of all technologies. In this chapter, we first study the myriad factors to be considered in making our data persistent; we then play with most of the freely available Perl persistence modules and hold them up against the checklist of factors, to clearly understand their strengths and weaknesses and what they provide and where they expect the developer to step in. In the next chapter, we will use some of these modules to create an object persistence framework to store an object transparently in files and databases.

---

[*] Or end-users, as a letter to *Byte* magazine once complained!

[†] We'll use the term "system" to mean a C implementation, such as a DBM library or a database, and "module" to refer to a Perl module.

Persistence Issues

Data ranges from simple comma-delimited records to complex self-referential structures. Users vary in level of paranoia and their ability (and need) to share persistent data. Application programmers attempt to juggle between solutions that are varying combinations of simple, robust, and efficient. The following list examines these differences in a slightly greater detail:

Serialization

Ordinary arrays and hashes can be written to a file using tabs, commas, and so on. Nested structures such as arrays of hashes or arrays of arrays have to be flattened, or *serialized*, before they can be dumped into a file. If you have ever packed the wiring for your holiday lights, you know that not only do you have to strive for a tight packing, you have to do it in a way that it can be easily and efficiently unscrambled the next time you need to use it. Further, data items can be typeglobs, can contain pointers to native C data structures, or can be references to other data items (making the structures cyclic or self-referential). In this chapter, we will study three modules that serialize data: FreezeThaw, Data::Dumper, and Storable.

Boundaries

Ordinary files, being byte streams, neither offer nor impose any kind of boundaries; you have to decide how you keep each data item distinct and recognizable on disk. DBM and ISAM systems impose a record-oriented structure. Relational databases provide record and column boundaries; if your data can be slotted into such a grid structure, you are in luck; otherwise, you have what is commonly called an "impedance mismatch." Newer technologies, such as object-relational and object-oriented databases, attempt to make this "restriction" or "failure" a nonissue.*

Concurrency

Multiple applications or users may want concurrent access to persistent data stores. Some systems ignore this issue altogether; others offer different types of locking schemes.

Access privileges

Most persistence solutions leave it to the operating system to enforce file-level privileges (create, update, read, or delete). Databases offer a finer level of access restriction.

---

* E.F. Codd, considered the father of relational database theory, has constantly maintained that this mismatch is not an inherent part of the theory itself; it is an artifact of the RDBMS implementation technology.

Random access and insertion

Databases make it easy to insert a new record or update a single attribute. With streams, you have no option but to serialize and rewrite the entire data into the file.

Queries

DBM and ISAM files allow you to selectively fetch records on the basis of the primary key, and databases allow you to selectively fetch records on the basis of any field. The more data you have, the less you can afford the luxury of examining each record to see whether it matches your criteria.

Transactions

Important commercial applications require "ACID" properties from persistence solutions [1]:

Atomicity: A series of actions that happen as one unit or not at all.

Consistency: The transaction must leave the system in a consistent state. Consistency is the responsibility of the application; a transaction monitor or a database knows nothing about specific application domains to judge what is consistent and what is not.

Isolation: Reads and writes from independent transactions must be isolated from each other; the result should be identical to what would result if the applications were forced to operate on the data in serial order, one at a time.

Durability: Once a transaction finishes, its results must be firmly committed to disk.

Currently, only databases provide this facility, and there are very few transactional file systems going around. The 2.0 release of the Berkeley DB library provides concurrency, transactions, and recovery, but the Perl wrappers have not been updated to take advantage of it, as of this writing.

Meta-data

If you have access to information that describes your data—*meta-data*—you can afford to hardcode less. Databases make meta-data explicitly available, while the other solutions simply translate from disk to in-memory Perl structures and let Perl provide the meta-information.

Machine independence

You may want to retrieve data from a file that has been created on a different type of machine. You have to contend with differences in integer and floating-point representation: size as well as byte order.

Portability and transparency

Finally, requirements change, and an application that accounts for some of the factors listed above may have to account for more factors—or worse, a different set of factors. There have been several attempts to provide a layer of uniformity between different solutions; for example, DBI and ODBC are two efforts that specify a consistent API across competing relational database implementations. We will be more ambitious in the next chapter: we will build ourselves a set of modules that hide the API differences between file and database storage. It is a fact that the more transparency you look for, the more of an impact there is on performance.

In the following pages we examine a variety of Perl modules that enable us to persistently store our data. We classify them by the boundary constraints: streamed (no boundaries), record-oriented, and grid-oriented (relational databases).

Streamed Data

We look at three modules, FreezeThaw, Data::Dumper, and Storable, in this section. All of them serialize Perl data structures to ASCII or binary strings; only Storable actually writes them to disk. The other two modules are important because they can be used in conjunction with other persistence mechanisms such as databases and DBM files. All of them correctly account for blessed object references and self-referential data structures, but trip up when it comes to typeglobs, tied variables, or scalars containing pointers to C data types (justifiably so). It is also impossible for these (or any) modules to understand implicit relationships. For example, if you use the ObjectTemplate approach described in Chapter 8, *Object Orientation: The Next Few Steps*, the "object" is basically an array index, and so the disk will get to see only a bunch of meaningless array indices minus the data. Another subtle error occurs when you use references as hash indices and Perl converts them to strings (such as `SCALAR(0xe3f434)`). This is not a real reference, so if you store the hash table to a file and recreate it, the implicit reference to the original structure is not valid any more.

Moral of the story: simple nests of Perl structures are handled easily; in all other cases, it is your responsibility to translate your application data into a structure containing ordinary Perl elements before sending it to disk.

FreezeThaw

FreezeThaw, written by Ilya Zakharevich, is a pure Perl module (no C extensions) and encodes complex data structures into printable ASCII strings. It does not deal directly with files and leaves it to you to send the encoded string to a normal file, a DBM file, or a database. Here's an example of the module's use:

```
use FreezeThaw qw(freeze thaw); # Import freeze() and thaw()
# Create a complex data structure: a hash of arrays
```

```
$c = { 'even' => [2, 4, 6, 8],
       'odd'  => [1, 3, 5, 7]};
# Create sample object
$obj = bless {'foo' => 'bar'}, 'Example';
$msg = freeze($c, $obj);
open (F, "> test") || die;
syswrite (F, $msg, length($msg)); # can also use write() or print()
```

The `freeze()` function takes a list of scalars to be encoded and returns one string. Arrays and hashes must be passed by reference. The **thaw** method takes an encoded string and returns the same list of scalars:

```
($c, $obj) = thaw ($msg);
```

We will use FreezeThaw in Chapter 13, *Networking: Implementing RPC*, to send data structures across a socket connection. Because the encoding is ASCII, we don't need to worry about machine-specific details such as byte order, or the length of integers and floating point numbers.

Data::Dumper

Data::Dumper, written by Gurusamy Sarathy, is similar in spirit to FreezeThaw, but takes a very different approach. It converts the list of scalars passed to its **Dumper** function into pretty-printed Perl code, which can be stored into a file and subsequently **eval**ed. Consider

```
use Data::Dumper ;
# Create a complex data structure: a hash of arrays
$c = { 'even' => [2, 4,],
       'odd'  => [1, 3,]};
# Create sample object
$obj = bless {'foo' => 'bar'}, 'Example';
$msg = Dumper($c, $obj);
print $msg;
```

This prints

```
$VAR1 = {
          even => [
                    2,
                    4
                  ],
          odd => [
                   1,
                   3
                 ]
        };
$VAR2 = bless( {
                 foo => 'bar'
               }, 'Example' );
```

Data::Dumper assigns an arbitrary variable name to each scalar, which is not really useful if you want to **eval** it subsequently and recreate your original data. The module allows you to assign your own variable names by using the **Dump** method:

```
$a = 100;
@b = (2,3);
print Data::Dumper->Dump([$a, \@b], ["foo", "*bar"]);
```

This prints

```
$foo = 100;
@bar = (
        2,
        3
      );
```

Dump takes two parameters: a reference to a list of scalars to be dumped and a reference to a list of corresponding names. If a "*****" precedes a name, **Dump** outputs the appropriate type of the variable. That is, instead of assigning to $b a reference to an anonymous array, it assigns a real list to @b. You can substitute **Dumpx** for **Dump** and take advantage of a C extension that implements the same functionality and gives you a speed increase of four to five times.

Data::Dumper gives you an opportunity to specify custom subroutines to serialize and deserialize data, which allows you to smooth the troublesome spots mentioned earlier. Please refer to the documentation for details.

Storable

Storable is a C extension module for serializing data directly to files and is the fastest of the three approaches. The **store** function takes a reference to a data structure (the *root*) and the name of a file. The **retrieve** method does the converse: given a filename, it returns the root:

```
use Storable;
$a = [100, 200, {'foo' => 'bar'}];
eval {
    store($a, 'test.dat');
};
print "Error writing to file: $@" if $@;
$a = retrieve('test.dat');
```

If you have more than one structure to stuff into a file, simply put all of them in an anonymous array and pass this array's reference to **store**.

You can pass an open filehandle to **store_fd** instead of giving a filename to **store**. The functions **nstore** and **nstore_fd** can be used for storing the data in "network" order, making the data machine-independent. When you use **retrieve** or **retrieve_fd**, the data is automatically converted back to the native machine format (while storing, the module stores a flag indicating whether it has stored it in a machine-independent format or not).

Record-Oriented Approach

In this section, we will study three modules that essentially depend on the DBM library. DBM is a disk-based hash table, originally written by Ken Thompson for the Seventh Edition Unix system. This library has since spawned many variants: SDBM (Simple DBM, a public-domain module bundled with Perl), NDBM (New DBM, which is packaged with some operating systems), and GDBM (from the Free Software Foundation). All these libraries can be accessed from equivalent Perl modules, which use Perl's `tie` facility to provide transparent access to the disk-based table. Performance and portability are the only criteria for selecting one of these systems. Be warned that the files produced by these approaches are not interchangeable.

DBM

We use SDBM here, because it is bundled with Perl. The SDBM_File module provides a wrapper over this extension:

```
use Fcntl;
use SDBM_File;
tie (%capital, 'SDBM_File', 'capitals.dat', O_RDWR|O_CREAT, 0666)
    || die $!;
$capital{USA}      = "Washington D.C.";
$capital{Colombia} = "Bogota";
untie %capital;
```

The `tie` statement associates the in-memory hash variable, `%capital`, with the disk-based hash file, *capitals.dat*. Read and write accesses to `%capital` are automatically translated to corresponding accesses to the file. `untie` breaks this association and flushes any pending changes to the disk. `O_RDWR` and `O_CREAT`, "constants" imported from `Fcntl`, specify that *capitals.dat* is to be opened for reading and writing, and to create it if it doesn't exist. The file's mode (bitmask for access privileges) is set to the 0644 in this case—the result of 0666 & ~022, where 022 is the umask.

The biggest problem with the DBM approaches mentioned earlier is that the value in a tied key-value pair has to be a string or number; if it is a reference, these modules do not dereference it automatically. So to associate a key with a complex data structure, you must serialize the structure using Data::Dumper or Freeze-Thaw, which is exactly what is done by MLDBM, described next.

MLDBM

Gurusamy Sarathy's MLDBM (multilevel DBM) stores complex values in a DBM file. It uses Data::Dumper to serialize any data structures, and uses a DBM module of your choice (SDBM_File is used by default) to send it to disk. This is how it is used:

```
use SDBM_File;
use MLDBM qw (SDBM_File);
use Fcntl;
tie (%h, 'MLDBM', 'bar', O_CREAT|O_RDWR, 0666) || die $!;
$sample   = {'burnt' => 'umber', 'brownian' => 'motion'} ;
$h{pairs} = $sample;    # Creating a disk-based hash of hashes
untie %h;
```

All parameters to `tie` following the string "MLDBM" are simply passed to the module specified in the `use` statement.

Berkeley DB

DB [3]—also referred to as *Berkeley DB*—is a public-domain C library of database access methods, including B+Tree, Extended Linear Hashing, and fixed/variable length records. The latest release also supports concurrent updates, transactions, and recovery. The corresponding Perl module, DB_File, puts a DBM wrapper around the B-tree and hashing implementations, and a tied array wrapper over the fixed/variable length record (also known as the `recno` access method).

The DBM usage is identical to the ones shown in the preceding sections. The `tie` statement is as follows:

```
use DB_File;
use Fcntl;    # For the constants O_RDWR and O_CREAT
tie (%h, 'DB_File', $file, O_RDWR|O_CREAT, 0666, $DB_BTREE);
```

The `$DB_BTREE` constant tells the library to use the btree format, allowing the key-value pairs to be stored in a sorted, balanced multiway tree; that is, the keys are stored in lexical order. You can also specify your custom sorting subroutine like this:

```
$DB_BTREE->{'compare'} = \&sort_ignorecase;
sub sort_ignorecase {
    my ($key1, $key2) = @_;
    $key1 =~ s/\s*//g;          # Get rid of white space
    $key2 =~ s/\s*//g;
    lc($key1) cmp lc($key2);    # Ignore case when comparing
}
```

Now, when you use `keys`, `values`, or `each` to retrieve data from the tied hash, you get them in your custom sorted order. An ordinary hash and the other DBM modules do not give you this facility.

You can use $DB_RECNO instead of $DB_BTREE, which uses TIEARRAY to treat a file as a collection of variable-length records:

```
use Fcntl;
use DB_File;
tie (@l, 'DB_File', 'foo.txt', O_RDWR|O_CREAT,0666, $DB_RECNO);
print $l[1];                    # Retrieve second line
$l[3] = 'Three musketeers';     # Modify fourth line
untie @l;
```

As was mentioned in Chapter 9, *Tie*, the current TIEARRAY implementation allows only array indexing; operators like push and splice are not supported. The DB_File module provides extra methods called push, pop, shift, unshift, and length, which can be used like this:

```
$db = tied @l;
$db->push($x);
```

Relational Databases

Relational databases have been around for a while, and while most commercial implementations have standardized on SQL, they differ significantly in the native C API. There have been several solutions to this. Microsoft popularized the ODBC (Open DataBase Connectivity) initiative, which has become the de facto standard in the (Wintel) PC world and provides a standard frontend to a large number of relational databases. PC Perl users using the ActiveWare port can access the ODBC library using the Win32::ODBC module.

Meanwhile in the Perl/Unix world, Tim Bunce and other developers, who had been writing mutually incompatible wrapper modules for different databases, came up with the DBI (Database Interface) specification and implementation to merge their efforts. DBI is similar in spirit and interface to the ODBC specification.

The ODBC specification has recently been accepted as the basis for the SQL CLI (Call-Level Interface) ISO standard, and it is expected that all database vendors will eventually provide a compliant-client library. When that becomes common-place, you can expect the DBI implementation to be rewritten to take advantage of this interface or go away completely.

In this section, we will take a look at both DBI and Win32::ODBC.

DBI (Database Interface)

Back in the days when modules and dynamic loading were not built into Perl, the database wrappers had to be linked in to create custom Perl executables called sybperl (for Sybase), oraperl (for Oracle), and so on. These libraries have since been rewritten to take advantage of Perl Version 5's features but have preserved the old API, which means that your scripts written for one database won't work for another. If you want portability, the DBI module is the only option. DBI makes calls to modules called DBDs (database drivers), which are specific to a database vendor and drive the native vendor API. If you use Oracle, for example, you can use oraperl for marginally better performance, or you can use the DBI and DBD::Oracle combination for portability. Oraperl and DBD::Oracle are both based on the same underlying code. The following web site, maintained by Alligator Descartes, is a wonderful repository of things DBI: *http://www.hermetica.com/technologia/DBI/*.

Using DBI is a simple matter of connecting to the appropriate database and firing off SQL queries:[*]

```
use DBI;
$dbname = 'empdb'; $user = 'sriram';
$password = 'foobar'; $dbd = 'Oracle';
$dbh = DBI->connect ($dbname, $user, $password, $dbd);
if (!$dbh) {
        print "Error connecting to database; $DBI::errstr\n";
}
```

connect returns a *database handle*, which represents the connection to a specific database. The **$dbd** parameter in this example tells it to load the DBD::Oracle module. This parameter can be followed by a reference to a hash of driver or connection-specific attributes. Some database vendors allow multiple connections to be created.

All DBI statements return **undef** on failure. The error code and errors strings can be obtained from $DBI::err and $DBI::errstr; these reflect the errors in the last executed DBI statement.

Basic SQL accesses

SQL statements can be executed like this (the equivalent of *execute immediate* in embedded SQL):

```
$dbh->do("delete from emptable where status != 'active'");
print "Error: $DBI::err .... $DBI::errstr" if $DBI::err;
```

If you make the same query or a similar-looking query a number of times, you force the system to parse it over and over again. To avoid this overhead, you can compile a parameterized query using **prepare**, and **execute** it many times.

The **prepare** method is given a query with parameter placeholders indicated by "?":

```
$sth = $dbh->prepare ('insert into emptable (name, age)
                                     values (?,    ?)');
```

---

[*] I'll assume that you are comfortable with SQL.

You can **execute** this statement over and over again using the returned *statement handle*, each time supplying it an array of values corresponding to each placeholder. These values are sometimes referred to as *binding* parameters. In fact, **do** internally prepares and executes the query given to it.

The following piece of code reads employee names and ages from standard input and uses the statement handle created above to insert rows into the database:

```
while (defined($line = <>)) {
    chomp($line);

    # id, name, age separated by tab
    ($id, $name, $age) = split (/\t/, $line);
    $sth->execute($id, $name, $age);
    die "Error: $DBI::err .... $DBI::errstr" if $DBI::err;
}
```

If the field is nullable, you can indicate a null value by passing **undef** to **execute**.

Select

The following example shows how to retrieve information in bulk, using the SQL **select** statement:

```
$cur = $dbh->prepare('select name, age from emptable where age < 40');
$cur->execute();
die "Prepare error: $DBI::err .... $DBI::errstr" if $DBI::err;
while (($name, $age) = $cur->fetchrow) {
    print "Name:$name, Age: $age \n";
}
$cur->finish();
```

The **prepare** statement returns a statement handle as before. When executed, this handle is associated internally with an open database cursor and is used to fetch each row returned by the database. **fetchrow** returns the values corresponding to the fields specified in the **select** query. **finish** closes the cursor.

Query meta-data

Once a statement is prepared and executed, DBI stores the following pieces of information as attributes of the statement handle:

$DBI::rows
: The number of rows affected or returned

$sth->{NUM_FIELDS}
: The number of fields returned by a select

$sth->{NUM_PARAMS}
: The number of parameters returned by any query

After a `select` query, the following attributes contain references to arrays of field-specific information:

`$sth->{NAME}`
>   Column names returned by the query

`$sth->{NULLABLE}`
>   Booleans indicating whether fields are nullable or not

`$sth->{TYPE}`
>   Field types

`$sth->{PRECISION}`
>   Floating-point precision of field

`$sth->{SCALE}`
>   Field lengths

Let us use what we have learned this far and create a Perl replacement for the interactive SQL frontends shipped with most relational databases (programs such as `sqlplus` and `isql`). Example 10-1 does this.

Example 10-1. sql.pl: Interactive SQL Frontend

```perl
use DBI;
$dbname = 'DEMO732'; $user = 'scott';
$password = 'tiger'; $dbd = 'Oracle';

$dbh = DBI->connect($dbname,$user,$password,$dbd) ||
    die "Error connecting $DBI::errstr\n";;

while(1) {
    print "SQL> ";                     # Prompt
    $stmt = <STDIN>;
    last unless defined($stmt);
    last if ($stmt =~ /^\s*exit/);
    chomp ($stmt);
    $stmt =~ s/;\s*$//;

    $sth = $dbh->prepare($stmt);
    if ($DBI::err) {
        print STDERR "$DBI::errstr\n";
        next;
    }
    $sth->execute() ;
    if ($DBI::err) {
        print STDERR "$DBI::errstr\n";
        next;
    }
    if ($stmt =~ /^\s*select/i) {
        my $rl_names = $sth->{NAME};        # ref. to array of col. names
        while (@results = $sth->fetchrow) { # retrieve results
            if ($DBI::err) {
```

Example 10-1. sql.pl: Interactive SQL Frontend (continued)

```
                print STDERR $DBI::errstr,"\n";
                last;
            }
            foreach $field_name (@$rl_names) {
                printf "%10s: %s\n", $field_name, shift @results;
            }
            print "\n";
        }
        $sth->finish;
    }
}
$dbh->commit;
```

The script prepares and executes all statements. If the statement is a **select** query, it fetches each row and prints out each value annotated by the corresponding column name. Note that **fetchrow** returns a reference to an array of values in a scalar context.

Transactions

When a database connection is created by using **connect**, DBI (or the database) automatically starts a transaction. To end a transaction, you can use the **commit** or **rollback** methods on the database handle; a new transaction is immediately started implicitly. Distributed transactions, as defined by the XA standard, are not supported.

Special functions

Driver-specific functions can be called by using the **func** method of the database handle. For example, the mSQL database driver provides an internal function called **_ListFields**, which returns information about columns in a table. It is invoked as follows:

```
    $ref = $dbh->func($table, '_ListFields');
```

Clearly, using **func** is a nonportable solution.

What DBI does not provide

It is instructive to list common database tasks for which DBI does not currently provide an interface. This is not meant as a slight on the DBI/DBD implementors; it is just an indicator of the fact that databases vary enormously in every aspect not touched by the standards committees.

Meta-data

DBI provides a **$dbh->tables()** method to fetch a list of all accessible table names. However, there is no function to return the names of columns in a given table. Fortunately, there is a simple, portable solution. Because a *select* query returns meta-information, we can use a dummy query that we know will definitely *not* fetch any rows but will execute successfully:

```
select * from $table where 1 = 0;
```

The **where** clause is perfectly valid, but the condition will never succeed. The "*" makes it return all the columns, which we can study using **$sth**'s attributes, as explained earlier in the section "Query meta-data."

Creating databases

Database APIs differ widely in how databases (not tables) are created; you have to use vendor-specific APIs or tools for this. Once a database is set up, however, DBI can be used to create or drop tables in that database.

Inserts/creates from arrays

Bulk insertion or updates of data from arrays is not a standard SQL CLI* feature. If there is truly a large amount of data to be inserted, you are likely better off dumping the data into a file and using the appropriate bulk copy utility (such as Sybase's **bcp**) to transfer it to the database at high speeds. (For even better performance, drop the indexes before loading the data and recreate them later.)

Stored procedures and triggers

Stored procedures and triggers are very different from vendor to vendor. All Perl database modules such as oraperl and sybperl provide such access to their native database facilities, but DBI does not attempt to generalize any of them. Please refer to the module documentation for details or to the DBI web site [4] for suggested approaches.

Uniform error numbers

DBI may be portable, but it doesn't provide a portable set of common error codes. For example, assume that you want to create a table if it is not already present. You might try something like this:

```
$dbh->do("create table emptable (id    char(15), name char(40),
                        age   integer)");
```

If **$DBI::err** contains an error code, you don't want to take it seriously if it says something like "table/view already present." Unfortunately, if you are using Oracle, this error code is 955, and for Sybase it is something entirely different. There goes portability out of the window!

---

* Call Level Interface—another name for the standardized C API that all RDBMS vendors are expected to support.

Win32::ODBC

The Win32::ODBC module is available on the ActiveWare port of Microsoft Windows systems and resembles the DBI approach. Consider the following script, which retrieves all records from an employee table:

```
use Win32::ODBC;
$dbh = new Win32::ODBC ($dbname);
if $dbh->Sql("select * from emptable") {
    print 'Error: ', $db->Error(), "\n";
    $dbh->Close();
    exit(1);
}
@names = $dbh->FieldNames();
while ($dbh->FetchFrow()) {
    # Data returns the values
    @values = $dbh->Data();
    ... do something with @names and @values.
}
```

The **Sql** statement is equivalent to DBI's **do**. ODBC does not have the concept of statement handles; instead, the database handle is used to fetch the results of the last query.

Meta-data is available in the form of two methods: **TableList**, which returns a list of table names, and **ColAttributes**, which returns the specified attribute of each of the supplied field names in the current record.

Resources

1. *Transaction Processing: Concepts and Techniques.* Jim Gray and Andreas Reuter. Morgan Kaufman, 1992.

   One of the most informative and readable computer texts around. If something about transactions is not covered here, maybe it doesn't exist!

2. *An Introduction to Database Systems, Volumes I and II.* C.J. Date. Addison-Wesley, 1994.

   A thorough treatment of persistence issues and database technology.

3. Berkeley DB library, at *http://mongoose.bostic.com/db/*.

4. DBI web site by Alligator Descartes: *http://www.hermetica.com/technologia/DBI/*.

11

Implementing Object Persistence

> *God gave us our memories so that we might have roses in December.*
>
> —James Matthew Barrie

The Amazon is formed by the confluence of two rivers: the Solimões, a yellowish, silt-laden river, and the dramatic Rio Negro, a river with jet-black water.* Twelve miles downstream of their meeting, the two rivers defiantly retain their separate identities while sharing the same bed. Somehow, this seems to bear a strange resemblance to the subject at hand: object persistence.

There are two important camps in the commercial computing world: purveyors of OO (language designers, object evangelists) and persistence vendors (database and TP† monitor implementors). Like the Solimões and the Rio Negro, the two camps (and multiple camps within their ranks) have their own agendas, even as they strive to merge at some point in the future.

The OO folks would like nothing more than commercial-grade persistence (in terms of performance, stability, and scalability) and propose methods to retrofit various persistence stores onto an object model. Some of their prominent efforts include the CORBA Persistence Services specification from the Object Management Group, Sun's PJava (Persistent Java), and the OLE Persistence framework from Microsoft. Meanwhile, the database folks are grafting OO features onto their offerings: RDBMS vendors such as Informix and Oracle have announced object-relational databases (supporting abstract data types, not just plain scalar data), and the various TP monitor products from Tandem, IBM, Tuxedo, and Encina are sporting object-oriented interfaces. There is a tiny object persistence camp, the

---

* The color comes from suspended minerals and decomposed organic matter from marginal swamps.

† Transaction-processing.

Object Database Management Group, comprising the OODB vendors, but their presence is quite negligible (commercially).

One of the hot topics in all these groups is the subject of "orthogonal" persistence—the ability to make an application or object persistent without embedding any, or much, persistence-specific code in the object. The idea is very seductive: Design your object model, implement it in memory, and then add persistence on the "side." This way, the objects don't have to be cluttered with the myriad details (and differences) of databases, nor do they have to deal with file-system errors, data formatting, and other problems.* You can think of it this way: if you never embed user-interface-specific code inside an object, why would you do so for persistence?

There have traditionally been two approaches to achieving the transparency mentioned above.

The first is to take advantage of the systems side of things, such as the hardware, operating system, and compiler. For example, object-oriented databases such as Object Store and the Texas Persistent Store (a public-domain library) use the Unix system's `mmap` and `mprotect` calls to transparently move data from memory to disk and back. Another interesting systems-oriented approach comes from a group at Bell Labs, which has built a library that stores the state of an application by having it simply dump core in a controlled fashion, thus faithfully rendering all memory-based data structures onto disk.† They have augmented this facility with recovery and transactions and made this approach almost completely transparent to the application.

The second approach for achieving transparent or orthogonal persistence is to supply application-level tools and libraries, an approach that is considerably more portable than the systems approach. CASE tools, for example, generate code to automate the task of sending objects to a persistent store (typically a relational database), while libraries such as Microsoft Foundation Classes ask the objects to stream themselves out to a file. In the latter case, the objects have to implement streaming methods. In either case, the code to be written by *hand* is fairly minimal, so it is still a reasonably transparent approach.

In this chapter, we will discuss a pilot project called Adaptor, a persistence frame-work for Perl objects (and written in Perl, of course). This is an application-level approach and doesn't expect the objects to implement persistence-specific methods. Unlike typical CASE tools, it does not generate any code files, because Perl is a dynamic language.

---

* For an excellent bibliography on the topic, please refer to the PJava design paper [4].

† Note that Perl's `dump` operator does produce a core file, but it also aborts the application, a somewhat unpleasant feature.

The primary objective of the Adaptor project was to study orthogonal persistence; this, I thought, could be done by "adapting" objects to specific types of persistent stores, using information completely outside the objects; the implementation described in this chapter depends on configuration files to describe which attributes map to which database columns, and how.

A secondary objective of this project was to study how you might code an application differently if you could *always* take queries and transaction atomicity for granted; that is, even if you didn't have a database at all, suppose you could ask some entity, "Give me all employees whose salary exceeds $100,000," and the application would be persistence-ready from the very beginning. I'm of the firm belief that you cannot simply *drop* persistence into an application; the object implementations look very different if they *know* that there is some kind of persistence up ahead (even if they don't quite have any specifics about the type of persistence). This is similar to the case of applications knowing that there may be a graphical user interface in the future and that it may be event-driven; for example, you may not write errors out to STDERR, and might make sure that no code gets indefinitely blocked on I/O. (We'll actually discuss these issues in Chapter 14, *User Interfaces with Tk.*)

This chapter is probably more important for the issues it brings up than the specifics of the implementation; however, an implementation is necessary to clearly understand the problem.

Adaptor: An Introduction

Adaptor is intended to be a group of modules that translate a uniform persistence interface to specific types of persistent stores, as shown in Figure 11-1. This chapter describes the two that have been implemented: Adaptor::File, capable of storing objects in plain files, and Adaptor::DBI, which can store them in relational databases. From here on, we will use the term "adaptor" to mean an object of any of these modules.

An adaptor represents a typical persistent store capable of accommodating a heterogeneous collection of objects; an Adaptor::File object is a wrapper over a file, and an Adaptor::DBI object is a wrapper over a database connection. All adaptors provide basic SQL queries* and transactions.†

---

* Only SQL where clauses, not the entire select clause; joins are not supported either.

† Adaptor::File implements a fairly limited model, but it does support the interface.

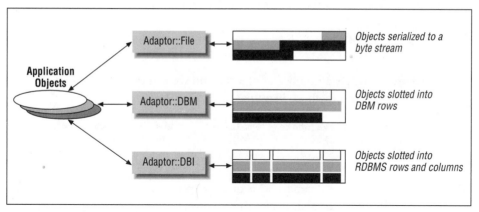

Figure 11-1. Adaptor modules

Before we use these modules, let us create a few test application objects. We use the ObjectTemplate library discussed in Chapter 8, *Object Orientation: The Next Few Steps*, for this task:

```
use ObjectTemplate;
#----------------------------------------
package Employee;
@ISA = ('ObjectTemplate');
@ATTRIBUTES = qw(_id name age dept);
#----------------------------------------
package Department;
@ISA = ('ObjectTemplate');
@ATTRIBUTES = qw(_id name address);
#----------------------------------------
$dept = new Department (name => 'Materials Handling');
$emp1 = new Employee   (name => 'John',  age => 23, dept => $dept);
$emp2 = new Employee   (name => 'Larry', age => 45, dept => $dept);
```

We now have three objects, free of database-specific code. To stow these objects into a persistent store, we start by creating an instance of a file or database adaptor as follows:

```
$db = Adaptor::File->new('test.dat', 'empfile.cfg');
```

The adaptor object, $db, is now associated with file *test.dat* and stores all objects given to it in this file. An object may have attributes that it doesn't wish to be made persistent: some attributes may be computed (`after_tax_salary`), while others may refer to filehandles, sockets, or GUI widgets. For this reason, the adaptor expects the developer to state, in a configuration file (*empfile.cfg*, in this example), which attributes must be made persistent. *empfile.cfg* looks like this:

```
[Employee]
attributes = _id, name, age
[Department]
attributes = _id, name, address
```

The adaptor can now be asked to store objects in its file, *test.dat*, as follows:

```
$db->store($dept);
$db->store($emp1);
$db->store($emp2);
```

Our "database" now has a number of objects, and we can query this database using the `retrieve_where` method, like this:

```
@emps = $db->retrieve_where ('Employee', "age < 40 && name != 'John'");
foreach $emp (@emps) {
    $emp->print();
}
```

This method takes a class name and a query expression and returns object references of the specified class that match this criteria.

The `flush` method is used to ensure that the data in memory is flushed out to disk:

```
$db->flush();
```

You can store objects under the purview of transactions:

```
$db->begin_transaction();
$db->store($emp1);
$db->store($emp2);
$db->commit_transaction(); # or rollback_transaction
```

The file adaptor keeps track of all objects given to its store method, and it flushes them to disk on `commit_transaction`. If, instead, you call `rollback_transaction`, it simply discards its internal structures and reloads the file, thus getting rid of all changes you may have made to the objects. This is by no means a real transaction (it doesn't protect the data from system failures), but it does support atomic updates, which can be used as an automatic undo facility.

To store these objects in a database instead of a file, all we need to do is make `$db` an instance of the Adaptor::DBI class. Everything else remains unchanged, except that you can feel a lot safer about your data because you get real transactions.

The Adaptor::DBI constructor's arguments are database-specific:

```
$db = Adaptor::DBI->new($user, $password, 'Sybase', 'empdb.cfg');
```

This method calls DBI::new with the first three parameters. The last parameter is, as before, a configuration file, with some extra database-specific *mapping* information:

```
[Employee]
table      = emp
attributes = _id, name, age
columns    = _id, name, age
```

```
[Department]
table       = dept
attributes = _id, name, address
columns    = _id, name, address
```

The *attributes* parameter specifies the list of attributes to be extracted out of an instance of a given module, and *columns* lists the corresponding column names in the database. Many adaptors can use the same configuration file.

Design Notes

The adaptor interface is undoubtedly simple; in this section, we will ask ourselves whether it is too simplistic. The Adaptor implementation is still at the level of a prototype but, as we shall see in the next few pages, is significant enough to challenge us on all the issues that the people working with object persistence are trying to grapple with.

Design Goals

I wanted the Adaptor API to be *transparent*; that is, to be able to change the type of persistent store at will. The idea was to write small prototypes without messing around with databases and then migrate to a database for the real thing by simply changing the adaptor. Further, I wanted to retain the flexibility of an object living in multiple persistent stores concurrently, because that is the only way to copy objects from one store to another.

I wanted to retain the best features of memory-based data structures (navigability, speed, ease of use) and those of databases (transactions, concurrency, queries), where available. Finally, I did not want the adaptor to break object encapsulation, which means that the implementation could not assume anything about how a module stores instance-specific information and, more subtly, how it constructs its objects.

Object Encapsulation

One important stricture that we easily forget is that an object is not just data. The three serialization modules we saw in the last chapter—FreezeThaw, Data::Dumper, and Storable—all make this assumption. They look past an object reference at the underlying structure and serialize whatever is reachable from there. This assumes that all instance-specific data is reachable from the reference: a false assumption. For example, an object reference of type ObjectTemplate is merely a reference to a scalar. By studying that reference, you have no idea of the object's attributes.

There is a worse problem with the above modules: when restoring objects from a byte stream, they simply recreate the original data structure in memory and bless it under the target module, without the module's involvement. This has the possibility of missing a few key initializations.

To avoid these problems, Adaptor requires each class that wants persistence to support three methods: a constructor, `new()`, and two attribute accessor methods, `get_attributes()` and `set_attributes()`, as follows:

1. `new()`: The module must provide this constructor (a "default constructor," in C++ parlance), capable of creating an object without any input parameters. The simplest default constructor for creating hash-table-based objects looks like this:

   ```
   sub new {
       bless {}; # bless a hash-table reference and return it.
   }
   ```

   Of course, an even simpler alternative is to use ObjectTemplate, which provides an inheritable default constructor. As it happens, it also provides the other two methods listed next.

2. `get_attributes(LIST)`: Given a list of attribute names, this method should return a list of corresponding values. For now, the restriction is that these values must be scalars (a big limitation; we will have more to say about this shortly). Because this method can be coded efficiently, it is preferable to Adaptor calling individual accessor functions. For example, if you use a hash table for your objects, you can implement this method as a hash slice:

   ```
   sub get_attributes {
       my $obj = shift; # @_ now contains names of attributes
       @{$obj}{@_};     # hash slice returns corresponding values
   }
   ```

   Adaptor uses the configuration file to specify the list of persistent attributes.

3. `set_attributes(LIST)`: Given a list of attribute name and value pairs, this method updates the appropriate attributes. Both this function and `get_attributes` above must allow an attribute called `_id`, for reasons to be outlined shortly.

These methods are perfectly general functions; they are not tied to persistence in any way. In contrast, some libraries, especially in the C++ world (Microsoft Foundation Classes and the NIH library), require the object to support a streaming interface. Since a streamed object is of no use to a database, I chose to keep the attributes distinct. Besides, if we wanted to send these attributes to a file, we know we can always rely on other modules to stream them, without having to ask the object to do it for us.

Object-Adaptor Protocol

When storing the object, the adaptor consults the configuration information for the list of persistent attributes for that class. It gives this list to `get_attributes` to retrieve the corresponding values and, depending on the type of the adaptor, either serializes it to a file or updates the database with an SQL query.

When retrieving an object from the database, the adaptor calls `new()` on the appropriate class and calls `set_attributes` to prime the newly constructed object with data from the persistent store.

Multivalued Attributes and Database Mapping

Adaptor::DBI simply translates an object to a single row in an RDBMS table. For this reason, it requires each value returned by `get_attributes` to be a simple scalar (number or string, not a reference). My hope is to eventually ease this restriction with the help of *typemaps*—pieces of code that can perform customized translations of data types.[*]

Here are the currently available choices for how to handle an object with one or more non-simple-scalar attributes:

1. *Customized* `{get,set}_attributes`: Adaptor::DBI allows multivalued attributes in memory. All it requires is that `get_attributes` translate such attributes to a simple scalar in a way that `set_attributes` will be able to convert back to the original structure, when the data is read back from disk. It can do this translation using FreezeThaw, Data::Dumper, `sprintf`, or `pack`; the last two are probably the best, because you can control the length of the resulting scalar (it matters because database columns have predeclared maximum sizes). The scalar can then be mapped to a database column capable of accommodating a variable number of characters (such as *VARCHAR*) or a binary string (such as Oracle's *RAW* or *LONG RAW*). Incidentally, there are still a lot of problems associated with BLOB (Binary Large OBjects) columns: some databases only allow one BLOB column, and others sport an API that is completely different from that of the conventional data types.

2. *Use file storage*: Adaptor::File doesn't care whether the attributes are references or ordinary scalars, because it simply hands over the attributes to Storable. In other words, `get/set_attributes` doesn't have to worry about multivalued attributes if you use Adaptor::File. Of course, the solution won't work if you decide to use a database adaptor tomorrow. There is also

---

[*] In Chapter 18, *Extending Perl: A First Course*, we will see how the concept of typemaps is used in creating extensions.

the danger that you might inadvertently store unrelated objects this way, just because they happen to be reachable from some attribute.

3. *Separate object class*: If an attribute is a reference to a sequence of homogenous records (an employee has multiple records of educational qualifications, for example), that attribute can be modeled as a separate class that gets its own table. More on this when we study object associations later in this section.

Since `{get,set}_attributes` are general methods, how do they know whether or not to serialize complex attributes? Well, they don't. If you want to make this distinction, you could have a different set of attribute *names* for persistence purposes (`db_address`, for example) and have these methods recognize these special cases. This strategy conflicts with our original intention of not embedding db-specific code within an object. Oh, well. As Jiri Soukup notes in his book *Taming C++: Pattern Classes and Persistence for Large Projects* [6], "It is popular to show elegant C++ programs, and elegance is not a feature of programs providing persistent data."

Inheritance and Database Mapping

The common strategy for mapping an inheritance relationship to a database is to have the superclass and derived class each map to its own table. The table representing the derived class contains all the attributes of all its superclasses; in other words, the inheritance hierarchy is flattened. Another strategy—less commonly used—is to create one table with the *union* of all attributes of an inheritance hierarchy and have all objects of all classes in that hierarchy use that one table. You can have an extra column identify the specific class of object. Adaptor does not have a problem with either strategy, because it puts the burden of interpreting the attribute names and values on the `get`/`set` methods.

Object Identity

One key notion in OO circles is that an object has properties separate from its identity. Two objects may have identical properties but still occupy different address spaces; they will be considered *equivalent*, not *identical*.

In memory, an object's address provides its identity, and in a database, the primary key does the same. Adaptor requires each object to support an attribute called `_id`, so a future implementation can automatically convert relationship attributes (those that point to other objects) to the `_ids` of the objects on the other end. For example, if you ask an Employee object for its `dept` attribute, it will ask the department object it is pointing to for its `_id` and return that. Note that the object doesn't necessarily have to allocate memory for its `_id`; the `get`/

`set_attributes` methods can compute it on the fly based on some other attribute. For example, an employee object can return the Social Security number or employee number when asked for its `_id.`

When `store()` is called, Adaptor supplies the object with a unique identity, if it doesn't already have one. The identity cannot be a simple global counter, because when the program restarts, it will get reset to 0, and the adaptor will start handing out numbers that might have been given to persistent objects in an earlier incarnation. Storing the counter's last value in a file is slow because you have to make sure you flush this value to the file every single time you store an object. (You never know when the program might crash.) The current implementation experiments with an alternate approach. When the program starts, it notes down the time (using `time`, which returns the seconds elapsed since January 1, 1970), and appends to it a five-digit counter; the combined number can be used as an object identifier. When the counter overflows, the time is again noted. If the program crashes and comes back again, the identifier is unique, unless it crashes and comes back up within one second. The trouble with this scheme is that it generates long identifiers (eight bytes, using `pack()`). It also does not work in a distributed setup, because there is the real possibility that two programs call `time()` within the same second, thus generating the same identifier. To avoid this, you have to create an even bigger identifier that incorporates the IP address of the machine.

Object Associations

An attribute that is a reference to some other object can be translated to the other object's `_id` value (a *foreign key*, in database-speak) when storing it in a database or file. As currently implemented, Adaptor does not automatically do this translation, because I don't have a good solution to handle the following problem.

Assume that an employee object's `dept` attribute points to a department object. When storing `dept`, we can simply store the department object's `_id`. No problems so far. Now, when we retrieve the employee record back from disk, what do we do with the encoded `dept` attribute? Do we immediately create a department object so that the in-memory `dept` attribute can refer to it? If so, what data should it contain? Should we read the database to correctly populate the department object? That has the problem that an innocuous query on an employee ends up loading all kinds of objects from the database. Alternatively, should we keep the department in an uninitialized state, and only populate it the first time it is used? Further, we must ensure that when the department data is read from disk, it doesn't create a fresh new object, because one with the same identity already exists in memory. We will have more to say on this subject in the following section. For now, it eases my life a little to leave it to the objects to implement foreign key attributes.

Now let us look at how associations of varying cardinalities can be implemented in a database regardless of how they appear in memory.

One-to-many associations such as a department containing a list of employees can be implemented as a foreign-key attribute on the *many* side. That is, in the database, the employee object points *back* to its containing department object, instead of the department maintaining a multivalued attribute.

Many-to-many associations can be modeled as a separate class; this way, each association becomes a single record in the database. For example, an employee can work on many projects; a project has many employees working on it; we can model this relationship in a separate class called `ProjectEmployee`. This scheme has the additional advantage that the relationships can be queried and updated, independent of the objects they are supposed to connect. Associations with cardinalities higher than two (ternary associations, for example) map to distinct tables. Rumbaugh et al. [1] give an excellent treatment of database-mapping approaches.

All these strategies (or limitations) will change dramatically once object-relational extensions become widely available.

Uniqueness of Objects in Memory

Close on the heels of object identity issues comes a very thorny problem. Consider the following query:

```
@emps = $db->retrieve_where ('Employee', 'age < 40');
```

This returns a list of object references that match the query criteria. Now if you re-issue this query, it is not too much to expect it to return an identical list of objects (the same object references, that is). This means that Adaptor has to keep an in-memory cache of objects that have been retrieved from disk in previous queries, so that if a database row is reread, the corresponding object is reused. The problem with this scheme is that if this cache is in script space, it increments the reference count of all its constituent objects, which means that once an object is in this cache, it will never be freed, even if no one else is interested in it. In other words, the cache can never shrink, and in the worst case, it has a copy of all the objects present in the database.

One solution to this problem is to implement the cache in C and not update the reference count at all.* If all persistent objects were to inherit from a module called Persistent, say, then this module's `DESTROY` method can be used to remove unwanted entries from this cache.

---

* You will know how to do this once you have read Chapter 20, *Perl Internals.*

The Adaptor::DBI module, as currently implemented, takes the easy way out and creates a fresh set of objects for each query, leaving it to Perl to automatically deallocate them when no other object refers to them. This means that the applications developer has to be careful when modifying an object returned from a query. This is a clumsy solution, I know. In addition, there is currently no provision for *cache inconsistency*—where the cache is out-of-date if someone else modifies the database.

The Adaptor::File module does not have this problem because it maintains a list of *all* objects given to its `store()` method (for reasons to be explained in the next section); hence successive identical queries return identical lists.

Queries

One big reason why object-oriented databases haven't caught on is the lack of a query language (or at least a standard query language). When you have a million objects in the database, it would be a terrible thing to load every single object in memory to see whether it matches your criteria; this is a job best left to the database. Adaptor::DBI simply translates queries to equivalent SQL queries, while Adaptor::File implements a simple-minded scheme for file based objects: it converts the query expression to an `eval`able Perl expression and cycles through all objects, matching them against the query specification.

Schema Evolution

Let us say you have sent your objects' data to a file, and tomorrow, some more attributes are added to the object implementation. The schema is said to have evolved. The framework has to be able to reconcile old data with newer object implementations.

Implementation

This section explains the implementation of Adaptor::DBI and Adaptor::File. We will cover only the key procedures that perform query processing and file or database I/O. Pay as much attention to the design gotchas and unimplemented features as you do to the code.

Adaptor::File

An Adaptor::File instance represents all objects stored in one file. When this adaptor is created (using `new`), it reads the entire file and translates the data to in-memory objects. Slurping the entire file into memory avoids the problem of having to implement fancy on-disk schemes for random access to variable-length data; after all, that is the job of DBM and database implementations. For this reason, this approach is not recommended for large numbers of objects (over 1,000, to pick a number).

The file adaptor has an attribute called `all_instances`, a hash table of all objects given to its `store` method (and indexed by their `_id`), as shown in Figure 11-2.

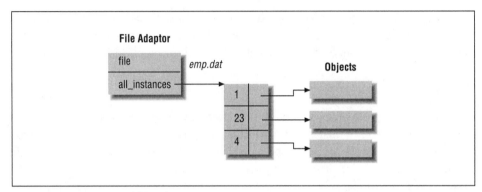

Figure 11-2. Structure of file adaptor

Storing objects

Let us examine the two methods for storing objects to files: `store()` and `flush`.

`store` allocates a new unique identifier for the object (if necessary) and simply pegs the object onto the `all_instances` hash. It doesn't send the data to disk.

```
sub store {                          # adaptor->store($obj)
    (@_ == 2) || die  'Usage adaptor->store ($obj_to_store)';
    my ($this, $obj_to_store) = @_;  # $this  is 'all_instances'
    my ($id) = $obj_to_store->get_attributes('_id');
    my $all_instances = $this->{all_instances};
    if (!defined ($id )) {
        # Haven't seen this object before. Generate an id (doesn't
        # matter how this id is generated)
        $id = $this->_get_next_id();
        $obj_to_store->set_attributes('_id'=> $id);
    }
    $all_instances->{$id} = $obj_to_store;
    $id;             # Return the object identifier
}
```

Note that the object is told about its new identifier (using `set_attributes`), so if it is given again to `store`, a new identifier is not allocated.

The real work of storing the data in the file is done by `flush`:

```
sub flush {     # adaptor->flush();
    my $this = $_[0];
    my $all_instances = $this->{'all_instances'};
```

```
    my $file          = $this->{'file'};
    return unless defined $file;
    open (F, ">$file") || die "Error opening $file: $!\n";
    my ($id, $obj);
    while (($id, $obj) = each %$all_instances) {
        my $class = ref($obj);
        my @attrs =
            $obj->get_attributes(@{$this->get_attrs_for_class($class)});
        Storable::store_fd([$class, $id, @attrs], \*F);
    }
    close(F);
}
```

`flush` simply walks the `all_instances` hash and, for each user-defined object, calls its `get_attributes` method. `get_attrs_for_class` returns a list of persistent attributes for each class (as an array reference) and is loaded from the configuration file supplied to the adaptor's constructor.

The attribute values, together with the class and instance identifier, are packaged in an anonymous array before being given to `Storable::store_fd`.

This implementation is unsatisfactorily slow (a second or two to store 1,000 objects), largely because so many lookups and accessor functions are called per object. At this stage of prototyping, I do not consider it a big issue. Retrieving objects

The `load_all` method, called from `new`, simply does the reverse of `flush`. It reads the file, recreates each object, and inserts it in the `all_instances` attribute as shown:

```
sub load_all {  # $all_instances = load_all($file);
    my $file = shift;
    return undef unless -e $file;
    open(F, $file) || croak "Unable to load $file: $!";
    # Global information first
    my ($class, $id, $obj, $rh_attr_names, @attrs, $all_instances);
    eval {
        while (1) {
            ($class, $id, @attrs) = @{Storable::retrieve_fd(\*F)};
            $obj = $all_instances->{$id};
            $obj = $class->new() unless defined($obj);
            $rh_attr_names = $this->get_attrs_for_class($class);
            $obj->set_attributes(
                    "_id" => $id,
                    map {$rh_attr_names->[$_] => $attrs[$_]}
                        (0 .. $#attrs)
            );
            $all_instances->{$id} = $obj;
        }
    };
    $all_instances;
}
```

`load_all` calls `Storable`'s `retrieve_fd` function, calls the constructor of the appropriate class (`new`) to construct an uninitialized object of that class, and invokes `set_attributes` on this newly created object. The `map` statement constructs a list of attribute name-value pairs. When `Storable::retrieve_fd` has no more data, it throws an exception (using `die`). It breaks the infinite loop but is trapped by the `eval`.

Query processing

The `retrieve_where` method accepts a class name and a query expression, which is a subset of the SQL syntax. The query is not guaranteed to work for SQL keywords such as `LIKE`, `BETWEEN`, and `IN`; however, it will work for the database adaptor because it is sent untranslated to the database.

Writing a query processor for parsing and executing arbitrary query expressions is not a trivial task. But we know that Perl itself deals with expression evaluation, so if we can convert a query to a Perl expression, we can simply use `eval` to do the dirty work for us, as we saw in Chapter 5, *Eval*.

`retrieve_where` hence invokes `parse_query` to convert the expression to an `eval`able Perl Boolean expression and dynamically creates a piece of code incorporating this expression to traverse all the objects in the `all_instances` attribute. That is, a call such as:

```
retrieve_where ('Employee', 'age < 45 && name != 'John')
```

is translated to the following piece of Perl code, and `eval`ed:

```
my $dummy_key; my $obj;
while (($dummy_key, $obj) = each %$all_instances) {
    next unless ref($obj) eq "Employee";
    my ($age, $name) = $obj->get_attributes(qw(age name));
    push (@retval, $obj) if $age < 45 && $name ne 'John';
}
```

The Boolean expression in the `push` statement and the list of attribute names are both returned by `parse_query`, discussed later. `retrieve_where` is implemented like this:

```
sub retrieve_where {
    my ($this, $class, $query) = @_;
    my $all_instances = $$this;
    # blank queries result in a list of all objects
    return $this->retrieve_all() if ($query !~ /\S/);

    my ($boolean_expression, @attrs) = parse_query($query);
    # @attrs contains the attribute names used in the query
    # Construct a statement to fetch the required attributes,
    # of the form:
    #   my ($name, $age) = $obj->get_attributes(qw(name age));
    my $fetch_stmt = "my (" . join(",",map{'$' . $_} @attrs) . ") = " .
```

```
                          "\$obj->get_attributes(qw(@attrs))";

    my (@retval);

    my $eval_str = qq{
        my \$dummy_key; my \$obj;
        while ((\$dummy_key, \$obj) = each \%\$all_instances) {
            next unless ref(\$obj) eq "$class";
            $fetch_stmt;
            push (\@retval, \$obj) if ($boolean_expression);
        }
    };
    print STDERR "EVAL:\n\t$eval_str\n" if $debugging ;
    eval ($eval_str);
    if ($@) {
        print STDERR "Ill-formed query:\n\t$query\n";
        print STDERR $@ if $debugging;
    }
    @retval;
}
```

Instead of constructing a list of objects for every query, `retrieve_where` should optionally take a callback reference as the third parameter, which can be called for every object that matches this query.

Now let us take a look at **parse_query**, which, as was mentioned earlier, translates the SQL **where** clause to a Perl expression. The input query expression is essentially a series of query terms of the form *variable op value*, strung together with logical operators (&& and ||). The rules of the transformation are as follows:

1. If query is blank, it should evaluate to TRUE.

2. Escaped quotes should be preserved. That is, a string such as `"foo\'bar"` should not cause confusion.

3. "=" is mapped to "==".

4. *variable* is mapped to *$variable*. When processing this step, **parse_query** also keeps a note of the attribute names encountered. This list is returned to its calling procedure, **retrieve_where**.

5. If *value* is a quoted string, then *op* gets mapped to the appropriate string comparison operator (see **%string_op** below).

parse_query is implemented like this:

```
my %string_op = ( # Map from any operator to corresponding string op
            '=='  =>  'eq',
            '<'   =>  'lt',
            '<='  =>  'le',
            '>'   =>  'gt',
            '>='  =>  'ge',
            '!='  =>  'ne',
            );
```

```
my $ANY_OP = '<=|>=|<|>|!=|==';          # Any comparison operator
sub parse_query {
    my ($query) = @_;
    # Rule 1.
    return 1 if ($query =~ /^\s*$/);
    # First squirrel away all instances of escaped quotes - Rule 2.
    # This way it doesn't get in the way when we are processing
    # rule 5.
    $query =~ s/\\[# Hopefully \200 and \201 aren't being
    $query =~ s/\\["]/\201/g; # being used.
    # Rule 3 - Replace all '=' by '=='
    $query =~ s/([^!><=])=/$1 == /g;
    my %attrs;
    # Rule 4 - extract fields, and replace var with $var
    $query =~
       s/(\w+)\s*($ANY_OP)/$attrs{$1}++, "\$$1 $2"/eg;
    # Rule 5 - replace comparison operators before quoted strings
    # with string comparison opersators
    $query =~
          s{
             ($ANY_OP)            (?# Any comparison operator)
             \s*                  (?#  followed by zero or more spaces,)
             ['  (?#  then by a quoted string )
          }{
             $string_op{$1} . ' \'' . $2 . '\''
          }goxse;    # global, compile-once, extended,
                     # treat as single line, eval
    # Restore all escaped quote characters
    $query =~ s/\200/\\'/g;
    $query =~ s/\201/\\"/g;
    ($query, keys %attrs);  # Return modified query, and field list
}
```

Adaptor::DBI

Adaptor::DBI is considerably simpler than Adaptor::File. It does not maintain a
table of objects in memory; when asked to store an object, it sends it to the database, and when asked to retrieve one or more objects, it simply passes the
request along to the database. This scheme is also its biggest failing, as was
pointed out earlier in the section "Uniqueness of Objects in Memory."

The **new** method simply opens a DBI connection, as was illustrated in Chapter 10,
Persistence, and creates an adaptor object with the connection handle as its sole
attribute. No rocket science here.

Storing objects

The adaptor's **store** method sends an object to the database:

```
sub store {     # adaptor->store($obj)
    (@_ == 2) || croak  'Usage adaptor->store ($obj)';
    my $sql_cmd;
```

```
my ($this, $obj) = @_;
my $class = ref($obj);
my $rh_class_info = $map_info{$class};
my $table = $rh_class_info->{"table"};
croak "No mapping defined for package $class"
    unless defined($table);
my $rl_attr_names = $rh_class_info->{"attributes"};
my ($id)         = $obj->get_attributes('_id');
my ($attr);
if (!defined ($id )) {
    $id = $this->_get_next_id($table);
    $obj->set_attributes('_id'=> $id);
    # Generate a statement like:
    #        insert into Employee (_id, name,    age)
    #                       values (100, "jason", 33)
    $sql_cmd  = "insert into $table (";
    my ($col_name, $type, $attr);
    my (@attrs) = $obj->get_attributes(@$rl_attr_names);
    $sql_cmd .= join(",",@$rl_attr_names) . ") values (";
    my $val_cmd = "";
    foreach $attr (@attrs) {
        my $quote = ($attr =~ /\D/)
                        ? "'"
                        : "";
        $val_cmd .= "${quote}${attr}${quote},";
    }
    chop ($val_cmd);
    $sql_cmd .= $val_cmd . ")" ;
} else {
    # Object already exists in the database. Update it
    # with a statement like:
    #        update Employee set name = "jason", age = 33
    #                    where _id  = 100;

    $sql_cmd = "update $table set ";
    my ($name, $quote);
    my @attrs = $obj->get_attributes(@$rl_attr_names);
    foreach $name (@$rl_attr_names) {
        if ($name eq '_id') {
            shift @attrs;   # Can't update primary row
            next;
        }
        $attr = shift @attrs;
        $quote = ($attr =~ /\D/)
                     ? "'"
                     : "";
        $sql_cmd .= "$name=${quote}${attr}${quote},";
    }
    chop($sql_cmd); # remove trailing comma
    $sql_cmd .= " where _id = $id";
}
# Sql query constructed. Give it to the appropriate db connection
# to execute.
$this->{dbconn}->do($sql_cmd); #
```

```
        die "DBI Error: $DBI::errstr" if $DBI::err;
        $id;
    }
```

The global variable **%map_info** stores database configuration information for every package mentioned in the configuration file: the name of the corresponding database table, the list of persistent attributes, and the corresponding database column names. If the object already has an attribute called **_id**, the corresponding database row is updated; otherwise, a new identifier is allocated and a new database row is inserted. All string valued attributes are automatically quoted.

Clearly, we can do much better than this implementation. If we create 1000 objects, the preceding code creates and evaluates 1000 fresh SQL insert statements. A better approach is to prepare **insert/delete/update/fetch** statements for each class the first time an object of that class is encountered, like this:

```
$insert{'Employee'} = $dbh->prepare (
                    "insert into Employee (_id, name, age)
                                 values (? , ?   , ? )");
$delete{'Employee'} = $dbh->prepare (
                    "delete from Employee where _id = ?";
$update{'Employee'} = $dbh->prepare (
                    "update Employee (name=?, age=?");
$fetch {'Employee'} = $dbh->prepare (
                    "select name, age, from Employee
                                 where _id = ?");
```

store can simply execute these statements with the appropriate statements. An even faster way is to take advantage of stored procedures. As it stands, the current implementation works reasonably well for prototypes.

Incidentally, Adaptor::DBI's **flush()** method does not do anything, because **store()** doesn't keep any object in memory.

Queries

retrieve_where creates a select query from the mapping information for that class. As was pointed out earlier, the same query executed twice will get you two different sets of objects, whose data are duplicates of the other:

```
sub retrieve_where {
    my ($this, $class, $query) = @_;
    my $where;
    $where = ($query =~ /\S/)
                    ? "where $query"
                    : "";
    my $rh_class_info = $map_info{$class};
    my $table = $rh_class_info->{"table"};
    croak "No mapping defined for package $class"
            unless defined($table);
```

```
    my $rl_attr_names = $rh_class_info->{"attributes"};
    my $rl_col_names  = $rh_class_info->{"columns"};
    my $sql_cmd       = "select "
                        . join(",", @{$rl_col_names})
                        . " from $table $where";
    print $sql_cmd if $debugging;
    my $rl_rows       = $this->{d}->do($sql_cmd);
    my @retval;
    my $size = @$rl_attr_names - 1;

    if ($rl_rows && @$rl_rows) {
        my $i; my $rl_row;
        foreach $rl_row (@$rl_rows) {
            my $obj = $class->new;
            $obj->set_attributes(map {
                               $rl_attr_names->[$_] => $rl_row->[$_]
                               }(0 .. $size));
            push (@retval, $obj);
        }
    }
    @retval;
}
```

The preceding **set_attributes** statement perhaps requires some explanation. The objective of this statement is to set all the attributes returned by the database. Since **set_attributes** requires a list of name-value pairs, we use the **map** built-in function to return a list. This function takes two parameters—a block of code and a list—and, for each element of the list, evaluates the block in a list context. The function returns a list containing the result executing that block across all iterations.

At this point, if your enthusiasm continues unabated, you may find it worthwhile to go back and understand how Adaptor handles the issues raised in the "Design Notes" section.

Resources

The following books and web sites have good treatments of object persistence:

1. *Object-Oriented Modeling and Design.* James Rumbaugh, Michael Blaha, William Premerlani, Frederick Eddy, and William Lorensen. Prentice-Hall, 1991.

   An excellent treatment of implementing OO models in relational databases.

2. *Object Persistence.* Roger Sessions. Prentice Hall, 1996.

   A discussion of the CORBA Persistence architecture. Interesting as much for the discussion of politics behind such committees, as the technical material.

3. CORBA Persistence Service Specification, Object Management Group (OMG), at *http://www.omg.org*.

4. PJava: Orthogonal Persistence for Java, at *http://www.dcs.gla.ac.uk/pjava/*. Look especially for the design paper entitled "Design Issues for Persistent Java: a Type-Safe, Object-Oriented, Orthogonally Persistent System."

5. Object Database Management Group (ODMG): *http://www.odmg.org*.

6. *Taming C++: Pattern Classes and Persistence for Large Projects*. Jiri Soukup. Addison-Wesley, 1994.

7. "Equal Rights for Functional Objects, or, The More Things Change, The More They Are the Same." Henry Baker.

   This paper shows you that there's much more to object identity than meets the eye. Download from *ftp://ftp.netcom.com/pub/hb/hbaker/ObjectIdentity.html*.

12

Networking with Sockets

> *I plugged my phone in where the blender used to be. I called someone. They went "Aaaaahhh..."*
>
> —Steven Wright

Programs can communicate with each other in a variety of ways. They can use files, anonymous/named pipes, System V interprocess messaging primitives, BSD sockets, and TLI (Transport Layer Interface). Socket and TLI communications come under the purview of "networking," a step up from the other IPC (interprocess communication) mechanisms, because they don't constrain the communicating processes to be on the same machine. This chapter provides a primer on socket communications and builds simple client/server configurations using Graham Barr's IO library (part of the standard Perl distribution). This knowledge is put to use in the next chapter, where we build an asynchronous message passing module, and another for doing remote procedure calls (RPC).

Networking is the second of four important technologies that we discuss in this book; the others are user interfaces, persistence, and code generation. This chapter, like the other three, is as much about the technology as it is about Perl's support for it. Andrew Tanenbaum's textbook on computer networks [2] is a *wonderful* introduction to computer networking. (I also rate it as one of the best computer books ever written.) This chapter provides just enough introduction to networks to work with Perl, sockets, and TCP/IP.

Networking Primer

Mail (paper and electronic) and telephones are two distinct forms of communication. A telephone conversation is *connection-oriented*, because the caller and the called "own" the line (have a continuous link) until the end of the conversation. Connection-oriented communication guarantees message delivery, preserves the order in which messages are sent, and allows a stream of data to be sent. Mail, in contrast, is a connectionless mode of transfer, which transports information in packets (or *datagrams*) and gives no guarantees about message delivery and the order in which the packets are received. It has a higher overhead because each packet identifies its sender and the intended receiver; in contrast, a connection-oriented conversation proceeds without further ado, once the parties have identified themselves. Computer networks offer you a similar choice of connection versus connectionless mode of data transfer. It must be mentioned that there are connectionless protocols such as reliable UDP that do offer guaranteed delivery and sequence integrity.

The networking world assigns each computer an internet address, also called an IP address (short for Internet Protocol), a sequence of four bytes typically written in a dot sequence, like this: 192.23.34.1. (This will change with IPv6, because the world is fast running out of four-byte IP addresses.) Just as you have convenient phone aliases such as 1-800-FLOWERS, computers are often given unique aliases, such as *www.yahoo.com*. Now, many programs can run on one machine, and it is not enough to deliver a message to the machine: it has to be handed over to the appropriate application program running on that machine. A program can ask for one or more *ports* to be opened, the equivalent of a private mailbox or telephone extension. To send a message to a program, you need its full address: its machine name and the port on which it is *listening*. Standard applications such as *ftp*, *telnet*, and *mail* actually come in pairs; for example, the *ftp* program you use talks to a counterpart server program called *ftpd* (ftp daemon) on the remote computer. Such server programs listen on standard port numbers; when you type *www.yahoo.com* on your web browser, the browser automatically connects to port 80 on that machine, where it assumes the corresponding web server to be listening. Port numbers 1–1024 are reserved for standard, well-known Internet applications. Many platforms reserve the name "localhost" (and the address 127.0.0.1) to mean the machine on which the program is running.

Once assigned a socket, your program has a choice of using a connection-oriented protocol called TCP/IP (Transport Control Protocol/IP) or a connectionless one, UDP/IP (User Datagram Protocol). Clearly, sender and receiver must use the same protocol. The TCP/IP model is usually preferred over UDP because it provides for data sequencing, end-to-end reliability (checksums, positive acknowledgments, time-outs), and end-to-end flow control (if the sender is sending data faster than the receiver can handle it, it will block the sender when the receiver's buffers are full). If the communications medium is very good, such as a LAN, UDP may perform much better because it doesn't spend time accounting for the worst case. In a production system, however, you can never really take a chance, so we will stick to TCP in this chapter.

The socket abstraction and API were introduced in BSD 4.2 to provide a uniform interface over different types of protocols (there are others besides TCP and UDP), and, depending on the protocol used, a socket behaves like either a telephone receiver or a mailbox. In either case, it takes one socket on each side to make a conversation (which is why sockets are also known as *communications endpoints*). The socket API allows you to specify the *domain* of the communicating entities—the "Unix domain" is used for processes on the same machine, and the "Internet domain" is used for processes on different machines. This chapter examines the more generally accepted (and useful) "Internet domain" option.

TLI (Transport Layer Interface), another API introduced in System V (Release 3.0, 1986), provides a very similar-looking alternative to the socket abstraction, but because it is not as widely used as the BSD socket interface, we will not discuss it in this chapter.

Socket API and IO::Socket

Perl provides native support for sockets and a module called Socket to smooth some of the rough edges associated with the native **socket** call. It turns out that there are still a large number of options to deal with, and since most applications use a fairly standard set of options, we instead use a truly convenient module called IO::Socket, which is built on Socket.

This section uses this module to build a sending and receiving program.

Receiver

Just as you would ask the phone company for a telephone number and a physical handset, both sender and receiver ask the module to create sockets. Sockets, like telephones, are bidirectional endpoints: once a connection is established, either side can send and receive data, as long as there is an understanding between the two programs about the direction of communication.

Because only the receiving side needs to have a well-known address, we create a receiving socket as follows:

```
use IO::Socket;
$sock = new IO::Socket::INET (LocalHost => 'goldengate',
                              LocalPort => 1200,
                              Proto     => 'tcp',
                              Listen    => 5,
                              Reuse     => 1,
                             );
die "Could not connect: $!" unless $sock;
```

The IO::Socket::INET module provides a nice wrapper for Internet domain sockets. The LocalHost and LocalPort parameters specify the host and port on which this socket is going to listen. The number 1200 is chosen arbitrarily, but you must make sure that it doesn't conflict with the port number used by some other application on that machine (otherwise, you get an error saying, "Address already in use"). We set the `Reuse` option, because if this program ends without properly closing the socket and is subsequently restarted, it will complain about the socket being in use. The `Listen` option specifies the maximum number of callers that can be put on hold while they are *dialing* this number, figuratively speaking.

Once created, the socket is all set to receive incoming calls. The `accept()` method listens on the given port until another program attempts to connect to it (we'll shortly see the calling side to see how this is done); at this point, `accept` returns a new socket:

```
$new_sock = $sock->accept();
```

This is analogous to a switchboard operator indicating a different handset for you to converse on, while he goes back to waiting for the main number to ring. Messages sent by the client can now be obtained by reading from `$new_sock`. You can use this socket as a filehandle and call any of the input operators, `<>`, `read`, or `sysread`, like this:

```
$buf = <$new_sock>;
# or,
$bytes_read = sysread ($new_sock, $buf, $num_bytes_to_read);
```

Both return `undef` on an end of file condition.

The following code summarizes the above discussion. It binds a socket to an address and waits for an incoming connection request. When that happens, it reads the new socket created until the other end closes its end of the connection. At this point, the `<>` operator returns `undef` (`sysread` returns 0, the number of bytes read).

```
use IO::Socket;
$sock = new IO::Socket::INET (LocalHost => 'goldengate',
                              LocalPort => 1200,
                              Proto     => 'tcp',
                              Listen    => 5,
                              Reuse     => 1
                              );
die "Socket could not be created. Reason: $!" unless $sock;
while ($new_sock = $sock->accept()) {
    while (defined ($buf = <$new_sock>)) {
        print $buf;
    }
}
close ($sock);
```

You can also use `$new_sock->get_line()` instead of `<$new_sock>`.

Sender

The calling side is even simpler. It creates a socket giving it the receiver's address and, if successful, starts sending data to it:

```
use IO::Socket;
$sock = new IO::Socket::INET (PeerAddr => 'goldengate',
                              PeerPort => 1200,
                              Proto    => 'tcp',
                            · );
die "Socket could not be created. Reason: $!\n" unless $sock;
foreach (1 .. 10) {
    print $sock "Msg $_: How are you?\n";
}
close ($sock);
```

Notice how the parameters to the `IO::Socket::INET::new` method define whether it is a server- or client-side socket. The `Listen` and `Reuse` parameters are ignored for sending ports.

Bidirectional Communications

You can read and write from sockets, but as the preceding scripts show, two communicating processes must have a common understanding of who is doing the talking and who the listening. The programs can *deadlock* if both are too polite and start reading their respective sockets (`sysread` and other input operators wait until they are able to read the requisite amount of data). They can also deadlock if both are too impolite and start speaking into the phone at the same time, figuratively speaking (`syswrite` blocks once the buffers fill up, and because the other end is not listening, deadlock is a likely possibility). In a typical client/server setup, this protocol is well established. The client program initiates the conversation, makes a request, and waits for an answer. The typical server never attempts to connect to a client program or initiate requests; it listens and responds. Deadlocks thus happen only in peer-peer conversations.

Handling Multiple Clients

The fact that `accept`, `read`, and `sysread` are blocking calls has more implications for the server.* A single-threaded process can invoke only one of these calls at a time, which is fine if there aren't too many clients clamoring for the server's attention *and* if no client ties the server up for too long a time. The real world is ugly, and you have to resolve this issue. There are three ways of doing this:

1. Create multiple threads of control (processes or threads) and have each call block in its own thread.

---

* `accept` blocks until someone tries to connect.

2. Make these calls only when you are absolutely sure they won't block. We'll call this the "select" approach, because we use the `select` call to ensure that a socket has something to offer.

3. Make these calls nonblocking using `fcntl` or `ioctl`.

As we shall see, option 2 should be used in conjunction with option 3 in production systems. In all cases, the client code remains unaffected while we try out these options.

Incidentally, there is a fourth option. Some systems support an asynchronous I/O notification: a `SIGIO` signal is sent to the process if a specified socket is ready to do I/O. We will not pay attention to this approach because there is no way for a signal handler to know *which* socket is ready for reading or writing.

Multiple Threads of Execution

Perl doesn't have threads yet (at least not officially[*]), but on Unix and similarly empowered systems, it supports `fork`, the way to get process-level parallelism. The server process acts as a full-time receptionist: it blocks on `accept`, and when a connection request comes in, it spawns a child process and goes back to `accept`. The newly created child process meanwhile has a copy of its parent's environment and shares all open file descriptors. Hence it is able to read from, and write to, the new socket returned by `accept`. When the child is done with the conversation, it simply exits. Each process is therefore dedicated to its own task and doesn't interfere with the other. The following code shows an example of a forking server:

```
# Forking server
use IO::Socket;
$SIG{CHLD} = sub {wait ()};
$main_sock = new IO::Socket::INET (LocalHost => 'goldengate',
                                   LocalPort => 1200,
                                   Listen    => 5,
                                   Proto     => 'tcp',
                                   Reuse     => 1,
                                   );
die "Socket could not be created. Reason: $!\n" unless ($sock);
while ($new_sock = $main_sock->accept()) {
    $pid = fork();
    die "Cannot fork: $!" unless defined($pid);
    if ($pid == 0) {
        # Child process
        while (defined ($buf = <$new_sock>)) {
            # do something with $buf ....
```

---

[*] Malcolm Beattie has a working prototype of a threaded Perl interpreter, which will be incorporated into the mainstream in the Perl 5.005 release.

```
            print $new_sock "You said: $buf\n";
        }
        exit(0);    # Child process exits when it is done.
    } # else 'tis the parent process, which goes back to accept()
}
close ($main_sock);
```

The `fork` call results in two identical processes—the parent and child—starting from the statement following the `fork`. The parent gets a positive return value, the process ID (`$pid`) of the child process. Both processes check this return value and execute their own logic; the main process goes back to `accept`, and the child process reads a line from the socket and echoes it back to the client.

Incidentally, the `CHLD` signal has nothing to do with IPC per se. On Unix, when a child process exits (or terminates abnormally), the system gets rid of the memory, files, and other resources associated with it. But it retains a small amount of information (the exit status if the child was able to execute `exit()`, or a termination status otherwise), just in case the parent uses `wait` or `waitpid` to enquire about this status. The terminated child process is also known as a *zombie* process, and it is always a good thing to remove it using `wait`; otherwise, the process tables keep filling up with junk. In the preceding code, `wait` doesn't block, because it is called only when we know for sure that a child process has died—the `CHLD` signal arranges that for us. Be sure to read the online documentation for quirks associated with signals in general and `SIGCHLD` in particular.

Multiplexing Using select

The reason we forked off a different process in the preceding section was to avoid blocking during `accept`, `read`, or `write` for fear of missing out on what is happening on the other sockets. We can instead use the `select` call, introduced in BSD Unix, that returns control when a socket (any filehandle, in fact) can be read from or written to. This approach allows us to use a single-threaded process—somewhat akin to firing the receptionist and handling all the incoming calls and conversations ourselves.

The interface to the native `select` call is not very pretty, so we use the IO::Select wrapper module instead. Consider

```
use IO::Socket;
use IO::Select;
$sock1 = new IO::Socket (....);
$sock2 = new IO::Socket (....);
$read_set = new IO::Select;
$read_set->add($sock1);
$write_set = new IO::Select;
$write_set->add($sock1, $sock2);
```

The IO::Select module's **new** method creates an object representing a collection of filehandles, and **add** and **remove** modify this set. The **select** method (which calls Perl's native **select** function) accepts three sets of filehandles, or IO::Select objects, which are monitored for readability, writability, and error conditions, respectively. In the preceding snippet of code, we create two such sets—a filehandle can be added to any or all of these sets if you so wish—and supply them to the **select** method as follows:

```
($r_ready, $w_ready, $error) =
    IO::Select->select($read_set, $write_set, $error_set, $timeout);
```

select blocks until an interesting event occurs (one or more filehandles are ready for reading, writing, or reporting an error condition) or the time-out interval has elapsed. At this point, it creates three separate lists of ready filehandles and returns references to them. The time-out is in seconds but can be expressed as a floating-point number to get millisecond resolution.

Let us use this information to implement a program that retrieves messages from one or more clients:

```
# Create main socket ($main_socket) as before ...
# ....

use IO::Select;
$readable_handles = new IO::Select();
$readable_handles->add($main_socket);
while (1) {  #Infinite loop
    # select() blocks until a socket is ready to be read or written
    ($new_readable) = IO::Select->select($readable_handles,
                                    undef, undef, 0);
    # If it comes here, there is at least one handle
    # to read from or write to. For the moment, worry only about
    # the read side.
    foreach $sock (@$new_readable) {
        if ($sock == $main_socket) {
            $new_sock = $sock->accept();
            # Add it to the list, and go back to select because the
            # new socket may not be readable yet.
            $readable_handles->add($new_sock);
        } else {
            # It is an ordinary client socket, ready for reading.
            $buf = <$sock>;
            if ($buf) {
                # .... Do stuff with $buf
            } else {
                # Client closed socket. We do the same here, and remove
                # it from the readable_handles list
                $readable_handles->remove($sock);
                close($sock);
            }
        }
    }
}
```

We create a listening socket, $main_socket, and configure it to listen on a well-known port. We then add this socket to a newly created IO::Select collection object. When `select` returns the first time, $main_socket has something to read from (or has an error, a possibility that we ignore for the moment); in other words, it has received a connection request and is guaranteed not to block when `accept` is called. Now, we are not interested in being blocked if the socket returned from `accept` has nothing to say, so we add it to the list of filehandles being monitored for readability. When `select` returns the next time, we know that one of the two sockets is ready for reading (or both are ready). If $main_socket is ready, we repeat the exercise above. If not, we have a socket with something to read.

`select` also returns if one or more remote sockets are closed. The corresponding sockets on the listening end return 0 when any of the I/O operators are used (0 bytes read or written). The server above removes these sockets from the IO::Select collections to prevent from `select` returning the same defunct sockets every time.

Blocking looms again

All we have done in this section is depend on `select` to tell us that a filehandle is ready for reading or writing before actually attempting to read or write from it. Unfortunately, we still don't know *how much* data has accumulated in the I/O buffers (for purposes of reading) or how much can be written to it (the other side may be reading slowly, and there's a limit to how much you can pump in from this side). Both `sysread` and `syswrite` return the number of bytes actually read or written, so you would have to invoke them in a loop until the entire message is read or written. Once you have drained the buffers (or filled them, as the case may be), there is the very real possibility that it might block the next time you attempt to read or write if the other side doesn't do something quick. One option is to invoke `select` in every iteration of the loop and proceed only if it confirms the socket's availability. This slows you down when the filehandle *can* accommodate your read or write requests. Besides, you have to quit the loop anyway when `select` tells you that a filehandle isn't ready and make the attempt later on when the file descriptor changes state.

For single-threaded programs the next option is to make the filehandle non-blocking. Read on.

Nonblocking Filehandles

Any filehandle can be made nonblocking by using the operating-system-specific `fcntl` or `ioctl` call, like this:

```
use POSIX;
fcntl($sock, F_SETFL(), O_NONBLOCK());
```

The Fcntl module (file control) makes the constants in the *fcntl.h* file available as functions. The `fcntl` function takes a command like `F_SETFL` ("set flag") and an argument that is specific to that command. Depending on the operating system, the flag to set nonblocking I/O may also be known as `O_NDELAY` or `FNDELAY`.

In any case, once this operation is carried out, `sysread` and `syswrite` return `undef` (not 0) and set `$!` to `EAGAIN` (or `EWOULDBLOCK` on BSD 4.3) if they cannot carry out the operation right away. The following code accounts for these return and error values when reading a socket:

```
# Want to read 1024 bytes
$bytes_to_read = 1024; $msg = '';
while ($bytes_to_read) {
    $bytes_read = sysread($sock, $buf, $bytes_to_read);
    if (defined($bytes_read)) {
        if ($bytes_read == 0) {
            # Remote socket closed connection
            close($sock);
            last;
        } else {
            $msg .= $buf;
            $bytes_to_read -= $bytes_read;
        }
    } else {
        if ($! == EAGAIN()) {
            # Can return to select. Here we choose to
            # spin around waiting for something to read.
        } else {
            last;
        }
    }
}
```

One simple option is to forget the `select` call and simply spin around in a polling loop, calling `read` (or `sysread`) on each socket (or `accept` on the main socket) to check whether it has anything to say, or calling `write` (or `syswrite`) if *we* have something to say, without fear that it would block. This approach is a constant drain on the CPU because the process is never idle. You should always strive to build a *quiescent** server, in client/server parlance.

You might have noticed that we have ignored clients in all these discussion. If a client is willing to block, there is no issue at all, since, unlike the server side, it is not talking to more than one entity. But if it contains a GUI, it clearly cannot afford to block, and we have much the same problem. We will revisit this issue in Chapter 14, *User Interfaces with Tk*. In a system in which there is no clear delineation between "clients" and "servers"—a cluster of bank computers is an example

---

* "Marked by inactivity or repose," as *Webster's Tenth Collegiate Dictionary* puts it.

of such a peer-to-peer system—every process is modeled on the more general server framework described in the preceding pages.

You can now see that all three approaches to creating servers have their individual quirks and failings. The next section introduces us to techniques and strategies used in typical production servers.

Real-World Servers

Single-threaded servers are essentially event-driven—they execute in response to a time-out or an I/O event. They typically don't spend much CPU time for a given request, because they need to get back to `select` to service other events that might have queued up in the meantime. Most production single-threaded servers also use nonblocking filehandles (combining the second and third options listed in the section "Handling Multiple Clients"). In the next chapter, we will build a small message-passing library using these techniques. The advantage of using single-threading is that frequent short-cycle requests are handled with very little overhead. In addition, data structures can easily be shared between all parallel conversations or cached for future conversations. A chat server, for example, benefits most from such an architecture.

The multiprocess solution is chosen when the server cannot guarantee how long a given request is going to take. Web servers follow this approach and simply spawn a CGI (Common Gateway Interface) program to handle the conversation with the corresponding web browser on the other end. Nowadays, the trend is to handle quick tasks in the web server itself and spawn programs only when the task might hold up the entire server. Of course, the problem is that spawning processes is expensive, so a popular option is to prespawn a fixed number of processes and hand the task to them whenever a request comes in. Clearly, if there are many more sockets than there are prespawned processes, the parent has no option but to use `select` to multiplex between them. As you can see, the options described in the previous section are by no means independent of each other.

Multithreading is an option if the environment supports it (Perl doesn't yet). Java is enthusiastic about this approach and expects a thread to block on I/O calls; in fact, it doesn't even provide an interface to `select`. The advantage of this approach is that it is much more lightweight in comparison to the multiprocess version. In addition, you get parallelism *and* data sharing. The disadvantage is that typical workstations tend to perform badly if you introduce, say, 40 or more kernel level threads, so they can support only a limited number of concurrent clients. Threads on Solaris are better off, because they make a distinction between lightweight, user-level threads and kernel threads. In any case, this is not an option currently available to a Perl programmer, so the discussion is moot.

IO Objects and Filehandles

Perl supports the BSD `socket` call, which returns a filehandle, as `open` does for files and pipes. This filehandle can be used as an argument for all the built-in input-output operators: `<>`, `read`, `sysread`, `print`, `write`, `syswrite`, and so on. In addition, it can be used by socket-specific functions such as `send`, `recv`, and `setsockopt`.

The IO::Socket module's `new` method returns an object that can also be used as a parameter to these I/O routines. Internally, it calls `socket` and uses the typeglob corresponding to the filehandle to store other attributes; we described this hideous-looking trick in Chapter 8, *Object Orientation: The Next Few Steps*, in the section "Efficient Attribute Storage." In other words, its return value is the same object that was given to `socket`, which is why it does not matter to the I/O operators which option you choose. My recommendation is to go for the considerably easier to use IO::Socket option.

IO::Select is another story, however. If performance is absolutely crucial, you may prefer to do yourself what IO::Select implements:

```
$r_bitset = $w_bitset = $e_bitset = '';
# Monitor $sock1 for reading
vec($r_bitset, $sock1->fileno(), 1) = 1;
# Monitor $sock2 for writing
vec($w_bitset, $sock2->fileno(), 1) = 1;
# Monitor both for errors
$e_bitset = $r_bitset | $w_bitset;

($nfound, $timeleft) =
    select ($r_bitset, $w_bitset, $e_bitset, $timeout);
```

The native `select` function requires three bit vectors representing collections of open files, sockets, or pipes. Each bit in these bit sets corresponds to an integer file descriptor, which in turn is tracked by the appropriate filehandles or IO objects. The `fileno()` method of IO::Socket, or the built-in function, `fileno`, can be used to retrieve this number. The rest is simple: we create three bit sets, for checking readability, writability, and error conditions, and use `vec` to set the appropriate bits in each bit set. Before `select` returns, it modifies the bit sets to indicate which file descriptors are ready for doing input or output.

Because these bit sets are modified, we have to construct them all over again before going back to `select`, which gets to be somewhat expensive. Instead, a common technique is to make a copy of these sets before getting them clobbered by `select`:

```
# Set up $r_bitset and $w_bitset once
...
```

```
while (1) {
    ($nfound, $timeout) = select ($r_copy = $r_bitset,
                                  $w_copy = $w_bitset,
                                  $e_copy = $e_bitset, $timeout);

    # Check $r_copy, $w_copy for readiness ...
}
```

Note that the assignment happens before **select** gets control, and **select** sees only $r_copy, $w_copy, and $e_copy, which it feels free to modify.

The only place where we really save time over using IO::Select is that we don't have to make a list of ready filehandles; we can process the bit set directly. For the applications I have built, this marginal gain in efficiency is not worth it, so I use IO::Select.

Prebuilt Client Modules

Applications such as mail clients, FTP, web browsers, telnet, and Usenet news-readers are built to use TCP/IP and sockets. Several libraries available on CPAN give you the client-side libraries to roll your own FTP or mail reader, for example, without having to worry about the application protocol. (Note that there are no libraries to write your own servers to handle these protocols.) In this section, we will take a brief look at a couple of interesting client modules packaged under the Net hierarchy and available as *libnet* from CPAN. These packages were also written by Graham Barr.

Net::FTP

This module implements the client side of the File Transfer Protocol and is used like this:

```
use Net::FTP;
$ftp = Net::FTP->new("ftp.digital.com");
die "Could not connect: $!" unless $ftp;
$ftp->login('anonymous', 'me@foo.com');    # Guest User; email as passwd
$ftp->cwd('/pub/plan/perl/CPAN');          # cwd:Change Working Directory
$ftp->get('index');
$ftp->quit();
```

This module supports all the commands that you can issue from a standard FTP program.

As currently implemented, the **get** call blocks until the entire file is transmitted, so while it is very useful for a batch application (such as mirroring an FTP site nightly), you cannot use it to write a graphical FTP client.

Net::POP3

This library gives an interface to programmatically access a POP (Post Office Protocol) server, used, for example, on dial-up connections. The POP server stores incoming email until the mail reader comes and "visits the post office." Let us study a small example based on Net::POP3.

The trouble with most PC-based mail readers is that they don't give you a preview of the messages and don't wait for you to decide whether you really want to download any of them. People take the Internet's bandwidth for granted all the time, and you might find yourself helplessly waiting as an email containing the latest photograph of Madonna's baby trickles slowly through your dial-up connection. The Perl-based POP client shown below provides a preview of the messages sitting on the POP server: it simply lists the first three lines of all available messages:

```perl
use Net::POP3;
$m = Net::POP3->new('pop.myhost.com'); # Name of POP server
die "Could not open account" unless $m;
$n = $m->login('sriram', 'foofoo');     # Login, passwd
print "Number of msgs received: $n\n";
$r_msgs = $m->list();                    # Returns a ref-to-hash mapping
                                         # msg_id to msg_size
foreach $msg_id (keys %$r_msgs) {
    print "Msg $msg_id (", $r_msgs->{$msg_id}, "):\n";
    print "----------------\n";
    $rl_msg = $m->top($msg_id, 3);  # Get top three lines from message
    $, = "\n";
    print @$rl_msg;
}
$m->quit();
```

I use a slightly beefier version of this script to optionally delete messages and then fire up my regular mail reader to download what's left.

Resources

1. *perlipc* documentation.

   Covers all available IPC mechanisms, including socket communications.

2. *Computer Networks*, 3rd edition. Andrew S. Tanenbaum. Prentice-Hall, 1996.

   The best book on computer networks ever written.

3. *Unix Network Programming*. W. Richard Stevens. Prentice-Hall, 1990.

4. *Advanced Programming in the Unix Environment*. W. Richard Stevens. Prentice-Hall, 1992.

13

Networking: Implementing RPC

> *I waited and waited and waited, and when no*
> *message came, I knew it must have been from you.*
>
> —Ashleigh Brilliant

In this chapter, we build on the lessons learned in the preceding chapter and implement two layers on top of sockets. The first is an asynchronous message-passing system, Msg, which takes advantage of nonblocking I/O where available. We then build a remote procedure call module, RPC, on top of the Msg substrate. RPC offers the convenience of synchronous procedure calls and accounts for exceptions, `wantarray`, parameter marshalling, and so on.

Before we proceed, let us get one basic definition out of the way. In Chapter 12, we glossed over the definition of a "message." A socket connection is simply a stream of bytes and leaves it to the application to define message boundaries, so the receiver can tell when one message ends and another starts. Some protocols insert an end-of-message character, an arbitrarily chosen byte such as ASCII 4 (Ctrl-D), or a lone period on a line, and some prepend message lengths so that the receiver knows how much to expect. We use the latter option in this chapter.

Msg: Messaging Toolkit

In this section, we implement a module called Msg, an event-driven, client-server, messaging framework,[*] using the IO::Select and IO::Socket modules. These are its key characteristics:

Queued messages

> You can instruct Msg to either send a message right away or queue it for later delivery.

---

[*] Talk about being fully buzzword-compliant!

Nonblocking I/O

Msg checks to see whether your system supports POSIX and, if so, uses its nonblocking I/O support (as shown in Chapter 12). On systems with nonblocking I/O support but no POSIX compliance, you can inherit from Msg and override two methods to set a filehandle's blocking properties. On systems with no support at all for this facility, a send or a receive will block, but because `select` is used to determine a good time when messages can be sent out or received, it minimizes the chances that these calls might block (or block for long).

Message boundaries

Msg simply prepends every outgoing buffer with 4 bytes containing the message's length. The receiving side knows to expect at least 4 bytes and subsequently knows how long a message to expect.

Message transparency

Msg doesn't bother to look inside your message; this means that you have to be careful about sending binary messages to some other architecture. One simple solution is to encode all your messages in ASCII (using `sprintf` or `pack`). The RPC module, described later in this chapter, uses the FreezeThaw library to obtain a network-transparent encoding.

The following code shows a client that uses Msg:

```
use Msg;
$conn = Msg->connect('localhost', 8080);
die "Error: Could not connect\n" unless $conn;
$conn->send_now("Message $i");
($msg, $err) = $conn->rcv_now();
```

`connect` is a static method that creates a *connection* object (one of its attributes is a socket connection). The `send_now` method pumps out messages on that connection, and a corresponding method called `rcv_now` blocks until it receives a message from the other side. We'll look at deferred (or queued) messaging shortly.

The following code shows a server built using Msg:

```
use Msg;
use strict;
my $host = 'localhost';
my $port = 8080;
Msg->new_server($host, $port, \&login_proc);
print "Server created. Waiting for events";
Msg->event_loop();
#-------------------------------------------------------------
sub login_proc {
    # Unconditionally accept an incoming connection request
    return \&rcvd_msg_from_client;
}
```

```
sub rcvd_msg_from_client {
    my ($conn, $msg, $err) = @_;
    if (defined $msg) {
        print "$msg\n";
    }
}
```

The script calls **new_server** to create a listening socket (the program's network address) and then calls **event_loop**, an event dispatcher, which is a thin wrapper over **select**.

When a client process attempts to connect, Msg creates a local connection object and calls the login procedure supplied by you (to **new_server**), with the connection object as an argument. In the login procedure, you can query the remote host and port if you want and refuse a connection request by returning **undef**. To accept the connection, you return the reference to a subroutine (**rcvd_msg_from_client** in this example), which will be called on every subsequent message received on that connection. Different connections can have different receiving procedures if you so wish.

This is how you send or receive messages in a deferred fashion:

```
$conn = Msg->connect($remote_host, $remote_port, \&msg_from_server);
$conn->send_later($msg);
Msg->event_loop();
```

The **connect** method takes a reference to a subroutine exactly like **new_server**. **event_loop** sends queued outgoing messages when the connection becomes writable, and is responsible for dispatching incoming messages to corresponding local subroutines (deferred receive). Note that if a client wants to use deferred messages, it has to call **event_loop**.

Do you see the lines between a "client" and "server" blurring? Both have event loops (although the client requires it only for deferred messages) and respond to incoming messages. In a traditional client/server setup such as a database connection, the client initiates the conversation (**connect**) and asks the questions. The server never initiates a request. In a peer-peer setup, as in a telephone conversation, one process initiates the conversation, but once the connection is established, either process can send messages. Msg supports this peer-peer model.

Other filehandles can be incorporated into the event loop, like this:

```
Msg->set_event_handler (\*STDIN, "read" => \&kbd_input);
```

The process can now respond to keyboard events and still keep an ear out for incoming messages, or send outgoing queued messages in the "background."

All event-driven frameworks support timer events to periodically trigger a background task. If you have a time-consuming task, you are expected to split it up into more manageable pieces and use a timer (with a 0 second time-out) to trigger the next subtask. This way, you can keep returning to the event loop after every subtask is over and get a chance to process other messages that might have trickled in since then. Since this chapter is about networking, I have not taken the trouble to add timer support to Msg. It is a rather trivial addition, because `select` supports a millisecond resolution time-out facility.

Msg Implementation

Msg exhibits the public interface shown in Table 13-1.

Table 13-1. Msg's Public Interface

Method	Description
`connect(host, port, [rcv_cb])`	Connects to a server at the remote host and port and returns a connection object. `rcv_callback` is the reference to a user-defined subroutine, which is called as follows when the remote process sends a message (at any time): `rcv_callback($conn, $msg, $err)` conn is the connection object, used to send messages or issue a disconnect. `msg` is the received message; it is `undef` if the connection is closed on the other side. (Msg automatically closes the connection on this side if this happens.) `err`, if present, contains the last error value on a `sysread`.
`$conn->send_now($msg)`	Sends the message right away and blocks if it needs to. If there are queued messages, it sends them first before attempting to send `msg`.
`$conn->send_later($msg)`	Puts the message in a queue associated with the connection object and leaves it to `event_loop` (described later) to dispatch it when the socket becomes writable. That is, you have to call `event_loop` at some point; otherwise, the message never goes out.
`$conn->disconnect()`	Closes the connection.
`($msg, $err) = $conn->rcv_now()`	Blocks until it receives a full message. It does not call the callback function given to `connect`. In a scalar context, it returns only the message; otherwise it returns the error code, if any.
`new_server($thishost, $thisport, [login_proc])`	A static method that creates a listening socket at `thishost`, `thisport`. When a remote socket attempts to `connect`, `login_proc` is called with the connection object and the connecting host and port as arguments. If `login_proc` returns `undef`, the connection is closed.

Table 13-1. Msg's Public Interface (continued)

Method	Description

`set_event_handler(`
`    $handle,`
`    ["read" => rd_cb],`
`    ["write" => wt_cb])`
	`handle` can be a socket, file, or pipe handle, or a derivative of IO::Handle. The callbacks are called by `event_loop` when the corresponding file descriptors become ready for reading or writing. A callback value of `undef` removes existing registered callbacks. Only one callback of a type can be registered for a given handle.

`event_loop ([count])`	Executes the select loop `count` times (infinite, by default). This loop quits if no handles are registered with the event loop. Look at RPC for an example of how `count` is used.

The Msg implementation is divided into four logical parts:

- *Send routines.* For connecting to a remote process and sending messages to it.

- *Receive routines.* For receiving notification when a message or a connection request comes in.

- *Support for nonblocking I/O.* Routines to make a socket blocking or nonblocking if the platform supports the POSIX module.

- *Event loop support.* For dispatching file-related events.

Let's start with the send-side routines:

```
package Msg;
use strict;
use IO::Select;
use IO::Socket;
use Carp;
use vars qw(%rd_callbacks %wt_callbacks $rd_handles $wt_handles);
%rd_callbacks = ();
%wt_callbacks = ();
$rd_handles   = IO::Select->new();
$wt_handles   = IO::Select->new();
my $blocking_supported = 0;
```

Msg: Send-side routines

```
sub connect {
    my ($pkg, $to_host, $to_port,$rcvd_notification_proc) = @_;
    # Create a new internet socket
    my $sock = IO::Socket::INET->new (
                                    PeerAddr => $to_host,
                                    PeerPort => $to_port,
                                    Proto    => 'tcp');

    return undef unless $sock;
    # Create a connection end-point object
    my $conn = bless {
        sock                    => $sock,
```

```
            rcvd_notification_proc => $rcvd_notification_proc,
    }, $pkg;

    if ($rcvd_notification_proc) {
        # Bundle _rcv and $conn together in a closure
        my $callback = sub {_rcv($conn)};
        set_event_handler ($sock, "read" => $callback);
    }
    $conn;
}
```

connect sets up a client socket and creates the connection object mentioned earlier. The connection object is a communications endpoint and has the following attributes:

sock
: The socket connection

rcvd_notification_proc
: A callback function to call on receipt of a message

queue
: A reference to a list of buffered messages

send_offset
: In nonblocking mode, Msg allows partial writes. If the socket blocks, we note down how much of the topmost message in the queue we have already sent.

msg
: In nonblocking mode, msg contains a partial incoming message...

bytes_to_read
: ....and bytes_to_read contains the bytes still expected.

Once the connection is established, each side can use its local connection object to talk to the other side.

If the user specifies a callback ($rcvd_notification_proc), we set up our event handler to call a private routine _rcv, which in turn calls this callback when an entire message has been received:

```
sub disconnect {
    my $conn = shift;
    my $sock = delete $conn->{sock};
    return unless defined($sock);
    set_event_handler ($sock, "read" => undef, "write" => undef);
    close($sock); undef $!; # Should ideally process errors from close
}

sub send_now {
    my ($conn, $msg) = @_;
    _enqueue ($conn, $msg);
    $conn->_send (1); # 1 ==> flush
}
```

send_now enqueues the message and tells **_send** to flush this message and other previous messages hanging around in the queue, if any.

```
sub send_later {
    my ($conn, $msg) = @_;
    _enqueue($conn, $msg);
    my $sock = $conn->{sock};
    return unless defined($sock);
    set_event_handler ($sock, "write" => sub {$conn->_send(0)});
}
```

send_later enqueues the message and registers a "write" callback. This is invoked later on when **event_loop** is called, and the file descriptor is writable.

```
sub _enqueue {
    my ($conn, $msg) = @_;
    # prepend length (encoded as network long)
    my $len = length($msg);
    $msg = pack ('N', $len) . $msg;
    push (@{$conn->{queue}}, $msg);
}
```

_enqueue prepends each message with a length and pushes it into a queue associated with the connection. The length is encoded as a "network-independent long" (a 32-bit number) so that the receiving side knows to read exactly four bytes to obtain this length. As was mentioned earlier, the message itself is assumed to be independent of byte-ordering issues.

```
sub _send {
    my ($conn, $flush) = @_;
    my $sock = $conn->{sock};
    return unless defined($sock);
    my ($rq) = $conn->{queue};    # rq -> ref. to queue.

    # If $flush is set, set the socket to blocking, and send all
    # messages in the queue - return only if there's an error
    # If $flush is 0 (deferred mode) make the socket non-blocking, and
    # return to the event loop only after every message, or if it
    # is likely to block in the middle of a message.

    $flush ? $conn->set_blocking() : $conn->set_non_blocking();
    my $offset = (exists $conn->{send_offset}) ? $conn->{send_offset}
: 0;
    while (@$rq) {
        my $msg            = $rq->[0];
        my $bytes_to_write = length($msg) - $offset;
        my $bytes_written  = 0;
        while ($bytes_to_write) {
            $bytes_written = syswrite ($sock, $msg,
                                       $bytes_to_write, $offset);
            if (!defined($bytes_written)) {
                if (_err_will_block($!)) {
                    # Should happen only in deferred mode. Record how
                    # much we have already sent.
```

```
                    $conn->{send_offset} = $offset;
                    # Event handler should already be set, so we will
                    # be called back eventually, and will resume sending
                    return 1;
                } else {      # Uh, oh
                    $conn->handle_send_err($!);
                    return 0; # fail. Message remains in queue ..
                }
            }
            $offset            += $bytes_written;
            $bytes_to_write    -= $bytes_written;
        }
        delete $conn->{send_offset};
        $offset = 0;
        shift @$rq;
        last unless $flush; # Go back to select and wait
                            # for it to fire again.
    }
    # Call me back if queue has not been drained.
    if (@$rq) {
        set_event_handler ($sock, "write" => sub {$conn->_send(0)});
    } else {
        set_event_handler ($sock, "write" => undef);
    }
    1;  # Success
}
```

_send does the real work of sending the message and is called either directly
from **send_now** or as a callback from the event loop. If called from **send_now**,
it sets the socket to blocking mode and flushes all messages in the queue. If
called from the event loop, it sets the socket to nonblocking mode and flushes at
most one message at a time before returning to the event loop. This way, other
connections get their share of time. If **syswrite** says it will block, _send notes
down how much of the message has already been sent (in the **send_offset**
attribute) and returns to the event loop. In all cases, it accounts for the fact that
syswrite might write only a part of the buffer.

```
sub handle_send_err {
    # For more meaningful handling of send errors, subclass Msg and
    # rebless $conn.
    my ($conn, $err_msg) = @_;
    warn "Error while sending: $err_msg \n";
    set_event_handler ($conn->{sock}, "write" => undef);
}
```

This is a wishy-washy error-handling procedure that doesn't do anything other
than turn off the event loop notification. It does not touch the connection object
in any way, so you can potentially resume from where you left off. To do this,
you must override this method in an inherited class (look at the RPC module
described later, for an example).

Msg: Receive-side routines

The procedures in this section implement the listening side:

```perl
my ($g_login_proc, $g_pkg); # The prefix g_ stands for global
my $main_socket = 0;
sub new_server {
    @_ == 4 || die "new_server (myhost, myport, login_proc)\n";
    my ($pkg, $my_host, $my_port, $login_proc) = @_;

    $main_socket = IO::Socket::INET->new (
                                    LocalAddr => $my_host,
                                    LocalPort => $my_port,
                                    Listen    => 5,
                                    Proto     => 'tcp',
                                    Reuse     => 1);
    die "Could not create socket: $! \n" unless $main_socket;
    set_event_handler ($main_socket, "read" => \&_new_client);
    $g_login_proc = $login_proc; $g_pkg = $pkg;
}
```

new_server is somewhat similar to **connect**. It creates a listening socket and registers the user-defined login procedure with the event handler. (Client programs that have no wish to send or receive deferred messages don't need to call **new_server** or **event_loop**.) This login procedure will not be called until the server calls **event_loop** *and* a connection request comes in. Unlike **connect**, **new_server** doesn't create a connection object yet; that is the job of _new_client:

```perl
sub _new_client {
    my $sock = $main_socket->accept();
    my $conn = bless {
        'sock' =>  $sock,
        'state' => 'connected'
    }, $g_pkg;
    my $rcvd_notification_proc = &$g_login_proc ($conn);
    if ($rcvd_notification_proc) {
        $conn->{rcvd_notification_proc} = $rcvd_notification_proc;
        my $callback = sub {_rcv($conn)};
        set_event_handler ($sock, "read" => $callback);
    } else {  # Login failed
        $conn->disconnect();
    }
}
```

_new_client is called when a connection request is received. After doing an **accept**, it gives the user-defined login procedure a chance to accept or reject the connection. If the login procedure accepts the request, it returns a reference to a subroutine. This code reference is promptly associated with the newly created connection object and will be called when a message arrives on that connection. _rcv is registered as the standard callback to process all incoming messages (for

all connections) and accumulates an entire message before calling the code reference mentioned above.

```perl
sub _rcv {                          # Complement to _send
    my ($conn, $rcv_now) = @_; # $rcv_now complement of $flush
    # Find out how much has already been received, if at all
    my ($msg, $offset, $bytes_to_read, $bytes_read);
    my $sock = $conn->{sock};
    return unless defined($sock);
    if (exists $conn->{msg}) {
        $msg           = $conn->{msg};
        delete $conn->{'msg'};                      # Have made a copy.
        $offset        = length($msg) - 1;  # sysread appends to it.
        $bytes_to_read = $conn->{bytes_to_read};
    } else {
        # The typical case ...
        $msg           = "";                        # Otherwise -w complains
        $offset        = 0 ;
        $bytes_to_read = 0 ;                        # Will get set soon
    }
    # We want to read the message length in blocking mode. Quite
    # unlikely that we'll get blocked too long reading 4 bytes
    if (!$bytes_to_read)  {                         # Get new length
        my $buf;
        $conn->set_blocking();
        $bytes_read = sysread($sock, $buf, 4);
        if ($! || ($bytes_read != 4)) {
            goto FINISH;
        }
        $bytes_to_read = unpack ('N', $buf);
    }
    $conn->set_non_blocking() unless $rcv_now;
    while ($bytes_to_read) {
        $bytes_read = sysread ($sock, $msg, $bytes_to_read, $offset);
        if (defined ($bytes_read)) {
            if ($bytes_read == 0) {
                last;
            }
            $bytes_to_read -= $bytes_read;
            $offset        += $bytes_read;
        } else {
            if (_err_will_block($!)) {
                # Should come here only in non-blocking mode
                $conn->{msg}           = $msg;
                $conn->{bytes_to_read} = $bytes_to_read;
                return ; # .. to event loop; _rcv will be called
                         # later when socket is readable again.
            } else {
                last;
            }
        }
    }
    # Message successfully read.
FINISH:
```

```
        if (length($msg) == 0) {
            $conn->disconnect();
        }
        if ($rcv_now) {
            return ($msg, $!);
        } else {
            &{$conn->{rcvd_notification_proc}}($conn, $msg, $!);
        }
    }
```

_read is the complement to **_send** and does the grunt work of reading from a
socket. Unlike **_send**, it does not know how much data it is going to deal with,
but does know that the first four bytes of any message contain the encoded
length (of the rest of the message). To simplify matters, it sets the mode to
blocking before attempting to read these four bytes with the (reasonable) hope
that if it blocks at all, it wouldn't be for too long. Once the length has been
decoded, it sets the mode back to nonblocking, if required, and proceeds to read
the socket. Like **_send**, it accounts for the fact that **sysread** may return less
data than asked for, or it might return an error saying it may block. If the socket
will block, **_rcv** copies the partial message into the connection object, notes
down the number of bytes still left to read, and returns, waiting for it to be triggered by the event loop again. If there's an error, it disconnects the connection
automatically.

```
    sub rcv_now {
        my ($conn) = @_;
        my ($msg, $err) = _rcv ($conn, 1); # 1 means receive immediately
        return wantarray ? ($msg, $err) : $msg;
    }
```

Msg: Support for nonblocking I/O

```
    BEGIN {
        eval {
            require POSIX; POSIX->import(qw(F_SETFL O_NONBLOCK EAGAIN));
        };
        $blocking_supported = 1 unless $@;
    }
```

BEGIN tests to see whether it can load the POSIX module and, if so, sets
$blocking_supported, which is used by the following routines:

```
    sub _err_will_block {
        if ($blocking_supported) {
            return ($_[0] == EAGAIN());
        }
        return 0;
    }
    sub set_non_blocking {
        if ($blocking_supported) {
```

```
            # preserve other fcntl flags
            my $flags = fcntl ($_[0], F_GETFL(), 0);
            fcntl ($_[0], F_SETFL(), $flags | O_NONBLOCK());
        }
    }
    sub set_blocking {
        if ($blocking_supported) {
            my $flags = fcntl ($_[0], F_GETFL(), 0);
            $flags  &= ~O_NONBLOCK(); # Clear blocking, but preserve others
            fcntl ($_[0], F_SETFL(), $flags);
        }
    }
```

set_blocking and set_non_blocking both call fcntl as explained in the last chapter. The F_SETFL sets the file descriptor's flags to the bitmask you supplied, so we take care not to obliterate the flags that may already have been set.

Msg: Event loop routines

The event loop support routines use IO::Select to manage collections of filehandles and socket handles. The send and receive side routines described earlier call these routines, but because these procedures do not make any assumptions about who is calling them, they are at a logically lower level. This means that for this module to coexist with another event-driven toolkit, you will just have to rewrite the routines shown below (while preserving the interface). For example, to make Msg work with Tk, you can have set_event_handler (described below) simply delegate its functionality to an equivalent Tk procedure called fileevent (described in Chapter 14, *User Interfaces with Tk*); similarly, event_loop can simply call Tk's *run* method, instead of calling IO::Select.

```
    sub set_event_handler {
        shift unless ref($_[0]); # shift if first arg is package name
        my ($handle, %args) = @_;
        my $callback;
        if (exists $args{'write'}) {
            $callback = $args{'write'};
            if ($callback) {
                $wt_callbacks{$handle} = $callback;
                $wt_handles->add($handle);
            } else {
                delete $wt_callbacks{$handle};
                $wt_handles->remove($handle);
            }
        }
        if (exists $args{'read'}) {
            $callback = $args{'read'};
            if ($callback) {
                $rd_callbacks{$handle} = $callback;
                $rd_handles->add($handle);
            } else {
```

```
                delete $rd_callbacks{$handle};
                $rd_handles->remove($handle);
            }
        }
    }
```

set_event_handler simply keeps track of read and write callbacks by using the handle as a hash index. To remove a callback, you call **set_event_handler** with a callback value of **undef**:

```
sub event_loop {
    my ($pkg, $loop_count) = @_;
    my ($conn, $r, $w, $rset, $wset);
    while (1) {
        # Quit the loop if no handles left to process
        last unless ($rd_handles->count() || $wt_handles->count());
        ($rset, $wset) =
            IO::Select->select ($rd_handles, $wt_handles,
                                    undef, undef);
        foreach $r (@$rset) {
            &{$rd_callbacks{$r}} ($r) if exists $rd_callbacks{$r};
        }
        foreach $w (@$wset) {
            &{$wt_callbacks{$w}}($w) if exists $wt_callbacks{$w};
        }
        if (defined($loop_count)) {
            last unless --$loop_count;
        }
    }
}
```

event_loop is normally an infinite loop but can be instructed to cycle a limited number of times. The idea of giving this a loop count is to be able to dispatch other events without forfeiting control to an infinite loop. Take a look at the RPC implementation, described in the following section, which uses a count of 1 to dispatch messages in a controlled fashion.

Remote Procedure Calls (RPC)

In this section, we use the Msg library to implement a Remote Procedure Call module, *RPC.pm*. The idea of RPC is to transparently invoke a subroutine in another process space and have it behave exactly as if it had been invoked in its own process. The following are the features we take for granted while calling ordinary subroutines, which the RPC module takes into account:

Synchronicity
    The caller waits until the called procedure finishes. The RPC module invokes **Msg::send_now** and **Msg::rcv_now** to get this blocking behavior.

Parameters

A Perl subroutine can take any number of parameters of any type (including references to objects, complex data structures, and subroutines). The RPC module uses the FreezeThaw module described in Chapter 10, *Persistence*, for *marshalling* parameters: all parameters are flattened and encoded into a single string (*frozen*) and recovered on the other side (*thawed*). This means that all data structures sent by reference are copied in their entirety so that the receiving subroutine on the other side can get a reference to an object (as it would if it were in the same process). FreezeThaw—and hence RPC—does not account for code references, because there is no way (in Perl) to decode a code reference and get the subroutine text (because it could be compiled into machine code). We could create a dummy subroutine on the remote side and have it make a nested RPC invocation back to the real code reference, but the current implementation does not have this feature (though it doesn't preclude it).

Context

A subroutine can use **wantarray** to find out whether the caller is specifying a list or scalar context. The fact that the subroutine is being called from a remote process should not be an issue. The RPC module arranges the necessary transparency. Another example of context (not to be confused with the Perl meaning of the word) is the caller's package. When you say `foo()`, you mean `foo()` in the current package.

Exceptions

A subroutine can invoke **die**, and expect its caller to trap it. The receiving side of RPC invokes the target subroutine inside an **eval**, and if it dies, it sends a message back to the calling process, which in turn invokes a **die** in its own space with the error received.

Mutual recursion

Subroutine A can call subroutine B, which in turn can call A—they are said to be mutually recursive. RPC allows this because of its ability to process incoming messages while it is blocked on a send.

No deadlocks

Traditional RPC systems are subject to deadlocks if two peer processes decide to call each other at the same time, because as we saw in Chapter 12, they are too impolite to listen to what the other is saying. Not so with RPC. In fact, it can dispatch incoming messages on all file descriptors while, from the caller's perspective, it is still blocked.

No code generation

Typical RPC systems generate client and server stub code, but RPC does not need to—a tribute to the dynamic aspects of Perl.

Using RPC

Let us take a look at a sample use of the RPC module. The client is shown first:

```
# Client stuff
use RPC;
my $conn = RPC->connect($host, $port);
my $answer = $conn->rpc('ask_sheep',
                        "Ba ba black sheep, have you any wool ?");
print "$answer\n";
```

The client sets up an RPC connection, given a host and port. A subroutine that is normally invoked as

```
$answer = ask_sheep ($question);
```

is invoked by using RPC as follows:

```
$answer = $conn->rpc ("ask_sheep", $question);
```

The client code *knows* it is making an RPC call. Making this transparent (as typical RPC systems do) is quite simple, really. Using **eval**, we can dynamically create a dummy client stub called **ask_sheep** on the caller's side and have it make the call to **rpc()**.

The called subroutine, however, does not know whether it has been invoked locally or from a remote process (unless of course, it uses **caller()** to find out).

The remote process (call it the RPC server) provides the required subroutines and invokes **new_server** and **event_loop** to accept incoming RPC calls; **ask_sheep** will get called at the right time. Simple!

```
# Server stuff
RPC->new_rpc_server($host, $port);
RPC->event_loop();

sub ask_sheep {  # Sample subroutine to be invoked from client
    print "Question: @_\n";
    return "No";
}
```

Now, let us look at an example of using RPC between *peer processes*. Process 1 (identified by **$host1, $port1**) calls subroutine **two** on Process 2 (**$host2, $port2**), which in turn calls subroutine **one** back on Process 1.

Process 1 looks like this:

```
sub one {
    print "One called\n";
}
$conn2 = RPC->new_rpc_server($host2, $port2);
$conn2->rpc ("two");
```

Process 2 looks like this:

```
sub two {
    print "Two called\n";
}
$conn1 = RPC->new_rpc_server($host1, $port1);
$conn1->rpc ("one");
```

Each process calls **new_rpc_server** to establish a listening port. Since the **rpc** call listens to incoming messages while it is still sending stuff out, neither process needs to call **event_loop** explicitly. A process that intends to hang around for a while should, of course, do so.

RPC: Implementation

The RPC implementation is surprisingly small, thanks to the Msg and FreezeThaw modules. It inherits from Msg to provide the same connection and event loop abstractions.

Let us examine the calling side first:

```
package RPC;
use Msg;
use strict;
use Carp;
@RPC::ISA = qw(Msg);
use FreezeThaw qw(freeze thaw);

sub connect {
    my ($pkg, $host, $port) = @_;
    my $conn = $pkg->SUPER::connect($host,$port, \&_incoming_msg);
    return $conn;
}
```

connect simply calls Msg's **connect**, with **_incoming_msg** as the subroutine to notify on all incoming messages (including responses to subroutine calls and end-of-file indications). It leaves it to Msg's **connect** to create a connection object and bless it under RPC's auspices. Both Msg and RPC have been written so that they can be inherited by another module; the package name is not hardcoded.

```
my $g_msg_id = 0;
my $send_err = 0;
sub handle_send_err {
    $send_err = $!;
}
```

handle_send_err overrides **Msg::handle_send_err** and stores any errors encountered while sending a message. This error code is checked in **rpc**, as shown next. The error handling in both RPC and Msg is definitely not up to snuff and needs a considerable amount of work before it can be reliably used in a production application.

```
sub rpc {
    my $conn = shift;
    my $subname = shift;

    $subname = (caller() . '::' . $subname) unless $subname =~ /:/;
    my $gimme = wantarray ?  'a' : 's';  # Array or scalar
    my $msg_id = ++$g_msg_id;
    my $serialized_msg = freeze ('>', $msg_id, $gimme, @_);
    # Send and Receive
    $conn->send_later ($serialized_msg);
    do {
        Msg->event_loop(1); # Dispatch other messages until we
                            # get a response
    } until (exists $conn->{rcvd}->{$msg_id} || $send_err);
    if ($send_err) {
        die "RPC Error: $send_err";
    }

    # Dequeue message.
    my $rl_retargs = delete $conn->{rcvd}->{$msg_id}; # ref to list
    if (ref($rl_retargs->[0]) eq 'RPC::Error') {
        die ${$rl_retargs->[0]};
    }
    wantarray ? @$rl_retargs : $rl_retargs->[0];
}
```

rpc uses the FreezeThaw module's `freeze` method to bundle the following pieces of information into one big string:

- Name of the remote subroutine. The caller's module is prepended to the subroutine name if it is not fully qualified, which is the behavior expected of a normal subroutine.

- Parameters to the subroutine.

- `wantarray` indicator ($gimme): "s" for scalar, "a" for array.

- Request or response indicator. ">" indicates request, and "<" indicates response. When the receiver gets a message, it should know whether it is a response to an outgoing message or an incoming request that it is expected to evaluate.

- A message identifier. This is to identify the response corresponding to this request.

The `freeze` method accounts for cyclic data structures and objects and returns one ASCII string, which means that we don't have to worry about the size of native integers or doubles or their memory layout (byte order). `Msg->send_later()` is used because it triggers nonblocking I/O where available. The message is really sent only when `event_loop` is called, because it determines when the socket is writable. At the same time, `event_loop` tracks other incoming messages and dispatches them. The count of 1 forces the event loop to return right after dispatching one round of messages, so we can retain control. When the response comes from the remote host, `event_loop` calls `_incoming_msgs`, which decodes it and hangs the return arguments on the connection object. Read on.

Let us now take a look at the receiving side:

```perl
sub new_server {
    my ($pkg, $my_host, $my_port) = @_;
    $pkg->SUPER::new_server($my_host, $my_port,
                            sub {$pkg->_login(@_)});
}
sub _login {
    \&_incoming_msg;
}
```

`new_server`, like `connect`, is a simple wrapper over its Msg counterpart. All incoming connections are unconditionally accepted by default, and messages are directed towards the subroutine `_incoming_msg`, shown next. Calling the `_login` procedure indirectly via `$pkg` gives you the opportunity to subclass RPC and supply your own `_login` procedure and refuse the connection if needed.

```perl
sub _incoming_msg {
    my ($conn, $msg, $err) = @_;
    return if ($err);    # Need better error handling.
    return unless defined($msg);
    my ($dir, $id, @args) = thaw ($msg);
    my ($result, @results);
    if ($dir eq '>') {
        # New request message
        my $gimme = shift @args;
        my $sub_name = shift @args;
        eval {
            no strict 'refs';  # Because we call the subroutine using
                               # a symbolic reference
            if ($gimme eq 'a') {  # Want an array back
                @results = &{$sub_name} (@args);
            } else {
                $result = &{$sub_name} (@args);
            }
        };
        if ($@) {
            $msg = bless \$@, "RPC::Error";
            $msg = freeze('<', $id, $msg);
        } elsif ($gimme eq 'a') {
            $msg = freeze('<', $id, @results);
        } else {
            $msg = freeze('<', $id, $result);
        }
        $conn->send_later($msg);
```

```
      } else {
          # Response to a message we had sent out earlier
          $conn->{rcvd}->{$id} = \@args;
      }
  }
```

`_incoming_msg` is the counterpart to the `rpc` method. It unpacks the message sent by `rpc` and checks the direction (whether it is a request or a response). If it is a request, it calls the required subroutine using a symbolic reference. Notice that depending on the `wantarray` indication, it provides a scalar or vector result parameter. If `eval` reports an error, the `$@` variable is stamped with an RPC::Error module tag and shipped back to the calling process (which invokes `die`).

Resources

The following resources have useful information on messaging and RPC:

1. EventServer

   EventServer, available on CPAN, provides a replacement for Msg's `event_loop` procedure and supports callbacks for file and time-out events.

2. *Unix Network Programming*. W. Richard Stevens. Prentice-Hall, 1990.

3. *Advanced Programming in the Unix Environment*. W. Richard Stevens. Prentice-Hall, 1992.

4. "A Note on Distributed Computing." Jim Waldo, Geoff Wyant, Ann Wollrath, and Sam Kendall. Available at *http://www.sunlabs.com/techrep/1994/abstract-29.html* (Technical Report TR-94-29).

   A very well-written report on the problems associated with RPC (the concept) and distributed computing in general. (In fact, other technical reports at SUN's research labs also make for good reading.)

14

User Interfaces with Tk

> *Programming the X Window System is like trying to find the square root of pi using Roman numerals.*
>
> —Anonymous

In this chapter, we learn how to build graphical user interfaces (GUIs) using one of the most feature-rich and professional-looking toolkits around: the Tk toolkit [1]. We start with a brief tour of most of the Tk widgets as well some of the Tix extension and then learn about *geometry management* (how to arrange widgets on a form). Next, we briefly examine Perl's support for timers, used extensively in Chapter 15, *GUI Example: Tetris*. We then cover event bindings, which allow us to map arbitrary combinations of mouse and keyboard events to callbacks. Finally, we deal with event loop issues similar to the ones we studied in Chapter 12, *Networking with Sockets*.

For the sake of simplicity, this chapter presents small snippets of code to illustrate the widgets and other Tk features in relative isolation; we will rely on the next two chapters to cut a broad swath through all these aspects and to apply them to practical problems.

While we are on the subject of building user interfaces, please do yourself (and your users) a favor by reading Alan Cooper's* excellent and refreshingly opinion-ated book, *About Face: The Essentials of User Interface Design* [3].

Introduction to GUIs, Tk, and Perl/Tk

At the most basic level, all windowing platforms (Apple Macintosh, X Windows, and Microsoft Windows) are very simple. They provide a low-level API to create

---

* Called the "father of Visual Basic."

and manage windows, to report interesting events such as mouse and keyboard events, and to draw graphical elements such as lines, circles, and bitmaps. The problem is that drawing even a simple form takes a considerable amount of code and reading thousands of pages of documentation (literally).

Often-used patterns of GUI code have evolved into *widgets* (called "controls" in the Microsoft Windows world); examples include buttons, scrollbars, and list-boxes. Building a GUI is now a simple matter of launching an interactive form designer and dragging and dropping these ready-made components into a layout of your choice. Object-oriented programming has never been easier.

It turns out that widgets and scripting languages are a perfect match. Widgets have simple interfaces, and form-based GUIs are not performance-critical. Both of these attributes make GUIs a very fertile ground for scripting. Combine that with the fact that GUIs need the most configurability (because that's the part of the application the user deals with, and for the most part, the GUI *is* the application), and you can understand the enormous popularity of tools such as Visual Basic, PowerBuilder, and Hypercard.

On Unix systems, X Windows has been the windowing platform of choice. Several widget toolkits have been built over X: Athena, InterViews, Motif, and Tk. For professional good looks, ease of use, and documentation, you can't beat Tk. To top it all, it is free!

Unlike other widget toolkits, Tk was developed expressly to be driven by a scripting language: Tcl.* Indeed, it can be argued that Tk is the chief reason for Tcl's popularity. There are a lot of people who don't like Tcl as a scripting language but love Tk, and have attempted to adapt it to their favorite scripting language—Scheme, Python, Guile, and, of course, Perl. Malcolm Beattie made the initial attempt to provide a Perl layer that internally used the Tcl interpreter to reach the Tk library.

Nick Ing-Simmons tried a more ambitious approach: he purged Tk of all embedded Tcl code and gave it a generic porting layer to make it easy to add other scripting languages; this effort is called pTk (portable Tk). To this, he added a Perl5 wrapper (with the intention of adding other language wrappers in the future). This combination of pTk and the Perl wrapper module *Tk.pm*, referred to as Perl/Tk, is the subject of this chapter.

Meanwhile, Dr. Ousterhout's team at Sun ported both Tcl and Tk to Microsoft Windows and the Mac, and the Perl/Tk combination has followed suit fairly closely. Other portable GUI options are Tcl/Tk, of course, and Python/Tk (which

---

* Both Tcl and Tk were developed by Dr. John Ousterhout, then at the University of California, Berkeley, and now at Sun Microsystems. See *http://www.sunlabs.com/research/Tcl*.

does not rely on pTk). Microsoft is porting its ActiveX (formerly OLE) and VBA (Visual Basic for Applications) to the Unix environment, so they might be formidable competition soon. The VB toolkit itself doesn't come anywhere close to Perl and Tk's functionality, but the development environment and third-party support is unbeatable. We live in interesting times!

Several new professional-looking widgets have been added to Tk in the form of an extension library called Tix, developed by Ioi Kim Lam. These include balloons (for help messages), notebooks, and spreadsheet-like grid widgets. The good news is that the Perl/Tk distribution contains a Perl layer over this effort also.

Starting with Perl/Tk

All user interfaces developed with Perl/Tk follow this general sequence:

1. Create a *main* window (also known as the *top-level* window).

2. Instantiate one or more widgets, configure them, and arrange them inside the main window. A widget is simply a collection of data and methods that produce some visible element of the interface, like a button or listbox, and make it behave properly when clicked or otherwise manipulated.

3. Start the event loop. After this, the user's actions (events) determine what the program does.

Example 14-1 shows these steps executed in serial order; they result in the simple GUI* shown in Figure 14-1.

Example 14-1. Simple UI Code

```
use Tk;                                          # Slurp the module in.
# ---------------------------------------------------------
# Create a main window
# ---------------------------------------------------------
$top = MainWindow->new();
$top->title ("Simple");
# ---------------------------------------------------------
# Instantiate widgets and arrange them
# ---------------------------------------------------------
$l = $top->Label(text    => 'hello',             # label properties
                 anchor => 'n',                   # anchor text to "north"
                 relief => 'groove',              # border style
                 width  =>  10, height => 3);# 10 chars wide, 3 high.

$l->pack();       # Give it a default place within the main window
# ---------------------------------------------------------
# Sit in an infinite loop dispatching incoming events.
# ---------------------------------------------------------
MainLoop();
```

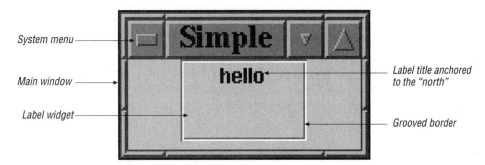

Figure 14-1. Our first Perl/TK screen

This example captures a number of significant Tk concepts (and those of most GUI toolkits in general).

The main window is the outermost shell and contains the resize handles, system menu, and minimize and maximize boxes (also known as *decorations*). An application can have any number of main windows.

The main window is then asked to create a label widget with preconfigured properties. You can change your mind about a widget's properties by invoking the `configure` method on it:

```
$label->configure (text => 'foobar', foreground => 'red');
```

Some widgets, such as Frame and Notebook, are themselves capable of containing other widgets, so the widget hierarchy can be arbitrarily nested. A main window is always at the root of the hierarchy.

The widget's `pack` method is then called to do *geometry management*: the scheme for allocating the position and the width and height for the widget. This call is simply delegated to the widget's *container*, the main window, which calculates the amount of screen real estate to apportion to each contained widget. This is akin to saying "`socks->pack`" and having the suitcase figure out where to put the socks and how much to bunch them up.

Packing is only one of many geometry management schemes available for placing widgets around. Tk supplies a *grid* geometry manager and a *placer*; we'll study both in the section "Geometry Management" later in this chapter.

You can create and pack a widget in one fell swoop, like this:

```
$l = $top->Label (text => 'Oh my')->pack ();
```

---

* Though there's nothing interactive about it—nothing much graphical either, actually.

In most cases, you don't even need to capture the return value unless you plan to invoke methods on that widget later. The typical approach is to set up all the parameters at creation time and call `MainLoop`. We will use this style extensively in this book.

We have already studied the concept of event loops in Chapter 12, and we will have more to say on this topic in the section "Event Loops" later in this chapter. Meanwhile, suffice it to say that `MainLoop` is an "event dispatcher," which returns only when you close the window by double-clicking on the system menu. It is essential to call this function; otherwise, you'll never see the form on your display. (Incidentally, it is essential to call `pack` on a widget; otherwise, you'll never see the widget on the display.)

That's all there is to it. Now it is a simple matter of knowing which widgets are available, what properties they support, and how to hook them up together. Read on!

GUI Forms: The Easy Way

Why write code to create static screens when you can draw them? Stephen Uhler, of the Tcl/Tk team at Sun Microsystems, has written a WYSIWIG GUI builder called SpecTcl (pronounced "spectacle"), with an intention to support multiple languages. This tool has since been customized for Perl/Tk, Java/Tk, and Python/Tk; the resulting variations are called SpecPerl, SpecJava, and SpecPython, respectively. Mark Kvale has done the port for Perl/Tk, and it is available from his home page:* *http://www.keck.ucsf.edu/~kvale/specPerl/*.

Using SpecPerl, you can lay the widgets out visually, set widget-specific properties in corresponding forms, and select colors and fonts from palettes—very convenient.

However, in this chapter (and the next two), we will hand-write GUI code instead of using SpecPerl, for a number of reasons. First, we don't build elaborate forms. Second, most of the examples focus more on the dynamic aspects of Tk, and a GUI builder can only help you build static forms. Third, once you understand this chapter, you'll know what SpecPerl produces.

Widget Tour

This section provides an introduction to most of the interesting widget classes implemented in Tk and Tix and exercises their commonly used configuration

---

* Sun has since started selling SpecTcl commercially, so SpecPerl is necessarily dependent on older (and free) SpecTcl code.

options and methods. To reduce clutter and to allow quick lookups later on (when you know what you are looking for), this extensive set of properties and methods is provided as a separate appendix: Appendix A, *Tk Widget Reference.* Be aware that this chapter, extensive as it is, is only a subset (though a significant subset) of the entire Tk widget feature set. It also does not cover all widgets provided by Tk and Tix. Perl/Tk comes with the entire original well-written and comprehensive Tk documentation.

Widget Properties

Please skim Table A-1 to get an idea of the kind of configurable properties that all widgets share. Most of these properties are ordinary strings or numbers, but three types of properties are worth delving into some detail before we proceed to discussing the actual widgets: fonts, images, and colors.

Fonts

Font values are specified in the XLFD format (X Logical Font Description), which consists of 14 fields separated by hyphens, as shown in Figure 14-2.

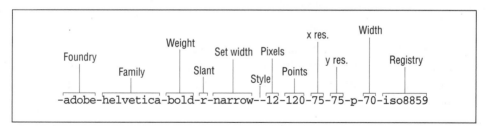

Figure 14-2. Fields in a font

Fortunately, we don't have to remember the purpose of most of these fields. Any of these fields can have the wildcard "*" or "?", but it is important to get the number of hyphens right. On the X Windows system, there are two utilities, a graphical one called *fontsel,* and a batch utility called *xlsfonts,* that list all combinations of these fields available, so it is a simple matter of picking one. Essentially, you have to look only for the foundry, family, weight, slant, and points fields; ignore the rest of the fields. Note that "points" is in tenths of points, so 120 means a 12-point font. The slant can be "i" for italic or "r" for regular. To set the font of a widget, you configure its font property:

```
$label->configure (
    font => '-adobe-helvetica-medium-r-normal--8-80-75-75-p-46-*-1');
```

Once Perl/Tk is ported to the Windows and Mac, font values can be specified in either the XLFD format or the simpler Windows style: `Helvetica 24 bold`. The former format will continue to be supported on all platforms.

Images

Some widgets, such as buttons and labels, can display two-color *bitmaps* or multi-color *pixmaps*. Because the same bitmap or image can be used to decorate more than one widget, Tk considers them to be objects that are rendered in one or more places. That is, the image object holds the data, and the widgets know how to render them in their own space. Hence, two steps are involved in displaying a bitmap or a pixmap on a widget: create an image object given an image file, and configure the widget's bitmap or pixmap property with the image object.

Depending on the type of image file you have, you have to make one of three calls to create the appropriate type of image object:

```
#For XBM (X Bitmaps) only
$image = $label->Bitmap(file => 'face.xbm');

#For XPM (X Pixmaps only)
$image = $label->Pixmap(file => 'smiley.xpm');

#For GIF or PPM (Portable pixmap) formats, use the Photo constructor
$image = $label->Photo(file => 'frown.gif');
```

Now you can change the label's image easily:

```
$label->configure (image => $image);
```

Note that if the image is a bitmap, you must use the "bitmap" option, and if it is an XPM or GIF files, use the "image" property. In the bitmap case, the "`fore-ground`" and "`background`" options dictate the two colors; for images, the file supplies its own colors.

Colors

Colors can be given symbolic names such as "red" and "yellow." The library directory in an X installation has a file called *rgb.txt* that enumerates all the available symbolic names. Alternatively, you can give RGB values in the form #RGB, #RRGGBB, #RRRGGGBBB, or #RRRRGGGGBBBB, where each R, G, or B represents one hexadecimal digit of red, green, or blue intensity, respectively.

Our detour is now complete; let us briefly visit Tk's and Tix's widgets.

Labels and Buttons

The standard widget properties described in Table A-1 pretty much cover everything that labels have to offer. They are also fairly self-explanatory, so we will not say more about them.

Buttons are labels with one additional property—the "command" option, which allows you to associate a callback with a button click. The next example shows the callback procedure, `change_label`, toggling the label of the widget:

```
use Tk;
$top = MainWindow->new();
$button = $top->Button(text    => 'Start',
                       command => \&change_label);
$button->pack();
MainLoop();
sub change_label {                    # Create
    $button->cget('text') eq "Start"        ?
        $button->configure(text => 'Stop') :
        $button->configure(text => 'Start');
}
```

The `cget` method retrieves the value of a configurable property.

The callback can instead be a closure, like this (omitting the rest of the boiler-plate code):

```
$button = $top->Button(
            text    => 'Start',
            command => sub {
                          $button->cget('text') eq "Start"    ?
                          $button->configure(text => 'Stop') :
                          $button->configure(text => 'Start')
                      }
}
```

A third way of configuring the **command** property is to give it an anonymous array whose first element is the callback procedure parameter. The other elements of this array are passed to the callback when it is invoked:

```
$button->configure (command => [\&change_label, "new label"]);
```

We'll use this style in application-defined scrolling later in this chapter.

Radiobuttons and Checkbuttons

A radiobutton is a widget that displays a textual string, bitmap, or image and a diamond called an indicator (see Figure 14-3). Radiobuttons, like buttons, support the "command" option. Unlike buttons, however, radiobuttons are typically used in groups to give the user an option to select one of many choices. For this reason, a radiobutton provides two properties called **variable** and **value** for synchronizing with the others in its group so that only one indicator is "on." If you click on a radiobutton, that enables its indicator and changes its associated variable's value to its own value property. Conversely, if that variable's value is changed, the radiobutton checks to see whether it matches its own **value** property; if so, it turns its own indicator on. As you may have guessed, the tie facility is used internally to monitor changes to the variable.

Figure 14-3. Radiobutton example

The following example builds a radiobutton group. $bev is the synchronizing variable.

```
$bev = "coffee";                           # Starting value
$coffee = $top->Radiobutton ( variable => \$bev,
                              text      => 'Coffee',
                              value     => 'coffee');

$tea    = $top->Radiobutton ( variable => \$bev,
                              text      => 'Tea',
                              value     => 'tea');

$milk   = $top->Radiobutton ( variable => \$bev,
                              text      => 'Milk',
                              value     => 'milk');
# Lay out the radiobuttons
$coffee->pack (side => 'left');
$tea->pack   (side => 'left');
$milk->pack  (side => 'left');
```

Because the radiobuttons have different values and because they share the same variable, we ensure that only one indicator is on at any time.

Please refer to Table A-3 for more radiobutton properties and methods.

A checkbutton is very similar to a radiobutton. It has a square indicator that toggles depending on its associated variable's value. Unlike a radiobutton, toggling its value is not expected to change some other checkbutton's value, though you can easily arrange it that way. A checkbutton is used where you want the user to be able to select all applicable options.

Canvas

A canvas widget implements structured graphics. It provides methods to create and manipulate graphic *items* such as circles, rectangles, arcs, lines, bitmaps, polylines, and text. It even allows you to embed other widgets and treat them as ordinary canvas items.

Unlike Java's Abstract Windowing Toolkit's support for canvases (and pretty much every other GUI toolkit I know of), Tk's canvas items are objects in their own right: they support configurable properties just like widgets and allow these properties to be applied to individual items or to entire named groups of items. They can also be associated with callbacks. (You can say, in effect, "if the mouse passes over this circle, call procedure foo.")

Canvas items are different from widgets in that while each widget gets its own window on the X server, a canvas item does not. Also, unlike widgets, canvas items do not take part in geometry management (they cannot be resized by their container). It has always been unclear to me why the toolkit chose to expose this distinction to the user. In the InterViews toolkit (a C++ based X Windows library, later available as "Fresco"), for example, widgets and structured graphics all inherit from a generic graphic object called a *glyph*. This feels like a much cleaner design. On the other hand, I am thankful that such a fine implementation for structured graphics is available for free, with nice documentation to boot, so my quibble is minor in the larger scheme of things.

To draw a line inside a canvas widget, you invoke the **Canvas::create** method:

```
$top = MainWindow->new();
# first create a canvas widget
$canvas = $top->Canvas(width => 200, height => 100)->pack();

# Create line inside the canvas
$id = $canvas->create ('line',
                       10, 10, 100, 100,  # from x0,y0  to x1, y1
                       fill => 'red');  # fill color of object
```

The first parameter to the **create** command is the type of canvas item, and the rest of the parameters depend on this item. **create** returns an identifier that can be used to refer to that object later on. For example, you can update the coordinates of the object using the **coords** method:

```
$canvas->coords ($id, 10, 100);
```

All coordinates in Tk are in reference to the top-left corner. The x coordinate increases from left to right, and the y coordinate increases from top to bottom.

You can move the object relative to its current position using **move**:

```
$canvas->move ($id, 15, 23); # 15 and 23 represent x and y offsets
```

Canvas items can be configured using the **itemconfigure** method; Table A-5 shows the properties and methods for each type of item, as well as the canvas widget as a whole.

One of the canvas widget's most convenient features is its ability to tag one or more objects with a string identifier. An object can be tagged with as many strings as you want. The tag string **all** represents all the canvas's objects. You can tag an object at creation time or with the **addtag** method. The tag **current** represents the item over which the mouse is currently hovering. All canvas methods that accept an item ID also accept a string tag instead. For example, to move all objects labeled "bunch" 10 pixels to the right, do this:

```
$canvas->move('bunch', 10, 0); # xoffset = 10, yoffset = 0
```

We will exploit this property extensively in Chapter 15.

Example 14-2 shows a set of circles whose centers are drawn along an Archimedean spiral (see Figure 14-4). An Archimedean spiral is defined by the equation $r = a\theta$, where r, the radius (as depicted by the lines) is proportionally dependent on the angle, θ. For added visual effect, the sizes of the circles are also made proportional to the angle.

Example 14-2. Drawing an Archimedean Spiral

```
use Tk;
$top = MainWindow->new();
$canvas = $top->Canvas(width => 300, height => 245)->pack();
# Draw a set of circles along an archimedean spiral
# The centers of these circles move along the spiral
# (radius of spiral = constant * theta)

$origin_x = 110; $origin_y = 70;            # origin of the spiral
$PI = 3.1415926535;
$circle_radius = 5;                         # radius of the first circle
$path_radius = 0;

for ($angle = 0; $angle <= 180;
     $path_radius += 7, $circle_radius += 3, $angle += 10)
{
    # offset of path coordinates: r.cos(θ) and r.sin(θ)
    # sin() and cos() like their angles in radians (degrees*π/90)
    $path_x = $origin_x + $path_radius * cos ($angle * $PI / 90);
    $path_y = $origin_y - $path_radius * sin ($angle * $PI / 90);
    # path_x and path_y are the coordinates of the center of the new
    # circle. Canvas::create likes top-left and bottom-right corners
    $canvas->create ('oval',
            $path_x - $circle_radius,
            $path_y - $circle_radius,
            $path_x + $circle_radius,
            $path_y + $circle_radius,
            fill => 'yellow');
    $canvas->create ('line',
            $origin_x, $origin_y,
            $path_x, $path_y,
            fill => 'slategray');

}

MainLoop();
```

Text and Entry

The text widget displays one or more lines of text and allows you to edit the text. (Its default key bindings are those of Emacs, so, ahem, those of you still using *vi...*) The widget is powerful enough to address the presentation needs of a web

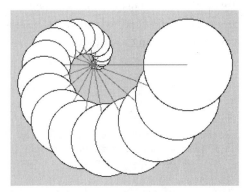

Figure 14-4. Structured graphics using canvas

browser, and several projects have done precisely that. The Perl/Tk distribution comes with an implementation of a web browser called *tkweb*, and Guido Von Rossum, Python's creator, has used Python and Tk for a web browser called *Grail*, capable of executing Python applets.

In this section, we will take a brief look at the text widget's capabilities, and in Chapter 16, *GUI Example: Man Page Viewer*, we will study it in greater depth and build an application based on it.

Inserting text at absolute positions

When you want to programmatically insert a piece of text at some position or select a range, you need to specify one or more indices. An index is a string such as "2.5," which means line 2, column 5 (line numbers start from 1, and columns start from 0). The following code creates a text widget and inserts a string at that position:

```
$t = $top->Text(width => 80, height => 10)->pack();
$t->insert('Sample', '2.5');
```

Inserting text at logical positions

The text widget supports the notion of a *mark*, a user-defined name assigned to a single position within the text widget. This position refers to the gap between two characters, not to a line and column pair. This makes it convenient to insert a character at a mark. A marked position is a logical entity; it does not change with insertion or deletion. The widget supports built-in mark names such as **insert** (where the insert cursor is), **current** (the character closest to the mouse pointer), **wordend** (end of the word on which the insert cursor is placed), **end** (the end of the insert cursor's line), and so on. These mark names can be used in place of the row and column numbers mentioned earlier:

```
$t->insert("Sample", "end");              # Insert text at end
```

Please take a look at the text preceding Table A-6 for details on index specifiers. The example code in the following sections creates a text widget and inserts strings at different locations using different types of indexing identifiers.

Insertion with relative indexing

Indices can also be relative to a base index. For example:

```
$t->insert('Sample',
           'insert +5'); # 5 chars after insert cursor's posiion.
$t->insert('Sample', 'insert linestart'); # go to insert position,
                                           # and then that line's start
```

Using tags to change properties of text ranges

The widget supports the concept of *tags* or tagged styles, which are user-defined strings representing a list of text properties (font, color, stippling style, and so on). Consider

```
$text->tagConfigure('foo',
                    foreground => 'yellow', background => 'red');
```

The string "foo" can be applied to one or more contiguous ranges of text within that widget, like this:

```
$text->tagAdd('foo', '3.5', '3.7');
```

This highlights the stretch of text on line 3, character indices 5 through 7. The indices specifying the range can also be absolute or relative mark positions. For example, the following snippet changes the properties of the line on which the insert cursor is positioned:

```
$text->tagAdd('foo', 'insert linestart', 'insert lineend');
```

Multiple tags can apply to overlapping ranges of text; conversely, one tag can be applied to many ranges. All text widgets support a special tag called `sel` that reflects the current range of selected text. You can insert new text and apply a section by supplying the tag name as the third parameter to insert:

```
$t->insert('Sample', '3.5','foo');
```

The text widget allows you to embed any other widget and treat it as a single character, which means that you can have buttons and listboxes in your text moving around as you insert more text.

The entry widget

For single-line text entries, Perl/Tk provides a widget called Entry, which does not support tags, marks, or embedded windows. It is essentially a lightweight version of the Text widget.

Perl/Tk (not the native Tk) also provides a widget called TextUndo, which is a subclass of the Text widget. It provides an unlimited undo facility (alas, there's no "redo"; you cannot undo an undo!) and has methods to load and save text from and to files. This widget is not part of the original Tcl/Tk distribution.

Text widget and ties

The text widget supports the `TIEHANDLE` and `print` methods, allowing it to be used as a module to simulate filehandles. Here's how you can use this facility to redirect filehandle activity to the text widget:

```
use Tk;
my $mw = MainWindow->new;              # Create a top-level window
my $t  = $mw->Scrolled('Text');        # Create a scrolled text window
$t->pack(-expand => 1,
         -fill => 'both');             # Configure it
tie (*TEXT, 'Tk::Text',$t);            # tie the filehandle and widget
print TEXT "Hi there\n";               # This shows up on the widget
```

Listbox

A listbox displays a list of strings, one per line, as shown in Figure 14-5. All strings have the same display characteristics. If you want to mix and match different fonts and colors, you can write a simple wrapper over the text widget and simulate a fancy listbox.

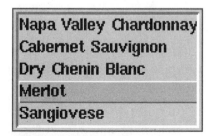

Figure 14-5. Listbox showing a choice of wines

The default bindings of a listbox select and deselect items, but if you want something extra, such as special handling for a mouse double-click, it is your responsibility to bind it to a function of your choice. Selection modes are "single," "browse" (default), "multiple," and "extended." Single or browse mode indicates that only one element can be selected at any time. Browse mode also allows you to drag the selection with button 1. In multiple mode, you can select any number of elements; selecting and deselecting one doesn't affect any other. The extended mode allows you to select multiple elements by clicking and dragging, but a single click deselects the previous selection before selecting the current element.

Like the text widget, the listbox has various ways of identifying list positions in addition to the index; examples include **end** and **active** (where the location cursor is poised). Table A-8 describes these indices as well as the listbox's properties and methods. Example 14-3 creates the listbox shown in Figure 14-5.

Example 14-3. Listbox with Callbacks

```
use Tk;
$top = MainWindow->new();
$wine_list = $top->Listbox("width" => 20, "height" => 5
                          )->pack();
$wine_list->insert('end', # Insert the following list at end
                "Napa Valley Chardonnay", "Cabernet Sauvignon",
                "Dry Chenin Blanc", "Merlot", "Sangiovese" );
$wine_list->bind('<Double-1>', \&buy_wine);
sub buy_wine {
    my $wine = $wine_list->get('active');
    return if (!$wine);  # Return if no list item is active
    print "Ah, '$wine'. An excellent choice\n";
    # Remove the wine from the inventory
    $wine_list->delete('active');
}
MainLoop();
```

The listbox does not provide a property such as **command**, so we have to use the more general method, **bind**, to set up a binding between a double mouse-click and a user-defined subroutine. More details on this technique are given in the section "Event Bindings."

Frame

Frame widgets are fairly uninteresting widgets, but come in very handy when you want sophisticated widget layouts or are creating composite widgets.

If you have a complex GUI form, you are better off dividing the screen into major chunks, each with a specific function, and putting each chunk into its own frame. Then at the top level, you can arrange and rearrange these chunks easily. There is more on this in the section "Geometry Management" later in this chapter. Frame widgets, being containers, can be asked to create other "fundamental" widgets such as buttons, text, and scrollbars.

Menus

The term "menu" commonly refers to an arrangement whereby a user clicks on a menu button and a collection of label or button widgets pops up. Menus come in one of three configurations: pulldown menu, option menu, or popup menu.

Tk provides a MenuButton widget, which, when clicked, can be made to pop up a Menu widget. The Menu widget is just a container of the menu item widgets; it does not refer to the whole arrangement. We'll use the difference in font styles to distinguish between the concept of menu and the Menu widget. Figure 14-6 shows the components.

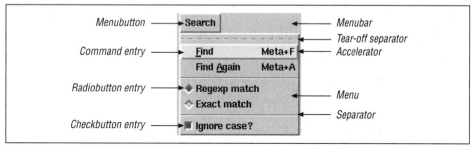

Figure 14-6. Pulldown menu and menubutton

To construct a menu, you need to go through the following steps:

1. Create a *menu bar* to hold the MenuButton widget. The menu bar is an ordinary Frame widget.

2. Create one or more MenuButton widgets and pack them into the menu bar.

3. Ask the MenuButton widgets to create and manage menu entry widgets.

The properties and API of the MenuButton and Menu widgets are listed in Tables A-9 and A-10, respectively. Example 14-4 shows how the menu in Figure 14-6 is created.

Example 14-4. Pulldown Menu for Text Search

```
use Tk;
$top = MainWindow->new();
# Use a Frame widget as a container for menubuttons
$menu_bar = $top->Frame()->pack(side => 'top');

#Search menu button
$search_mb = $menu_bar->Menubutton(text       => 'Search',
                                   relief      => 'raised',
                                   borderwidth => 2,
                                   )->pack(side => 'left',
                                           padx => 2
                                           );
# "Find" menubutton
$search_mb->command(label       => 'Find',
                    accelerator => 'Meta+F',
                    underline   => 0,
                    command     => sub {print "find\n"}
                    );
```

Example 14-4. Pulldown Menu for Text Search (continued)

```perl
# "Find Again" menubutton
$search_mb->command(label      => 'Find Again',
                    accelerator => 'Meta+A',
                    underline   => 5,
                    command     => sub {print "find again\n"}
                    );

$search_mb->separator();
$match_type = 'regexp';    # Default search is by regexp.
$case_type = 1;            # Ignore case, by default (enable checkbutton)
# Regexp match
$search_mb->radiobutton(label    => 'Regexp match',
                        value    => 'regexp',
                        variable => \$match_type);
# Exact match
$search_mb->radiobutton(label    => 'Exact match',
                        value    => 'exact',
                        variable => \$match_type);
$search_mb->separator();
# Ignore case
$search_mb->checkbutton(label    => 'Ignore case?',
                        variable => \$case_type);

MainLoop();
```

This example invokes methods such as **command**, **separator**, **checkbutton**, and **cascade** on the MenuButton widget (**$search_mb**). Curiously enough, these methods actually belong to the Menu widget's interface, not the MenuButton's (see Tables A-9 and A-10). For convenience, Perl/Tk's MenuButton accepts these commands and silently delegates them to its associated Menu widget.

Normally, the menu entries are stacked in the order in which they are created, but you can specify the index position explicitly using the **add** method. The indexing syntax is similar to that of the listbox and is described in Appendix A. We'll use this method to dynamically create menus in Chapter 16.

Scrollbars and Scrolling

Although scrollbars are full-fledged widgets, they are seldom used by themselves; they always control associated widgets. Because of this close association, Perl/Tk provides a convenience function called **Scrolled** that wraps scrollbars around a widget of your choice without having to explicitly create, size, and pack them. The following example creates a scrolled listbox:

```perl
$scrolled_list = $top->Scrolled('Listbox', listbox options,
                                scrollbars => 'se');
```

Internally, this creates a Frame widget, horizontal and vertical scrollbars (if required), and a listbox; packs all of them together; and returns the reference to the Frame widget (the container). Isn't that nice? In fact, for the most common case of scrolled listboxes and scrolled text boxes, Perl/Tk provides convenient methods called `ScrlListBox` and `ScrlText`, respectively, reducing your typing even further:

```
$scrolled_list = $top->ScrlListBox(listbox options);
```

This is typically all you need to know about scrolling, and you can safely go on to the "Scale" section without loss of continuity.

Custom scrolling

There are times, though, when you want to handle your own scrolling. For example, suppose you have three listboxes and want to synchronize their scrolling. This means that you need to arrange to have the scrollbar send messages to all three widgets whenever its slider is moved. The subtle issue here is that the inverse also holds true: the widgets also should send messages when they are themselves scrolled by using other means. For example, if you click on one listbox and drag the cursor, the listbox will scroll its own contents. It must then make sure that the scrollbar and the other two listboxes are in sync. In other words, the scrollbar is not always in the driver's seat; it is very much a "I'll scroll you, you scroll me" kind of relationship.

As Table A-11 shows, there is no explicit property tying a scrollbar to a widget, but the scrollbar does have a callback property called `command` that is notified when the slider is moved. Meanwhile, it so happens that all widgets that are scrollable (listboxes, text widgets, frames, and canvases) support two methods called `xview` and `yview` (Table A-12), which tell the scrollable widget what part of its contents to show in its window. Hence, to make a scrollbar send a message to a widget to scroll itself, we configure the scrollbar's `command` property like this:

```
$scrollbar->configure (command => [N$widget]);
```

The scrollbar automatically calls the specified method (`xview` or `yview`) on the widget. How does the widget know where to scroll to? Ah, unbeknownst to you, the scrollbar supplies some arguments to the `yview` invocation, so internally, the message from the scrollbar to the widget might look like this:

```
$widget->yview('moveto', 30);
```

This tells the widget to align its contents such that the top line or pixel represents the 30% mark.

Now let us look in the other direction, where the widget informs the scrollbar.

All scrollable widgets support two methods called `xscrollcommand` and `yscrollcommand`, which should be set up to call the scrollbar's `set` method as follows:

```
$listbox->configure ('yscrollcommand', [N$scrollbar]);
```

Figure 14-7 shows this symbiotic relationship. The details of the commands and properties described above are provided in Tables A-11 and A-12.

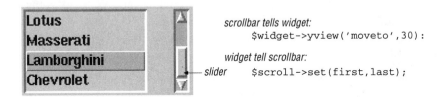

Figure 14-7. Interaction between a scrollbar and an associated widget (a listbox)

Note that in this example, you don't have to make each listbox drive the other two listboxes. It is enough if each of them drives the scrollbar, because the scrollbar is tied to the other two.

Example 14-5 puts the various configuration commands together for one list.

Example 14-5. Setting up a Scrollbar and Listbox to Scroll Each Other

```perl
use Tk;
$top = MainWindow->new();
$car_list = $top->Listbox("width" => 15, "height" => 4,
                     )->pack(side => 'left',
                             padx => 10);

$car_list->insert('end', # Insert at end, the following list
             "Acura", "BMW", "Ferrari", "Lotus", "Maserati",
             "Lamborghini", "Chevrolet"
             );

# Create scrollbar, and inform it about the listbox
$scroll = $top->Scrollbar(orient  => 'vertical',
                     width   => 10,
                     command => ['yview', $car_list]
                    )->pack(side => 'left',
                            fill => 'y',
                            padx => 10);

# Inform listbox about the scrollbar
$car_list->configure(yscrollcommand => ['set', $scroll]);
MainLoop();
```

Scale

The Scale widget is like a thermometer. It displays tick marks along a horizontal or vertical "trough" and provides a slider inside the trough that can be moved programmatically or manually (with the mouse or keyboard). Table A-13 shows the scale's properties and methods.

Figure 14-8 shows two scales displaying Celsius and Fahrenheit values (corresponding to 0–100 degrees Celsius). The scales are coordinated so that a movement of one slider causes a corresponding movement in the other.

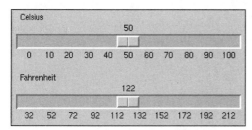

Figure 14-8. Coordinated Celsuis and Fahrenheit scales

Example 14-6 shows how you might implement it.

Example 14-6. Celsius/Fahrenheit Conversion Shown Using Two Scale Widgets

```
use Tk;
# Show Celsius/Fahrenheit equivalence using scales.
$top = MainWindow->new();

$celsius_val = 50;
compute_fahrenheit();
#--------------------- CELSIUS Scale -----------------------------
$top->Scale(orient       => 'horizontal',
            from         => 0,                   # From 0 degrees C
            to           => 100,                 # To 100 degrees C
            tickinterval => 10,
            label        => 'Celsius',
            font         => '-adobe-helvetica-medium-r-normal' .
                            . '--10-100-75-75-p-56-iso8859-1',
            length       => 300,                 # in pixels
            variable     => \$celsius_val,       # global variable
            command      => \&compute_fahrenheit # Change fahrenheit
            )->pack(side => 'top',
                    fill => 'x');
#--------------------- FAHRENHEIT Scale --------------------------
$top->Scale(orient       => 'horizontal',
            from         => 32,                  # From 32 degrees F
            to           => 212,                 # To 212  degrees F
            tickinterval => 20,                  # tick every 20 deg.
            label        => 'Fahrenheit',
            font         => '-adobe-helvetica-medium-r-normal'
                            . '--10-100-75-75-p-56-iso8859-1',
```

Example 14-6. Celsius/Fahrenheit Conversion Shown Using Two Scale Widgets (continued)

```
        length      => 300,              # In pixels
        variable    => \$fahrenheit_val,  # global variable
        command     => \&compute_celsius  # Change celsius
    )->pack(side => 'top',
            fill => 'x',
            pady => '5');

sub compute_celsius {
    # The Celsius scale's slider automatically moves when this
    # $celsius_val is changed
    $celsius_val = ($fahrenheit_val - 32)*5/9;
}

sub compute_fahrenheit {
    $fahrenheit_val = ($celsius_val * 9 / 5) + 32;
}

MainLoop();
```

In this example, the Celsius scale calls `compute_fahrenheit()` when its slider is moved. This procedure changes `$fahrenheit_val`, which is associated with the Fahrenheit scale. As you can see, using the `command` and `variable` properties is typically enough to work with scales. You don't have to invoke the `set()` method explicitly.

HList

Hierarchical data, like filesystem structures or organization charts, can be represented with the hierarchical list widget, HList. Each entry is indented one level to the right of its parent entry. HList optionally draws branches and can associate icons or other widgets with each entry. An entry is identified not by its index (as the listbox does) but by its "entry path," which is like a file pathname with a separator character of your choice. Table A-14 describes some of the interesting properties and methods of this widget.

Example 14-7 builds a directory browser using HList. Double-clicking on a directory entry expands or collapses the directory and changes the icon correspondingly.

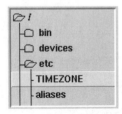

Figure 14-9. HList widget used for a directory browsing application

Example 14-7 shows one of way of building the browser in Figure 14-9. Pay particular attention to the code that opens and sets bitmaps and the part that changes the shape of the cursor when it is doing its work.

Example 14-7. Directory Browser Built Using an HList Widget

```perl
use Tk;
require Tk::HList;
$top = MainWindow->new();
$hlist = $top->Scrolled('HList',
                           drawbranch    => 1,    # yes, draw branches
                           separator     => '/', # filename separator
                           indent        => 15,   # pixels
                           command       => \&show_or_hide_dir);
$hlist->pack(fill    => 'both',expand => 'y');
# Read bitmap files and create "image" objects.
$open_folder_bitmap   = $top->Bitmap(file => './open_folder.xbm');
$closed_folder_bitmap = $top->Bitmap(file => './folder.xbm');

# Start with the root directory
show_or_hide_dir("/");
MainLoop();


#----------------------------------------------------------------------
sub show_or_hide_dir {    # Called when an entry is double-clicked
    my $path = $_[0];
    return if (! -d $path);  # Not a directory.
    if ($hlist->info('exists', $path)) {
        # Toggle the directory state.
        # We know that a directory is open if the next entry is a
        # a substring of the current path
        $next_entry = $hlist->info('next', $path);
        if (!$next_entry || (index ($next_entry, "$path/") == -1)) {
            # Nope. open it
            $hlist->entryconfigure($path, image => $open_folder_bitmap);
            add_dir_contents($path);
        } else {
            # Yes. Close it by changing the icon, and deleting its children
            $hlist->entryconfigure($path,
                                    image => $closed_folder_bitmap);
            $hlist->delete('offsprings', $path);
        }
    } else {
        die "'$path' is not a directory\n" if (! -d $path);
        $hlist->add($path, itemtype => 'imagetext',
                          image    => $icons{"open"},
                          text     => $path );
        add_dir_contents($path);
    }
}

sub add_dir_contents {
    my $path = $_[0];
    my $oldcursor = $top->cget('cursor'); # Remember current cursor, and
```

Example 14-7. Directory Browser Built Using an HList Widget (continued)

```
$top->configure(cursor => 'watch'); # change cursor to watch
$top->update();
my @files = glob "$path/*";
foreach $file (@files) {
    $file =~ s|//|/|g;
    ($text = $file) =~ s|^.*/||g;
    if (-d $file) {
        $hlist->add($file, itemtype => 'imagetext',
                    image => $icons{"closed"}, text => $text);
    } else {
        $hlist->add($file, itemtype => 'text',
                    text => $text);
    }
}
$top->configure(cursor => $oldcursor);
}
```

That concludes our tour of Tk and Tix's widgets. Please look at the Tk documentation for the other widgets and the *contrib* directory in the Tk distribution for contributed widgets. Now let us look at the rest of the facilities provided by Tk: geometry management, timers, event bindings, and event loops.

Geometry Management

You've already seen the purpose of the **pack** method. The name of the game is "geometry management," the art of arranging widgets on the screen and specifying a policy for rearranging themselves when the screen is resized. Tk supports three types of geometry managers: placer, packer, and grid. The placer is the simplest of the lot. Like Motif's Bulletin Board widget or Visual Basic's geometry management policy, you have to specify the *x* and *y* coordinates of each widget. I'll just refer you to the Tk documentation for more details on the placer.

Packer

The packer, like Motif's Form widget, is a powerful constraint-based geometry manager. The packer is not an object; it is simply the algorithm implemented by the **pack()** method. In other words, the call **$widget->pack()** is a request to the widget to pack itself in the next available space inside its containing widget.

When you pack a suitcase, you typically start at one end and, for every item, proceed to fill in the remaining space. The packer works exactly like this, but there's one crucial difference. Once it sticks a widget onto an edge of a container widget, it slices off that entire edge and takes it off the remaining available space. Figure 14-10 illustrates the packing algorithm.

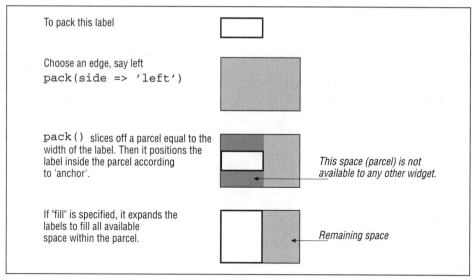

To pack this label

Choose an edge, say left
`pack(side => 'left')`

`pack()` slices off a parcel equal to the width of the label. Then it positions the label inside the parcel according to 'anchor'.

This space (parcel) is not available to any other widget.

If "fill" is specified, it expands the labels to fill all available space within the parcel.

Remaining space

Figure 14-10. Packing algorithm

In this figure, if the **side** were specified as **top** or **bottom**, the *height* of the label would dictate the height of the sliced parcel.

You can use **pack** to accomplish three things:

- Specify the order in which a widget is considered for packing.

  The order in which you invoke **pack** determines the packing order, which in turn determines the amount of available space that a widget has access to. When the container is resized, the packing algorithm is run again in the same order.

- Specify how it fills up its parcel.

  This option is dictated by the **fill** value: **x** (expand the widget in the *x* direction to fill up the width of the parcel), **y** (expand to fill up the height), **both**, or **none**. The **ipadx** and **ipady** options reserve some internal padding space around the widget, so the allocated parcel can be made that much bigger than the dimensions required by the widget. The **anchor** option specifies the edge or corner of the parcel to which the widget sticks. It defaults to "**center**".

- Specify what should be done with the remaining space left over in the parent after all widgets have been inserted.

  This is provided by the **expand** parameter. Normally, the last widget to be inserted gets the rest of the available space, and it can "fill" up that space. But if other widgets have been packed with an expand value of "y" (yes), then any extra horizontal space is equally divided up among all widgets that have specified this option and whose side is left or right. Similarly, extra vertical space is divided between all widgets that have the values "top" or "bottom." Note that the packing algorithm can never overlap widgets.

You might be wondering how to insert three widgets on the left side (as shown in Figure 14-11) if the first widget to be inserted takes over the entire side.

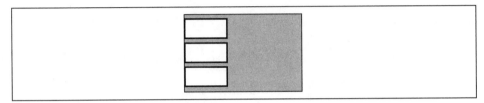

Figure 14-11. Packing three widgets to the left

The only way to solve this problem is to create a frame widget and stick it in the left side of the top window. Since a frame is a container for other widgets, these three widgets can be packed inside this frame, as shown in the following code:

```
$frame->pack(-side => 'left', -fill => 'y', -expand => 'y');
# Now create buttons b1, b2 and b3 as children of frame, and
# pack top to bottom
$b1 = $frame->Button (-text => 'Oh   ')->pack();
$b2 = $frame->Button (-text => 'Hello')->pack();
$b3 = $frame->Button (-text => 'There')->pack();
```

pack inserts the widgets from top to bottom, by default.

Alternatively, you might just find it easier to work with the grid geometry manager.

Grid

The grid method tells the widget to use the grid geometry manager. All child widgets within one parent must use the same geometry manager, but you are free to use any geometry manager of your choice for a given combination of a parent and its contained widgets or for widgets nested within each child.

The grid geometry manager allows you to slot widgets in rows and columns, much like HTML's table tag. The maximum width of any widget in a column determines the width of that column, and the height of a row is determined by the maximum height of any widget. This is how you use gridded geometry management:

```
$button->grid (row => 0, column => 0);
```

This command puts the button on the top-left corner.

Like HTML's tables, a widget can be made to span any number of rows and columns, using the `rowspan` and `columnspan` options. The widget still belongs to the row and column specified by "`row`" and "`column`" but straddles the required span of columns and/or rows, as shown in the following example:

```
$button->grid(row => 1, col => 2,
              columnspan => 2, sticky => 'ns');
```

The button in this example straddles two columns but doesn't use up all the space. The `sticky` option instructs the grid to make the widget stick to the north and south walls of the cell in this case. If you configure it as "`nsew`," the widget is stretched to fill the entire cell. By default, the widget is centered inside the parcel and occupies only as much space as it requires. Like the packer, the grid also understands the `ipadx` and `ipady` options.

Timers

Tk provides a lightweight timer mechanism that can call back a procedure after a specified delay (specified in milliseconds). To create one-shot timers, use the `after` method on any widget; for repeating timers, use `repeat`. In the following example, the button changes its label when pressed and resets its label after 300 milliseconds:

```
$button->configure (text => 'hello',
                    command => \&change_title));
sub change_title {
    my ($old_title) = $button->cget('text');
    $button->configure (text => 'Ouch');
    $button->after (300,
                    sub {$button->configure(text => $old_title)});
}
```

We will use `after` extensively in Chapter 15 for animation.

Both `after` and `repeat` return timer objects. Because these mechanisms are quite efficient and lightweight (unlike using `alarm()` and `SIGALRM`), you can have a large number of timers. To cancel a timer, use `cancel`:

```
$timer = $button->after(100, sub {print "foo"});
$timer->cancel();
```

Tk's time-out facility, unlike `SIGALRM`, is not preemptive. It requires that control return to the event loop before it can check if it is time for the next timer to fire. A long subroutine can delay the timed event.

Event Bindings

An event binding associates a callback function with any type of event. You have already seen instances of event bindings—the button widget's **command** property arranges for a user-defined procedure to be called on a mouse click, for example. The **bind()** command provides a more general (and hence low-level) access to the most fundamental events such as keyboard and mouse button presses and releases. (A mouse click is a press and release, so we are talking about really low-level events here.) Other "interesting" event types include mouse motion, the mouse pointer entering or leaving a window, and windows getting mapped or resized on the display. All widgets themselves rely on the **bind** method for their own functionality, and allow you to create extra bindings yourself. The bound procedure executes if the event you're tracking happens inside that widget or is related to that widget (such as a window resize).

The syntax of bind is as follows:

```
$widget->bind(event sequence, callback);
```

The event sequence is a string containing a sequence of basic events, with each basic event contained in angle brackets. Examples of event sequences are as follows:

```
"<a>"                    # Key "a" pressed (Control/shift/meta not
                         # pressed)
"<Control-a>"            # Control and a pressed
"<Escape> <Control-a>"   # Two-event sequence
"<Button1>"              # Mouse button 1 clicked
"<Button1-Motion>"       # Mouse moves while Button 1 is down
```

A single event (within angle brackets) has the following generic syntax:

```
"<modifier-modifier...-modifier-type-detail>"
```

Examples of *modifiers* are **Control**, **Meta**, **Alt**, **Shift**, **Button1** (or **B1**), **Button2**, **Double** (double click), and **Triple**. The modifier **Any** is a wildcard—all possible modifiers (including none of them) match the basic event.

The *type* of the event is one of **KeyPress**, **KeyRelease**, **ButtonPress** (or **Button**), **ButtonRelease**, **Enter**, **Leave**, and **Motion**.

For keyboard event specifications, the *detail* is a textual string describing the exact key. X Windows calls this a *keysym*. For printable ASCII characters, the keysym is the printed character itself. Other examples of keysyms are **Enter**, **Right**, **Pickup**, **Delete**, **BackSpace**, **Escape**, **Help**, **F1** (function key), and so on.

The most common event types are key presses and button clicks, so Tk allows an abbreviated form of binding: instead of saying <KeyPress-a>, you can say, <a>; instead of writing <Button1-ButtonPress>, you can say, <1>.

The text and canvas widgets support bindings at a finer level of granularity. They support event bindings for different tags in addition to bindings for the widget itself. bind allows you to specify the name of the tag as the first parameter and the event sequence and callback as the second and third parameters, respectively:

```
$text->bind('hyper-link', '<1>', \&open_page);
```

This code ensures that any stretch of text tagged with "hyper-link" will respond to a button click event and call the procedure open_page.

Multiple Bindings

It is possible to have several bindings to respond to the same event. For example, when a mouse button is pressed, both <Button1> and <Double-Button1> are candidates. If there's a conflict for a given widget (or tag), the rule is that the most specific binding is called. <Double-Button1> is more specific than <Button1>, since it is a longer specification.

In addition to matching the most specific binding at the widget level, Tk matches the most specific bindings at the class level (the class that represents all buttons, for example), then at the widget's top level, then at a level called "all." All four categories of bindings are executed. This order itself can be changed using the bindtags() method, but I recommend that you avoid doing this.

Although Tk allows you to change default widget bindings, I recommend that you don't modify them because people get used to them working in a certain way. For example, a double-click inside a text widget usually selects the word under the mouse pointer, and it would be quite disconcerting for a user if you happened to change that behavior. On the other hand, there are plenty of other places where you can, and need to, add your own bindings. Canvas and text widget tags are the most frequent target of event bindings, as we shall see in the next two chapters.

Event Details

We have seen how to specify an event accurately. There are times when we do exactly the opposite—make the event specifier most general, such as <Any-KeyPress>. For instance, you probably don't want to specify a unique binding for each character on the keyboard. But when a key is pressed, the callback might like to know which key was pressed. This is where event details come in.

Each event carries with it all the details related to that event, and the function Ev() is used to get at those details. The parameter to Ev() is a single character that specifies the part of the event record you are interested in. Ev('k') specifies the keycode, Ev('x') and Ev('y') specify the x and y coordinates of the mouse pointer, and `Ev('t')` specifies the time of the event. There are over 30 such parameters to `Ev`. The following example shows how you can use this facility:

```
$label->bind("<Any-KeyPress>" => [\&move, Ev('k')]);
sub move {
    my $key = shift;
    if ($key eq 'k') {
       move_left();
    } elsif ($key eq 'l') {
       move_right();
    }
}
```

In this example, the **bind** specification registers its interest in key events and specifies that it wants the keycode supplied to the callback procedure whenever it is invoked.

Event Loops

MainLoop executes an event loop that picks up events from the underlying windowing system and dispatches it to the appropriate widgets. When a callback procedure is called in response to an event, it is the responsibility of the callback to return (or "yield") as soon as possible; otherwise, it holds up all events that have since arrived.

For long-running activities that are CPU-intensive, it is your responsibility to chop that activity up into manageable pieces and arrange for a timer to call the processing routine at regular intervals. This gives the event loop a chance to dispatch pending events. This kind of CPU sharing is called cooperative multi-tasking. Early versions of Microsoft Windows (until Version 3.1) similarly depended on your application being a good citizen; otherwise, it would hang the entire operating system.

For tasks such as ray-tracing and animations that are both CPU- and GUI-intensive, you can use the `$widget->update` method to process all events. This method doesn't return until all pending event messages (including repaint events) in the event queue have been processed.

Blocking system calls are not a very good idea in an event-driven environment, as we discussed in Chapter 12. The most common of these are the **read** and **write** calls, especially if they are talking to pipes and sockets. For example, the diamond operator (<>) blocks until it can get a line of text. Instead of directly calling an I/O call, you must let Perl/Tk tell you that it is safe to use that call, since it won't block. Tk provides a procedure called **fileevent** that notifies a callback when the file descriptor becomes readable or writable. This is how you use it:

```
open (F, "/tmp/foo");
$button->fileevent(F, "readable", \&read_file);
sub read_file {
    if (eof(F)) {
        $button->fileevent(F, "readable", undef); # cancel binding
            return ;
    }
    if (sysread (F, $buf, 1024)) {
        $text->insert('end', $buf); # Append the data read
    } else {
        # sysread returned undef. Problem with file
        $text->insert('end', "ERROR !!!";
        button->fileevent(F, "readable", undef); # cancel binding
    }
}
```

When the callback is invoked, Tk (which on Unix uses the **select** call internally) guarantees that at most one character is ready to be read or written. Beyond that it may or may not block; no assurances are given. The callback is also called if there's an end-of-file or error, so you must check both these conditions. Otherwise, the callback is called again as soon it returns, resulting in an infinite loop. As we discussed in the networking chapters, it is best to use nonblocking I/O if your system supports it.

In this chapter, we have studied widgets, event loops, timers, and event bindings. The next two chapters are designed to pull all these concepts together and to apply them to some practical problems. They also give us a chance to go beyond a mere test run of the two really neat widgets in the Tk pantheon: canvas and text.

Resources

1. Tcl/Tk libraries and papers, available at *http://www.sunlabs.com/research/Tcl* for the Sun Tcl/Tk pages; *http://www.neosoft.com* for everything related to Tcl/Tk.

2. *Perl/Tk* documentation.

   All widgets are extensively documented. Look for the file *index.html.*

3. *About Face: The Principles of User-Interface Design.* Alan Cooper. IDG Books Worldwide, 1995.

   Forceful, opinionated writing on how GUIs should be designed.

4. *Bringing Design to Software.* Terry Winograd. Addison-Wesley, 1996.

   Has specialists from different fields talking about good design, especially user interfaces.

15

In this chapter:
• Introduction to Tetris
• Design
• Implementation

GUI Example: Tetris

– Is this a game of chance?
– Not the way I play it, no.
—W.C. Fields

Writing a game is the best ways to test your understanding of GUI programming, because it covers three important user interface areas: forms, structured graphics, and animation. In this chapter, we build the popular game of Tetris and reward ourselves with hours of unproductive fun afterward. These are the specific bits of Tk knowledge that we will exercise in this chapter:

- Using canvas tags to efficiently move or delete groups of canvas items.

- Using the timer to control pieces of animation: moving the blocks and shooting them. (Yes, we will add a cheesy arcade style shooting of the blocks too!)

- Using **pack** effectively for form layout. This chapter just has two buttons and a canvas widget, so this is a very minor exercise.

It is estimated (or commonly quoted, at least) that most applications with a user interface devote around 70% of their code in GUI-specific details. In this chapter, you'll see how Tk reduces the burden to, say, a 30% effort, even in an application as GUI-intensive as a game.

Introduction to Tetris

Tetris hit the PC world in 1985 when its creators, Alexey Paszhitnov, Dmitry Pavlovsky, and Vadim Gerasimov, ported the game to the IBM PC. Shortly thereafter, Nintendo converted it into a huge success by implementing it on their Gameboy line of hand-held computer games. The continued availability of the line at a time when Nintendo is marketing 64-bit systems is a testimony to the game's appeal.

If you have never played the game, I suggest you play it a few times to get a feel for it.* In each iteration, a block† falls down from the top (ticking along one row at a time), and finally merges with the heap at the bottom (see Figure 15-1). At this point, Tetris collapses any row (of the heap) that has become full; that is, it deletes that row and moves all the heap rows above it one row down. Then the next iteration starts, this time possibly with a differently shaped block. The object of the game is to keep the heap from piling up all the way to the top. To do this, you can move the block to the left and right (using the keys "j" and "l") and rotate it (using "k") as it falls such that you can get the rows to fill up and collapse frequently. If you press the spacebar, the block falls down to the heap instantly (instead of gradually ticking along) and is merged with the heap.

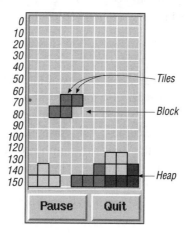

Figure 15-1. Tetris screen

Design

Let us look at the design of the user interface (specifically, our strategy for using the canvas widget effectively) and the data structures that record the state of the game and are not dependent on the user interface.

User Interface

Tetris's screen layout, shown in Figure 15-1, is straightforward. You need two button widgets for "Start/Pause" and "Quit," a canvas widget for the graphics, and a main window to contain all this stuff.

---

* The complete code is available as *tetris.pl* at the O'Reilly FTP site.

† Consisting of four tiles, hence the name of the game.

The grid and the blocks are drawn on the canvas. Each block is composed of several square tiles moving as one unit. The heap is a similar collection of tiles. Each tile is a canvas item. An alternative for drawing the block is a filled polygon, but the tiled version is much simpler to implement. The block's tiles are tagged with the string "block," so it is easy to move them around as one unit, using the canvas's move method. We also remember each tile's canvas item ID so that they can be individually deleted or moved.

One concern with animation is flicker when the monitor's periodic refresh picks up changes to video memory as they are happening. To prevent flicker, you need to resort to *double-buffering*: first render the new animation frame into a pixmap and then copy that pixmap quickly into video memory. Fortunately, the canvas widget already does double-buffering, so we can simply move canvas items around without fear of flicker.

Data Structures

Both the block and the heap carry two pieces of information for each tile: its position on the grid (the cell) and the ID given by the canvas widget. The position can be expressed either as a row and a column or as a cell index expressed as (row * (columns in grid) + column). The formula assumes that both row and column are 0-based. That is, the cells are numbered from left to right and from top to bottom in increasing numbers starting from 0. Figure 15-1 shows the numbers assigned to the leftmost cells in each row. This approach is convenient, since it encodes both row and column into one number and easily fits into the data structures discussed next.

My first attempt was to model the block and the heap as objects. A tile has two attributes, *tile_id* (the ID given by the canvas widget) and *position*, and the block and heap have one attribute each, a sequence of tiles. But because there is only one block and one heap at any time, and because a tile belongs to either the block or the heap, I chose a simpler approach. The block is represented by the array @block_cells, each element of which contains the cell number occupied by the corresponding tile. Similarly, each element of the array @tile_ids contains the ID of the canvas widget item representing the block's tile in that position. The heap is organized in a different way. The array @heap contains as many elements as there are cells in the grid; an element of this array either is undef or contains the appropriate canvas item ID of a tile belonging to the heap. Of the different ways in which I tried organizing the block and heap information, I found that this scheme is the most convenient for the two complex operations: rotating the block and merging the block and heap.

Implementation

We will focus only on those routines that either are central to the game or illustrate Tk in action.

The main program simply consists of the two calls to init() and MainLoop(). init creates the screen, sets up the key bindings, and configures a timer to call tick. Let us jump into the meat of the action by starting with this procedure.

tick moves the block down and then reloads the timer, specifying itself as a callback:

```
sub tick {
    return if ($state == $PAUSED);
    if (!@block_cells) {
        if (!create_random_block()) {
            game_over();            # Heap is full:could not place block
            return;                 # at next tick interval
        }
        $w_top->after($interval, \&tick);
        return;
    }
    move_down();                    # move the block down
    $w_top->after($interval, \&tick); # reload timer for nex
}
```

fall() is called when the space bar is hit; it keeps moving the block down until it hits any tile in the heap or hits bottom. move_down returns a false when either of these happens.

```
sub fall {                 # Called when spacebar hit
    return if (!@block_cells);   # Return if not initialized
    1 while (move_down()); # Move down until it hits heap or bottom.
}
```

move_down() simply adds $MAX_COLS to each of the block tile's cell positions to effectively move it one row down. It then checks whether any of these new positions touch the bottom of the grid or intersect with any preexisting heap tile's cell position. If so, it calls the merge_block_and_heap routine and returns a false value. If not, it simply remembers the set of new positions and uses the move method to move all the block tiles down in one fell swoop ($TILE_HEIGHT pixels down). It returns a 1 so that fall above knows to keep continuing.

```
sub move_down {
    my $cell;
    my $first_cell_last_row = ($MAX_ROWS-1)*$MAX_COLS;
    # if already at the bottom of the heap, or if a move down
    # intersects with the heap, then merge both.
    foreach $cell (@block_cells) {
        if (($cell >= $first_cell_last_row) ||
            ($heap[$cell+$MAX_COLS])) {
```

```
                    merge_block_and_heap();
                    return 0;
                }
        }
        foreach $cell (@block_cells) {
            $cell += $MAX_COLS;
        }
        $w_heap->move('block', 0,  $TILE_HEIGHT);
        return 1;
    }
```

`merge_block_and_heap` does two major things: it hands over all of the block's tiles to the heap, and it nullifies `%block`. Then it marches through `@heap` looking for rows that have tiles in all columns. If it finds any, it marks all those tiles with an additional tag called `delete`, using the addtag method:

```
$w_canvas->addtag('delete', 'withtag' => $heap[$i]);
```

The straightforward way to delete a row would be to remove the corresponding entries in the heap and to delete the corresponding tiles on the canvas. But that method doesn't give the user an idea of which rows are being consolidated; besides, it's too boring. So `merge_block_and_heap` fills all the tiles tagged `delete` with a white background and, after 300 ms, deletes all these items. This way the user sees a full row change color to white for a brief instant before vanishing. Notice how the closure supplied to `after` makes it convenient to supply a piece of code to execute in the future. The same closure also moves the rest of the heap's tiles to their new places (because some rows have collapsed).

```
my $last_cell = $MAX_COLS * $MAX_ROWS;
sub merge_block_and_heap {
    my $cell;
    # merge block
    foreach $cell (@block_cells) {
        $heap[$cell] = shift @tile_ids;
    }
    $w_heap->dtag('block'); # Forget about the block - it is now merged
    # check for full rows, and get rid of them
    # All rows above them need to be moved down, both in @heap and
    # the canvas, $w_heap
    my $last_cell = $MAX_ROWS * $MAX_COLS;
    my $filled_cell_count;
    my $rows_to_be_deleted = 0;
    my $i;
    for ($cell = 0; $cell < $last_cell; ) {
        $filled_cell_count = 0;
        my $first_cell_in_row = $cell;
        for ($i = 0; $i < $MAX_COLS; $i++) {
            $filled_cell_count++ if ($heap[$cell++]);
        }
        if ($filled_cell_count == $MAX_COLS) {
            # this row is full
            for ($i = $first_cell_in_row; $i < $cell; $i++) {
```

```
                        $w_heap->addtag('delete', 'withtag' => $heap[$i]);
                    }
                    splice(@heap, $first_cell_in_row, $MAX_COLS);
                    unshift (@heap, (undef) x $MAX_COLS);
                    $rows_to_be_deleted = 1;
            }
    }
    @block_cells = ();
    @tile_ids = ();
    if ($rows_to_be_deleted) {
        $w_heap->itemconfigure('delete',
                            '-fill'=> 'white');
        $w_top->after (300,
                    sub {
                        $w_heap->delete('delete');
                        my ($i);
                        my $last = $MAX_COLS * $MAX_ROWS;
                        for ($i = 0; $i < $last; $i++) {
                            next if !$heap[$i];
                            # get where they are
                            my $col = $i % $MAX_COLS;
                            my $row = int($i / $MAX_COLS);
                            $w_heap->coords(
                                $heap[$i],
                                $col * $TILE_WIDTH,          #x0
                                $row * $TILE_HEIGHT,         #y0
                                ($col+1) * $TILE_WIDTH,      #x1
                                ($row+1) * $TILE_HEIGHT);    #y1
                        }
                    });
    }
}
```

Let us now look at two of the other routines to manipulate the block: `move_left` and `rotate`. We'll skip `move_right` because it is similar to `move_left`.

`move_left` moves each of the block's tiles to the left by simply subtracting 1 from their respective cell positions. The function does nothing if any of the new positions go past the left edge or intersect with an occupied heap cell. If moving is allowed, the canvas items tagged "block" are simply moved `$TILE_WIDTH` pixels to the left:

```
sub move_left {
    my $cell;
    foreach $cell (@block_cells) {
        # Check if cell is at the left edge already
        # If not, check whether the cell to its left is already
        # occupied
        if ((($cell % $MAX_COLS) == 0) ||
            ($heap[$cell-1])){
            return;
        }
    }
}
```

```
    foreach $cell (@block_cells) {
        $cell--; # This affects the contents of @block_cells
    }

    $w_heap->move('block', - $TILE_WIDTH, 0);
}
```

rotate is a trifle more complex. It computes a *pivot* row and column from the block's tile positions and calculates new tile positions by a simple transformation explained in the following code. It also ensures that the newly computed positions are not illegal in any way (moving out of the grid or intersecting with the heap). It then calls the canvas's **coords** method to move each of the tiles individually to their new places.

```
sub rotate {
    # rotates the block counter_clockwise
    return if (!@block_cells);
    my $cell;
    # Calculate the pivot position around which to turn
    # The pivot is at (average x, average y) of all block_cells
    my $row_total = 0; my $col_total = 0;
    my ($row, $col);
    my @cols = map {$_ % $MAX_COLS} @block_cells;
    my @rows = map {int($_ / $MAX_COLS)} @block_cells;
    foreach (0 .. $#cols) {
        $row_total += $rows[$_];
        $col_total += $cols[$_];
    }
    my $pivot_row = int ($row_total / @cols + 0.5); # pivot row
    my $pivot_col = int ($col_total / @cols + 0.5); # pivot col
    # To position each cell counter_clockwise, we need to do a small
    # transformation. A row offset from the pivot becomes an equivalent
    # column offset, and a column offset becomes a negative row offset.
    my @new_cells = ();
    my @new_rows = ();
    my @new_cols = ();
    my ($new_row, $new_col);
    while (@rows) {
        $row = shift @rows;
        $col = shift @cols;
        # Calculate new $row and $col
        $new_col = $pivot_col + ($row - $pivot_row);
        $new_row = $pivot_row - ($col - $pivot_col);
        $cell = $new_row * $MAX_COLS + $new_col;
        # Check if the new row and col are invalid (is outside or
        # something is already occupying that  cell)
        # If valid, then no-one should be occupying it.
        if (($new_row < 0) || ($new_row > $MAX_ROWS) ||
            ($new_col < 0) || ($new_col > $MAX_COLS)  ||
            $heap[$cell]) {
            return 0;
        }
        push (@new_rows, $new_row);
```

```
            push (@new_cols, $new_col);
            push (@new_cells, $cell);
        }
        # Move the UI tiles to the appropriate coordinates
        my $i= @new_rows-1;
        while ($i >= 0) {
            $new_row = $new_rows[$i];
            $new_col = $new_cols[$i];
            $w_heap->coords($tile_ids[$i],
                             $new_col * $TILE_WIDTH,       #x0
                             $new_row * $TILE_HEIGHT,      #y0
                             ($new_col+1) * $TILE_WIDTH,   #x1
                             ($new_row+1) * $TILE_HEIGHT);
            $i--;
        }
        @block_cells = @new_cells;
        1; # Success
    }
```

When this mutant version of Tetris starts, it draws a small red triangular "gun"
(cell number 70 in Figure 15-1). shoot is called when the "a" or "s" key is
pressed. The "a" key shoots an arrow from the gun and blows off the leftmost tile
of the block in the gun's row if the block happens to be passing by. The "s" key
takes a shot at the rightmost tile. This is quite cheesy, really, but useful if you
want to see how an animation sequence can be staged by using the canvas. The
first part of the procedure simply determines which block tile is to be removed, if
any. It then creates an arrow (a line with an arrowhead) from the gun to the
selected tile, changes its stippling, and after a 200-ms interval, deletes both the tile
and the arrow. This has the visual effect of blowing up a tile.

```
    sub shoot {
        my ($dir) = @_;
        my $first_cell_shoot_row = $shoot_row*$MAX_COLS;
        my $last_cell_shoot_row = $first_cell_shoot_row + $MAX_COLS;
        my $cell;
        my (@indices) =
            sort {
                $dir eq 'left' ?
                    $block_cells[$a] <=> $block_cells[$b] :
                        $block_cells[$b] <=> $block_cells[$a]
                    } (0 .. $#block_cells);
        my $found = -1;
        my $i;
        foreach $i (@indices) {
            $cell = $block_cells[$i];
            if (($cell >= $first_cell_shoot_row) &&
                ($cell < $last_cell_shoot_row)) {
                $found = $i;
                last;
            }
        }
        if ($found != -1) {
```

```perl
        my $shot_tile = $tile_ids[$found];
        ($cell) = splice (@block_cells, $found, 1);
        splice (@tile_ids, $found, 1);
        my $y = ($shoot_row + 0.5)*$TILE_HEIGHT;
        my $arrow = $w_heap->create(
                                    'line',
                                    0,
                                    $y,
                                    (($cell % $MAX_COLS) + 0.5)
                                                * $TILE_WIDTH,
                                    $y,
                                    '-fill' => 'white',
                                    '-arrow' => 'last',
                                    '-arrowshape' => [7,7,3]
                                    );

        $w_heap->itemconfigure($shot_tile,
                            '-stipple' => 'gray25');
        $w_top->after (200,sub {
            $w_heap->delete($shot_tile);
            $w_heap->delete($arrow);
        });
    }
}
```

Let us now see the two routines responsible for setting up the screen: **create_screen** and **bind_key**. Both these functions are called by **init()**. Note the way the **pack** method is used in **create_screen** and how the space character is translated to an event-binding in **bind_key**.

```perl
    sub create_screen {
        $w_top = MainWindow->new('Tetris - Perl/Tk');
        $w_heap = $w_top->Canvas('-width'  => $MAX_COLS * $TILE_WIDTH,
                                 '-height' => $MAX_ROWS  * $TILE_HEIGHT,
                                 '-border' => 1,
                                 '-relief' => 'ridge');
        $w_start = $w_top->Button('-text' => 'Start',
                                  '-command' => \&start_pause,
                                  );
        my $w_quit = $w_top->Button('-text' => 'Quit',
                                    '-command' => sub {exit(0)}
                                    );
        $w_heap->pack();
        $w_start->pack('-side'=> 'left', '-fill' => 'y', '-expand' => 'y');
        $w_quit->pack('-side'=> 'right', '-fill' => 'y', '-expand' => 'y');
    }

    sub bind_key {
        my ($keychar, $callback) = @_;
        if ($keychar eq ' ') {
            $keychar = "KeyPress-space";
        }
        $w_top->bind("<${keychar}>", $callback);
    }
```

In this chapter:
• *man and perlman*
• *Implementation*
• *Resources*

16

GUI Example:
Man Page Viewer

Help wanted. Telepath. You know where to apply.
—Anonymous

The primary objective of this chapter is to exercise some of the most important capabilities of Tk's text widget; a man page viewer called *perlman* provides an ideal test case.* In this chapter, you will familiarize yourself with the widget's text insertion, deletion, and retrieval capabilities; use a variety of indexing primitives; create and configure tags; and perform regular expression searching and highlighting of text. Along the way, you'll also learn to use entry widgets and construct menus dynamically.

perlman is modeled after *TkMan* [1], a very nice man page viewer written by Thomas Phelps at the University of California at Berkeley, using Tcl/Tk. *perlman* contains only a small subset of *TkMan*'s functionality.

Thomas has also written an experience paper entitled "Two Years with TkMan: Lessons and Innovations. Or, Everything I Needed to Know about Tcl/Tk I Learned from TkMan" [2]. It presents a good case for writing the entire utility in a scripting language and unwittingly convinces us, smug Perl programmers that we are, why Perl would have been the ideal choice. Please see the "Resources" section at the end of this chapter for pointers to *TkMan* and this paper.

man and perlman

Unix manual pages are normally viewed by the `man(1)` command. When you say man perl at the command line, it searches the list of directories indicated by the environment variable **MANPATH**, a colon-separated list of pathnames. (If **MANPATH**

---

* For a more ambitious workout of the text widget, you could try writing an HTML page viewer.

is not specified, man(1) looks at standard locations, such as */usr/man.)* Once it finds a file called *perl.1*, it calls *tbl* to format the tables and *nroff* to format the text, and pipes the output through a suitable pager, such as more(1) or less(1).

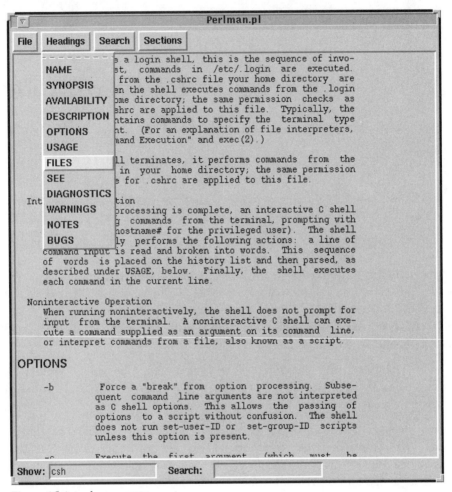

Figure 16-1. perlman screen

perlman, shown in Figure 16-1, is a GUI wrapper over man. To view a topic, you have to enter a string in the "Show" box and press the Return key. To highlight all pieces of text matching a given regular expression, simply enter it in the "Search" box and press Return. You can also perform exact string searches and ignore case optionally. In addition, *perlman* provides the following features:

Hypertext

If you double-click on any word, *perlman* displays the man page on that topic, if it exists. In man(1), you have to quit the current man page before looking at the other documentation. In contrast to other help systems such as those found on Microsoft Windows or HTML pages, *perlman* doesn't require a piece of text to be specially marked as a hypertext link. In addition, if you click on a string such as `strcmp(3)`, *perlman* looks for the corresponding documentation in section three of the manual. This helps immensely with the "SEE ALSO" sections.

Section headers

Some manual pages such as `csh(1)`, `gcc(1)`, and `perlfunc(1)` are very big. *perlman* helps the user navigate faster through such documents by creating a special menu called "Headings." Under this menu, it shows all the section headings in that document, such as "NAME," "DESCRIPTION," and "SEE," as shown in Figure 16-1. When the user selects one of these options, the corresponding section is brought into view.

Sections

perlman shows all the sections available, in a menu called "Sections," and when you select one of them, it shows all the topics available in that section. You can then double-click on any of these topics to get help.

Implementation

perlman's implementation can be logically divided into four chunks:

- Formatting and displaying man pages in the text widget: the routines `show_man` and `get_command_line`.

- Search facility: `search`.

- Screen layout: `create_ui`.

- Displaying the list of help topics available in every section. We will not look at this particular piece of functionality, because it does not have much user interface code.

Before we barrel into each of the subroutines mentioned above, let us briefly study all the capabilities of the text widget used by *perlman*:

- Inserting text at end, and marking it with a tag ("section"):

    ```
    $text->insert('end', 'sample text', 'section');
    ```

- Retrieving a stretch of text between two indices:

    ```
    $line = $text->get($start_index, $end_index);
    ```

- Ensuring that a particular index is visible:

    ```
    $text->see($index)
    ```

- Deleting entire contents:

    ```
    $text->delete('1.0', 'end'); # From line 1, column 0, to end
    ```

- Creating and configuring a tag:

```
$text->tagConfigure('search',
                'foreground' => yellow, 'background' => 'red');
```

- Deleting a tag:

```
$text->tagDelete('search');
```

- Applying a tag to a range of text, given an index position and number of characters:

```
$text->tagAdd('search', $current, "$current + $length char");
```

- Listing all mark names and deleting each of them:

```
foreach $mark ( $text->markNames() ) { $text->markUnset($mark); }
```

- Getting the line and column number (the index) from logical positions:

```
# row and col of current end position
$index = $text->index('end');

# go to current insert position, then to the beginning of the word
# and report the line and column
$start_index = $text->index('insert wordstart');

# Go to 10th row, column 3, advance 5 chars, and report the new
# row and column
$i = $text->index("10.3 + 5 char");
```

Note that the **index** method does not change the state of the widget.

- Doing an exact or regular expression search, specifying where to start and where to end:

```
$current = $text->search('-count' => \$length,
                    '-regex', '-nocase','--', # search options
                    $search_pattern,
                    $current, 'end');          # from , to
```

The **search** method returns the index of the text at which the search succeeds and sets the variable associated with the **-count** property. It returns **undef** if the search failed.

- Binding a mouse double-click to a subroutine:

```
$text->bind('<Double-1>', \&pick_word);
```

Showing Man Pages

Let us dive into the meat of the application, the procedure **show_man**. As can be seen in Figure 16-1, an entry widget labeled "Show:" accepts a topic name. When the user types text into this widget, **$show**, and hits the Return key, **show_man** is called. This procedure fetches the string from **$show** and calls **get_command_line** to construct a command pipeline to read from **man** (for **open**'s purposes). It then reads this pipe a line at a time and examines the line to see whether it is a likely heading (such as "NAME" or "DESCRIPTION"). Headings in man pages are typically in all caps and start from the first column. If a line looks like a heading, show_man inserts the line with a tag called "section"; otherwise, it inserts it as regular untagged text. The "section" tag is preconfigured with a larger size font. In addition, show_man appends a new entry to the "Headings" menu and arranges the callback associated with this entry to scroll the text widget to the line containing that section header.

```perl
sub show_man {
    my $entry = $show->get();    # get entry from $show
    # $entry can be something like 'csh', or 'csh(1)'
    my ($man, $section) = ($entry =~ /^(\w+)(\(.*\))?/);
    if ($section && (!is_valid_section($section))) {
        undef $section ;
    }
    my $cmd_line = get_command_line($man, $section); # used by open

    # Erase everything to do with current page (contents, menus, marks)
    $text->delete('1.0', 'end');   # erase current page
    # Insert 'working' message; use the 'section' tag because
    # it has nice large fonts.
    $text->insert('end',
                    "Formatting \"$man\" .. please wait", 'section');
    $text->update();   # Flush changes to text widget
    $menu_headings->menu()->delete(0,'end'); # Delete current headings
    my $mark;
    foreach $mark ($text->markNames) {   # remove all marks
        $text->markUnset($mark);
    }

    # UI is clean now. Open the file
    if (!open (F, $cmd_line)) {
        # Use the text widget for error messages
        $text->insert('end', "\nError in running man or rman");
        $text->update();
        return;
    }
    # Erase the "Formatting $man ..." message
    $text->delete('1.0', 'end');
    my $lines_added = 0; my $line;

    while (defined($line = <F>)) {
        $lines_added = 1;
        # If first character is a capital letter, it's likely a section
        if ($line =~ /^[A-Z]/) {
            # Likely a section heading
            ($mark = $line) =~ s/\s.*$//g;   # $mark has section title
            my $index = $text->index('end');# note current end location
            # Give 'section' tag to the section title
            $text->insert('end', "$mark\n\n", 'section');
            # Create a section heading menu entry. Have callback
            # invoke text widget's 'see' method to go to the index
            # noted above
            $menu_headings->command(
```

```
                      '-label' => $mark,
                      '-command' => [sub {$text->see($_[0])},$index])
           } else {
               $text->insert('end', $line); # Ordinary text. Just insert.
           }
       }
       if ( ! $lines_added ) {
           $text->insert('end', "Sorry. No information found on $man");
       }
       close(F);
   }
```

get_command_line takes the name of a man page and an optional section and
returns an appropriate command line that can be used for the open command.
Different systems might need different command lines, and the following listing
shows the command line for Solaris. Since *man* (actually, *nroff*) formats the page
for a terminal (inserting escape sequences to show words in bold and headers and
footers for every page), we use a freely available utility called *rman* ("RosettaMan";
see the "Resources" section at the end of this chapter) to filter out this noise.

```
   sub get_command_line {
       my ($man, $section) = @_;
       if ($section) {
           $section =~ s/[()]//g; # remove parens
           return "man -s $section $man 2> /dev/null | rman |";
       } else {
           return "man $man 2> /dev/null | rman |";
       }
   }
```

The pick_word procedure is called when you double-click on the text widget. It
uses the index method to compute the index of the beginning of the word
clicked on, and that of the end of the line, and extracts this range of text. pick_
word then looks for an ordinary string (the topic), followed by an optional string
within parentheses (the section). Before invoking show_man, it inserts this string
into the entry widget, $show, thus pretending to be a user who has typed in that
text.

```
   sub pick_word {
       my $start_index = $text->index('insert wordstart');
       my $end_index = $text->index('insert lineend');
       my $line = $text->get($start_index, $end_index);
       my ($page, $section) = ($line =~ /^(\w+)(\(.*?\))?/);
       return unless $page;
       $show->delete('0', 'end');
       if ($section && is_valid_section($section)) {
           $show->insert('end', "$page${section}");
       } else {
           $show->insert('end', $page);
       }
       show_man();
   }
```

Searching for Text

The menu bar contains a search menu exactly as described in the example under "Menus" in Chapter 14, *User Interfaces with Tk*. When the "Find" menu item is selected, the subroutine `search` is called. It first calls `tagDelete` to remove all highlights (which may be present from a previous search). Then it starts from the top (line 1, column 0) and invokes the widget's `search` method to find the first piece of matching text. When a match is found, this method updates the variable supplied to the `-count` parameter with the length of the matched text. This stretch of text is then highlighted using a tag called "search." The cursor is advanced beyond the matching text, and the search is resumed.

```perl
sub search {
    my $search_pattern = $search->get();
    $text->tagDelete('search');   # Removing the tag restores the
                                  # associated regions of text to their
                                  # default style
    $text->tagConfigure('search',
                        '-background' => 'yellow',
                        '-foreground' => 'red');

    my $current = '1.0';# Start at line 1, column 0 (beginning of file)
    my $length = '0';
    while (1) {
        if ($ignore_case) {
            $current = $text->search('-count' => \$length,
                                     $match_type, '-nocase','--',
                                     $search_pattern,
                                     $current,
                                     'end');
        } else {
            $current = $text->search('-count' => \$length,
                                     $match_type, '--',
                                     $search_pattern,
                                     $current,
                                     'end');
        }
        last if (!$current);
        # Tag the matching text range with the tag name 'search'
        $text->tagAdd('search', $current, "$current + $length char");
        # Move the cursor ahead, and continue searching
        $current = $text->index("$current + $length char");
    }
}
```

Screen Layout

`create_ui` sets up the simple user interface. Pay particular attention to the padding options given to **pack** and the event bindings set up on the text and entry widgets.

```perl
sub create_ui {
    my $top = MainWindow->new();
    #----------------------------------------------------------------
    # Create menus
    #----------------------------------------------------------------
    # Menu bar
    my $menu_bar = $top->Frame()->pack('-side' => 'top',
                                       '-fill' => 'x');


    #----------- File menu ----------------------
    my $menu_file = $menu_bar->Menubutton('-text' => 'File',
                                          '-relief' => 'raised',
                                          '-borderwidth' => 2,
                                          )->pack('-side' => 'left',
                                                  '-padx' => 2,
                                                  );
    $menu_file->separator();
    $menu_file->command('-label' => 'Quit',
                        '-command' => sub {exit(0)});


    #----------- Sections Menu ----------------------
    $menu_headings = $menu_bar->Menubutton('-text' => 'Headings',
                                           '-relief' => 'raised',
                                           '-borderwidth' => 2,
                                           )->pack('-side' => 'left',
                                                   '-padx' => 2,
                                                   );
    $menu_headings->separator();


    #----------- Search Menu ----------------------
    my $search_mb = $menu_bar->Menubutton('-text'        => 'Search',
                                          '-relief'       => 'raised',
                                          '-borderwidth'  => 2,
                                          )->pack('-side' => 'left',
                                                  '-padx' => 2
                                          );
    $match_type = "-regexp"; $ignore_case = 1;
    $search_mb->separator();

    # Regexp match
    $search_mb->radiobutton('-label'    => 'Regexp match',
                            '-value'    => '-regexp',
                            '-variable' => \$match_type);
    # Exact match
    $search_mb->radiobutton('-label'    => 'Exact match',
                            '-value'    => '-exact',
                            '-variable' => \$match_type);
    $search_mb->separator();
    # Ignore case
    $search_mb->checkbutton('-label'    => 'Ignore case?',
                            '-variable' => \$ignore_case);
    #----------- Sections Menu ----------------------
    my $menu_sections = $menu_bar->Menubutton('-text' => 'Sections',
                                              '-relief' => 'raised',
```

```
                                                 '-borderwidth' => 2,
                                      )->pack('-side' => 'left',
                                                 '-padx' => 2,
                                                 );
        # Populate sections menu with keys of %sections
        my $section_name;
        foreach $section_name (sort keys %sections) {
            $menu_sections->command (
                    '-label' => "($section_name)",
                    '-command' => [\&show_section_contents, $section_name]);
        }


        #-----------------------------------------------------------------
        # Create and configure text, and show and search entry widgets
        #-----------------------------------------------------------------
        $text = $top->Text ('-width' =>  80,
                            '-height' => 40)->pack();
        $text->tagConfigure('section',
                            '-font' =>
        '-adobe-helvetica-bold-r-normal--14-140-75-75-p-82-iso8859-1');
        # Used xlsfonts(1) for this font spec.
        $text->bind('<Double-1>', \&pick_word);
        $top->Label('-text' => 'Show:')->pack('-side' => 'left');

        $show = $top->Entry ('-width'   => 20,
                             )->pack('-side' => 'left');
        $show->bind('<KeyPress-Return>', \&show_man);

        $top->Label('-text' => 'Search:'
                    )->pack('-side' => 'left', '-padx' => 10);
        $search = $top->Entry ('-width' => 20,
                             )->pack('-side' => 'left');
        $search->bind('<KeyPress-Return>', \&search);
    }
```

Please take a look at the file *perlman.pl*, packaged with the rest of this book's software and available from O'Reilly's FTP site. You can, if you wish, make a few valuable (and simple) additions to this utility: Add caching of formatted manual pages and the ability to show all man pages for a given topic name (not just the first one in MANPATH).

Resources

1. TkMan and RosettaMan (*rman*). Thomas Phelps. Download from *ftp:// ftp.cs.berkeley.edu/pub/people/phelps/tcl*

2. "Two Years with TkMan: Lessons and Innovations. Or, Everything I Needed to Know about Tcl/TK I learned from TKMan." Thomas Phelps.

   Interesting case study of Tcl/Tk usage. See address above.

17

Template-Driven Code Generation

> *I'd rather write programs to write programs than write programs.*
> —Programming Pearls
> *Communications of the ACM, Sept. 1985*

This chapter builds a template-driven code generator, an indispensable tool in a C, C++, or Java programmer's toolbox. The chapter has two objectives: to make the case for code generation as a method of code reuse and to present a small but nontrivial problem that can exercise all the Perl concepts you learned in the first half of the book: complex data structures, modules, objects, and `eval`. Enjoy!

On Code Generation

Programmers create and use tiny specification languages all the time. Database schemas, resources (*rc* files in Unix such as *.mwmrc* and *.openwinrc*), user interface specifications (Motif UIL files), network interface specifications (RPC or CORBA IDL files), and so on are all examples of such languages. These languages enable you to state your requirements in a high-level, compact, and declarative format; for example, in Motif's UIL (User Interface Language), you can simply state that you want two buttons inside a form and spare yourself the effort of writing 20 or so statements in C to achieve the same effect.

The semantic gap between these specification languages and conventional systems-programming languages such as C or C++ can be bridged in one of two ways. The first approach is for the C application to treat the specification as metadata; that is, the application embeds the specification parser and exchanges information with it using C data structures and an internal API. The second approach is to have a standalone compiler to translate the specification to C, which in turn is linked to the application. RPC systems and CASE tools prefer this approach.

In the following pages, we will study the second alternative and build ourselves a configurable code generation framework called Jeeves.*

The code generators we mentioned previously are clearly domain-specific. In practice, I have also found most of them to be needlessly specific in their output capabilities. Consider the following examples:

RPC

NOTE   The Remote Procedure Call facility allows you to call a procedure in a different address space, possibly on a different machine. You specify a list of procedures that you wish to export in an Interface Definition Language (IDL) and feed it to an IDL compiler, which produces some C code for the client and server ends. Link these pieces of code to your application, and voilà, you have network transparency.

Most commercial IDL compilers are remarkably inflexible about changing their output code. They make it hard for you to insert probes for monitoring network performance or auditing data flowing across the network. If you want to transparently encrypt the data before it is put "on the wire," you are often out of luck. Sure, you can change the C code output by the IDL compiler, but your changes will get overwritten the next time you run the IDL compiler.

CASE

Many CASE tools generate C code from object model specifications. The following sample specification lists entity classes and their attributes and specifies the degree and cardinality of relationships between these classes:

```
Employee {
    int         emp_id    key
    string[40]  name
    Department  dept_id
    double      salary
}
Department {
    int         dept_id   key
    string[20]  name
}
Relationship Department(1) contains Employee (n)
```

Given this tiny specification language, we can, for example, automatically generate C and embedded SQL code to maintain database tables, as shown below:

```
int create_employee_table {
```

---

* Jeeves is the efficient butler in P.G. Wodehouse's novels, who does all the work for his bumbling master with at most a twitch of an eyebrow.

```
        exec sql create table employee_table (
            employee_id integer,
            name varchar, salary float);
        return check_db_error();
    }
    int create_employee (employee *e) {
        if (!check_dept(e->dept))
            return 0;
        e->employee_id = ++g_employee_id;
        exec sql insert into table employee_table (
                employee_id, name, salary)
                values (:*e);
        return check_db_error();
    }
```

The specification also provides enough information to generate code for creating C++ classes for each entity and for managing referential integrity constraints ("cannot delete a department object if it contains one or more employees").

Most CASE tools suffer from the restriction that they can generate only a fixed pattern of code. Buy an object-oriented database tomorrow, and the output code shown earlier doesn't help much. If this pattern is hardcoded, you are left with a mere diagramming tool (a mighty expensive one too).

POD, Javadoc

The entire Perl documentation is written in a format called POD (plain old documentation). It provides simple, high-level primitives for specifying paragraph styles (=head1, =item) and character styles (B<foo> prints the word in boldface, for example). The distribution comes with tools such as *pod2text*, *pod2html*, *pod2man*, and so on. POD documents can be embedded in code, and extracted by these tools (the Perl interpreter ignores these directives). This facility reduces the possibility of mismatches between code and documentation since they are all in one place.

Similarly, all Java libraries are documented using a format known as Javadoc. The documentation is extracted and converted to HTML by a tool called *javadoc*.

Both sets of tools are limited to specific outputs (ASCII, HTML, and so on). For example, if you want to write a *pod2rtf* translator (Rich Text Format, used on Microsoft Windows systems), you have to start from scratch, because the POD parser is not available as a separate package. The better option would have been to centralize the POD parser and allow several different plug-and-play back ends.

SWIG, XS

In Chapter 18, *Extending Perl: A First Course*, we will have occasion to study two tools called SWIG and XS. Given an interface specification, they generate code to bind Perl and custom C extensions together. In fact, SWIG is a classic example of the type of code generators we would like to build: From one specification language, this tool is capable of producing a variety of output code, because its back end is template-driven.

In most of these cases, the demand for different types of output typically exceeds the number of changes made to the input specification format. We can make two observations as a consequence. First, parsing the input and producing the final output are related but separate tasks. Second, the output needs to be configurable. This can be arranged either by having one *parameterizable* output generator or by having a number of output generators that can be used interchangeably with the input parser. In my experience, the first option is not often practical. For example, it is pointless to write one output generator in the POD case, which can output HTML or ASCII or RTF just by tweaking a few parameters; they are very different sets of outputs.

The Jeeves framework goes for the second option. It helps you write a configurable translator by supplying a template-driven code-generating back end. This module allows you to write configurable templates with loops, if/then conditions, variables, and bits of Perl code, so it is no ordinary cookie-cutter cookie-cutter (otherwise, it might have been called *yacccc*).

An example serves to better explain this framework.

Jeeves Example

We will consider a very simple object model specification file consisting of a list of classes, each of which contains a list of typed attributes:

```
// File: emp.om (om stands for object model)
class Employee {
    int        id;
    string     name;
    int        dept_id;
};
class Department {
    int    id;
    string name;
};
```

From this specification, we wish to produce a C++ header file for each class. Assume, for example, that the file *Employee.h* is expected to look like this (and similarly for *Department.h*):

```
#ifndef _Employee_h_
#define _Employee_h_
#include <Object.h>
// File : 'Employee.h'
```

```
// User : "sriram"
class Employee : Object {
    int id;
    string name;
    int dept_id;
    Employee(); // private constructor. Use Create()
public:
    // Methods
    Employee* Create();
     ~Employee();
    // Accessor Methods;
    int    get_id();
    void set_id(int);
    string    get_name();
    void set_name(string);
    int    get_dept_id();
    void set_dept_id(int);
}
#endif
```

Instead of succumbing to the temptation of writing a throwaway script to handle this specific job, we use Jeeves. This approach has three steps:

1. Write a parser module for the object specification.

2. Write a template to create the output required.

3. Invoke Jeeves with the name of the specification parser, the template file, and the example specification file.

This approach forces you to separate the parsing and output stages into two different modules. You might think it is simpler to write a throwaway script, but that's not quite true: you still have the problem of parsing the specification and producing the output. If you play by Jeeves's rules, you can take advantage of its template-processing facility. Jeeves expects the parser to boil the specification down to a data structure known as an *abstract syntax tree* (AST). Jeeves does not help you with parsing; after all, how can it know about a language we randomly cooked up not too long ago?

The syntax tree is a simple hierarchical arrangement of properties and property lists and is shown in Figure 17-1 for our example problem. Shaded boxes represent AST nodes, and outer boxes represent collections of these nodes (vector properties). Each node in this syntax tree has one or more properties (or name-value pairs). A property value is either a scalar (*class_name, attr_name, attr_type*) or a vector of other nodes (*attr_list* and *class_list*). As currently implemented, Jeeves does not expect nodes to contain any other type of values (references to other types of arrays, or to hashes, for example).

To get a quick overview of the Jeeves process, we will assume for now that the input specification parser has already been written and is capable of producing

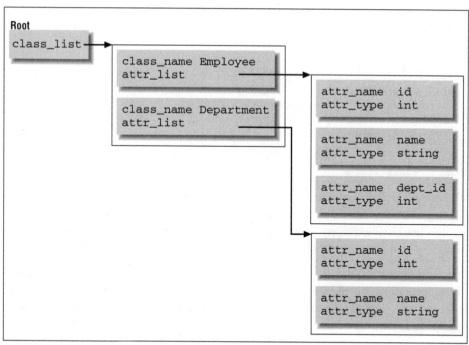

Figure 17-1. Example syntax tree

the syntax tree in Figure 17-1. The implementation is explained later, in the section "Sample Specification Parser."

The next step is to write a template file (call it *oo.tpl*) to output the requested files. Jeeves allows you to use the properties in the syntax tree as variables and provides keywords to iterate through vector properties. The template in Example 17-1 produces the two files in one fell swoop.

Example 17-1. oo.tpl: Template File

```
@foreach class_list
@//-----------------------------------------------------------------
@// Note: we are opening a new ".h" file within the foreach above ...
  @openfile ${class_name}.h
#ifndef _${class_name}_h_
#define _${class_name}_h_
#include <Object.h>
  @perl $user = $ENV{"USER"};
// File : '${class_name}.h'
// User : "$user"
class $class_name : Object {
  @foreach attr_list
  $attr_type $attr_name;
  @end
  $class_name(); // private constructor. Use Create()
```

Example 17-1. oo.tpl: Template File (continued)

```
public:
    // Methods
    $class_name* Create();
     ~$class_name();
    // Accessor Methods;
  @foreach attr_list
    $attr_type    get_${attr_name}();
    void set_${attr_name}($attr_type);
  @end .. attr_list
}
#endif
@end .. class_list
```

The template file contains a mixture of control statements (the highlighted lines starting with @), attributes (indicated by *$varname*), and ordinary text. The highlighted lines are indented to indicate nesting of control structures. Ordinary text is simply output after variable interpolations, and whitespace is faithfully preserved.

It is important for the template writer to know the kind of syntax tree that is being produced by the input parser and the set of properties at each type of node. In the preceding example, the template writer has to know that the list of classes is known as `class_list`, each element of which has properties such as `class_name` and `attr_list`.

Ordinarily, a line in the template is simply interpolated (all scalar variables are expanded *in situ*) and written to the file last opened by the `@openfile` construct. If the line belongs inside an `@foreach ... @end` block, it gets interpolated and written several times. The `@foreach` block iterates through a list-valued property in the syntax tree and makes the properties of the *current* AST node available as global variables. For example, `@foreach class_list` "visits" each node pointed to by the *class_list* property and makes the variables `$class_name` and `$attr_list` (refer to Figure 17-1) available for the text following the `@foreach` directive. In the sample template shown earlier, because `@open_file` is within such a block and uses the variable `$class_name` for the filename, the template produces a new file during each iteration. Ordinary template lines are simply funneled into the currently open file. The `@perl` command allows you to intersperse Perl code when the built-in primitives don't quite cut it. We'll cover some more template directives when we discuss the template parser implementation.

Having written the object model specification parser, *OO_Schema.pm*, the template *oo.tpl*, and our example specification, *emp.om*, we invoke Jeeves as follows:

```
% jeeves -s OO_Schema -t oo.tpl emp.om
Translated oo.tpl to oo.tpl.pl
```

```
Parsed emp.om
% ls *.h
Department.h Employee.h
```

This template is now capable of generating C++ code for any class in your specification. One small change in the template can be instantly reflected in all pieces of code.

Oh, and Can You Do This Too?

As soon as you finish doing this and are ready to go home, your remarkably prescient boss comes in and asks you to generate one more file: an SQL script to create the corresponding relational database schema. The script, *db.sql*, is expected to look like this:

```
create table Employee (
     id       integer,
     name     varchar,
     dept_id integer,
)
create table Department (
     id       integer,
     name     varchar,
)
```

Luckily, the Jeeves template makes this a two-minute task. Just create one more template file (or add the piece in Example 17-2 to the earlier template).

Example 17-2. sql.tpl: Template File to Create a Relational Database Schema

```
@openfile db.sql
@perl %db_typemap = ("int" => 'integer', string => 'varchar');
@foreach class_list
create table $class_name (
  @foreach attr_list
    @perl my $db_type = $db_typemap{$attr_type};
      $attr_name $db_type,
  @end
)
@end .. class_list
```

The template maps each attribute's type to the corresponding SQL datatype, using a snippet of Perl code.

As you can see, this architecture allows us to reuse specification parsers; we have used the information generated by the parser to fashion a completely different output.

Jeeves Overview

Figure 17-2 illustrates how various components of a Jeeves-based translator relate to each other. Gray rectangles constitute the Jeeves framework.

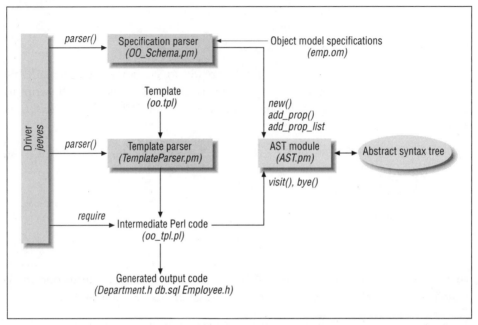

Figure 17-2. Components of a running Jeeves-based translator

The Jeeves framework supplies a driver program, `jeeves`, a template-parsing module, *TemplateParser.pm*, and a utility module for creating and accessing the syntax tree, *AST.pm*.

You supply a specification parser for a given application domain, such as *OO_Schema.pm*, a specification file (*emp.om*), and one or more templates, such as *oo.tpl*.

The driver starts by calling the **parse** function of the specification parser. This calls the AST functions **new**, **add_prop**, and **add_prop_list** to convert all "relevant" data from the specification file to a tree of properties.

The driver then calls the template parser's **parse** function, which converts the given template file to an intermediate perl file. (Note the line `Translated oo.tpl to oo.tpl.pl` in the command-line invocation shown earlier.) The template contains variables along with looping and conditional constructs, all of which are more than adequately supported by Perl itself, so by converting the template to Perl code, we are able to leverage all of Perl's power. This is similar to early versions of C++ compilers (`cfront`), which simply converted C++ files to intermediate C files, thus taking advantage of the power, optimization features, and portability of existing C compilers.

Finally, the driver loads the intermediate file using `require`, which is an `eval` in disguise. When evaluated, this code traverses the syntax tree and produces the required output files.

Advantages of This Architecture

So what have we gained by this seemingly complicated arrangement? The input parser is written once to produce a standardized data structure. The template parser knows how to make this data structure available to the template and traverse it in a controlled fashion. The result is that you can write all kinds of templates while reusing the input parser.

This arrangement works very well in big projects. Someone with parsing experience writes the parser, and another who knows the application well writes templates. Others simply write different specifications and run the tool. Tomorrow, if you, an applications developer, write a template to automatically generate a Motif-based user interface from an object model, the others don't have to learn Motif to generate custom UIs for their object models.

The `jeeves` driver takes the name of a specification parser on the command line. This means that you can have a library of specification parsers for all kinds of problems and a library of templates corresponding to these parsers. The framework itself is independent of application domains.

The advantage of writing it in Perl is that no other language comes anywhere close to Perl's text-processing abilities. Besides, you can use modules such as Tk and IO::Socket within your templates.

Intermediate Perl Code

Most of Jeeves is extremely simple; the only piece of code that warrants some attention is the template parser.

The following snippet shows a sample conversion of a template to the intermediate Perl file:

```
@foreach class_list
Name: $class_name
  @foreach attr_list
  Attr: $attr_name, $attr_type
  @end
@end
```

Stripped to its essence, the corresponding intermediate file looks like this:

```
$ROOT->visit();
foreach $class_list_i (@class_list) {
    $class_list_i->visit();
    print "Name : $class_name\n";
    foreach $attr_list_i (@attr_list) {
        $attr_list_i->visit();
        print "Attr: $attr_name, $attr_type\n";
        Ast->bye();
    }
    Ast->bye();
}
```

Ast::visit converts all properties of the AST node being visited to global Perl variables in package `main`. The root node of the syntax tree is "visited" first, which results in the creation of one global variable, `@class_list`, since that is the sole property of the root node. `@class_list` consists of one or more AST nodes itself, and when one of them is visited, the properties *class_name* and *attr_list* become available as `$class_name` and `@attr_list`. This code has to account for the possibility that a given global variable already exists, either because of a similarly named property at an outer level of nesting or because one was defined by the template writer using an `@perl` directive. For this reason `visit()` keeps track of the old value of a variable if necessary; `bye()` restores it to the old value at the end of a `@FOREACH` block. This arrangement hence implements dynamic scoping.

Jeeves Implementation

In the following pages, we implement all the components of the Jeeves framework. You may find it helpful to run `jeeves` for a sample problem and have a copy of the output handy.

AST Module

The AST module is a very simple library, so we will look at only a few of the more interesting procedures below.

An AST node is a container of properties, so a hash table suits the job perfectly. Each node is given a name for ease of debugging:

```
package Ast;
use strict;
sub new {
    my ($pkg, $name) = @_;
    bless {'ast_node_name' => $name}, $pkg;
}
```

new, add_prop, and add_prop_list are used by all specification parsers to create AST objects:

```perl
sub add_prop {
    my ($node, $prop_name, $prop_value) = @_;
    $node->{$prop_name} = $prop_value;
}
sub add_prop_list {
    my ($node, $prop_name, $node_ref) = @_;
    if (! exists $node->{$prop_name}) {
        $node->{$prop_name} = [];
    }
    push (@{$node->{$prop_name}}, $node_ref);
}
```

add_prop simply adds a name-value pair to the AST object. add_prop_list creates a list-valued property. The property value is an anonymous array that contains references to other AST nodes. You can have your own list-valued properties, but you should never use them as an argument to @foreach because it assumes that the elements of that list are AST nodes.

```perl
my @saved_values_stack;
sub visit {
    no strict 'refs';
    my $node = shift;
    package main;
    my ($var, $val, $old_val, %saved_values);
    while (($var,$val) = each %{$node}) {
        if (defined ($old_val = $$var)) {
            $saved_values{$var} = $old_val;
        }
        $$var = $val;
    }
    push (@saved_values_stack, \%saved_values);
}
```

The visit and bye methods are used by the intermediate Perl file. $node is the node being visited, so %$node is the corresponding hash table. $var is a property name such as class_name, so to check whether a variable such as $class_name already exists, we use symbolic references: if defined($$var). All such variables that existed before are squirreled away into a hash table (%saved_values), which is then pushed into a stack. This stack represents collections of such saved values.

```perl
sub bye {
    my $rh_saved_values = pop(@saved_values_stack);
    no strict 'refs';
    package main;
    my ($var,$val);
    while (($var,$val) = each %$rh_saved_values) {
        $$var = $val;
    }
```

```
}
```

bye() simply pops this stack and restores the global variables to their former values. Incidentally, since **use strict** doesn't encourage symbolic references, we have to explicitly turn it off for a short while with **no strict 'refs'**.

Template Parser

The template parser supports the directives in Table 17-1.

Table 17-1. Directives Recognized by Jeeves

Directive	Description
`@//`	Comment. This line is not output
`@foreach var [condition]` `@end`	This loops through each element of **var** (it is assumed that **var** is an array) and executes the body if the (optional) condition is true. Conditions are simply pieces of embedded Perl code and can be used like this: `@FOREACH attr_list ($className eq "Test")`
`@if @elsif @else @end`	Translates directly to Perl's **if** statement.
`@openfile filename` `           [options]`	All statements following this line are simply sent to this file until another **@OPENFILE** is encountered. Options are: `-append`: open the file in append mode `-no_overwrite`: do not overwrite the file if it already exists `-only_if_different`: overwrites the file only if it is different. Useful in a **make** environment, where you don't want to unnecessarily touch files.

`@perl`	For embedding Perl code, provided as an escape to a higher power.
	`@perl $user_name = $ENV{USER};`
	`@perl print $user_name;`

The following template parser code simply translates all template directives to corresponding pieces of Perl code in the intermediate files. Explanations follow each subroutine definition.

```
package TemplateParser;
use strict;

sub parse {
    # Args : template file, intermediate perl file
    my ($pkg,$template_file, $inter_file) = @_;
    unless (open (T, $template_file)) {
        warn "$template_file : $@";
        return 1;
    }
    open (I, "> $inter_file") ||
```

```
                    die "Error opening intermediate file $inter_file : $@";

            emit_opening_stmts($template_file);
            my $line;
            while (defined($line = <T>)) {
                if ($line !~ /^\s*\@/) { # Is it a command?
                    emit_text($line);
                    next;
                }
                if ($line =~ /^\s*\@OPENFILE\s*(.*)\s*$/i) {
                    emit_open_file ($1);
                } elsif ($line =~ /^\s*\@FOREACH\s*(\w*)\s*(.*)\s*/i) {
                    emit_loop_begin ($1,$2);
                } elsif ($line =~ /^\s*\@END/i) {
                    emit_loop_end();
                } elsif ($line =~ /^\s*\@PERL(.*)/i) {
                    emit_perl("$1\n");
                };
            }
            emit_closing_stmts();

            close(I);
            return 0;
    }
```

TemplateParser::parse is called by the driver, with the name of the template file. For every line in the template, it checks to see whether that line is a command or ordinary text and calls the appropriate "emit" routine. All emitted code is shown in italics.

```
    sub emit_opening_stmts {
        my $template_file = shift;
        emit("# Created automatically from $template_file");
        emit(<<'_EOC_');
    use Ast;
    use JeevesUtil;

    $tmp_file = "jeeves.tmp";
    sub open_file;
    if (! (defined ($ROOT) && $ROOT)) {
        die "ROOT not defined \n";
    }

    $file = "> -";    # Assumes STDOUT, unless @OPENFILE changes it.
    open (F, $file) || die $@;
    $code = "";
    $ROOT->visit();
    _EOC_
    }
```

All pieces of code that go into the intermediate file (*emitted*) are shown in italics. Perl's "here document" feature is used extensively because we can use quotes and newlines without restrictions. emit_opening_statement visits the syntax tree's root node (the driver makes it available as a global variable called $ROOT). By default, all output from the intermediate file is to standard output until it comes across an @openfile directive.

```
sub emit_open_file {
    my $file = shift;
    my $no_overwrite      = ($file =~ s/-no_overwrite//gi) ? 1 : 0;
    my $append            = ($file =~ s/-append//gi) ? 1 : 0;
    my $only_if_different = ($file =~ s/-only_if_different//gi) ? 1 :
0;
    $file =~ s/\s*//g;
    emit (<<"_EOC_");
# Line $.
open_file(\"$file\", $no_overwrite, $only_if_different, $append);
_EOC_
}
```

emit_open_file contains the translation for @openfile and simply emits a call to the utility function *open_file* (discussed later).

```
sub emit_loop_begin {
    my $l_name = shift; # Name of the list variable
    my $condition = shift;
    my $l_name_i = $l_name . "_i";
emit (<<"_EOC_");
# Line $.
foreach \$$l_name_i (\@\${$l_name}) {
    \$$l_name_i->visit ();
_EOC_
    if ($condition) {
        emit ("next if (! ($condition));\n");
    }
}
sub emit_loop_end {
    emit(<<"_EOC_");
#Line $.
    Ast->bye();
}
_EOC_
}
```

We saw earlier the code generated for a @foreach directive. Note how we manufacture the iterator name and protect certain expressions from getting interpolated. This code can be better understood by looking at the sample output.

```
sub emit {
    print I $_[0];
}
sub emit_perl {
    emit($_[0]);
}
sub emit_text {
    my $text = $_[0];
    chomp $text;
```

```
        # Escape quotes in the text
        $text =~ s/"/\\"/g;
        $text =~ s/'/\\'/g;
        emit(<<"_EOC_");
output("$text\\n");
_EOC_
}

    sub emit_closing_stmts {
        emit(<<'_EOC_');
Ast::bye();
close(F);
unlink ($tmp_file);
sub open_file {
    my ($a_file, $a_nooverwrite, $a_only_if_different, $a_append) = @_;

    #First deal with the file previously opened
    close (F);
    if ($only_if_different) {
        if (JeevesUtil::compare ($orig_file, $curr_file) != 0) {
            rename ($curr_file, $orig_file) ||
            die "Error renaming $curr_file  to $orig_file";
        }
    }
    #Now for the new file ...
    $curr_file = $orig_file = $a_file;
    $only_if_different = ($a_only_if_different && (-f $curr_file))
                        ? 1 : 0;
    $no_overwrite = ($a_nooverwrite && (-f $curr_file))  ? 1 : 0;
    $mode =  ($a_append) ? ">>" : ">";
    if ($only_if_different) {
        unlink ($tmp_file);
        $curr_file = $tmp_file;
    }
    if (! $no_overwrite) {
        open (F, "$mode $curr_file") || die "could not open $curr_
file";
    }
}

sub output {
    print F @_ (! $no_overwrite);
}
1;
_EOC_
}
```

The open_file and output routines are present in all intermediate code files (for no particular reason—they might as well have been put in the JeevesUtil package). open_file closes the previously opened file. If you say, @openfile foo -only_if_different, the intermediate file dumps the template output into a temporary file, and when it is done, it compares this temporary file to the contents of foo, and overwrites it only if it is different.

Jeeves Driver

The *jeeves* script is merely a driver that first calls the template parser to produce the intermediate file, then calls the input parser (its **parse()** method, actually) to produce the syntax tree, and finally **eval**s the intermediate file. The template file is recompiled only if it is newer than the intermediate file.

Example 17-3 gives the code for *jeeves*, minus the uninteresting stuff (such as **process_args()**).

Example 17-3. Jeeves

```
#!/opt/bin/perl
# process_args initializes the following global variables:
#    $spec_file      - Name of the input specification (emp.om)
#    $template_file - Name of the template file (oo.tpl)
#    $inter_file    - name of the intermediate file
#                       (defaults to "${template_file}.pl"
process_args();
#------------------------------------------------------------------------
# Parse the template file
#------------------------------------------------------------------------
# Use "require" to allow process_args() to set @INC first
require 'TemplateParser.pm';
my $compile_template = 1;
if ((-e $inter_file) &&
    (-M $inter_file) >= (-M $template_file)) {
        $compile_template = 0; # Don't compile if inter-file is newer.
}
if ($compile_template) {
    if (TemplateParser->parse ($template_file, $inter_file) == 0) {
        print STDERR ("Translated $template_file to $inter_file\n")
            if $verbose;
    } else {
        die "Could not parse template file - exiting\n";
    }
}
#------------------------------------------------------------------------
# Parse the input specification file
#------------------------------------------------------------------------
require "${spec_parser}.pm"; $spec_parser->import;
$ROOT = $spec_parser->parse($spec_file);
print STDERR ("Parsed $spec_file\n") if $verbose;
$ROOT->print() if $debugging;
#------------------------------------------------------------------------
# Eval the intermediate Perl file
#------------------------------------------------------------------------
require "$inter_file";
die "$@\n" if $@;
exit(0);


#------------------------------------------------------------------------
```

Example 17-3. Jeeves (continued)

```
sub Usage {
    print STDERR <<"_EOT_";

Usage: jeeves <options> <specification file>
 where options are:
 -t <template file>                : Name of the template file.
                                     Default : "./jeeves.template"
                                     Default template directory = ".", which
                                     can be modified by setenv-ing
                                     "JEEVESTEMPLATEDIR"
 -q                                : Quiet Mode
 -d                                : Set a debugging trace. This is NOT quiet!
 -s <specification parser>         : Parser module that can parse the input
                                     specification file
                                     Default : "oo_schema"
[-ti <intermediate perl file>]  : jeeves translates the template file to
                                  : perl code. Default : "<template>.pl"
-D var[=value]                    : Define variables on the command line

The command line can be specified in the envt. variable "JEEVESOPTIONS".

The pathname to all Jeeves modules can be set in the envt. variable
    "JEEVESLIBDIR" (colon-separated);
_EOT_
    exit(1);
}
```

Sample Specification Parser

The input specification parser is particular to an application domain. In this section, we look at the parser that is required for our toy object model specification, primarily to review how the AST library is used; the parsing code itself is quite trivial. For more involved parsing tasks, you can use a version of Berkeley *yacc*, which has been hacked up to output Perl instead of C (available from *http://ftp.sterling.com:/local/perl-byacc.tar.Z*). I have successfully used this combination to produce IDL parsers for the CORBA specification.

The parser in Example 17-4 allows attributes to have additional annotations like this:

```
class Foo {
    int id,  access=readonly, db_col_name=id, index=yes;
};
```

In the template, these attribute properties can be used just like "standard" properties such as *attr_name* and *attr_type*.

Example 17-4. OO_Schema.pm: The Specification Parser

```
package SchemaParser;
use Ast;
use Carp;
sub parse{
    my ($package, $filename) = @_;
    open (P, $filename) || die "Could not open $filename : $@";
    my $root = Ast->new("Root");
    eval {
        while (1) {
            get_line();
            next unless ($line =~ /^\s*class +(\w+)/);
            $c = Ast->new($1);
            $c->add_prop("class_name" => $1);
            $root->add_prop_list("class_list", $c);
            while (1) {
                get_line();
                last if $line =~ /^\s*}/;
                if ($line =~ s/^\s*(\w+)\s*(\w+)//) {
                    $a = Ast->new($2);  #attribute name
                    $a->add_prop ("attr_name", $2);  #attribute type
                    $a->add_prop ("attr_type", $1);  #attribute type
                    $c->add_prop_list("attr_list", $a);
                }
                $curr_line = $line;
                while ($curr_line !~ /;/) {
                    get_line();
                    $curr_line .= $line;
                }
                @props = split (/[,;]/,$curr_line);
                foreach $prop (@props) {
                    if ($prop =~ /\s*(\w*)\s*=\s*(.*)\s*/) {
                        $a->add_prop($1, $2);
                    }
                }
            }
        }
    };
    # Comes here if "END OF FILE" exception is thrown
    die $@ if ($@ && ($@  !~ /END OF FILE/));
    return $root;
}
sub get_line {
    while (defined($line = <P>)) {
        chomp $line;
        $line =~ s#//.*$##;           # remove comments
        return if $line !~ /^\s*$/;   # return if not white-space
    }
    die "END OF FILE";
```

Example 17-4. OO_Schema.pm: The Specification Parser (continued)

```
}
1;
```

OO_Schema::parse starts by creating a new AST root node, and whenever it encounters a new class declaration, it adds it to the root's *class_list* property. Similarly, for each attribute, it creates a new node and adds it to the *attr_list* property of the AST node representing the class being examined.

The procedure `get_line` throws an end of file exception when there's nothing more to read. This way, the user of `get_line` can wrap multiple calls to `get_line` inside an `eval` without having to check at each place if it has prematurely reached the end of input.

Resources

1. Berkeley *yacc* for Perl, availabe at *http://ftp.sterling.com:/local/perl-byacc.tar.Z*

2. Lex for Perl. `Parse::Lex`, available on CPAN.

   Generates lexical analyzers *à la* Lex. The documentation is in French, but the library is easy enough to figure out even if you don't speak the language.

3. "Research Issues with Application Generators," *Proceedings of the 6th Annual Workshop on Software Reuse*. Prem Devanbu.

4. "A Configurable Code Generator for OO Methodologies." A. Aimar, A. Khodabandeh, P. Palazzi, and B. Rousseau. From *http://www1.cern.ch/WebMaker/ examples/CHEP94_codegene_1/www/codegene_1.html*

5. "Little Languages," *More Programming Pearls: Confessions of a Coder*. John Bentley. Association for Computing Machinery, 1988.

6. "Building Application Generators." J. Craig Cleaveland. *IEEE Software*, July 1988.

7. "Tools for Building Application Generators." J. Craig Cleaveland and Chandra M.R. Kintala. *AT&T Technical Journal*, July/August 1988.

8. *Thank You, Jeeves*. P.G. Wodehouse. Aeonian Press, 1983.

18

Extending Perl: A First Course

> *Thompson's rule for first-time telescope makers:*
> *"It is faster to make a four-inch mirror, then a six-inch mirror, than to make a six-inch mirror."*
>
> —Programming Pearls
> *Communications of the ACM, Sept. 1985*

Scripting is almost always a more pleasant and productive alternative to using a systems programming language. Scripting languages aren't designed to do everything,[*] however, and there comes a time when you need to dig down to C/C++ for speed, fine-grained data structures, type safety, and access to existing libraries. The ability of languages such as Perl, Visual Basic, Python, and Tcl to integrate well with C accords them the status of a serious development language, in contrast to *awk* and early versions of BASIC, which were seldom used for production applications.

In this chapter, we will examine what it takes to cement Perl and C code together and then study two tool sets that do a remarkable job of performing this binding for us. The first is a pair of tools called *h2xs* and *xsubpp*, packaged with the Perl distribution. For brevity, we will refer to this pair as XS,[†] because it involves an intermediate language of the same name. The other tool is SWIG (Simplified Wrapper and Interface Generator), written by Dave Beazley at the University of Utah.

We'll cover an often-used subset of these tools' capabilities and learn that a lot can be achieved without having to know anything at all about the internal Perl API. But a number of powerful features will have to wait until the section "Meaty Extensions" in Chapter 20, *Perl Internals*.

---

[*] In Perl's case, the definition of *everything* may be a bit hard to nail down!

[†] Both XSUB and XS stand for eXternal SUBroutine.

This chapter requires you to have the following modules handy: C::Scan, Data::Flow, both required by *h2xs* and available from CPAN, and the *gd* library for creating GIF files, downloadable from *www.boutell.com*.

Writing an Extension: Overview

Figure 18-1 shows a file called *testmatrix.pl* making a call to an underlying Matrix library written in C. To bind the two sets of code together, we need to have some *glue* code, indicated by the dark gray boxes.

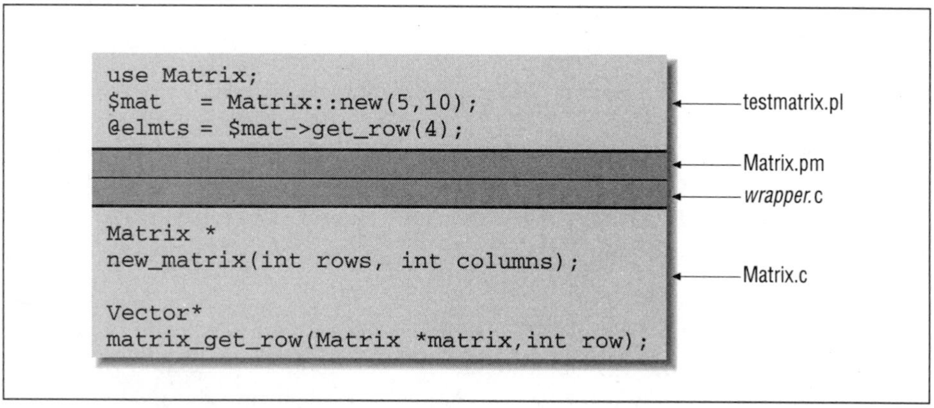

```
use Matrix;
$mat    = Matrix::new(5,10);               ←———— testmatrix.pl
@elmts = $mat->get_row(4);

                                           ←———— Matrix.pm
                                           ←——— wrapper.c

Matrix *
new_matrix(int rows, int columns);         ←———— Matrix.c

Vector*
matrix_get_row(Matrix *matrix,int row);
```

Figure 18-1. Calling C from Perl

XS and SWIG both create this glue code in two files—a Perl module and a C wrapper file—and address the following issues:

Data type translation

A Perl scalar argument can be translated to a fundamental C data type such as *int, double,* or *char *(and vice versa) with ease. Dealing with a user-defined structure such as **Matrix *** or **Vector *** is trickier. $mat in Figure 18-1 holds a C pointer to a user-defined data type. Both *xsubpp* and SWIG are equipped with a *type-mapping* facility, which allows you to write custom code for handling translations between Perl and unfamiliar C data types. You have to know some internal API before you can write typemaps, so we will visit this issue again in Chapter 20.

Memory management

Perl automatically manages the memory allocated for user-defined variables, while C expects the programmer to spell out everything. This issue is especially important when data crosses the Perl-C interface. Unfortunately, a C function's signature gives no clue about its memory management protocol; it is difficult for humans to divine it, let alone automated tools such as SWIG and XS. Let us assume that the C matrix library stores its data as a series of Vector objects internally (each row is represented as a Vector), and that `matrix_get_row` returns the Vector corresponding to that row. As you can see, both `new_matrix` and `matrix_get_row` return a pointer to an object, but in the first case, the caller is expected to take ownership of the object (delete it when it is no longer required), and in the latter, the matrix library owns the memory. While the extension tools provide certain default choices, you have to be constantly on the watch. You should also ensure that the appropriate function deletes the memory—`free`, `delete`, or `delete[]`, for objects allocated by `malloc` or C++'s `new` or `new[]`, respectively.

Perl conveniences

A simple call such as

```
($a,$b,$c) = $mat->get_row(10);
```

exercises Perl features such as packages, variable number of function arguments, multiple return values from functions, OO notation, the `wantarray` functionality, and so on. An extension should strive to make a Perl programmer feel at home.

Bootstrapping and initialization

For the C library to be called from Perl, it needs to be statically or dynamically linked in to the Perl interpreter. The Perl module generated by XS and SWIG contains the code for bootstrapping and initializing the C library. (The rest of the functions described above are present in the C wrapper code.)

The Extension Process

C header files (such as *Matrix.h*) contain data structure declarations, preprocessor macros, publicly accessible variables, and function prototypes—essentially, the interface for a C library. You are typically not interested in making everything available to a Perl script; there's nothing worse than attempting C programming in Perl. In most cases, it suffices to export a subset of public functions, and some constants (which are available as initialized variables, `#define`'s, or `enum`s). We refer to them collectively as the public interface and extract them into a public header file.

Figure 18-2 shows how the Matrix library's header file is used as input for the two sets of tools.

The public header file may contain complex C declarations. SWIG expects you, the extension developer, to boil the interface down to a still simpler form and express it in its interface definition language. Fortunately, this language is close enough to ANSI C and simple C++ that a large number of header files don't need any translation at all. From the interface description, SWIG generates the glue

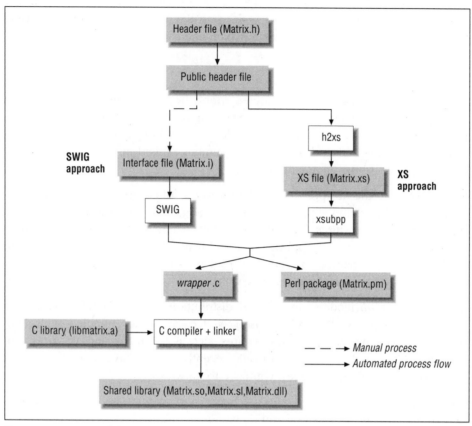

Figure 18-2. SWIG and XS processes

code; in the Matrix case, it will be *Matrix.pm* and *Matrix_wrap.c*. If your system supports dynamic linking (shared libraries on Unix, and DLLs on Windows), and if the Perl executable has been built to use it, all that is left to be done is to convert the glue code and your C library into a dynamic library. If dynamic linking is not an option, then a new Perl executable is generated by statically linking the Perl archive library (*libperl.a* on Unix or *perl.lib* on Microsoft Windows) with the pieces of code mentioned above.

h2xs and *xsubpp* take a slightly different approach. *h2xs* understands C header files (but not C++) and converts all constants and function prototypes to a meta language called XS. But a function declaration may still be too complex for scripting purposes, so this approach expects you to twiddle with the *.xs* file produced by *h2xs* and take the necessary steps to simplify the interface. Of course, the hand conversion is unnecessary if the interface is already simple enough. The XS language is a mixture of C and funny keywords and provides directives for you to override the glue code produced by *xsubpp*.

Incidentally, the code generated by both tools is quite similar, and it is perfectly acceptable to have some extensions built using the XS approach and some using SWIG. Which brings us to the question: which one should you use?

SWIG or XS?

Differences in SWIG's and XS's features spring from differences in their design goals. SWIG is designed to help create a scripting language wrapper over a C library and supports Python, Tcl, and Guile in addition to Perl. In contrast, XS is designed only for Perl and allows for a number of Perlisms that SWIG cannot easily generalize to the other languages.

I prefer SWIG to the XS approach because it *feels* a lot cleaner, is far less internals-oriented than XS is, and supports multiple languages. In addition, it has excellent support for data structures (not just functions), whereas XS supports only functions. I build C++ and Java applications for a living, so my focus is typically more on the application than on the scripting frontend—I leave the choice of scripting language to the user. Your mileage may vary.

You'll find that *all* modules in the Perl distribution and on CPAN are currently written by using XS. The chief reason is that XS comes bundled with Perl. Besides, it has supported powerful features such as typemaps since its inception, whereas SWIG has been beefed up only recently. If you have to understand or modify any of the CPAN modules, you have to know XS.

Both tools provide significant degrees of freedom to compensate for most deficiencies, so my advice is to pick one and go with it.

Example: Fractals with Perl

Enough general talk! Let us test-drive both tools using a simple piece of fractal-drawing code. This problem is tailor-made for C, because generating a fractal image involves performing a series of computations on every pixel, which calls for compact data structures *and* fast number-crunching. This exercise creates the familiar Mandelbrot set image shown in Figure 18-3.

Our Mandelbrot code is implemented in *mandel.c* and *mandel.h*. To avoid a non-portable GUI solution, we use a public domain library, *gd*, written by Tom Boutell [6], which allows you to treat a GIF file as a canvas and render points, lines, and circles on it. This GIF file can then be viewed by using any web browser.

Figure 18-3. Mandelbrot set

mandel.c implements one function called **draw_mandel**, with the signature shown in Example 18-1.

Example 18-1. Mandel.h

```
extern int
draw_mandel (char *filename,
             int width, int height,
             double origin_real, double origin_imag,
             double range, double depth);
```

The meaning of the parameters will be explained in the "A Detour into Fractals," later in this chapter. First, we'll first concentrate on making it callable from Perl.

Fractals Using SWIG

We start by writing a SWIG interface file, *Fractal.i*, as in Example 18-2.

Example 18-2. Fractal.i—SWIG Interface File

```
%module Fractal
%{
#include "mandel.h"
%}
%include mandel.h
```

The **%module** statement gives a unique namespace to all the interface declarations in that file. We call the module Fractal because we would like to have one namespace for all fractal drawing code, and the Mandelbrot set is only one of many choices.

The statements between %{ and %} are meant for "raw" C code. We include *mandel.h* here because the interface file is soon going to be converted to C glue code, which in turn needs this header. Now comes the portion where all data structures and exported functions (with complete signatures) are to be listed. Since the interface file format is very close to ANSI C, we can simply %include *mandel.h*. Unlike the first include, which began with a # because it is called later from C code, this include starts with % because it is called immediately within SWIG.

Next, we invoke SWIG on this interface file and specify perl5 as the scripting language:

```
% swig -perl5 Fractal.i
Generating wrappers for Perl 5
% ls
mandel.h       mandel.c         Fractal_wrap.doc
Fractal.i      Fractal.pm       Fractal_wrap.c
```

SWIG creates four files from the interface file. *Fractal.pm* contains some code to make the C library dynamically loadable. *Fractal_wrap.c* contains the wrapper code; for a function *foo* listed in the interface file, this wrapper file contains a function called _wrap_foo that translates Perl argument values to C, calls foo, and packages the return results back into Perl data types. You don't have to understand the contents of *Fractal.pm* and *Fractal_wrap.c*. SWIG also extracts all documentation out of the interface file into *Fractal_wrap.doc* (ASCII), or *Fractal_wrap.html* (HTML), or *Fractal_wrap.tex* (LaTeX).

All we have left to do is to compile the two *.c* files and make them dynamically loadable.* SWIG (as well as XS) simplifies this part again by helping you create a makefile. Because a makefile is dependent on machine- and site-specific details such as operating system peculiarities, compiler, linker options, Perl installation directories, the name and location of the C compiler, and so on, these tools do not generate a makefile directly. Instead they generate a Perl script called *Make-file.PL*, which, when executed, produces a makefile that is customized for your system. This script is very simple, shown here after manually adding the LIBS and OBJECT lines:

```
use ExtUtils::MakeMaker;
WriteMakefile(
    'NAME'   => 'Fractal',    # Name of module
    'LIBS'   => [M     # All custom libraries to be linked with
    'OBJECT' => 'mandel.o Fractal_wrap.o'  # All object files
);
```

---

* Since this is a much simpler option than static linking, and since most self-respecting operating systems support it, we consider only dynamic linking in this book.

The standard ExtUtils::MakeMaker module does all the magic of finding out about the configuration of your system and creating a custom makefile.

The next three steps build and install this extension:

```
% perl Makefile.PL      # create Makefile
% make                  # compiles sources and creates shared library
% make install          # optional. installs library
```

(How much easier and more portable do you want it to get?)

We are now all set to create fractal images. The following call to `draw_mandel()` creates the beautiful image shown in Figure 18-3.

```
use Fractal;
Fractal::draw_mandel('mandel.gif', 300, 300,   # file, width, height
                     -1.5, 1.0,                 # origin x, y
                      2.0, 20);                 # range, max iterations
```

Since the chief purpose of this chapter is to illustrate writing extensions, we'll (reluctantly) put off the discussion of *draw_mandel* to the end.

Fractals Using XS

The XS process is also extremely straightforward. *h2xs* understands normal C header files, so a fractal extension is produced as follows:

```
% h2xs -x -n Fractal mandel.h
```

This creates *Fractal.pm*, the Perl module, *Makefile.PL*, the makefile-generating script, and *Fractal.xs*. At this point, you don't need to know what this file contains.

Since *Makefile.PL* is automatically generated, you will need to add or modify the OBJECT and LIB lines, as shown earlier. The build and install are identical to what we saw earlier:

```
% perl Makefile.PL
% make
% make install
```

The makefile generated in the first step notices *Fractal.xs*, and feeds it to `xsubpp` to create the glue code in *Fractal.c*. Note that the name is not *Fractal_wrap.c* as with SWIG, so the OBJECT line in *Makefile.PL* should look like this:

```
'OBJECT' => 'mandel.o Fractal.o' # mandel.o contains the real function
                                 # Fractal.o contains the glue code
```

SWIG Features

Having completed a tour of the extension process, let's zoom in for a closer look at SWIG's compendium of features. We mentioned earlier that SWIG handles a useful subset of ANSI C/C++, which means support for data structures as well as functions. Specifically, it supports the following:

Constants and global variables

A C variable can be exported into Perl space as a scalar variable of the same name. SWIG supports the fundamental C data types, enums, and #defined constant values. Variables of complex or user-defined types are automatically mapped to a pair of get/set accessor functions.

Pointers

Every pointer is treated as a `void *` by default, regardless of whether it is a `char**` or `Matrix*` or `double ***`. This strategy works especially well for user-defined types, because most C libraries don't expect you to dereference such pointers. For example, `fopen` returns a `FILE *`, which is simply handed over to `fread()` and `fwrite()`. In Perl, this pointer is available as a scalar, and Perl doesn't have to know whether the pointer refers to an array, structure, or a typedef. On the other hand, if you want a `Vector *` to a list of integer-valued scalars, you will have to help SWIG out by providing a typemap.

Typemaps

Not every data type is a simple conversion from Perl to C or vice versa. SWIG (like *xsubpp*) provides a way for you to write arbitrary transformations, such as converting a Perl array to a 10-by-10 matrix. To write a typemap, you need to know Perl's API for accessing its internal data types, so we'll cover this topic in the section "SWIG Typemaps" in Chapter 20. Typemaps can be applied not just to function parameters, but also to structure members and global variables. You can also optionally create named typemaps, which apply to specific named entities (function arguments, variable names, function names), instead of all entities of that type.

Arrays

Both simple arrays (`vector[100]`) and multidimensional arrays (`vector[10][10]`) are mapped to a simple pointer (`vector *`). Typemap support for arrays exists, but there are still a number of thorny issues for which SWIG cannot provide a general solution; please read the SWIG documentation for details.

Structures and C++ classes

SWIG automatically creates accessor functions for each member of a structure or class defined in the interface file. As with the other facilities, these declarations cannot have the full generality of a C structure or a C++ class, but they are powerful enough for handling most common interface issues.

Methods

SWIG provides constructor and destructor procedures, which allow you to allocate and free C structures from Perl space. You can convert basic C structures to objects in Perl space with a primitive called `%addmethods`.

Ordinary functions

SWIG creates function wrappers that look pretty similar to their C equivalents. Each parameter can be optionally typemapped, but since a typemap provides a translation in isolation (from other parameters), the *number* of parameters cannot be changed. This is not a constraint in XS.

In other words, with SWIG you cannot map the C function

```
char ** permute(char *string); // returns permutations of string
```
to
```
@array = permute ($str);
```

because one parameter, `char**`, needs conversion to a variable number of scalars (to be assigned to `@array`). You can instead write a typemap to convert the `char**` to an array and *return its reference*, so in Perl space, it is accessible this way:

```
$rarray = permute ($str);
print join(' ', @$rarray);
```

Of course, you can always write a wrapper Perl function and insert it in the *.pm* file created automatically by SWIG:

```
sub fancy_permute {
    @{permute($_[0])}; # dereferences array
}
```

Default and optional parameters

Parameters can have default values but, as in C++, can be applied only to the rightmost parameters. This is how you specify the function signature in the interface file:

```
draw_mandel (file,width,height,orig_real,orig_imag,range,depth=30);
```

This allows you to optionally skip the last parameter when calling from Perl.

Centralized exception handling

SWIG provides a `%except` directive to wrap all external library calls inside a generic exception handler. This way you can trap all user-defined errors and C++ exceptions in one central place and translate them into Perl exceptions. Please see the SWIG documentation for examples.

Shadow classes

SWIG optionally creates wrapper Perl code that allows you to access member attributes and functions of C or C++ objects using the Perl hash notation,

`$person->{age}`. This mechanism is built on top of the attribute accessor functions mentioned earlier.

Nested structures

An embedded structure gets the same treatment as an outermost structure—accessor functions and support from shadow classes.

The following interface file shows an example of using classes, accessing methods, and creating shadow classes:

```
%module Graphics

class Shape {
public:
    int x, y; // origin
    int w, h; // width, ht (defines bounding area)
    draw();
};
class Polygon : public Shape {
public:
    Polygon(int x, int y, int w, int h);
    draw();
};
```

We invoke SWIG with the −c++ option, since it is not enabled by default, and the −shadow option for creating shadow classes:

> **% swig -c++ -shadow Graphics.i**

SWIG sets up an identical inheritance hierarchy in script space, and using this class in Perl feels completely natural:

```
use Graphics;
$poly = new Polygon(10, 10, 30, 40);
printf "Origin: %d %d \n", $poly->{x}, poly->{y};
$poly->draw();
```

You'll be happy to know that SWIG properly handles the relationship between base classes and derived classes. For example, a function involving a base class will recognize pointers that have been blessed into a derived class. In the case of multiple inheritance, SWIG performs proper C++ type-casting to make sure the pointer values are correct. XS has no such feature.

While the shadow class feature is convenient, you should be aware that for every instance generated using **new**, an additional object is created internally. The reason is that to support the member access notation (`$poly->{x}`), **new** returns a tied hash, whose FETCH subroutine calls the appropriate accessor function. You know by now that the tie facility interposes an intermediate object.

XS Features

XS, as we mentioned earlier, is an interface definition language. Unlike SWIG, XS concentrates solely on C functions and `#define`'d constants and does not provide any support for `struct` or `class` definitions (although there are plans for doing so in the future). In practice, I haven't missed this support for structures and classes too much because I rarely export data structures, in keeping with encapsulation principles.

The XS approach allows you to modify the XS file and supply glue code (in C) in varying degrees. It is analogous to C or Pascal compilers that allow you to insert native assembly code within a program. This gives a lot of power if you know what you are doing, but requires you to be conversant with the internal Perl API and protocols.

By modifying the XS file, you can create `write` function wrappers that take a variable number of input parameters, modify some input parameters (as `read` does), and return an array of result values. Combine this with the ability to write custom typemaps and modify the Perl module (produced by *h2xs*), and you have several ways of creating extensions.

Let us take a brief look at XS syntax. *Fractal.xs*, from our earlier example, looks like this in its most essential form:

```
#include <mandel.h>

MODULE = Fractal    PACKAGE = Fractal

int
draw_mandel (filename,width,height,origin_real,origin_imag,range,depth)
      char*  filename
      int    width
      int    height
      double origin_real
      double origin_imag
      double range
      double depth
```

All text preceding a `MODULE` statement is considered to be raw C code and is sent untranslated into the *Fractal.c*, the glue code (like the `%{ ... %}` block in SWIG). An XS module can contain more than one package, but since this is not typical, the `MODULE` and `PACKAGE` keywords have the same value. All exportable functions are listed in a special way. The return type comes first, on its own line (you must specify `void` in the absence of a return type), then the name of the function with a list of parameter names, and, finally, each parameter on a separate line. It is important to keep the "*" along with the type, not the name—you must say `char* filename`, not `char *filename`. The next function declaration simply starts after a blank line.

What Does xsubpp Do?

It pays to understand a little bit about the glue code generated by *xsubpp*. When *xsubpp* is given the XS snippet shown above, it creates a function called `Fractal_xs_draw_mandel` (in *Fractal.c*) with the same signature as the XS declaration. This function translates the arguments supplied in Perl space to the C function's parameters, calls the real `draw_mandel` function, and finally packages its return value into a Perl value.

XS provides several keywords to either inject your own code at suitable locations inside the generated function or completely replace the generated glue code with your own. For example, you can write typemap functions that handle how Perl arguments get translated to C; you can use the CODE keyword (described later) to specify that you are supplying your own code.

With this brief overview in mind, let us now look at a few of the important aspects of the XS language.

Default and Optional Parameters

Parameters can have default values but, as in C++, can be applied only to the rightmost parameters:

```
draw_mandel (file,width,height,orig_real,orig_imag,range,depth=30)
```

This allows you to optionally skip the last parameter when calling from Perl.

Modifying Parameters

XS allows you to modify parameters before they are given to the real `draw_mandel` function:

```
int
draw_mandel (filename,width,height,origin_real,origin_imag,range,depth)
      char*  filename
      int    width
      int    height
      double origin_real
      double origin_imag
      double range
      double depth
   INIT:
   if (width > 400) {
       fprintf (stderr, "Width cannot exceed 400. Truncating.\n";
       width = 400;
   }
```

The INIT: keyword tells XS to insert the code following it between the argument translation (from Perl to C) and the call to the real function.

In SWIG, you would use a named typemap for the same effect. The XS approach, however, allows you to make a decision based on more than one parameter. For example, if you had to maintain a certain aspect ratio, you would have to look at both width and height and modify one of them. A typemap cannot give you this flexibility because it looks at each parameter in isolation.

Incidentally, the `PREINIT:` keyword can be used to insert variable declarations; *xsubpp* puts these declarations ahead of any generated code. Of course, this keyword is not important if you compile the glue code with a C++ compiler, since it allows you to declare variables anywhere in the code.

Special Code

You can write the glue code yourself if you want. Consider the `sin()` function in the math library, which requires you to supply the angle in radians. You can create a new function in Perl to accept the angle in degrees using the `CODE` keyword, like this (the indentation scheme is arbitrary):

```
double
d_sin(angle)
   double angle
   CODE:
   RETVAL = sin(angle * PI / 180);
   OUTPUT:
   RETVAL
```

When *xsubpp* sees the `CODE` keyword, it just maps the arguments from Perl data types to C types and leaves you to supply the rest of the code, which means that you have to make the call to the underlying external subroutine yourself. The `CODE` directive does not change the essential structure of the C call; you can modify input parameters and you can return at most one result value.

The `OUTPUT:` directive tells *xsubpp* to supply some code to package the returned result and load it back into Perl space. `RETVAL` is automatically declared by *xsubpp* to match the return value of the function. In the preceding example, the return value of `sin()` is the only output parameter and is listed under `OUTPUT`.

The `CODE` directive does not help if you want a variable number of input parameters or returned results. In this case, you use the `PPCODE` directive and explicitly manage the entire argument stack. We will have more on this in Chapter 20.

Please take a look at the XS documentation for other keywords, details, and examples.

C++ Code

XS supports two special procedures for automatically creating and deleting C++ objects. Consider the following XS code for a module called `Car`:

```
Car*
Car::new()

void
Car::DESTROY()

void
Car::turn_left()
```

When you say `new Car` in Perl, the wrapper code corresponding to `Car::new` makes the C++ invocation, `new Car()`. Later on, when you say in Perl space, `$car->turn_left()`, the appropriate C++ function is automatically called. If you want to supply CODE or PPCODE directives for C++ interfaces, you can refer to the object as `THIS` and to the class as `CLASS`.

This example has one hitch. It has no clue what's in the data type `Car`. Unlike SWIG, which quite unconcernedly treats a `Car*` like a `void*`, *xsubpp* expects help in the form of a typemap. Since we need to know the internal Perl API to create a typemap, we'll leave this issue unresolved until Chapter 20.

Degrees of Freedom

Before we conclude the essential part of this chapter, let us quickly recap all the places where you can plug in code to help XS and SWIG produce a smooth interface (for the script programmer):

Perl module
> So far, the Perl module produced by these tools has been used only to bootstrap the C code, but there's no reason why it shouldn't have some custom subroutines too. The XS example presented earlier, in the "Modifying Parameters" section, could easily have been implemented in Perl space.

Typemaps
> Supply snippets of code to convert between Perl and C data types.

Wrapper code in the interface files
> The CODE and PPCODE directives allow you to insert a variety of custom translation tasks. In SWIG, you can inline custom C code as follows:

```
%module FunMath
%inline %{
    int factorial(int n){return (n == 1) ? 1 : n *(n -1)};
%}
```

A Detour into Fractals

This chapter would be incomplete and dry without a small foray into Mandelbrot sets and the implementation of `draw_mandel`.

For starters, I highly recommend Ivars Peterson's book *The Mathematical Tourist* [5] for its engaging style and treatment of a surprisingly wide set of mathematical topics. We'll begin by assuming that you already know about complex numbers.

We know that a complex number $a + bi$ is composed of two parts, the real part a, and the imaginary part b, that taken together constitute a point on a graph. Now consider the expression $z = z^2 - 1$, where z is a complex number. We start with a complex number (z^0) and plot it. We then substitute it in the above expression to produce a new complex number and plot this number. This exercise is repeated, say, 20 or 30 times. We find that different starting values of z^0 result either in this series trailing off to infinity, or remaining confined within a boundary. All z^0's that result in a bounded series belong to a *Julia set*, named after the mathematician Gaston Julia. In other words, if we plot all the z^0's that result in a bounded series, we will see a nice fractal picture (no, not the one we saw earlier).

Now, let us make the equation a bit more general: $z \leftarrow z^2 + c$, where c is a complex number (the discussion above was for $c = -1 + 0i$). Now, if we plot the Julia sets for different values of c, we find that some plots show beautiful connected shapes while other disperse into a cloud of disconnected dots. Clearly, we are interested only in the former; all values of c that result in such nice-looking Julia sets are said to belong to the Mandelbrot set, after Benoit Mandelbrot.

Calculating the Mandelbrot set is obviously a pain, because for every c (an infinite set), you have to plot the Julia set to see whether it disperses or not. Enter mathematicians John Hubbard and Adrien Douady. They proved that for a given value of c, it is enough to check whether a starting point of $z^0 = 0$ (that is, $0 + 0i$) results in a bounded sequence. If it does, then that value of c yields a connected (nondispersing) Julia set. It has also been proven that all c's belonging to the Mandelbrot set are contained within a small area that "looks like a small pimply snowman on his side," as Ivars Peterson puts it. This is the white central area inside Figure 18-3, extending from −2 to +0.5 on the x-axis, and from −1.0 to +1.0 on the y-axis. So as soon as the series goes beyond 2, you know that it is not bounded, and, consequently, c is not going to be a part of the Mandelbrot set. To lend some more visual interest to the figure, we attempt to assign a color to every point within our viewing window, whether it belongs to the Mandelbrot set or not. Those that belong to this set are colored white, and those that don't are given a gray color, depending on how far the corresponding series attempts to jump out of the boundaries.

`draw_mandel` (contained in the file *Fractal.c* and shown in Example 18-3) implements the algorithm described previously. The parameters are explained below, and the values that generated Figure 18-3 are shown in parentheses:

filename
> The name of the GIF file to produce.

width, height (400, 400)
> The width and height of the GIF image in number of pixels.

origin_real, origin_imag (-1.4,1.0)
> What the top-left pixel corresponds to, given as a complex number.

range (2.0)
> The width and height spanned in the complex number plane. If the origin is $-1.0 + 1.4i$ and the range is 2, the figure spans $-1.0 + 1.4i$ to $1.0 - 0.6i$ (*y* decreases from top to bottom, *x* increases from left to right). If you reduce this number, the canvas is devoted to a smaller area of the complex plane. Consequently, range works as a zoom factor, the image varying inversely with this value.

max_iterations (20)
> The number of times one should iterate through $z \leftarrow z^2 + c$ before giving up to check before deciding whether the series is bounded.

Example 18-3. mandel.c

```
#include <math.h>
#include <stdio.h>
#include <gd.h>
typedef struct {
    double r, i;
} complex;

int draw_mandel (char *filename,
                 int width, int height,
                 double origin_real,
                 double origin_imag,
                 double range,
                 double max_iterations)
{
    complex     origin;
    int         colors[51], color, white, x, y, i;
    FILE        *out;
    gdImagePtr im_out;

    origin.r = origin_real;  /* Measured from top-left */
    origin.i = origin_imag;
```

Example 18-3. mandel.c (continued)

```
if (!(out = fopen(filename, "wb"))) {
    fprintf(stderr, "File %s could not be opened\n");
    return 1;
}


im_out = gdImageCreate(width, height); /* Create a canvas */
/* Allocate some gray colors. Start from black, and increment r,g,b
   values uniformly. This has the effect of varying the luminosity,
   while keeping the same hue.
   (Black = 0,0,0 and white = 255, 255,255 */
for (i = 0; i < 50; i++) {
    color = i * 4;
    colors[i] = gdImageColorAllocate(im_out, color,color,color);
}
white = gdImageColorAllocate(im_out, 255,255,255);
/* For each pixel on the canvas do ... */
for (y = 0; y < height; y++) {
    for (x = 0; x < width; x++) {
        complex z, c ;
        int  iter;
        /* Convert the pixel to an equivalent complex number c,
           given the origin and the range. The range acts like an
           inverse zoom factor.*/

        c.r = origin.r + (double) x / (double) width * range;
        c.i = origin.i - (double) y / (double) height * range;

        /* Examine each point calculated above to see if repeated
           substitutions into an equation like z(next) = z**z + c
           remains within a definite boundary.
           If after <max_iterations> iterations it still hasn't gone
           beyond the white area, it belongs to the Mandelbrot set.
           But if it does, we assign it a color depending on how
           far the series wants to jump out of bounds*/
        color = white;
        z.r = z.i = 0.0; /* Starting point */
        for (iter = 0; iter < max_iterations; iter++) {
            double dist, new_real, new_imag;
            /*calculate  z = z^2 + c */
            /* Recall that z^2 is a^2 - b^2 + 2abi, if z = a + bi, */
            new_real = z.r * z.r - z.i * z.i + c.r;
            new_imag = 2 * z.r * z.i + c.i;
            z.r = new_real; z.i = new_imag;
            /* Pythagorean distance from 0,0 */
            dist = new_real * new_real + new_imag * new_imag;
            if (dist >= 4) {
                /* No point on the mandelbrot set is more than 2 units
                   away from the origin. If it quits the boundary, give
                   that 'c' an interesting color depending on how far
                   the series wants to jump out of its bounds */
                color = colors[(int) dist % i];
```

Example 18-3. mandel.c (continued)

```
                    break;
                }
            }
            gdImageSetPixel(im_out, x,y, color);
        }
    }
    gdImageGif(im_out,out);
    fclose(out);
    return 0;
}
```

Resources

1. SWIG. David Beazley.

   Download freely from *http://www.cs.utah.edu/~beazley/SWIG/swig.html*. SWIG is packaged with around 200 pages of *wonderful* tutorial-style documentation, containing plenty of interesting examples. While you are there, please take a look at Dave's papers on applying SWIG to large-scale projects.

2. *perlxstut*, by Jeff Okamoto, and *perlxs*, by Dean Roehrich.

   These two standard Perl documents provide a tutorial and a reference, respectively, for XS. You must be conversant either with Chapter 20 or the Perl internals documentation (*perlguts*). (The former is a slightly gentler introduction.)

3. Standard extensions

   The Socket, POSIX, and SDBM modules supplied with the Perl distribution make good case studies for applying XS.

4. XS Cookbook. Dean Roehrich.

   These cookbooks are available from CPAN (look under the *authors/Dean_ Roehrich* directory) and provide solutions to a number of sample problems covering all XS features. Highly recommended. You may also find it a good exercise to solve these problems using SWIG.

5. *The Mathematical Tourist.* Ivars Peterson. W.H.Freeeman and Co., 1988

6. GD library for rendering into GIF files. Tom Boutell. Download from *http:// www.boutell.com/*.

19

Embedding Perl:
The Easy Way

*A rock pile ceases to be a rock pile the moment a
single man contemplates it, bearing within him
the image of a cathedral.*

—Antoine de Saint-Exupery

Much as there are reasons for writing C extensions for Perl, there are any number of reasons to execute Perl scripts from within C/C++ applications; we refer to this activity as *embedding* the Perl interpreter. Embedding does not mean that we wish to conceal the interpreter; it just indicates that the application retains overall control and, when required, makes calls to the Perl internal API.

This chapter introduces a simple API for embedding the Perl interpreter in your C application. These functions are not standard (that is, they have been introduced in this book), and shield you from having to know anything at all about Perl internals, reference counting, memory management, and calling conventions. Although these details will be discussed in the next chapter, you shouldn't *have* to know them to get useful work done. The *perlembed* document written by Jon Orwant and Doug MacEachern [1] provides a fine tutorial-style coverage of this subject, but expects you to be conversant with the internals.

Why Embed?

A C application can make use of a scripting language in different ways:

Power through scripted extensions

Applications such as Emacs, Microsoft Office, and Autocad provide scripting language frontends. Although they work reasonably well on their own, their real power comes from the large community of developers writing scripted extensions. To paraphrase Brian Kernighan, a good tool is one that is used in ways its developers never thought of. The *calc* package in Emacs is capable of doing symbolic mathematics, for example. Who would have thought of putting this in a text editor?! *

As glue

Emacs is an excellent example of an application that implements its basic functionality in C for speed and operating system interfaces and everything else in LISP (it has an embedded LISP interpreter), which provide the necessary glue for the C code. The editor won't even start without some crucial LISP code.

Using the scripting language's power

I once had to work on a Unix-based application talking to a mainframe. The files coming off the mainframe were curiously formatted, and of course, wouldn't match the specifications. Since munging files is so much easier in Perl than in C, I used Perl scripts and an embedded Perl interpreter to parse these files so that I could change the parsing strategy at will.

I could have chosen the easier option of spawning an external Perl script using `system(3)` or `popen(3)` and fetching its output from a temporary file or a pipe. This approach works very well for a large number of applications, as is evident from the success of CGI. There is much to be said for separating application functionality into two separately debuggable programs. But it wasn't fast enough for my application. Additionally, the data flowing across the interface wasn't simple enough, so I would have had to write a lot of code to format this data on one end and to parse it on the other. Spawning external scripts has the additional problem that it doesn't give you a persistent context. That is, every time you launch a Perl script, it doesn't remember anything from the time it was last invoked, and it would have to reopen socket connections, database connections, restart transactions, and so on. An identical approach is taken by the Apache web server [2].

Better C code

Writing a scripting frontend forces you to simplify the interface functions to ease the integration with the scripting language. Happily enough, this also makes life easy for other C programmers using your libraries.

Instrumentation

A scripting facility presents an opportunity to provide programmatic access to instrumentation probes embedded in the code (for monitoring performance, memory usage, dynamic assertions, etc.). For example, you can automatically set up an audit trail of all inbound user connections when the number of users exceeds 50.

---

* Of course, *vi* folks would ask *why?*

Powerful configuration files

Applications may not be satisfied with simple configuration files (name-value properties, such as those provided by the Microsoft Windows Registry).

Embedding Overview

Strange as it may seem, there are no tools to automate the task of embedding Perl as there are for extending Perl. Why is that? After all, extensions also have to account for translating data from Perl to C and back (input and output parameters). The reason is that when Perl drives C code, it specifies precisely how and when a C extension is loaded. As an extension writer, you have the job of simply writing XSUBs in a callback style, providing some initializations; the XSUBs will be called when the script invokes the appropriate corresponding functions. In contrast, since there is no standard way to write a C application, you have to decide when to initialize an embedded Perl interpreter and how to give control over to a Perl script.

To simplify embedding, this chapter shows you an easy-to-use veneer over Perl's internal API. These routines have been developed for this book to save you the bother of assimilating over 50 pages of internal documentation. But if you are the type who thrives on such details, Chapter 20, *Perl Internals*, should provide the needed fix. It also explains the code for these convenience routines.

It so happens that the Perl executable is made up of two parts: a library of core Perl routines[*] (*libperl.a* on Unix systems and *perl.lib* on Microsoft Windows systems, or dynamically loadable equivalents of the same) and a simple driver file, *perlmain.c*, containing `main()`, which, shorn of all its portability aspects, looks like this:

```
#include <EXTERN.h>
#include <perl.h>
static PerlInterpreter *my_perl;
int main(int argc, char **argv, char **env)
{
    my_perl = perl_alloc();                      #
    perl_construct(my_perl);                     # Initialize

    perl_parse(my_perl, xs_init, argc, argv, env); #
    perl_run(my_perl);                           # Run

    perl_destruct(my_perl);                      # Shut down
    perl_free(my_perl);
}
```

---

[*] Not to be confused with the *lib* directory in a Perl distribution.

`perl_alloc` and `perl_construct` create an interpreter object. `perl_parse` does some more initializations, parses the command-line parameters provided to it via `argc` and `argv`, calls an initialization routine, `xs_init`, to load other extensions (or to at least initialize the dynamic loader), and finally parses the script provided as part of the command line. `perl_run` executes the script. Finally, `perl_destruct` and `perl_free` shut down and deallocate the interpreter.

To take advantage of the power of Perl, all you need to do is link the Perl library to your application and essentially clone the code in *perlmain.c.* We will talk about `xs_init` in the section "Adding Extensions" later in this chapter; until then, we will assume that we don't need any extensions and pass NULL to `perl_parse` instead of `xs_init`. The interpreter is fully primed once `perl_parse` is done, after which you can call all functions exported by the Perl library. In this chapter, however, we will restrict ourselves to a few high-level calls, listed in Table 19-1.

Table 19-1. Perl API Calls for Easy Embedding

Function Name	Description

`perl_call_argv(`
    `char *sub,`
    `I32   flags,`
    `char **argv);`
	This call is available in the standard Perl distribution. It calls a subroutine with an array of string arguments terminated by NULL. Unfortunately, it doesn't return results in a convenient way. For this reason, the only flag we will use in this chapter is G_DISCARD, to tell Perl to silently discard all returned results.

`perl_call_va (`
    `char *sub,`
    `[char *type, arg,]*`
    `["OUT",]`
    `[char *type, arg,]*`
    `NULL`
`);`
	This provides a convenient interface for passing a null-terminated list of typed parameters to a Perl subroutine and to collect the returned results into a list of parameters (similar to `printf` and `scanf`). The `type` argument can be `i`, `s`, or `d` (integer, string, double). The string OUT begins a list of return parameters, which are pairs of type specifiers and appropriately typed pointers. String output parameters are copied into the buffers supplied, which consequently should have enough space to absorb the returned strings.
	The parameter list must always be NULL-terminated. The function returns –1 on failure and the number of parameters returned by the procedure, if successful.

`int perl_eval_va(`
    `char *str,`
    `[char *type,`
          `*arg],`
    `NULL);`
	Evaluates an arbitrary string, not just a subroutine. The string can be followed by any number of out parameters in the style discussed above. It does not need input parameters because they are already encoded in the string. `perl_eval_va` returns –1 on failure, or the number of result parameters returned by the evaluation.

`set_int(char *var,`
        `int  value);`
`int get_int(`
        `char *var,`
        `int *pvalue);`
	Gets or sets a globally accessible, integer-valued scalar. `var` can contain ordinary scalar variable names or array and hash indices as follows: `foo`, `foo[10]`, or `foo{hello}`.
	`get_int` takes a pointer to an integer and returns 1 if successful (or 0 on failure).
	`set_int` creates a variable if it doesn't already exist.

Table 19-1. Perl API Calls for Easy Embedding (continued)

Function Name	Description

`set_double(char *var,`
`          double`
`          value);`
`int get_double(`
`          char *var,`
`          double`
`          *pvalue);`
	Similar to above.

`set_str(char *var,`
`        char *value);`
`int get_str(char *var,`
`          char **value);`
	`get_str` returns the address of the string. You are expected to copy it into your own buffer.

The `get_*` and `set_*` functions can be used only to manipulate a scalar at a time. The reason I allowed this limitation is that Perl already provides a nice chunk of functions that can slice, dice, and iterate through arrays and hashes; we'll take a detailed look at them in Chapter 20. These functions, while faster and more fine-grained, are tied to internals-related details (memory management, temporary variables, and so on); hence any discussion of them necessitates discussing these other aspects too. The `get_*` and `set_*` functions are simpler.

Examples

Let us now write some code to see this API in action. Suppose you have a Perl script, *search.pl*, containing subroutine `search_files`, defined in Example 19-1.

Example 19-1. search.pl

```
# search_files - a simple grep. Called as ...
#    search_files ("struct", "*.h")
sub search_files {
    my ($pattern, $filepattern) = @_;
    local (@ARGV) = glob($filepattern);
    return unless (@ARGV);
    while (<>) {        # Can do this because @ARGV has been primed
        if (/$pattern/o) {
            print "$ARGV\[$.\]: $_"; # File, line number, match line
        }
    }
}
```

`search_files` takes two string parameters and returns nothing. There are several ways of calling this procedure from C. Let's start with `perl_call_argv()`, since it takes string arguments. The piece of code in Example 19-2 searches for the word "struct" in all C header files.

Example 19-2. ex.c: Embedding Perl

```
#include <EXTERN.h>
#include <perl.h>
static PerlInterpreter *my_perl;
main(int argc, char **argv, char **env) {
    char *my_argv[] = {"struct", "*.h", NULL};
    my_perl = perl_alloc();
    perl_construct(my_perl);
    perl_parse(my_perl, NULL, argc, argv, env);

    perl_call_argv("search_files", G_DISCARD, my_argv);

    perl_destruct(my_perl);
    perl_free(my_perl);
}
```

By passing NULL instead of **xs_init**, we indicate to **perl_parse** that we are
not interested in loading any extensions. In addition, instead of calling **perl_
run**, we call **search_files** using **perl_call_argv** (with the G_DISCARD
flag to tell it to discard all returned results). This is how I compile and link this
code on a Linux box:[*]

```
% gcc -o ex -I/usr/local/lib/perl5/i586-linux/5.004/CORE \
           -L/usr/local/lib/perl5/i586-linux/5.004/CORE \
           -Dbool=char -DHAS_BOOL                        \
        ex.c -lperl -lm
```

We have created our first custom Perl interpreter. Since **perl_parse** is given all
the command-line arguments, *ex* can be invoked just like Perl, as shown:

```
% ex search.pl
```

This outputs something like this (when invoked in the Perl source directory):

```
av.h[10]: struct xpvav {
cop.h[58]: struct cop {
cop.h[60]:     char *  cop_label;     /* label for this construct */
cop.h[75]: struct block_sub {
cop.h[98]:      { struct block_sub cxsub;
...
```

We need to give the name of the script as an argument because **perl_parse** is
given the command-line arguments untranslated.

Instead of using **perl_call_argv**, we could have used the other two calls
instead, as follows:

```
perl_eval_va("search_files (qw(struct *.h))",
            NULL);             // No return parameters
```

---

[*] You don't have to remember or look up the include and library directory paths. The last section in this
chapter discusses a module called ExtUtils::Embed that makes creating embedded interpreters a snap.

or

```
perl_call_va ("search_files",
             "s", "struct",    // First parameter of type string
             "s", "*.h",       // Second parameter also of type string
             NULL) ;
```

Clearly, the `perl_eval_va` approach is the easiest of the lot in this particular example. Incidentally, did you notice how we used the **qw** operator to avoid embedded quotes?

Let us now take a look at another small example that requires us to pass in a mixture of parameter types. This time we call a Perl subroutine, `nice_number`, to insert commas into big numbers (1000000 is formatted as "1,000,000"). The subroutine, shown below, interposes a comma whenever it sees a group of four consecutive digits, and continues to do so until it no longer matches this pattern. To test this subroutine, we use an additional subroutine called `test_nice`, which, given a number n, generates an n-digit number composed of 1's and feeds it to nice_number:

```
sub nice_number {
    my $num = shift;
    1 while ($num =~ s/(.*\d)(\d\d\d)/$1,$2/g);
    $num;
}
sub test_nice {                      # test_nice(4) produces 1,111
    my $len = shift;
    nice_number(1 x $len);
}
```

Instead of putting this code into a file and parsing it using `perl_parse` (as we did earlier), we use `perl_eval_va` to parse and load this subroutine. It so happens that `perl_parse` does some crucial initializations, so we *have* to call it.* If we give it a null `argc`/`argv` array, it has the unfortunate property of waiting on standard input, as you normally expect Perl to do. For this reason, we give it the shortest possible script that compiles cleanly and doesn't take any time to finish, as shown in the following command line:

```
perl -e 0
```

The only way to have a shorter script is to reduce the font size! Note the call to `perl_parse` in Example 19-3.

Example 19-3. ex2.c: Embedding Perl

```
#include <EXTERN.h>
#include <perl.h>
static PerlInterpreter *my_perl;
```

---

* In fact, `perl_parse` should be called at most once, because it reinitializes the interpreter without checking that it has already been done.

Example 19-3. ex2.c: Embedding Perl (continued)

```
main() {
    static char *dummy_argv[] = {"","-e","0"}; int num;
    my_perl = perl_alloc();
    perl_construct(my_perl);

    perl_parse(my_perl, NULL, 3, dummy_argv, env);

    if (perl_eval_va (                         # define code inline
                "sub main::nice_number {"
                    "my $num = shift;"
                    "1 while ($num =~ s/(.*\\d)(\\d\\d\\d)/$1,$2/g);"
                    "$num;"
                "}"
                "sub main::test_nice {"
                    "my $num = shift;"
                    "nice_number (1 x $num);"
                "}",
                NULL ) == -1) {
        fprintf (stderr, "Eval unsuccessful. Aborted\n");
        exit(1);
    }
    # Subroutines defined. Now call test_nice
    for (num = 1; num <= 7; num++) {
        char buf[20];*buf = '\0';
        perl_call_va ("test_nice",
                    "i",   num,        /* Input parameters */
                    "OUT",
                    "s",   buf,        /* Output parameter */
                    NULL);             /* Don't forget this! */
        printf ("%d: %s\n", num, buf);
    }
    perl_close();
}
```

This prints

```
1: 1
2: 11
3: 111
4: 1,111
5: 11,111
6: 111,111
7: 1,111,111
```

Adding Extensions

In the preceding pages, we created C applications that made calls to the Perl library, parsed scripts, and sent data between Perl and C space. In the meantime, we studiously avoided the issue of extensions, if you recall, by passing **NULL** to **perl_parse** instead of the address of an initialization subroutine. This means that we could not make use of any C-based extensions in the scripts, even common ones such as Socket and SDBM—clearly an unacceptable solution for real applications.

In this section, we learn a simple way of making standard and custom extensions accessible to the embedded Perl interpreter.

The initialization subroutine, which we will refer to as `xs_init`, is responsible for calling the initialization routines for all *statically linked* extensions. If you prefer dynamic loading, `xs_init` simply needs to initialize the built-in dynamic loader.

Instead of handcoding `xs_init`, we rely on a very convenient module called ExtUtils::Embed to produce it for us. This module is packaged with the Perl distribution, and is used like this:

```
perl -MExtUtils::Embed -e xsinit -- -o xsinit.c -std IO::Socket DBI
```

The `-M` option is identical to saying "`use ExtUtils::Embed;`". This invocation produces a file called *xsinit.c* with a publicly available function called `xs_init`, which in turn contains the code to initialize all the standard modules (thanks to the `-std` argument), and the two custom modules, IO::Socket and DBI.

How does this module know what is standard or whether we want these packages linked statically or dynamically? Well, when Perl is compiled and installed, it keeps an inventory of all statically linked extensions (if any) and the parameters supplied to the `configure` script, such as compilation and linking options, location of the Perl installation, and so on. This inventory is kept in a module called *Config.pm*. The Embed module taps this information to produce the right set of initializations. In addition, Embed can be asked to print out the compilation and linking options, and we can leverage it on the command line as follows:

```
% cc -c xsinit.c         `perl -MExtUtils::Embed -e ccopts`
% cc -c ex.c             `perl -MExtUtils::Embed -e ccopts`
% cc -o ex ex.o xsinit.o `perl -MExtUtils::Embed -e ldopts`
```

In addition to sparing us the bother of hand-writing the initialization code, and filling in the appropriate compiler and linker command-line options, this module makes it simple to drop in other extensions in the future. Of course, if the embedded interpreter is set up for dynamic loading, there is no need to recreate *xsinit.c*, because it only contains one call to initialize the dynamic loader.

Resources

1. *perlembed* (Standard Perl document). Doug MacEachern and Jon Orwant.

2. Apache and `mod_perl` at *http://www.apache.org/*.

Apache is a freely available web server that embeds a Perl interpreter. mod_
perl, written by Doug MacEachern, is a Perl module that provides the glue
between the Apache C API and Perl, and allows you to write to the Apache
API instead of CGI scripts. People have reported 400–2000% improvement in
speed over the CGI approach.

20

Perl Internals

It cannot be seen, cannot be felt,
Cannot be heard, cannot be smelt.
It lies behind stars and under hills,
And empty holes it fills.[*]
—J.R.R. Tolkien
The Hobbit

This chapter is a modest attempt to shed light on most of the critical data structures and functions of the Perl interpreter. Getting a handle on such (admittedly dry) detail will give you the confidence to write powerful extensions, and will inform your judgment about how (and how much) Perl should be used in a given application. The mark of a good Perl programmer is the ability to answer questions that *don't* figure in the Frequently Asked Questions list, such as these:

• Why are objects so much preferable to closures?

• Why is my faster than local?

• The easy-embedding API presented in the last chapter isn't convenient enough. How can I roll my own?

• What do *xsubpp* and SWIG really produce?

• Why not join the Java revolution by making the Perl interpreter output Java byte-code?

And so on. All you require is fluency in C, an enquiring mind, and a comfortable chair.

---

[*] Answer: dark.

If you are into instant gratification and can't wait to churn out a cool extension, you may opt for the low-fat thread running through this chapter; read the following sections: "Perl Value Types," "Stacks and Messaging Protocol," and "Meaty Extensions." You can definitely skip all sections entitled "Inside..." on a first reading without loss of continuity.

Reading the Source

There was this programmer, the story goes, who was deeply mystified by a piece of code. It had no comments at all, and he couldn't for the life of him figure out how it did what it did. For years, he cursed the author of that code, but it continued to fascinate and trouble him. One day, it came to him in a flash. He understood it all. In fact, it was so obvious that he also understood why it didn't need any comments!

While the Perl source may be the final repository of all answers, it is a fairly reluctant informant. A lack of comments, generous use of macros, and some breathtaking optimizations make for a rather forbidding task of understanding the code, even for the true die-hard. If you are one of those who just wants to hack it and achieve all kinds of greatness, this chapter should get you adequately primed. In addition, here are some ways of understanding the system better:

The –D option

Perl can be optionally compiled with the *–DDEBUGGING* option, which enables the *–D* command-line switch. This takes several flags, all of which are documented in the *perlrun* document. Like a CAT scan, these flags provide unobtrusive snapshots of important structures at run time. For example, invoking Perl as `perl –Dts` tells it to display a trace of opcode execution (`-t`) and to dump the argument stack before each opcode is executed (`-s`).

Devel tools

Three modules available under the *Devel* hierarchy on CPAN provide script-level access to some important data structures. These are Devel::Peek (to dump internal information associated with a variable), Devel::Symdump (to dump the symbol table), and Devel::RegExp (to examine a regular expression). We will use the Devel::Peek module often in this chapter.

Debugger (gdb, dbx, Microsoft Developer Studio)

Examining Perl under a debugger gives a firsthand view of the entire process. At run-time, the process goes through three major phases: initialization, parsing, and execution; these can be examined quite independently. I suggest that you understand Perl value types and the stack protocol first, then attempt to understand the execution phase by setting a breakpoint at `run.c:runops`,[*] and proceed from there. The parser and code generator are the most complex part of the tool; I recommend that you attempt to understand them only after you are comfortable with the rest of the system. Incidentally, tools such as *cxref* do not help much because most interesting accesses are hidden by macros, casts, and pointer indirections, so single-stepping with a source-level debugger is often the sole option.

This chapter makes frequent references to source files, and while you may find it handy to have them in front of you, it is by no means necessary to do so.

Architecture

Figure 20-1 shows the various components of a running Perl system. Shaded rectangles represent data structures, some of which can have multiple instances in a program. The source code can also be partitioned roughly along these lines.

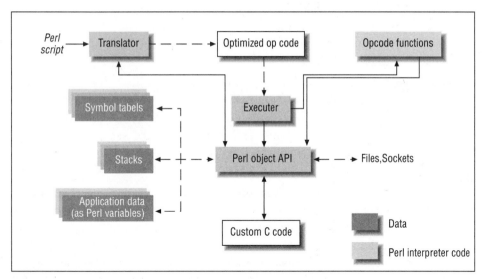

Figure 20-1. Snapshot of a running system

Perl Objects

The box "Perl object API" in Figure 20-1 represents the API to manipulate all internal data structures, such as variables, symbol tables, stacks, and resources such as files and sockets.

---

[*] I did mean *true* die-hard.

Variables

We saw in Chapter 3, *Typeglobs and Symbol Tables*, that the term "variable" refers to a name-value pair. In this chapter, we will look at the API to manipulate the different types of *values* and to optionally bind them to names. A value can be one of the following:

SV: Scalar value

AV: Array value

HV: Hash value

CV: Code value

GV: Glob value (or typeglob)

RV: Reference value

An SV can further be classified as an IV (integer value), PV (string value), or NV (double). The abbreviations are part of a uniform naming convention, so you can easily guess the intent of a function named `newSViv`, for example.

These value types provide a simple API, resize themselves automatically, and follow simple memory management protocols. For this reason, most Perl internal data structures such as stacks and symbol tables are also implemented in terms of these values.

Symbol tables

Symbol tables are plain old HVs, whose keys are identifier names (strings) and whose values are pointers to GVs. But aren't values in a hash table supposed to be scalars? The answer coming up, in the section "Glob Values and Symbol Tables."

Stacks

As Perl executes a script, it keeps run-time information in several stacks, the most important one being the "argument stack," or `stack` as it is simply known in the Perl source. The idea is simple: if `foo` wants to call `bar` with two arguments, it pushes these two scalars on the top of `stack` and calls `bar`. `bar` picks up these scalars, does its stuff, and dumps the results back on the stack. The stack is a simple AV, and every nested call occupies a stretch of the stack with its own parameters.

C programmers think of a stack as containing subroutine parameters, temporaries, and auto variables (those local to that scope). The Perl interpreter implements a different model. The `stack` described above holds only subroutine parameters; there are other stacks to track temporary variables generated during computations, local variables, and other miscellaneous tidbits of information such as loop iterators, the next opcode to execute on encountering last, redo, or return, and so on. The section "Stacks and Messaging Protocol" has more details.

I/O abstraction

Perl internally uses an object called `PerlIO` for all its I/O needs. This abstraction is essentially a thin porting layer for two libraries: *stdio*, and the much faster alternative, *sfio* [4]. We will not cover the I/O abstraction in this chapter, primarily because it is simple and offers no great insights. Please read the *perlapio* document for details.

Multiple interpreters

The data structures described above are normally kept in global C variables. If Perl is compiled with *–DMULTIPLICITY*, it lumps all these global variables into a structure called `PerlInterpreter`. This allows you to have multiple instances of the interpreter, each with its own "global" space. (Recall from Chapter 19 the API to allocate and construct an object of type `PerlInterpreter`.) In the absence of this compile-time option, the `PerlInterpreter` object is a dummy structure, and the internal data structures are truly global, for maximum performance. The API remains the same in either case.

You can use multiple interpreters to enforce completely isolated namespaces. Each interpreter has its own "main" package and its own tree of loaded packages. I have not seen this feature used in production Perl applications, but Tcl provides a framework called SafeTcl for security purposes, which uses a similar feature of multiple interpreter objects. These interpreters can be unrestricted or restricted. The equivalent module in Perl, Safe, uses a different mechanism, though the result (of isolated name spaces) is similar. More on this in the next section.

Translator

The translator converts a Perl script into a tree of *opcodes* (explained below). It comprises a hand-coded lexer (*toke.c*), the *yacc*-based parser (*perly.y*), and the code generator (*op.c*). Regular expressions—which form a distinct sublanguage—are recognized in *toke.c* and compiled to an internal format in *regcomp.c*.

Opcodes are similar in concept to machine code; while machine code is executed by hardware, opcodes (sometimes called byte-codes or p-code) are executed by a "virtual machine." The similarity ends there. Modern interpreters never emulate the workings of a hardware CPU, for performance reasons. Instead, they create complex structures primed for execution, such that each opcode directly contains a pointer to the next one to execute and a pointer to the data it is expected to work on at run-time. In other words, these opcodes are not mere instruction types; they actually embody the exact unit of work expected at that point in that program.

Java and Perl are both examples of such interpreters. While many of Java's byte-codes resemble a RISC machine's instruction set, Perl's opcodes represent a much higher level of abstraction. A large number of these opcodes directly correspond to the facilities available at the scripting level, such as regular expression matching and substitution, `chop`, `push`, `index`, `rindex`, `grep`,* and so on, which explains why there are 343 opcodes as of this writing! It also explains why Perl is so fast: instead of spending time in the interpreter, most of the work is done in lovingly hand-optimized C code. You can also see why it is hard to create a Perl-to-Java byte-code translator: there is no correspondence between the two sets.

Inside opcodes†

op.h defines a basic structure called `op`, shared by all opcodes. The important fields, discussed in this section, are:

```
OP*         op_next;
OP*         op_sibling;
OP*         (*op_ppaddr)();
OPCODE      op_type;
```

The `op_type` field contains the actual type of the opcode. A listing of all opcode types is present in *opcode.h*, produced automatically by the script *opcode.pl* while building the interpreter. The script contains a nicely tabulated description of all opcodes and hence is a much better source of information than *opcode.h*.

The `op_ppaddr` pointer represents the essence of the opcode: it is a pointer to a built-in function—call it an *opcode function*—that implements the functionality of the opcode. All opcode functions are prefixed with `pp` (`pp_push`, `pp_grep`, and so on) and are distributed over *pp.c*, *pp_ctl.c*, *pp_sys.c*, and *pp_hot.c*. The last one contains the opcode functions that are "hot," or frequently executed, so it is likely to remain within the cache of most RISC systems. Tom Christiansen once mentioned that this feature is also true of the regular expression-matching code, which is why regex matchers written in Java won't come anywhere close in performance. (I'll reevaluate this claim once Sun's Java processors are freely available.) As you will see later on, the opcode functions look strikingly similar to the glue code output by *xsubpp/SWIG*; this is because they interoperate using the argument stack and obey the same parameter passing protocols.

---

* Perl's `grep` operator, not the Unix utility. It hasn't come to a point at which entire utilities are represented by opcodes!

† Unless you want a gut feeling for what goes on deep inside, you don't have to digest—or even read —this section on a first pass over this chapter. Sections entitled "Inside..." are meant to be reasonably standalone pieces.

Opcodes have additional structure members depending on their type. For example, the **add** opcode is a binary operator, and hence contains two pointers to its *children*, which it evaluates before adding up the results. The **print** opcode is a list operator, and hence contains a pointer to the first opcode in its list of children, which are then linked to their *siblings* using the **op_sibling** pointer (possessed by all opcodes), and so on.

This complex interlinked mesh of opcodes is referred to as a *syntax tree*. Figure 20-2 shows such a tree, a result of parsing the expression **print $a + 2**.

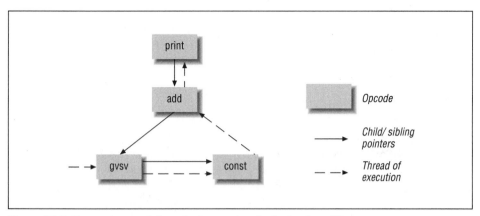

Figure 20-2. Syntax tree and thread of execution for "print $a + 2"

The syntax tree's top-down hierarchy indicates the precedence of expressions; the subexpression **$a + 2** must be computed before printing can commence. By the same token (pun unintended), **$a**'s value and the constant 2 must be retrieved and placed on the stack before addition can happen. The **gvsv** opcode (which fetches **$a**'s value) and the **const** opcode are thus children of the **add** opcode, and have a sibling relationship to each other. The **add** opcode is in turn a child of the **print** opcode. As you can see, the network of child and sibling pointers reflect the syntactic structure of the program.

The **op_next** pointer points to the next opcode to be *executed* and hence reflects the flow of control. Executing the code is thus a simple matter of moving to the next opcode and calling its opcode function. The dashed lines in Figure 20-2 indicate this thread of execution.

If you compile Perl with *-DDEBUGGING*, you can use the **-Dx** command-line option to tell it to dump its syntax tree after it finishes parsing a script. The output of an example invocation, **perl -Dx -e 'print $a + 2'**, is shown in Example 20-1. The nesting level reflects the hierarchy—Figure 20-2 turned on its side—and the numbering scheme shows the order of execution. (I've added the comments on the right; the rest of the output is Perl's.)

Example 20-1. Opcode Sequence and Hierarchy for "print $a + 2"; Using–Dx

```
{
8   TYPE = leave  ===> DONE                 # Clean up. The last instruction
    FLAGS = (SCALAR,KIDS,PARENS)
    {
1       TYPE = enter  ===> 2                # Enter here
    }
    {
2       TYPE = nextstate  ===> 3            # nextstate inserted after every
                                            # statement to clean up temporaries
        FLAGS = (SCALAR)
        LINE = 1
    }
    {
7       TYPE = print  ===> 8                # call print. Contains child
                                            # expressions to be evaluated first
        FLAGS = (SCALAR,KIDS)
        {
3           TYPE = pushmark  ===> 4
            FLAGS = (SCALAR)
        }
        {
6           TYPE = add  ===> 7              # add requires two arguments
            TARG = 1                        # to be available on top of the
            FLAGS = (SCALAR,KIDS)           # argument stack (discussed below)
            {
                TYPE = null  ===> (5)
                  (was rv2sv)
                FLAGS = (SCALAR,KIDS)
                {
4                   TYPE = gvsv  ===> 5 # Get the scalar value associated
                    FLAGS = (SCALAR)    # with the name "main::a"
                    GV = main::a
                }
            }
            {
5               TYPE = const  ===> 6    # Put the constant "2" on the stack
                FLAGS = (SCALAR)
                SV = IV(2)
            }
        }
    }
}
```

Each pair of braces represents information about a specific opcode. The first opcode to execute is enter. It then hands control over to nextstate, which in turn leaves it to pushmark, and so on. The nextstate opcode cleans up all temporaries introduced in a statement and prepares for the next statement in that scope. The intent of the pushmark opcode will be clear when we study the parameter-passing protocol later in this chapter.

At compile time, the `gvsv` opcode (which fetches global or local variables) is primed with the address of the value it intends to fetch and place on the stack when it is executed. This means that at run-time, it does not have to refer to the symbol table at all—it already possesses the value. The symbol table is consulted only when you use features such as symbolic references, dynamic binding of functions, and `eval`, which do not have all the information at compile-time.

Compilation and code generation stages

yacc works in a bottom-up fashion, so the opcodes at the leaf-level of the syntax tree are produced first. As parsing proceeds, opcodes at a higher level in the syntax tree thread together the nodes below. Each unary and binary opcode (an arithmetic operator, for example) is checked to see whether it can be immediately executed; this is called *constant folding*. If it can, that opcode and its children are removed, and a new `const` opcode is substituted in place. Next, opcodes corresponding to built-in functions are verified to see that they have the right number and type of parameters.

Then comes *context propagation*. On creation, each opcode gets to specify a context (void, Boolean, list, scalar, or lvalue) for itself and its child opcodes. Consider the expression `substr(foo(), 0, 1)`. The opcodes representing a call to `foo` and the constants 0 and 1 are created first. When the opcode for `substr` is subsequently created, it tells the opcode representing the call to `foo` that it wants a scalar as its result. Context propagation hence works top-down.

When parsing is complete, a *peephole optimizer* goes to work (function `peep` in *op.c*). It traces all branches of execution, following the `op_next` pointers just as it would during run-time, and scouts for local optimizations. (That is, it does a dry run of the execution path.) The procedure typically examines the next few opcodes in sequence (currently, at most two) and checks to see whether they can be reduced to simpler or lesser opcodes; it looks through a peephole, in other words. Let us investigate this a little with a small example.

A '$' can be followed by an identifier name ($a), an array element ($1[0]), or, in the most general case, an expression resulting in a scalar reference ($$ra or ${foo()}. In the first pass, the parser assumes the most general approach, so even something as simple as $a boils down to two opcodes: `gv` and `rv2sv`. The first one retrieves a GV (a typeglob, which, if you think about it, is a reference to a scalar value) and places it on the stack, and the second opcode converts this to an SV. Along comes the peephole optimizer and replaces this sequence to one opcode, `gvsv`, which can do the same thing in one shot. The problem is that deleting unwanted opcodes is time-consuming and tedious, since these opcodes contain links to other opcodes. For this reason, useless opcodes are simply marked as null, and the `op_next` pointer of the previous opcodes simply bypasses them (the nullified opcodes). Example 20-1 shows an example of a nullified opcode; look for the line TYPE = NULL (was rv2sv).

Security features

Perl provides the *-T* switch to enable *taint checking*, which marks all variables containing data derived from outside the program as tainted. It implements a data flow mechanism, whereby all variables derived from these variables are also considered tainted. (Pushing a tainted scalar into an array marks the array as suspicious.) Essentially, this means you trust the code to do the right thing and to discriminate between tainted and untainted data. But if the code itself is suspicious, you can use the standard module Safe and its companion package Opcode.* These modules allow you to create a *safe compartment* and specify an operator mask (a list of allowed opcodes) for that compartment. You can eval a piece of untrusted code inside this compartment, and if the compilation process produces an opcode that is not present in the opcode mask, it returns an error. In the next few versions, Perl is expected to account for other kinds of malicious attacks, such as unlimited allocation of memory (@1 = (1..1000000)) or CPU starvation (1 while (1)). These are also known as *denial of resource* attacks.

Executor

The executor (function runops in *run.c*) is a simple driver that traverses the execution chain in the syntax tree and calls each corresponding opcode function in sequence. But because Perl is such a dynamic language, the path of execution cannot always be determined at the outset, so every opcode function is expected to return the next opcode to execute. For the most part, it is the next opcode in sequence (the op_next pointer set during compile time). But some, such as conditional operators like if or indirect expressions like $foo->func(), can determine the next opcode to execute only at run-time.

This concludes our brief tour of Perl's architecture.

Perl Value Types

In this section, we'll study the functions and macros for manipulating the internal value types. We will also examine each object's internal makeup in sections entitled "Inside SV," "Inside AV," and so on. Although they will help you in making seasoned judgments about memory overhead and performance, you can skip these sections if the detail weighs you down.

---

* Both designed by Malcolm Beattie (check the *ext/Opcode* subdirectory in the standard Perl library).

Scalar Values

A scalar value (SV) contains the value of the scalar, a reference count, and a bitmask to describe the state of the scalar. The scalar may be an integer value ("IV"), a double ("NV"), a string ("PV" for pointer value), a reference ("RV"), or a special-purpose object ("magical"). We'll discuss magical variables separately.

Table 20-1 shows the functions and macros to create, delete, and modify SVs. They are listed in *sv.h* and implemented in *sv.c*. Macros, by convention, have their first letter capitalized. All the tables in this chapter make use of two important typedefs, `I32` and `U32`, which represent signed and unsigned integral quantities that are *at least* 32 bits wide and big enough to hold a pointer (it will be 64 bits on a 64-bit machine).

Table 20-1. API for Scalar Values

Function/Macro	Description

`SV* newSViv(I32);`
`SV* newSVnv(double);`
`SV* newSVpv(char* str,`
`          int   len);`
	Create a new SV from an integer, double, or string respectively. `newSVpv` calculates the length of the string if `len` is 0.

`SV* newSVsv(SV *);`	Create a clone of an existing SV. To create an empty SV, use the global scalar `sv_undef`, instead of NULL, like this: `    newSVsv(&sv_undef);` This is true of all functions that expect an SV as an argument.

`SV* newSVrv`
`   (SV*  rv,`
`    char *pkgname);`
	Creates a new SV and points `rv` to it. Additionally, if `pkgname` is nonnull, it blesses `rv` into that package.

`SV *newRV (SV* other)`
`SV* newRV_inc (SV* other)`
`SV* newRV_noinc(SV *)`
	Create a reference pointing to any type of value, not just SVs. You can cast other values to an SV*, as will be evident when we examine AVs, HVs, and CVs.
	`newRV_inc` increments the reference count of the entity referred to (and is an alias for `newRV`).

`SvIOK(SV*), SvNOK(SV*),`
`SvPOK(SV*), SvROK(SV*),`
`SvOK (SV*), SvTRUE(SV*)`
	These macros check whether the SV has a value of the corresponding type and, if so, return 1. They do not trigger a conversion. `SvOK` returns 1 if the value is not `undef`. `SvTRUE` returns 1 if the scalar is true.

`IV      SvIV(SV*)`
`double SvNV(SV*)`
`char*  SvPV(SV*,int len)`
`SV*    SvRV(SV*)`
	These macros retrieve the values inside an SV and, except for `SvRV`, force an implicit conversion to the appropriate values if necessary. `SvIV` yields 0 if the scalar contains a nonnumeric string. `SvPV` returns a pointer to a string and updates `len` with its length. The scalar owns that string, so don't free it. Before invoking `SvRV`, make sure that it is indeed a reference, using `SvROK`.

Table 20-1. API for Scalar Values (continued)

Function/Macro	Description

`sv_setiv (SV*, int)`
`sv_setnv (SV*, double)`
`sv_setsv (SV* dest,`
`        SV* src)`
	Modifies an SV's values. The SV automatically gets rid of its old value and morphs to the new type.
	`sv_setsv` copies the `src` SV to the `dest` SV after checking that the two pointers are different.

`sv_setpv (SV*, char *)`
`sv_setpvn(SV*, char *,`
`          int  len`
`sv_catpv (SV*, char*);`
`sv_catpvn(SV*, char*,`
`          int);`
`sv_catsv (SV*, SV*);`
	String functions, which force the scalar to be a string if necessary. `sv_setpv` assumes a null-terminated string, while `sv_setpvn` takes the length. Both functions make a copy of the given string.
	The `cat` series of functions does string concatenation.

`SVTYPE(SV*)`	Returns an enum value, and is equivalent to the `ref` function. These are the common values listed in *sv.h:* `SVt_IV` (Integer) `SVt_NV` (Double) `SVt_PV` (String) `SVt_RV` (Reference) `SVt_PVAV` (Array) `SVt_PVHV` (Hash) `SVt_PVCV` (Code) `SVt_PVGV` (Glob) `SVt_PVMG` (Blessed or magical scalar)

`sv_setref_iv(`
`    SV* rv,`
`    char* classname,`
`    int i)`
`(and similarly for nv and pv)`
	Creates a new SV, sets it to the value `i`, and makes `rv` refer to this new SV. The other two functions are similar.
	Note that `sv_setref_pv` stores the pointer; it does not make a copy of the string.
	If `classname` is nonnull, these functions bless the reference under that package.

`svREFCNT_dec(SV *)`	Decrements the reference count and calls `sv_free` if this count is 0. You should *never* call `sv_free` yourself.

`SV* sv_bless (`
`    SV *rv, HV* stash);`
`int sv_isa(`
`    SV *, char *pkgname);`
`int sv_isobject(SV*);`
	`sv_bless` blesses `rv` under a package represented by `stash`. Please refer to the section "Glob Values and Symbol Tables" for an explanation of stashes. `sv_isa` returns 1 if it inherits from a class `pkgname`.

`SV* sv_newmortal()`
`SV* sv_2mortal(SV*)`
`SV* sv_mortalcopy(SV*)`
	By default, if you create an SV, you are responsible for deleting it. If you create a *mortal* or temporary variable, Perl automatically deletes it the end of the current scope (unless someone else holds a reference to it).
	`sv_2mortal` tags an existing SV as a mortal, and `sv_2mortalcopy` creates a mortal clone.

Table 20-1. API for Scalar Values (continued)

Function/Macro	Description
| ```
SV* perl_get_sv(
      char* varname,
      int    create)
``` | To get a scalar variable as you are used to seeing in script space, you have to explicitly bind an SV to a name. create, if TRUE, forces it to create a variable if it didn't exist earlier. varname must always be qualified by the name of the package. To create $Foo::a, for example:<br>```SV *s = perl_get_av("Foo::a", 1);``` |
| `sv_dump(SV*)` | The name is a misnomer, since it is capable of pretty-printing the contents of all Perl value types (casting them to SV* if necessary). This is extremely useful if you have Perl under a debugger: for example, inside gdb, use
```call sv_dump(sv)``` |

The `mortal` series of calls in Table 20-1 create a temporary SV or tag an existing value as temporary. These calls essentially tell Perl to shove the SV onto a stack called `tmps_stack` and call svREFCNT_dec on the SV at the end of the current scope. (More on this in the section "Inside Other Stacks.") Typically, all parameters passed between functions are tagged mortal, because neither the caller nor the called function wants to worry about the appropriate time to delete the SV and its contents; Perl automatically takes care of the memory management.

Using this API

Perhaps your eyes are somewhat glazed and your mind is numbed, so we will relieve the tedium by writing a custom interpreter using the API we have seen so far. (For now, this is our idea of fun!) Example 20-2 shows a function called `create_envt_vars` that creates a scalar variable for every environment variable.

Example 20-2. Creating Scalars for Environment Variables—the Hard Way!

```
#include <EXTERN.h>
#include <perl.h>
void create_envt_vars (char **environ)
{
    /*
     * Each element in environ is in the form <envt. var name>=<value>"
     */
    SV * sv = NULL;
    char **env = environ; /* for iterating through environ */
    char buf[1000];         /* will contain a copy of an envt variable */
    char *envt_var_name;  /* Name of the envt. variable, like PATH */
    char *envt_var_value; /* Its corresponding value */
    char var_name[100];    /* Fully qualified name of environment var */
    while (*env) {
        strcpy (buf, *env);
```
```

Example 20-2. Creating Scalars for Environment Variables—the Hard Way! (continued)

```
                /* Search for "=", replace it with '\0', thus splitting it into
                 *  logical parts - envt variable name and the value
                 */
                envt_var_name = buf; envt_var_value = buf;
                while (*envt_var_value != '=') envt_var_value++;
                *envt_var_value++ = '\0';
                /* Qualify the environment var with the package name.
                 * PATH becomes $main::PATH
                 */
                strcpy (var_name, "main::"); strcat(var_name, envt_var_name);
                sv = perl_get_sv (var_name, TRUE); /* TRUE => Force Create */
                /* Set the string value for the sv);
                sv_setpv(sv, envt_var_value);
                env++;  /* On to the next environ variable */
        }
}

static PerlInterpreter *my_perl;
main(int argc, char **argv, char **env) {
    my_perl = perl_alloc();
    perl_construct(my_perl);
    perl_parse(my_perl, NULL, argc, argv, env);
    create_envt_vars();
    perl_run(my_perl);
    perl_destruct(my_perl);
    perl_free(my_perl);
}
```

On a DEC Alpha box, you might compile and link it as follows:

```
% cc -o ex  -I/usr/local/lib/perl5/alpha-dec_osf/5.004/CORE \
            -L/usr/local/lib/perl5/alpha-dec_osf/5.004/CORE \
            ex.c -lperl -lsocket -lm
```

Now for the big test:

```
% ./ex -e 'print $USER'
sriram
```

Amazing, it works—try doing that with your regular Perl! Okay, so it's not a big deal, but you are definitely on your way to dirtying your hands more than you thought you could. Or would!

Inside SVs

An SV has the potential of being large, to accommodate the worst case of it morphing to any one of its subtypes. To avoid this, Perl keeps track of the information in two parts, as illustrated in Figure 20-3: a generic structure called "sv", which contains a bitmask flag, a reference count, and a pointer, **sv_any**, which refers to a "specific part."

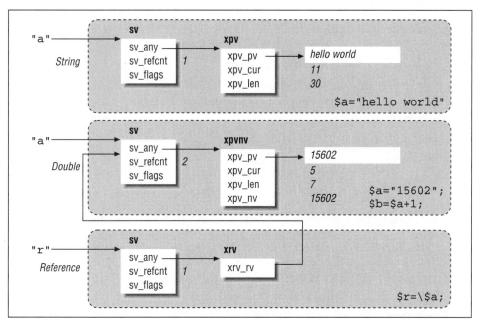

Figure 20-3. An inside view of scalars. Each shaded box represents one SV.

The specific part is a structure of the appropriate type and is one of several structures called **xpv**, **xpviv**, **xpvnv**, and so on, depending on what the bitmask flag says is contained by the scalar. A scalar may start life as a number, but the moment it is used in a string context, it morphs to a structure containing both the number and a string. Figure 20-3 shows an example of the SV (the middle one) containing a double and a string at the same time. If you modify its value with, say, **sv_setnv**, it sets a bit flag in **sv_flags** to indicate that the string part of it is not valid any more. Perl doesn't morph a structure unless absolutely necessary.

The Devel::Peek module gives you script-level access to the internal information discussed previously:

```
use Devel::Peek 'Dump';   # Import the Dump subroutine
$a = 15602;
Dump ($a);
```

This outputs

```
SV = IV(0x663f1c)
  REFCNT = 1
  FLAGS = (IOK,pIOK)
  IV = 15602
```

Modify $a to a string and see what happens to it:

```
use Devel::Peek 'Dump';
$a = 10;            # Start off with an integer value
$a .= " Ten";       # Convert to a string
Dump ($a);
```

Its output is as follows:

```
SV = PVIV(0x7b2ef0)
  REFCNT = 1
  FLAGS = (POK,pPOK)
  IV = 10
  PV = 0x7b2f00 "10 Ten"
  CUR = 6
  LEN = 11
```

Note that the SV still contains the old integer value (10) but that field will be ignored because the **FLAGS** field indicates that only its string contents are valid.

A basic integer value costs you at least 28 bytes on a typical workstation (`sizeof(SV)` + `sizeof(XPVIV)` + `malloc` overhead). Strings and arrays are more expensive than what you might infer from the length or count alone. The dump above shows that Perl allocated 11 bytes for the string (the `xpv_len` field) instead of the minimum 6 bytes (the length of the string, as stored in the `xpv_cur` field); this means that you can append 5 more bytes to the string without triggering a reallocation. Because it is geared for performance and convenience (being able to treat numbers and strings as one entity), it is not frugal with space at all. In fact, Perl applies this strategy of trading off space for performance for practically all data structures.*

There are no simple **xiv** or **xnv** structures that contain just an integer or a floating-point number. I do not know the reason for this, and idly speculate that it's so because a typical script requires numbers to morph into strings (while doing a `print`, for example) or vice versa (reading from files).

Figure 20-3 also shows the reference counts of the three scalars. The reference count of the middle scalar is 2 because of two arrows pointing to it; the arrows coming from the left imply a symbol table entry (for global and local variables) or a scratchpad for lexical variables, as we saw in Chapter 3. Note that all pointers to an SV (to any Perl value, actually) refer to the outer structure, never to the "specific" part.

---

* One notable exception being hashes, which share their key strings in one string table, thus minimizing space requirements but taking a small hit in performance.

SVs and object pointers

As an extension writer, you are often interested in storing a pointer to a C or C++ object returned from an XSUB. Recall that the integer (IV) slot of a scalar is guaranteed to be big enough to hold a pointer. We use this facility as follows:

```
Matrix *m = new_matrix();
sv_setiv(sv, (IV) m);          # Cast pointer to an IV.  Ugh!
```

Crufty, to say the least, but that's the way it is.

In practice, C/C++ objects are always associated with blessed references because it allows the Perl programmer to use the arrow notation (`$matrix->transpose()`). Consider

```
RV *rv = newRV();
sv_setref_iv(rv, "Matrix", (IV) m);
```

This creates a new integer SV internally, sets it to the "integer" **m**, and makes **rv** point to this freshly allocated SV. It also blesses **rv** under the module Matrix. This is exactly as if you had said, in Perl space,

```
my $m = 0xfffa34a;      # Some pointer value, converted to an int
bless \$m, "Matrix";    # Return a blessed reference to $m.
```

We will use this snippet when discussing typemaps for objects, in the section "Object Interface Using XS Typemaps."

Array Values (AV)

An AV is a dynamic, contiguous array of pointers to SVs, and as we are used to seeing in script space, storing a value at an index beyond its current capacity triggers an automatic expansion of the array. Table 20-2 shows the API for manipulating an AV as a whole and for accessing its elements individually. Take note that unless you clear or undef an AV, it does not touch the reference counts of its constituent SVs.

Table 20-2. API for Array Values

Function/Macro	Description

`AV * newAV()`
`AV * av_make(int num,`
`          SV  **ptr)`
	Creates an empty AV or a clone of another array of SV*.

`I32  av_len(AV*);`	Returns the highest index of the array (such as `$#array`).

`SV** av_fetch (AV*,`
`            I32 index,`
`            I32 lval)`
	Retrieves the SV* from the given index. If `lval` is non-zero, it replaces the existing value (at that location) with an `undef`. Note that `av_fetch` returns an SV** (not SV*); this is the pointer to the position in the array where the SV was stored. This way you can not only make changes to the SV, but also modify the array itself (splice the array at that location, for example).

Table 20-2. API for Array Values (continued)

Function/Macro	Description

`SV** av_store(AV*,`
`          I32 index,`
`          SV* val)`
	Stores an SV* at that index and returns an SV** just like `av_fetch`. Neither function updates the reference counts of the indexed element.

`void av_clear (AV*)`	Decrements the reference counts of its constituent scalars and replaces those positions with `undef`. It leaves the array intact.
`void av_undef (AV*)`	Decrements ref counts of all its scalars as well as of the array itself. In the typical case, this function deallocates the array. This is different from SVs in that they are deleted implicitly by decrementing the ref count (`SvREFCNT_dec`).
`void av_extend(AV*,` `           int num)`	Extends the array to `num` elements. Even though the other functions automatically extend the array, they can only heuristically determine how much to extend it. If you expect to store a lot of entries, you'll save time and many potential reallocations by preextending the array.
`void av_push (AV*, SV*)`	Pushes *one* SV at the end of an AV. You have to write more code if you want to append an entire list. This and the following functions do not touch the SV's reference count.
`SV* av_pop (AV* )`	Pops an SV from the end but doesn't touch its reference count, so you must call `SvREFCNT_dec` or tag it as a temporary variable with `sv_2mortal`, in which case Perl deletes it at the end of the scope.
`SV* av_shift(AV*)`	Like `av_pop` but pops an SV from the front of the AV.
`void av_unshift(AV*,` `            I32 num)`	Creates `num` empty spaces in front of the list (fills them with `undef`). You have to call `av_store()` to set each element's value.

`AV *perl_get_av (`
`     char* varname,`
`     int   create)`
	Gets the AV corresponding to `varname`. Create the variable if `create` is TRUE.

Inside AVs

AVs, like SVs, are split into a generic part and a specific part. As it happens, this is true for the other value types also.

As shown in Figure 20-4, the `xav_alloc` field points to a dynamically allocated array of SV*s, the real meat of the AV. `av_fill` contains the last valid (or filled) index in this array, and `av_max` contains the total number of SV*s allocated for the array. Perl always strives to make sure it allocates memory in some "reasonable" quantities so that it doesn't have to `realloc` every time you push an element into this array. `xav_array` points to the first valid element. It starts off by pointing to `xav_alloc[0]`, and gets incremented on an `unshift` to avoid having to move the rest of the elements to the left. In other words, the real contents of the AV are bounded by `xav_array` and `av_fill`.

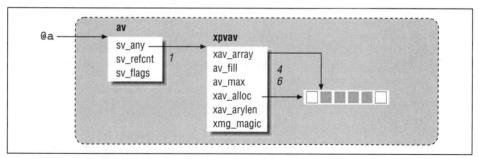

Figure 20-4. AV internal structure. The shaded squares contain real data.

The `xmg_magic` pointer is typically NULL but refers to a "magic" structure if the array is special (such as `@ISA`), represents a blessed object, or is tied to a package.* `xav_arylen` is an SV* that starts off being NULL but springs into existence as a magical scalar when you use the `$#` notation on the array (to get or set the array length).

Devel::Dump gives you script-level access to the internal details of an array and of all its constituent scalars. Dump expects nonscalar values to be passed by reference:

```
use Devel::Dump;
@l = (1,2,3,4);
Dump(\@l);  # Pass @l by reference
```

Hash Values (HVs)

An HV is a table of hash entries (HEs), each representing a pair consisting of a string key and an SV*. No two hash entries in a hash table can have the same key. The API listed in Table 20-3 allows you to act on the HV as a whole, to fetch or store single elements, or to iterate through it one entry at a time.

Table 20-3. API for Hash Values

Function/Macro	Description
`HV * newHV()`	Creates a hash value.

`SV**`
`hv_store(`
`    HV *hash,`
`    char* key, U32 klen,`
`    SV* val,    U32 hash)`
	Stores the key-value pair. It doesn't assume the key is a *text* string, so you *have* to supply the key length, `klen`. If `hash` is 0, Perl computes the hash automatically, which works very well for normal ASCII keys. Like AVs, these functions do not touch the reference count of the value `val`.

---

* You don't have to understand this paragraph until we have covered magical variables.

Table 20-3. API for Hash Values (continued)

Function/Macro	Description

SV**
hv_fetch(
    HV *hash,
    char* key, U32 klen,
    I32 lval)
	As with AVs, an SV** is returned for efficiency, not for your convenience. When storing an entry, the interpreter has to call hv_fetch to see whether an entry corresponding to that key already exists. If so, it can simply replace the value part of the entry without having to traverse the structure all over again. Typically, you should dereference the result and dispose of the returned SV* (call SvREFCNT_dec) or arrange to have it disposed of (sv_2mortal).

SV*
hv_delete(
    HV *hash,
    char* key, U32 klen,
    I32 flags)
	Deletes an entry and decrements the ref count of the value. If you don't want the deleted value, pass G_DISCARD for the flags; otherwise, it returns a mortal copy of that value.
	Since the entry is removed from the hash's data structures, it needs to return only an SV*, instead of SV**.

void hv_clear(HV *hash)	Equal to %h=(). Like av_clear(), it retains the outer array but gets rid of the hash entries, keys, and values. It also decrements the reference count of each value (not the hash itself).
void hv_undef(HV *hash)	Clears the HV and decrements its reference count.
I32 hv_iterinit(HV *hash)	Prepares to iterate through its list of entries and returns the number of elements in the HV. hv_iterinit and hv_iternextsv are used by the operators each, keys, and values.

SV*
hv_iternextsv(
    HV *hash,
    char** key,
    I32* pkeylen)
	Get the next key and value. The key is returned by reference (along with its length). Unlike hv_fetch(), this function returns only an SV*. This is similar to calling each().

HV *
perl_get_hv (
    char * varname,
    int create)
	Gets the HV corresponding to varname. Creates the variable if create is TRUE. varname must be qualified with the name of a package.

The iterating functions (hv_iter*) are safe for deletion but not for insertion. That is, you can invoke hv_delete on the current entry while iterating on a hash value using hv_iternextsv, but you should not call hv_store, because that might trigger a complete reorganization of the hash table.

Inside HVs

The HV is a straightforward implementation of a hashing technique called *collision chaining*. The basic idea is to reduce a string key to an integer and use this number as an index into an ordinary dynamic array. Clearly, we cannot expect to reduce all possible string keys to unique array indices, so each element of this dynamic array points instead to a linked list of all hash entries that reduced to that index. Figure 20-5 shows this arrangement.

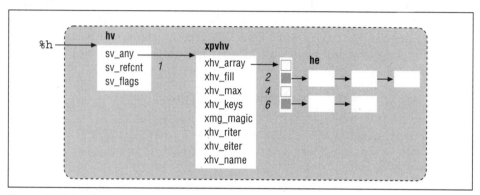

Figure 20-5. Hash value, containing hash entries

xhv_array is the dynamic array we mentioned above, **xhv_fill** indicates the number of elements that have linked lists hanging off them, and **xhv_keys** contains the total number of hash entries. Given a string, **hv_fetch()** computes the appropriate index and traverses the corresponding linked list, comparing the key to each hash entry's key value.

The translation of a string to an array index is a two-step process (for reasons to be discussed soon). First the string is run through an algorithm called a *hash function*, which computes an integer from a string without worrying about whether or not that number is practical to use as an array index. Perl's hash function is implemented as follows:

```
int i = klen;
unsigned int hash = 0;
char *s = key;
while (i--)
    hash = hash * 33 + *s++;
```

The resulting number is known as a *hash*. There is no guarantee that different strings hash to different hash values. Note that if you have a different hash algorithm, you can compute the hash yourself and supply it to **hv_store** (refer to Table 20-3).

To convert the hash to a practical array index, Perl folds it into the array's maximum size:

```
index = hash & xhv_max;
```

Ideally, we want the entries to spread out evenly around the array to keep the linked lists short. Perl's hashing algorithm does this surprisingly well for typical ASCII strings, but as we mentioned earlier, there's no guarantee that a given set of strings disperses well. So if **xhv_keys** exceeds **xhv_fill**, Perl takes it as an indication that one or more linked lists are unnecessarily long and that **hv_fetch** is likely to spend a considerable amount of time traversing these lists. Therefore, when such a condition occurs, Perl immediately reorganizes the hash table: the dynamic array **xhv_array** is doubled in size, and the entries are reindexed. Each hash entry stores its hash value, so it doesn't have to be hashed again when the table is reorganized.

You can get an idea of the hash efficiency by printing an associative array in a scalar context, as follows:

```
# Create a hash
for (1 .. 1000) {$h{'foo' . $_} = 1;} # Create 1000 entries
print scalar(%h);
```

This prints "406/1024" on my machine, which is simply a ratio of **xhv_fill** and **xhv_max**. The lower the ratio, the faster the hash access, because, on average, the linked lists are short.

If you know you are going to be performing a large number of insert operations on a hash, you can improve its efficiency in script space by telling it to preallocate a certain-sized dynamic array, like this:

```
keys %h = 400; # set xhv_max
```

Perl rounds it up to the next higher power of two: 512.

The **xhv_riter** and **xhv_eiter** fields are used by the iterator functions, **hv_iterinit** and **hv_iternextsv**, and constitute a cursor over the hash entries. **xhv_riter** contains the current row index, and **xhv_eiter** contains the pointer to the current entry.

Most object-oriented Perl implementations use hash tables for storing object attributes, which means that all instances of a given class would typically have the same set of key strings. To prevent unnecessary duplication, the actual key strings are maintained in a systemwide shared string table (**strtab** in *strtab.h*). **strtab** is a simplified HV: each value here keeps a reference count of the number of uses of that string. When you say "$h{'foo'}", the string **foo** is first entered into **strtab** if it is not already present. Then the hash entry for $h{foo} is created in the HV for %h. It turns out that performance suffers very little; if there are lots of duplicates, shared storage saves time because the key is **malloc**'ed only once. Also, since the hash algorithm needs to be executed only once, the performance is pretty good even when there aren't too many duplicates.

The shared string table is used only for immutable strings (remember that hash key strings cannot be changed). User-defined SVs containing strings do not get to use this table.

Glob Values and Symbol Tables

We saw in Chapter 3 that typeglobs, also known as glob values, or GVs, connect other value types with a symbol table entry. An identifier name, such as "foo", is linked by the GV to $foo, @foo, %foo, &foo, a filehandle called foo, and a format called foo.

GVs and symbol tables work so much in cahoots that all symbol table manipulation code is also lumped into *gv.c*. Symbol tables are internally implemented as hash tables (HVs) and hence are referred to as *stashes* (short for symbol table hash). Each package has its own stash and contains pointers to nested packages' stashes. The main stash, available from a global variable* called defstash, contains pointers to other "top-level" packages' stashes. Table 20-4 shows the important functions for accessing GVs and the symbol table.

Table 20-4. API for Glob Values and Stashes

Function/Macro	Description
GvSV, GvAV, GvHV, GvIO, GvFORM	Return the appropriate value pointers hanging off the GV.
HV *gv_stashpv(char *name, int create)	Given a package name, get the corresponding HV. The names don't need the trailing "::", unlike in script space.
HV *gv_stashsv(SV *, int create)	Same as above. SV* contains the name of the package.
HV *SvSTASH (SV* sv)	Get the stash from a blessed object. If sv is a reference, dereference it first: SvSTASH (SvRV(sv)).
char* HvNAME(HV* stash)	Given a stash, return the package name.

Standard variables in script space such as $_, $@, $&, $`, and $' are available as global variables in C space: defgv, errgv, ampergv, leftgv, and rightgv, respectively. For example, if you know that $_ contains a number, you can extract it in C as follows:

```
int i = SvIV(GvSV(defgv)); /* $_ and @_ are represented by defgv */
```

Inside glob values and symbol tables

Figure 20-6 shows most of the interesting components of a GV.

The xgv_name field stores the name of the variable (without the prefix). The pointers to the contained values ($foo, @foo, and so on) are encapsulated in a separate structure called gp to enable fast aliasing. In the typical case in which

---

* Or per-interpreter variable if MULTIPLICITY is defined.

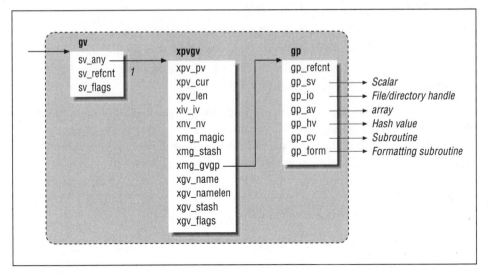

Figure 20-6. Glob value structure

you don't reuse the same name for different types of variables, all but one of the value pointers are NULL.

Symbol tables are HVs that map variable names to GVs. But aren't HVs supposed to store SVs only? Well, you may have noticed that all value types have identical-looking wrapper structures that maintain the reference count, flags, and the pointer to an internal structure. Because they are identical, you can cast an AV*, HV*, CV* to an SV* and thus fool the HV into storing anything you want. If you were to do this yourself, be careful of the HV calls that decrement the reference count of a contained "SV" (hv_delete, for example). This is because they will trigger an sv_free() if the reference count becomes 0, and if it is not an SV, you are in trouble.

Code Values

We have now finished studying all the fundamental data types used in Perl. Next we study code values, which represent subroutines, eval blocks, and format declarations. This explanation will enable you to call Perl subroutines efficiently from C and also give you a visceral understanding of how lexical variables and closures are implemented.

Table 20-5 shows the API for CVs; there's not much you can do with CVs except call them. Except for perl_call_sv, all the other API functions accept the name of a procedure rather than the CV itself.

Table 20-5. API for Code Value

Function/Macro	Description

`CV*`
`perl_get_cv(char *name,`
`            int create)`
	Get the CV for a given name. You should always set `create` to FALSE, because a TRUE value automatically creates a blank CV, which is useless to an application writer.

`int`
`perl_call_sv(SV* cv,`
`            int flags)`
	Call a subroutine indicated by the `cv` parameter. (Yes, you'll need to cast the CV to an SV.) It returns the number of return parameters pushed onto the stack. `flags` is explained below.

`perl_call_argv(`
`    char *sub,`
`    I32  flags,`
`    char **argv);`
	Discussed in Table 19-1.

`perl_call_va (`
`    char *sub,`
`    [char *type, arg],*`
`    ["OUT",]`
`    [char *type, arg,]*`
`);`
	Discussed in Table 19-1. We will implement this convenience function later in the section "Easy Embedding API."

`int perl_call_pv (`
`        char* sub_name,`
`        int flags)`
	Call a subroutine by name. A thin wrapper over `perl_call_sv`.

`int perl_call_method(`
`        char *method_name,`
`        int flags)`
	Call a method of a class by name. The first parameter on the stack must be either an SV containing the name of the class or a blessed reference of the class.

There are other ways of calling Perl subroutines, such as `perl_call_argv` and `perl_call_va`, which we saw in the last chapter. All these functions are wrappers around `perl_call_sv` and attempt to hide the messaging protocol details to some extent. The *flags* parameter is a combination of any of the following bitmasks defined in *perl.h*:

G_DISCARD

Discards all return parameters from the function.

G_SCALAR, G_ARRAY

Specifies a scalar or array context, scalar being the default. The called subroutine can use `wantarray` to find out the caller's intention. These flags can also be used in conjunction with `G_DISCARD`. This is useful when you want to affect the way a function invoking `wantarray` works, even if you are not interested in the results.

G_EVAL, G_KEEPERR

Wraps an `eval` block around the call. `perl_eval_sv()` assumes this flag automatically. When an `eval`'d block dies, Perl assigns `die`'s string argument to `errgv` (`$@`) and clears all temporary variables created in that block. Perl checks to see whether any of these variables is a blessed object and, if so, calls its `DESTROY` routine. There's a chance that this routine might invoke `die` (after all, it is user-defined code). Here we have a situation in which `errgv` is already computed and an additional exception is thrown. Using `G_KEEPERR`, you instruct Perl to concatenate this new exception string to `errgv` instead of overwriting it.

Inside CV

A CV has the same overall structure as the other value types: a generic part and a specific part. Consider the following piece of code, which defines a function in another package (by fully qualifying the name) and examines the function using Devel::Peek:

```
package Foo;
sub main::bar {    #Introduce a function in a different package
    my $a = 10;
}
use Devel::Peek;
Dump(\&main::bar);
```

The dump looks like this:

```
SV = PVCV(0x774300)
  REFCNT = 2
  FLAGS = ()
  IV = 0
  NV = 0
  COMP_STASH = 0x6635f0 "Foo"
  START = 0x7744d0
  ROOT = 0x774650
  XSUB = 0x0
  XSUBANY = 0
  GVGV::GV = 0x66365c    "main" :: "bar"
  FILEGV = 0x660418      "_<foo.pl"
  DEPTH = 0
  PADLIST = 0x66362c
```

The `COMP_STASH` field indicates that the "Foo" stash would be active when `bar()` executes, although this subroutine is defined in package `main`. The `ROOT` field indicates the root opcode of the syntax subtree for the CV, and `START` is the address of the opcode to get control when the function starts. The `XSUB` field either is NULL or contains a pointer to a C subroutine. The `DEPTH` field indicates the depth of recursion, and `PADLIST` refers to a list of *scratchpads* for storing lexical variables defined inside that subroutine. More on this next.

How local and my work

Perl variables, as we are well aware, can be global, dynamic (tagged with `local`), or lexical (`my`). Global variables are accessible via the stash and the corresponding typeglob. When Perl encounters the global variable `$a`, it produces the opcode `gvsv`, which places the corresponding GV's scalar value on the stack, at run-time.

When Perl parses "`local $a`," it still outputs the same `gvsv` opcode, but this time it sets a special flag in that opcode to "localize" the scalar. At run-time, the corresponding opcode function `pp_gvsv` checks this flag and, if it is set, replaces the GV's scalar value with a new scalar value and pushes this new value onto the argument stack. Meanwhile, the old SV sits safely in something called a savestack (discussed later, in the section "Inside Other Stacks"). Subsequent accesses of `$a` within that scope (or a nested scope) lead you, via a's GV, to the newly allocated scalar value.

`my` variables are stored and treated very differently. We mentioned earlier that each CV contains a *padlist*, a list of scratchpads, as illustrated in Figure 20-7.

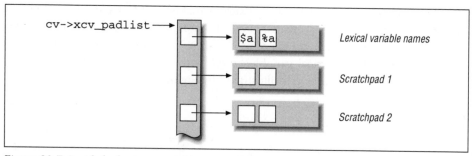

Figure 20-7. Inside look at my variables

The padlist is an ordinary AV. Its 0th element points to an AV containing all lexical variable names *used* within that subroutine (not just *declared* within that subroutine). The names contain their prefix symbols, so `$a` and `%a` have their own unique entries. The padlist's first element points to a *scratchpad* array (also an AV), whose elements contain the values corresponding to the lexical variables named in the 0th row. As you can see, the padlist is an alternative symbol table because it contains a logical pairing of variable names and values.

When the subroutine recurses, a new scratchpad is allocated for that recursion level. You'll notice that a CV requires at least three AVs (one for `xcv_padlist`, one for storing the names, and one or more for storing values).

When multithreading is introduced into Perl (Version 5.005 onward), each thread will get its own scratchpad,* which means that lexical variables will continue to be completely private to a recursion level and thread. (Package global variables will continue to be global, of course.)

`my` variables are a shade faster than `local` variables. The reason is that `local` allocates a new value at run-time to temporarily occlude the global value. In contrast, `my` variables are already unique to a CV, so they are typically allocated once, at parse time. The only reason to create a fresh `my` value is in case of recursion, which is not a typical occurrence. In future releases of Perl, multiple threads executing the same CV will also require run-time allocation of lexical variables.

When you access a lexical variable, Perl's code generator outputs an opcode called `padsv`, equivalent to `gvsv` (which is used for global or local variables). `padsv` remembers the offset of the variable inside the scratchpad (1 for `$a` in Figure 20-7). At run-time, Perl wastes no time at all fetching the corresponding value and pushing it on the stack.

Closures

This brief introduction to CVs and lexical variables leads us to the subject of closures. When a closure is created, Perl allocates a CV, points it to the starting opcode for the subroutine, and supplies it with its own private padlist. The padlist contains pointers to all lexical variables *used* by that closure, whether or not they were created within that block, as illustrated by Figure 20-8.

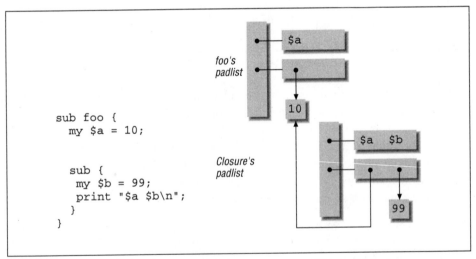

Figure 20-8. Scratchpad picking up lexicals from containing CVs' scratchpads

---

* This is according to Malcolm Beattie's current prototype patches for supporting POSIX threads.

For those lexicals picked up from the CV containing the closure ($a in Figure 20-8), the scratchpad contains direct pointers to the appropriate values, and the reference count of those values is incremented. Lexicals such as $b, created within the closure, are freshly allocated. Either way, the space allocated for a lexical variable is not deallocated as long as any subroutine using it can be called.

Objects versus closures

In Chapter 4, *Subroutine References and Closures*, we noted the similarity between objects and closures: both represent a binding between code and data. In other words, an object with three member functions can instead be represented as three closures acting on private variables borrowed from their containing environment.

Clearly, the closure approach is a lot more expensive in space; to represent 100 objects' worth of information, you require 300 unique closures, which works out to 900 AVs. In contrast, if you use a hash representation for storing object attributes, you need 100 hash tables and 9 AVs (three per subroutine).

On the other hand, calling a closure is faster than invoking an object's method. This is because a closure's variables are ready to be used as soon as the procedure is called, whereas an object's method has to dereference the object reference and then make a hash access for each attribute. The following benchmark compares the speed of an object accessor method to an equivalent closure—the latter approach is two to three times faster on my PC:

```
#------------------------------------------------------------
package OBJECT;                      # Pkg for timing object accessors
sub new {
   bless {'abc' => 10};
}
sub abc {                            # Fetch the abc attribute
    $_[0]->{'abc'};
    }
sub increment {                      # Increment the abc attribute
    $_[0]->{'abc'}++;
}
#------------------------------------------------------------
package CLOSURE;                     # Pkg for timing closures
sub new {
   my $abc = 10;                     # member data.
   $rs_increment = sub {$abc++};     # equivalent of OBJECT::increment
   $rs_abc       = sub {$abc}  ;     # equivalent of OBJECT::abc
   ($rs_increment, $rs_abc);
}
#------------------------------------------------------------
package main;
use Benchmark;
$a = OBJECT->new();                  # Create a new object
```

```
($inc, $fetch) = CLOSURE->new();   # Create two closures
timethese(1000000, {
    Object  =>  '$a->increment',   # call an object method
    Closure =>  '&$inc'            # call a closure
});
```

On my PC, this prints

```
Benchmark: timing 1000000 iterations of Closure, Object...
    Closure: 13 secs (14.39 usr  0.00 sys = 14.39 cpu)
     Object: 45 secs (45.14 usr  0.00 sys = 45.14 cpu)
```

Magic Variables*

There are ordinary user-defined variables containing strings, numbers, and references; then there are *magical* variables, those that have one or more special properties. A tied variable, for example, is magical because it contains pointers to a tied object and invokes that object's FETCH and STORE methods when read from and written to, as we saw in Chapter 9, *Tie*. Built-in variables such as $! and %SIG are also special: when $! is read from, Perl implicitly reads the C variable errno; when %SIG is written to, Perl resets the signal handler.

A magical scalar variable is shown in Figure 20-9. It contains the normal scalar fields that you saw earlier and, in addition, points to a linked list of properties. A structure called MAGIC represents each property and provides a semblance of uniformity over the different types of properties, as we shall soon see. Let us look at this structure in some detail before we use this facility to our advantage.

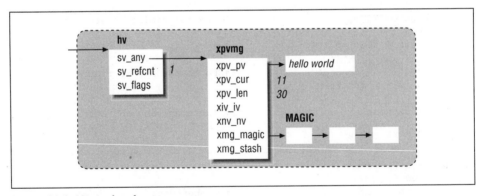

Figure 20-9. Magical scalar

A property, as seen in Figure 20-10, is an object containing a property type, a pointer to some data private to that property, and a pointer to a *virtual table* (or *vtbl*, a table of pointers to functions, in C++ parlance). When a variable is read

---

* This section can be skipped on a first reading.

from, written to, cleared, or destroyed, or if its length is accessed, Perl first updates the variable's value (the string, integer, or double fields) and then calls the accessor function responsible for the appropriate action (reading, writing, clearing, and so on; refer to Figure 20-10). If the variable has more than one property, the corresponding accessor function from each property is called, to give all of them a chance to affect the value of that variable as they please. An accessor can have side-effects too. For example, when you modify %SIG, each of its properties' svt_ set function is invoked. One of these functions updates the signal handler.

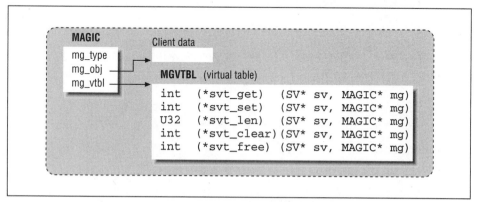

Figure 20-10. MAGIC: Uniform interface for representing special properties

Perl comes with a set of prebuilt virtual tables associated with unique *property types*, which are simply unique characters. For example, the virtual table to handle tied arrays is indicated by the character "P." Please take a look at the *perlguts* document if you are interested in the other built-in types. A value can have at most one property of a given type in its list. There's one property type, identified by the character ~, which is a hook for an extension writer to supply a custom virtual table. Let us see how to use this particular type.

To attach special properties to a scalar, use the **sv_magic** function, like this:

```
sv_magic(sv, obj, '~', "foo", 3);
```

This function upgrades the scalar value to an XPVMG structure internally and tells Perl not to attach any of its predefined virtual tables (because of ~). In addition, it creates one MAGIC structure and hangs it off the scalar. **obj** is an SV of your choice, containing user-defined data and meant for the accessor functions to distinguish between one magical variable and another. The last two parameters simply give a name to the property: an identifier string and length. Typically, you use the variable's name.

To access a certain property structure from a scalar, use the **mg_find** function:

```
MAGIC *m = mg_find(sv(,'~'));
```

Let us use these two functions to create a low-level tie mechanism: call a custom function when something happens to the variable. The procedure `foo_tie` in the following example shows how to associate a variable `$foo` in Perl space to a C variable `my_foo`:

```
int my_foo;  /* to be tied to $foo at script level */
int foo_get (SV *sv, MAGIC *mg)
{
    sv_setiv(sv, my_foo);   /* return my_foo's value */
    printf ("GET foo => %d\n", my_foo);
    return 1; /* return value not used */
}
int foo_set (SV *sv, MAGIC *mg)
{
    my_foo = SvIV(sv);      /* set my_foo's value     */
    printf ("SET foo => %d\n", my_foo);
    return 1; /* return value not used */
}
MGVTBL foo_accessors = {    /* Custom virtual table */
    foo_get, foo_set, NULL,   NULL,   NULL
};
void foo_tie ()
{
    MAGIC *m;
    /* Create a variable*/
    char *var = "main::foo";
    SV *sv = perl_get_sv(var,TRUE);
    /* Upgrade the sv to a magical variable*/
    sv_magic(sv, NULL, '~', var, strlen(var));
    /* sv_magic adds a MAGIC structure (of type '~') to the SV.
       Get it and set the virtual table pointer */
    m = mg_find(sv, '~');
    m->mg_virtual = &foo_accessors;
    SvMAGICAL_on(sv);
}
```

Since `foo_tie` uses the '~' property type, Perl does not supply a prebuilt virtual table. `foo_tie` makes up for the omission by supplying its own custom virtual table, `foo_accessors`, which contains pointers to `foo_get` and `foo_set`. Note that these two functions access the integer slot of the scalar given to them.

The `tie` mechanism that is available at the scripting level is slightly more involved. It first asks the module to return an object (using TIESCALAR, TIEHASH, etc.) and uses that object as a parameter to `sv_magic`. Later, when the tied variable is read from, the `sv_get` accessor is called, which relays the call to the private object's FETCH method.

Stacks and Messaging Protocol

Whew! We have now finished a reasonably in-depth look at all the value types offered by Perl. The next half of this chapter is devoted to understanding the data structures, API, and protocol used between caller and called subroutines.

We mentioned earlier that the argument stack is the data structure used for passing parameters and results between functions. Figure 20-11 shows the stack after calling `foo(10,20)`, which in turn has called `bar("hello", 30.2, 100)`.

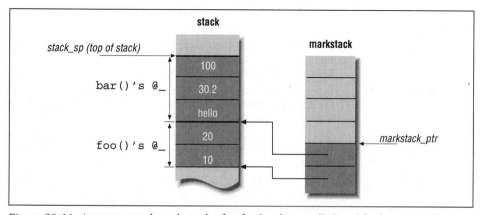

Figure 20-11. Argument and mark stack after foo has been called and foo has just called bar

How does `bar` know how many parameters it should pick up from the top of `stack`? Well, Perl keeps track of the stretches of the argument stack using another stack called a `markstack` (a stack of bookmarks, in a sense). `bar` knows the parameters meant for it by simply computing the difference between the current top of `stack` and the bookmark stored at the top of `markstack`. This stretch of the stack corresponds to `bar`'s `@_` array. Conversely, when `bar` is ready to return, it dumps one or more results in its stretch of stack, and `foo` knows how many scalars have been returned by looking at the markstack.

All these manipulations happen transparently when you are in script space. But if you write C routines that are called by Perl (extending Perl) or call Perl functions from C (embedding Perl), there are some details to contend with. Although tools such as XS and SWIG help you write extensions easily, you will find that the following sections will pave the way for even more powerful and intuitive extensions (intuitive, that is, for the script writer).

Calling a Perl Subroutine

Let's start with the case in which you call a Perl subroutine from C, normally done when you embed the Perl interpreter in your application. Table 20-6 contains the macros (defined in *pp.h*) that you will need to use, *in the order given*. These macros may be difficult to remember on one reading, but the good news is that they are called exactly in the same order every time, and they sort of grow on you after a while.

Table 20-6. Macros Used in Calling a Perl Routine (Embedding)

Function/Macro	Description
dSP	Declare a few variables used by the following macros.
ENTER	Start scope.
SAVETMPS	All mortal variables created after this call will be deleted when FREETMPS is called. See explanation of `tmps_stack` in the next section.
PUSHMARK	Remember the current top of `stack` (updates `markstack`). ENTER, SAVETMPS, and PUSHMARK are called to prepare the stack for a subroutine call.
XPUSHs(SV*)	Now you can push any number of arguments onto the stack. If you push newly created SVs, you can mark them as mortal, and Perl will automatically delete them at end of scope.
PUTBACK	Indicates that all arguments have been pushed in. PUSHMARK and PUTBACK bracket the arguments, in a sense. At this stage, the Perl procedure can be called using `perl_call_pv` or `perl_call_sv`. (See the following example.)
SPAGAIN	Like PUSHMARK, it provides the opening bracket for the returned results. Even if there aren't any returned results, you must call it anyway.
POPi POPl POPn POPp POPs	Pop a scalar from the stack and return the appropriate type: integer, long, double, pointer (typically to string), and SV. `perl_call_pv` returns the number of result parameters pushed onto the stack, and you must take care to call these macros only that many times. Keep in mind that POP returns the results in the inverse order in which the Perl procedure pushed its results on the stack.
PUTBACK	Call this after all result parameters have been popped.
FREETMPS	See SAVETMPS.
LEAVE	Ends scope. See ENTER.

The code snippet shown next illustrates how to invoke a Perl procedure called `add`, with two input parameters 10 and 20, and how to retrieve the results. Note again that the macros are used in the order given in Table 20-6.

```
#include <perl.h>
void foo() {
```

```
    int n;           /* number of parameters returned by add      */
    dSP;
    ENTER;           /* Tell perl we are entering a new scope      */
    SAVETMPS;        /* Ensure that FREETMPS will free only those
                        mortals created after this stmt            */
    PUSHMARK(sp);    /* Remember the current stack pointer. sp is
                        declared by dSP                            */
    /* Push arguments */
    XPUSHs(sv_2mortal(newSViv(10)));            /* push an integer  */
    XPUSHs(sv_2mortal(newSViv(20)));            /* push another     */
    PUTBACK;                                    /* End of arguments */

    /* Call subroutine by name, and expect it to return a scalar */
    n = perl_call_pv ("add", G_SCALAR);

    SPAGAIN;                    /* Start looking at return results */

    /* Retrieve returned value from stack */
    if (n == 1)
        printf ("Result: %d \n", POPi);
    /* Closing details                                             */
    PUTBACK;                /* Finished removing results from stack */
    /* Time to clean up and leave ..                               */
    FREETMPS;  /* Frees the two mortal parameters passed to add    */
    LEAVE;        /* Leave scope                                   */
}
```

This is all you need to understand the section "Easy Embedding API," which implements the `perl_call_va` convenience function introduced in Chapter 19.

The Called Side: Hand-Coding an XSUB

Having seen what it takes to call a Perl subroutine, let's look at the stack from the viewpoint of a called subroutine. This is precisely the situation that all XSUBs are in, and after this section, you'll be able to completely understand the code produced by SWIG and *xsubpp*.

First, let's settle the issue of how Perl discovers your XSUB. That is, if someone writes "add($a,$b,$c)" in a script, how does Perl know to call the C procedure `add`, or `my_add`, or whatever? Well, you have to create a binding between a subroutine name (as known in script space) and a C procedure, using the procedure `newXS` like this:

```
    extern XS(add);          /* XS macro explained in Table 20-7 next */
    newXS("add", add, "add.c"); /* Filename given for debugging reasons */
```

For a module called `foo`, XS and SWIG generate a procedure called `boot_foo`, which uses `newXS` to bind all XSUBs in that module to the corresponding names. The elegant thing about this approach is that `boot_foo` itself is an XSUB, and if you use dynamic loading, this procedure is called by the Dynaloader module at run-time.

XSUBs use the macros (defined in *XSUB.h*) listed in Table 20-7 to examine the stack and return results.

Table 20-7. Macros Used to Manipulate the Stack (Embedding)

Function/Macro	Description

XS	Supplies the standard signature required for your XSUB. For example, the procedure `foo` should be declared thus:
	`XS(foo) {`
	`}`

dXSARGS	Defines some local variables used by the other macros. The important one is an integer called `items`, which contains the number of parameters pushed onto the stack by the caller.
SV* ST(n)	Retrieves the *n*th parameter (an SV*) from the stack. `ST(0)` refers to the first parameter (`$_[0]`), and `ST(items-1)` is the last parameter.
XSRETURN(n)	Indicates that you have left *n* result parameters on the stack and returns. In the typical case in which you have only one value to return, you can use one of the more convenient macros listed below.
XSRETURN_NO XSRETURN_YES XSRETURN_UNDEF	Issues `XSRETURN(1)` after leaving an SV on the stack with a value of 0, 1, or undef.
XSRETURN_EMPTY	The same as `XSRETURN(0)`.
XSRETURN_IV (int) XSRETURN_NV (double) XSRETURN_PV (char *)	Leaves a new mortal scalar with the appropriate value type. This scalar will be deleted when the caller invokes `FREETMPS`.

The following snippet shows the hand-coded XSUB **add**, which adds all its input parameters and returns the result:

```
#include <perl.h>
#include <XSUB.h>
XS(add)                              /* All XSUBs have this signature*/
{
    int sum = 0;
    dXSARGS;                         /* defines 'items', and inits it*
                                      * with the number of params    */

    if (items == 0)
        XSRETURN_IV(0);     /* Return 0 if param list is empty       */

    for (--items ; items >= 0 ; --items) {
        if (SvIOK(ST(items))         /* If SV contains an integer     */
            sum += SvIV(ST(items));
    }
    XSRETURN_IV (sum);
}
```

Returning a variable list of results

The subroutine in the preceding example returns one parameter. Returning multiple parameters is straightforward too. The following example shows how a null-terminated array of strings (`argv`) is converted to an equal number of result parameters on the stack:

```
int i = 0;
for ( ; *argv; argv++, i++) {
    ST(i) = sv_2mortal(newSVPV(*argv,0));
}
XSRETURN(i);
```

As you can see, returned parameters occupy the stretch of argument stack between `ST(0)` and `ST(n-1)`. `XSRETURN` adjusts the markstack so that the caller can see the number of scalars being returned. It is important to note that the preceding code does not modify the *input arguments* that happen to live in the same stretch; it updates the *stack* to point to new SVs. (Remember that the stack is an array of SV*s.) To modify an input parameter directly, you would instead write:

```
sv_setpv(ST(i), "hello", 0); /* Like modifying $_[i] */
```

While functions such as **read** do this, I recommend that you refrain from taking advantage of it, and create new SVs instead. In addition, to save the calling code from worrying about memory management or reference counting issues, give that responsibility to Perl by making these new values mortal. They will then be automatically deleted at the end of scope.

Ensuring that the stack is big enough

The `ST` macro refers directly to the corresponding spot on the stack. Because the stack may not have been extended enough to accommodate the argument in the macro, you cannot arbitrarily say, for example, `ST(100)` without risking a crash. The `EXTEND` macro ensures that the stack is big enough to hold your data:

```
EXTEND(sp, 100); /* Extend stack by 100 elements */
```

This macro can be used in both the caller and the called subroutines. The variable `sp` (the stack pointer) is defined automatically for you (by the `dSP` and `dXSARGS` macros). `ST()` could have used **av_store()** to automatically extend the stack, but that would be considerably slower.

There's an alternative approach. If we reset the stack pointer back to the bottom of our stretch of stack, then we can use the `XPUSHs` macro, which automatically extends the stack for you:

```
i = 0;
sp -= items;            /* Resets stack pointer to beginning */
for ( ; *argv; argv++, i++) {
```

```
        /* Push fresh mortal string-valued scalars */
        XPUSHs(sv_2mortal(newSVpv(*argv, 0)));
    }
    XSRETURN(i);
```

This is precisely the strategy adopted by the **PPCODE** directive in XS, as we shall soon see. As I said earlier, this code doesn't modify the input parameters; it simply replaces those pointers in the stack with new ones. Note that if we forgot to reset the stack pointer, we would be piling stuff on top of the input parameters, and all hell would break loose when this procedure returns.

Inside Other Stacks

Let us take a brief look at the stacks available inside Perl (besides the argument and mark stacks) to understand what the macros described in the preceding sections do internally. Unless you are curious about these kind of details, you can safely skip this section without loss of continuity.

Save stack (`savestack`*)*

This stack is used as a repository for storing all pieces of global information that are liable to change within a nested scope. To safely squirrel away an integer, for example, Perl uses a macro called **SSPUSHINT** (in *scope.h*). This macro pushes three pieces of information on **savestack**: the value of the integer, the address of the integer, and the fact that an integer has been stored. The value of this integer can now be changed freely within a nested scope. At the end of the current scope, Perl pops the savestack and knows that because an integer has been stored, it must also have stored the old pointer and value. Thus the original integer is efficiently restored.

A statement such as `local($a)` is implemented by saving the GV corresponding to "a" and its scalar value on the save stack; the scalar value is replaced with a new scalar. When the scope ends, the GV and its scalar pointer are automatically restored.

Scope stack (`scopestack`*)*

The scope stack is used to remember positions along the save stack that correspond to different scopes (analogous to the markstack providing bookmarks for the argument stack). When the scope ends (upon **LEAVE**), Perl knows exactly how many objects to pop off the save stack and restores them to their former values.

Temporaries stack (`tmps_stack`*)*

When you create a mortal variable or mark a variable as mortal (using `sv_2mortal` or `local`, in script space), Perl pushes this SV on to this stack (without touching its reference count). At the end of scope, it decrements the reference count of all temporary variables pushed into the stack in that scope.

Recall that **my** variables (lexicals) sit in CV-specific scratchpads, so they never touch the temporaries stack.

Return stack (`retstack`)

Before calling a subroutine, Perl remembers the starting opcode of the statement following that subroutine call by pushing it on the **retstack**.

Context stack (`cxstack`)

This stack keeps track of the context information for the current block, such as the block label and the CV to execute when **last**, **redo**, or **next** are invoked. These are restored to the previous elements when the block is exited. I do not know why there are two stacks to deal with scope-related context information.

Meaty Extensions

Having armed ourselves to the teeth with information, and having hand-built a few extensions, we are now ready to exploit SWIG and XS to their hilts. In this section, we'll first look at the type of code produced by XS. As it happens, SWIG produces almost identical code, so the explanation should suffice for both tools. Then we will write typemaps and snippets of code to help XS deal with C structures, to wrap C structures with Perl objects, and, finally, to interface with C++ objects. Most of this discussion is relevant to SWIG also, which is why we need study only one SWIG example. That said, take note that the specific XS typemap examples described in the following pages are solved simply and elegantly using SWIG, without the need for user-defined typemaps.

Anatomy of an XS Extension

To understand XS typemaps, and the effect of keywords such as **CODE** and **PPCODE**, it pays to take a good look at the glue code generated by *xsubpp*. Consider the following XS declaration of a module, **Test**, containing a function that takes two arguments and returns an integer:

```
MODULE = Test  PACKAGE = Test
int
func_2_args(a, b)
    int    a
    char*  b
```

xsubpp translates it to the following (comments in italic have been added):

```
XS(XS_Test_func_2_args) /* Mangled function name, with package name */
                        /* added to make it unique                 */
{
    dXSARGS;            /* declare "items", and init it with       */
    if (items != 2)     /* the number of items on the stack        */
```

```
        croak("Usage: Test::func_2_args(a, b)");

    {   /* Start a fresh block to allow variable declarations    */
        /* Built-in typemaps translate the stack to C variables  */
        int     a = (int)SvIV(ST(0));
        char*   b = (char *)SvPV(ST(1),na);
        /* RETVAL's type matches the function return             */
        int     RETVAL;

        RETVAL = func_2_args(a, b);
        ST(0)   = sv_newmortal();

        /* Outgoing typemap to translate C var. to stack         */
        sv_setiv(ST(0), (IV)RETVAL);
    }
        XSRETURN(1);  /* Let Perl know one return param has been put back */
}
```

This is practically identical to the code we studied in the section "The Called Side: Hand-Coding an XSUB." Notice how the arguments on the stack are translated into the two arguments **a** and **b**. The XS function then calls the real C function, `func_2_args`, gets its return value, and packages the result back to the argument stack.

Let us now add some of the more common XS keywords to see how they are accommodated by *xsubpp*. The XS snippet

```
int
func_with_keywords(a, b)
    int     a
    char*   b
  PREINIT:
    double c;
  INIT:
    c = a * 20.3;
  CODE:
    if (c > 50) {
        RETVAL = test(a,b,c);
    }
  OUTPUT:
    RETVAL
```

gets translated to this:

```
XS(XS_Test_func_with_keywords)
{
    dXSARGS;
    if (items != 2)
        croak("Usage: Test::func_with_keywords(a, b)");
    {
        int     a = (int)   SvIV(ST(0));
        char*   b = (char *)SvPV(ST(1),na);
        double  c;                    /* PREINIT section        */
        int     RETVAL;
```

```
        c = a * 20.3;              /* INIT section           */
        if (c > 50) {              /* CODE section           */
            RETVAL = test(a,b,c);  /* Call any function      */
        }
        ST(0) = sv_newmortal();    /* generated due to OUTPUT */
        sv_setiv(ST(0), (IV)RETVAL);
    }
    XSRETURN(1);
}
```

As you can see, the code supplied in **PREINIT** goes right after the typemaps to ensure that all declarations are complete before the main code starts. The location is important for traditional C compilers, but would not be an issue for ANSI C or C++ compilers, which allow variable declarations anywhere in a block. The **INIT** section is inserted before the automatically generated call to the function or, in this case, before the **CODE** section starts. The **CODE** directive allows us the flexibility of inserting any piece of code; without it, *xsubpp* would have simply inserted a call to `func_with_keywords(a,b)`, as we saw in the prior example.

The **CODE** keyword behaves like a typical C call: you can modify input parameters, and you can return at most one parameter. To deal with a variable number of input arguments or output results, you need the **PPCODE** keyword. To illustrate the implementation of **PPCODE**, consider a C function, **permute**, that takes a string, computes all its permutations and returns a dynamically allocated array of strings (a null-terminated `char**`). Let's say that we want to access it in Perl as follows:

```
@list = permute($str);
```

We use **PPCODE** here because the function expects to return a variable number of scalars. The following snippet of code shows the XS file:

```
void
permute(str)
    char *      str
  PPCODE:
    int i = 0;

    /* Call permute. It returns a null-terminated array of strings */
    char ** ret = permute (str);

    /* Copy these parameters to mortal scalars, and push them onto
     * the stack */
    for ( ; *ret ; ret++, ++i) {
        XPUSHs (sv_2mortal(newSVpv(*ret, 0)));
    }
    free(ret);
    XSRETURN(i);
```

This gets translated to the following:

```
XS(XS_Test_permute)
{
```

```
dXSARGS;
if (items != 1)
    croak("Usage: Test::permute(str)");

/* PPCODE adjusts stack pointer (CODE does not do this) */
SP -= items;

{
    char *  str = (char *)SvPV(ST(0),na);
    int     i  = 0;
    /* Call permute.It returns a null-terminated array of strings */

    char ** ret = permute (str);
    /* Copy these parameters to mortal scalars, and push them onto
     * the stack */
    for ( ; *ret ; ret++, ++i) {
       XPUSHs (sv_2mortal(newSVpv(*ret, 0)));
    }
    free(ret);
    XSRETURN(i);
    PUTBACK;           /* These two statements are redundant */
    return;            /* because XSRETURN does both         */
}
}
```

The **PPCODE** directive differs from **CODE** in one small but significant way: it adjusts the stack pointer SP to point to the bottom of the Perl stack frame for this function call (that is, to **ST(0)**), to enable us to use the **XPUSHs** macro to extend and push any number of arguments (recall our discussion in the section "Ensuring that the stack is big enough"). We'll shortly see why we cannot do this using typemaps.

XS Typemaps: An Introduction

A typemap is a snippet of code that translates a scalar value on the argument stack to a corresponding C scalar entity (int, double, pointer), or vice versa. A typemap applies only to one direction. It is important to stress here that both the input and the output for a typemap are scalars in their respective domains. You cannot have a typemap take a scalar value and return a C structure, for example; you can, however, have it return a *pointer* to the structure. This is the reason why the **permute** example in the preceding section cannot use a typemap. We could write a typemap to convert a **char**** to a *reference* to an array and then leave it to the script writer to dereference it. In SWIG, which doesn't support a **PPCODE** equivalent, this is the only option.

Another constraint of typemaps is that they convert one argument at a time, with blinkers on: you cannot take a decision based on multiple input arguments, as we mentioned in Chapter 18, *Extending Perl: A First Course*, ("if argument 1 is 'foo', then increase argument 2 by 10"). XS offers the **CODE** and **PPCODE** directives to help you out in this situation, while SWIG doesn't. But recall from the section "Degrees of Freedom" in Chapter 18 that the two SWIG restrictions mentioned are easily and efficiently taken care of in script space.

While *xsubpp* is capable of supplying translations for ordinary C arguments, we have to write custom typemaps for all user-defined types. Assume that we have a C library with the following two functions:

```
Car*  new_car();
void  drive(Car *);
```

In Perl, we want to access it as

```
$car = Car::new_car;
Car::drive($car);
```

Let us first write the XS file for this problem:

```
/* Car.XS */
#include <EXTERN.h>
#include <perl.h>
#include <XSUB.h>

#include <Car.h>  /* Don't care what Car* looks like */

MODULE = Car  PACKAGE = Car
Car *
new_car ()

void
drive (car)
   Car *   car
```

As you can see, we need two typemaps: an output typemap for converting a `Car*` to `$car` and an input typemap for the reverse direction. We start off by editing a typemap file called *typemap,*[*] which contains three sections: `TYPEMAP`, `INPUT`, and `OUTPUT`, as follows:

```
TYPEMAP
Car *       CAR_OBJ

INPUT
CAR_OBJ
        $var = (Car *)SvIV($arg);
OUTPUT
CAR_OBJ
        sv_setiv($arg, (I32) $var);
```

The `TYPEMAP` section creates an easy-to-use alias (`CAR_OBJ`, in this case) for your potentially complex C type (`Car *`). The `INPUT` and `OUTPUT` sections in the

---

[*] We choose this particular name because the *h2xs*-generated makefile recognizes it and feeds it to *xsubpp*. It also allows for multiple typemap files to be picked up from different directories.

typemap file can now refer to this alias and contain code to transform an object of the corresponding type to a Perl value, or vice versa. When a typemap is used for a particular problem, the marker $arg is replaced by the appropriate scalar on the argument stack, and $var is replaced by the corresponding C variable name. In this example, the output typemap stuffs a Car* into the integer slot of the scalar (recall the discussion in the section "SVs and object pointers").

The advantage of the TYPEMAP section's aliases is that multiple types can be mapped to the same alias. That is, a Car* and a Plane* can both be aliased to VEHICLE, and because the INPUT and OUTPUT sections use only the alias, both types end up sharing the same translation code. The Perl distribution comes with a typemap file that supplies all the basic typemaps (see *lib/ExtUtils/typemap*), and you can freely use one of the aliases defined in that file. For example, you can use the alias T_PTR (instead of CAR_OBJ) and thereby use the corresponding INPUT and OUTPUT sections for that alias. In other words, our typemap file need simply say:

```
TYPEMAP
Car *      T_PTR
```

It so happens that the T_PTR's INPUT and OUTPUT sections look identical to that shown above for CAR_OBJ.

Object Interface Using XS Typemaps

Let us say we want to give the script writer the ability to write something like the following, without changing the C library in any way:

```
$car = Car::new_car(); # As before
$car->drive();
```

In other words, the OUTPUT section of our typemap needs to convert a Car* (returned by new_car) to a blessed scalar reference, as discussed in the section "SVs and object pointers." The INPUT section contains the inverse transformation:

```
TYPEMAP
Car *      CAR_OBJ

OUTPUT
CAR_OBJ
        sv_setref_iv($arg, "Car", (I32) $var);

INPUT
CAR_OBJ
        $var = (Car *)SvIV((SV*)SvRV($arg));
```

sv_setref_iv gives an integer to a freshly allocated SV and converts the first argument into a reference, points it to the new scalar, and blesses it in the appropriate module (refer to Table 20-1). In this example, we cast the pointer to an I32, and make the function think we are supplying an integer.

Making XS Typemaps More Generic

The typemap in the preceding example is restricted to objects of type `Car` only. We can use the TYPEMAP section's aliasing capability to generalize this typemap and accommodate any object pointer. Consider the following typemap, with changes highlighted:

```
TYPEMAP
Car *        ANY_OBJECT

OUTPUT
ANY_OBJECT
      sv_setref_pv($arg, CLASS, (void*) $var);

INPUT
ANY_OBJECT
      $var = ($type) SvIV((SV*)SvRV($arg));
```

All we have done is generalize the alias, the cast, and the class name. `$type` is the type of the current C object (the left-hand side of the alias in the TYPEMAP section), so in this case it is `Car*`. Because we want to make the class name generic, we adopt the strategy used in Chapter 7, *Object-Oriented Programming*—ask the script user to use the arrow notation:

```
$c = Car->new_car();
```

This invocation supplies the name of the module as the first parameter, which we capture in the `CLASS` argument in the XS file:

```
Car *
new_car (CLASS)
    char *CLASS
```

The only thing remaining is that we would like the user to say `Car->new` instead of `Car->new_car`. Just because C doesn't have polymorphism doesn't mean the script user has to suffer. The `CODE` keyword achieves this simply:

```
Car *
new (CLASS)
    char *CLASS
  CODE:
    RETVAL = new_car();
  OUTPUT:
    RETVAL
```

The `drive` method doesn't need any changes.

Having generalized this alias, we can apply the `ANY_OBJECT` alias to other objects too, as long as they also follow the convention of declaring and initializing a `CLASS` variable in any method that returns a pointer to the type declared in the TYPEMAP section. In the preceding example, the initialization happened automatically because Perl supplies the name of the class as the first argument.

C++ Objects and XS Typemaps

Suppose you have a C++ class called `Car` that supports a constructor and a method called `drive`. You can declare the corresponding interfaces in the XS file as follows:

```
Car *
Car::new ()

void
Car::drive()
```

xsubpp translates the `new` declaration to an equivalent constructor call, after translating all parameters (if any):

```
XS(XS_Car_new)
{
    dXSARGS;
    if (items != 1)
        croak("Usage: Car::new(CLASS)");
    {
        char *  CLASS = (char *)SvPV(ST(0),na);
        Car *   RETVAL;
        RETVAL = new Car();
        ST(0) = sv_newmortal();
        sv_setref_pv(ST(0), CLASS, (void*) RETVAL);
    }
    XSRETURN(1);
}
```

Unlike the previous example, *xsubpp* automatically supplies the `CLASS` variable. You still need the typemaps, however, to convert `Car*` to an equivalent Perl object reference. The `drive` interface declaration is translated as follows:

```
XS(XS_Car_drive)
{
    dXSARGS;
    if (items != 1)
        croak("Usage: Car::drive(THIS)");
    {
        Car *    THIS;
        THIS = (Car *) SvIV((SV*)SvRV(ST(0)));;
        THIS->drive();
    }
    XSRETURN_EMPTY;
}
```

xsubpp automatically generates the `THIS` variable to refer to the object. Both `CLASS` and `THIS` can be used in a `CODE` section.

Dean Roehrich's XS Cookbooks [3] provide several excellent examples of XS typemaps, so be sure to look them up before you start rolling your own.

Memory Management Using XS

We have conveniently ignored the issue of memory management so far. In the preceding sections, the **new** function allocates an object that is subsequently stuffed into a scalar value by the typemapping code. When the scalar goes out of scope or is assigned something else, Perl ignores this pointer if the scalar has not been blessed—not surprising, considering that it has been led to believe that the scalar contains just an integer value. This is most definitely a memory leak. But if the scalar is blessed, Perl calls its **DESTROY** routine called when the scalar is cleared. If this routine is written in XS, as shown below, it gives us the opportunity to delete allocated memory:

```
void
DESTROY(car)
    Car *car
  CODE:
    delete_car(car); /* deallocate that object */
```

The C++ interface is simpler:

```
void
Car::DESTROY()
```

In this case, *xsubpp* automatically calls "**delete THIS**", where **THIS** represents the object, as we saw earlier.

Recommended memory allocation and deallocation routines

The Perl library provides a set of functions and macros to replace the conventional dynamic memory management routines (listed on the left-hand side of the table):

Instead of:	Use:
malloc	New
free	Safefree
realloc	Renew
calloc	Newz
memcpy	Move
memmove	Copy
memzero	Zero

The Perl replacements use the version of **malloc** provided by Perl (by default), and optionally collect statistics on memory usage. It is recommended that you use these routines instead of the conventional memory management routines.

SWIG Typemaps

SWIG produces practically the same code as *xsubpp*. Consequently, you can expect its typemaps to be very similar (if not identical) to that of XS. Consider the **permute** function discussed earlier. We want a **char**** converted to a list, but since typemaps allow their input and output to be scalars, the following typemap translates it to a list *reference*:

```
%typemap(perl5,out) char ** {    // All functions returning char **
                                 // get this typemap
    // $source is of type char **
    // $target is of type RV (referring to an AV)
    AV *ret_av = newAV();
    int i      = 0;
    char **p   = $source;
    /* First allocate a new AV, of the right size */
    while (*p++)
         ;                /* Incr. p while *p is non-null */
    av_extend(ret_av, p - $source);

    /* For each element in the array of strings, create a new
     * mortalscalar, and stuff it into the above array */
    p = $source;
    for (i = 0, p = $source; *p; p++, i++ {
        av_store(ret_av, i, sv_2mortal(newSVPV(*p, 0)));
        p++;
    }
    /* Finally, create a reference to the array; the "target"
       of this typemap */
    $target = sv_2mortal(newRV((SV*)ret_av));
}
```

SWIG typemaps are specific to language, hence the **perl5** argument. **out** refers to function return parameters, and this typemap applies to *all* functions with a **char**** return value. **$source** and **$target** are variables of the appropriate types: for an **in** typemap, **$source** is a Perl type, and **$target** is the data type expected by the corresponding function parameter. Note that unlike XS's **$arg** and **$val**, SWIG's **$source** and **$target** switch meanings depending on the direction of the typemap.

If you don't want this typemap applied to all functions returning **char****'s, you can name exactly which parameter or function you want it applied to, like this:

```
%typemap(perl5,out) char ** permute {
    ...
}
```

Please refer to the SWIG documentation for a number of other typemap-related features.

Easy Embedding API

We have learned enough (and more) to implement the convenience API introduced in Chapter 19. They are `perl_call_va`, `perl_eval_va`, and the set of
functions for accessing or modifying scalar values: `get_int`, `set_int`, and so
on. We'll implement only `perl_call_va` in this section. `perl_eval_va` is a
shorter form of this procedure since it doesn't expect any input parameters (the
string to be `eval`'d contains all the information). The API functions to modify
scalars are simple wrappers over `sv_set*`, `av_store`, and `hv_store`, and are
left as an exercise to the reader.*

Recall that `perl_call_va` takes a NULL-terminated list of typed arguments. This
list contains both input and output parameters. The following implementation
processes the entire list by XPUSH'ing the input parameters and storing the output
parameters in an array of `Out_Param` structures. Knowing the number of output
parameters expected by the caller allows us to specify G_SCALAR, G_ARRAY, or
G_DISCARD. The full code is shown in Example 20-3.

Example 20-3. perl_call_va Implementation

```
#define MAX_PARAMS 20
typedef struct {
    char type;
    void *pdata;
} Out_Param;               /* To remember the "Out" section */

int perl_call_va (char *subname, ...)
{
    char       *p   = NULL;
    char       *str = NULL; int i = 0; double d = 0;
    int        nret = 0;                 /* number of return params expected*/
    int        ii   = 0;
    va_list    vl;
    int        out = 0;
    int        result = 0;
    Out_Param op[MAX_PARAMS];

    dSP;                               /* Standard ...    */
    ENTER;                             /*    ... Prologue */
    SAVETMPS;
    PUSHMARK(sp);
    va_start (vl, subname);
    while (p = va_arg(vl, char *)) {   /* Fetch next argument */
        switch (*p) {
        case 's' :                     /* String */
```

---

* I've always wanted to say that! (See the Preface for the FTP site where you can download this code and
other examples in this book.)

Example 20-3. perl_call_va Implementation (continued)

```
            if (out) {
                /* Comes here if we are processing the "Out" section */
                op[nret].pdata = (void*) va_arg(vl, char *);
                op[nret++].type = 's';
            } else {
                str = va_arg(vl, char *);
                ii = strlen(str);
                XPUSHs(sv_2mortal(newSVpv(str,ii)));
            }
            break;
        case 'i' :                          /* Integer */
            if (out) {
                op[nret].pdata = (void*) va_arg(vl, int *);
                op[nret++].type = 'i';
            } else {
                ii = va_arg(vl, int);
                XPUSHs(sv_2mortal(newSViv(ii)));
            }
            break;
        case 'd' :                          /* Double */
            if (out) {
                op[nret].pdata = (void*) va_arg(vl, double *);
                op[nret++].type = 'd';
            } else {
                d = va_arg(vl, double);
                XPUSHs(sv_2mortal(newSVnv(d)));
            }
            break;
        case 'O':
            out = 1;                        /* Out parameters starting */
            break;
        default:
             fprintf (stderr, "perl_eval_va: Unknown option \'%c\'.\n"
                             "Did you forget a trailing NULL ?\n", *p);
            return 0;
        }
        if (nret > MAX_PARAMS) {
            printf (stderr, "Can't accept more than %d return params\n",
                    MAX_PARAMS);
            return -1;
        }
    }
    va_end(vl);
    PUTBACK;
    /* All input parameters have been pushed on stack, and "nret" contains
     * the number of values expected back from the Perl function */
    result = perl_call_pv(subname, (nret == 0) ? G_DISCARD :
                                   (nret == 1) ? G_SCALAR  :
                                                 G_ARRAY  );
    /* Process output arguments */
    SPAGAIN;
    if (nret > result)
```

Example 20-3. perl_call_va Implementation (continued)

```
        nret = result;

    for (i = --nret; i >= 0; i--) {
        switch (op[i].type) {
        case 's':
            str = POPp;
            strcpy((char *)op[i].pdata, str);
            break;
        case 'i':
            *((int *)(op[i].pdata)) = POPi;
            break;
        case 'd':
            *((double *) (op[i].pdata)) = POPd;
            break;
        }
    }

    FREETMPS ;
    LEAVE ;
    return result;
}
```

A Peek into the Future

In this section, I'll describe a few of the exciting things that we can look forward to, possibly in the next few major releases of Perl.

Multithreaded interpreter

Malcolm Beattie has released an early version of a thread-safe Perl interpreter based on POSIX threads. (Search for the "thrperl" in the Perl 5 Porters archive [2].) This modified interpreter is not thread-hot; that is, it does not use threads itself (unlike the Java environment, for example, which uses separate threads for updating the user interface and for garbage collection). It allows the user to create as many threads as required and provides support for standard thread primitives such as monitors and condition variables. As currently implemented, all global data structures introduced in this chapter have simply become per-thread entities. That is, each thread gets its own set of stacks, its own stashes, and thread-local variables such as errgv ($@). Lexical variables are allocated out of subroutine and thread-specific scratchpads.

Static typing hints

Give hints to the interpreter for better optimization and type-checking. Larry's example, which has acquired near "hello world" status on the *p5p* list, is as follows:

```
    my Dog $spot = new Dog;
```

Now `$spot` is tagged at compile time as belonging to a class called `Dog`, so a call such as `$spot->meow()` will be a compile-time error, unless you have a mutant dog.

Faster objects

Expect better support for objects and a possible standard replacement for the ObjectTemplate module. You may be able to say something like this:

```
package Dog;
use Fields qw(breed color);
$spot = new Dog;
print $spot->{color};
```

What looks like a hash access in the last statement may in fact be optimized at *compile-time* to an array access, by replacing the attribute name with the field offset; that is, `$spot->{color}` becomes `$spot->[1]`.

Perl compiler

Malcolm has also submitted a Perl compiler extension [5], which is in its early stages as of this writing. It can be asked to translate a script to C code, which can be compiled to form an executable; as it happens, this executable is not much faster than the interpreted script, because most of the action still takes place in opcode functions as they exist now. Static typing hints may usher in some aggressive optimizations. For example, if you say:

```
my integer $i;
```

the compiler would use C's native integer type, rather than an SV—this would speed up loops and arithmetic expressions.

The compiler can alternatively produce a byte-code file and have the interpreter `eval` it subsequently, similar to the facilities provided by Python and Java. It also supports much better debugging options than those currently provided with *–D*.

Resources

These are the places to go trolling for further information, should this chapter not slake your thirst:

1. *perlguts* documentation. Jeff Okamoto and others.

   The *perlguts* documentation, along with *perlembed* and *perlcall*, is a fairly exhaustive source of information. The API reference in this document contains many more functions and macros than are covered in this chapter.

2. Perl 5 Porters news gateway and archive.

   The *perl.porters-gw* Usenet newsgroup is a gateway to the *p5p* mailing list, where vigorous discussions of Perl internals overshadow porting issues.

Archived articles can be searched at *http://www.rosat.mpe-garching.mpg.de/ mailing-lists/Perl5-Porters/*

3. XS Cookbooks. Dean Roehrich.

These cookbooks, available from CPAN (look under the *authors/Dean_ Roehrich* directory), provide solutions to a number of sample problems covering all XS features.

4. *sfio* (Safe/Fast I/O Library). David Korn and Kiem-Phong Vo.

Faster, extensible, and an overall better alternative to `stdio`, with backward compliance to `stdio`. Works only on Unix. Get it from CPAN's *Misc* directory, or check the following URL for a summary: *http://www.research.att.com/ sw/tools/reuse/packages/sfio.html*

5. Perl compiler. Fetch from CPAN's *authors/Malcolm_Beattie/* directory.

> *The Road goes ever on and on*
> *Now far ahead the Road has gone,*
> *And I must follow, if I can,*
> *Pursuing it with eager feet,*
> *Until it joins some larger way*
> *Where many paths and errands meet.*
> *And whither then? I cannot say.*
>
> —J.R.R. Tolkien
> *The Lord of the Rings*

Tk Widget Reference

The least flexible component of any
system is the user.
—Lowell Jay Arthur

This appendix covers the most commonly used properties and methods of Tk widgets. Please refer to the extensive online documentation accompanying the Tk distribution for more details.

Table A-1 shows all the properties and methods shared by almost all widgets.

Table A-1. Generic Widget Properties

Properties	Description
font	Discussed in the section "Fonts" in Chapter 14.
background, foreground	A name ("red") or an RGB value ("#FF00FA"). The options can also be abbreviated to `bg` and `fg`. Discussed in the section "Colors" in Chapter 14.
text	The string to be displayed inside the widget. This is displayed in the foreground color in the font specified above.
image, bitmap	Specifies a bitmap to be displayed inside the widget. Refer to the section "Images" in Chapter 14 for a discussion on creating and managing bitmaps.
relief	Border style: one of `raised`, `sunken`, `flat`, `ridge`, or `groove`. Should be accompanied by a nonzero borderwidth option.
height, width	Typically the height and width in pixels, except for labels, buttons, and text widgets, in which it is in number of characters (a multiple of average character width and height in that widget's font).
textvariable	Specifies the name of a variable. When the value of a widget changes, this variable is updated, and vice versa.

Table A-1. Generic Widget Properties (continued)

Properties	Description
anchor	Specifies how the widget or the information within it is positioned. Must be one of n, ne, e, se, s, sw, w, nw, or center. For example, an anchor value of "nw" tells a label widget to display its label text at its top-left corner.
Methods	
configure()	Change many attributes at once: `$widget->configure ('bg' =>'red','width' => 20);`
cget()	Get the current value for a given option: `$color = $widget->cget('bg');`

Note that properties such as text and textvariable are not applicable to all widgets; for example, text is wasted on a scrollbar. The properties can optionally be preceded by a hyphen (it is necessary to do so in Tcl/Tk but is optional in Perl/Tk).

Button

Buttons are labels with one additional property: the command option, shown in Table A-2. As was mentioned earlier, these properties are in addition to many of the ones mentioned in Table A-1.

Table A-2. Button Methods and Properties

Properties	Description
command	Specifies a reference to a Perl subroutine, which is called when mouse button 1 (by default) is released over the button.
width, height	Specifies the width and height in characters.
Methods	
flash()	Flashes the button by briefly toggling its colors.
invoke()	Invokes the Perl subroutine associated with the button, if any.

Radiobutton

Table A-3. Radiobutton Properties and Methods

Properties	Description
command	Specifies a reference to a Perl subroutine, which is called when mouse button 1 (by default) is released over the radiobutton. The variable associated with "variable" is updated before the command is invoked.

Table A-3. Radiobutton Properties and Methods (continued)

Properties	Description
variable	Takes a reference to a variable and updates it with the "value" property's value when the button is clicked. Conversely, when it is updated to have the same value as the "value" property, it selects the button (or deselects it in all other cases).
value	Specifies the value to store in the button's associated variable whenever this button is selected.
Methods	
select()	Selects the radiobutton and sets the associated variable to the value corresponding to this widget.
flash()	Flashes the button by briefly toggling its colors.
invoke()	Invokes the Perl subroutine associated with the button, if any.

Checkbutton

Table A-4. Checkbutton Properties and Methods

Properties	Description
command	Specifies a reference to a Perl subroutine, which is called when mouse button 1 (by default) is released over the button. The variable associated with "variable" is updated before the command is invoked.
variable	Takes a reference to a variable and updates it with the "onvalue" or "offvalue" property's value, depending upon the state of the indicator. Conversely, when it is updated, it matches itself with one of these values and appropriately selects or deselects itself.
onvalue, offvalue	Toggles the indicator depending upon which of these values match the variable's value. They default to 1 and 0, respectively.
indicatoron	If false, it does not display the indicator. Instead, it toggles the "relief" property of the entire widget (which makes it looked like a pressed button).
Methods	
select()	Selects the checkbutton and sets the associated variable to the "onvalue" value.
flash()	Flashes the button by briefly toggling its colors.
invoke()	Invokes the Perl subroutine associated with the command property, if any.
toggle()	Toggles the selection state and the variables value of the button.

Canvas

Table A-5 shows the properties of each item that is supported by the canvas widget and configured by using the widget's `itemconfigure` method. The widget itself has no particularly interesting properties. However, the methods shown in the latter half of the table are the widget's, even if they mostly apply to the individual canvas item types. Please note that all methods that take an item ID as a parameter can also take a preconfigured tag name as a parameter.

Table A-5. Canvas Class

Item Properties	Description
Common properties	
fill, outline	Colors for filling the region and outline.
tags	A list of strings. These are tags applicable to this item. You can add more to this list with `addtag`.
stipple, outlinestipple	Draw the interior or outline with a stipple pattern. The bitmap value specifies the stipple pattern.
width	Width of the outline.
Arc	
start, extent	Angles in degrees, moving counterclockwise.
style	`pieslice`, `chord`, `arc`. In the last case, the `fill` option is ignored.
Bitmap	
anchor	As in widget properties shown earlier.
bitmap	The bitmap to display.
background, foreground	Colors for each of the bitmap pixels.
Image	
anchor	As in widget properties shown earlier.
image	The image to display.
Line	
arrow	`First`, `last`, `both`, or `none`. The end at which an arrow should be drawn.
arrowshape	A reference to a list containing three dimensions a, b, and c like this:
fill	Color.
smooth, splinesteps	If 1, draws a bezier curve instead of a polyline. Each spline is approximated with the number of spline steps.
Polygon	
smooth, splinesteps	See "Line" above.
Oval	
Standard item properties	

Table A-5. Canvas Class (continued)

Item Properties	Description
Rectangle	
Standard item properties	
Text	
text, anchor	Position text with respect to anchor.
justify	Text justification: `left`, `right`, or `center`.
Window	
window	Specifies the widget to associate with this item. The widget must have been created as the canvas's child.
Methods	
create (type, x, y [x1, y1], [options...])	Type can be one of the above item types (non-capitalized). Returns a unique integer ID.
itemconfigure (ID, options..)	Configures one or more of the above parameters.
addtag, dtag	Add tags to items and delete them. Please see Tk documentation for tag specifications.
bind	Discussed in the section "Event Bindings" in Chapter 14.
coords (ID [x0, y0 ...]), move (id, xamount, yamount)	Move the item to the new location. `coords` is an absolute move, while `move` does it relative to current position.
delete (ID, [ID, ...])	Delete the item (or items) that correspond to the tag or ID.
find (searchCommand? arg ...?)	Find all items that meet a certain constraint. Constraints are of the form "above $id," "all," "below $id," "closest x y," "enclosed x1 y1 x2 y2," "withtag id," and so on.
postscript (?option value option value ...?)	Generate PostScript representation for part or whole of the canvas. Please check the Tk canvas documentation for the postscript rendering options.
raise, lower	Raise or lower the item.
scale (ID, xOrigin, yOrigin, xScale, yScale)	Rescale all of the items given by ID.

Text

Many of the text widget methods take one or more indices as arguments. An index can be an absolute number ("base") or a relative number ("base" + modifier). Both types of indices are specified as strings. The commonly used base indices are the following:

line.char

Indicates *char*'th character on line. Lines are numbered from 1 for consistency with other Unix programs that use this numbering scheme. Within a line, characters are numbered from 0.

end

Indicates the end of the text (the character just after the last newline).

insert

Where the insertion cursor is currently poised.

mark

. Indicates the character just after the mark whose name is mark.

tag.first, *tag*.last

Indicates the first and last character of a tag.

These absolute positions can be modified with one or more qualifiers:

+count chars, *−count* chars, *+count* lines, *−count* lines

Adjust the base index by *count* characters or lines.

wordstart, wordend, linestart, lineend

Adjust the index to point to the first character on the word or line referred to by the index, or just after the word or line.

Table A-6 shows some of the more interesting text properties and methods.

Table A-6. Text Properties and Methods

Text	Description
tabs	Specifies a set of tab stops for the window, as a reference to list of strings. Each string is a number followed by "l," "c," or "r" (left, center, right—to specify how the text is aligned respective to the tab).
height, width	Specifies height and width in number of characters.
state	normal or disabled
Methods	
Text Manipulation	
insert (index, {string, [tag]}+,)	Insert one or more strings with an optional tag at index. Index can be any of the index forms explained earlier.
delete(index1, [index2])	Delete character at index1, or the range index1 .. index2.
get (index1, [index2])	Get character at index1, or the range index1 .. index2.
see (index)	Scroll widget so that the index position is visible.
search([switches], pattern, index, [stopIndex])	Searches for text and returns the first index that matches the pattern. The search stops at stopIndex, if it is specified; otherwise it wraps around. Switches include forward, backward, exact (exact match—default), regexp, -nocase (ignore case), -count *var* (*var* is the reference to a variable, into which search stores the length of the matched string). The list of switches is terminated by "--".

Table A-6. Text Properties and Methods (continued)

Text	Description
Indexing	
index (index)	Returns an absolute index of the form *line.col*, given any of the other index forms.
see (index)	Ensures that the text at *index* is visible.
markSet (markName, index)	Give a logical bookmark name to that index.
markUnset (markName)	Remove bookmark.
Tag Manipulation	
tagAdd (tagName, {index1. [index2]}+)	Add tags to positions or ranges of characters. `insert` is another way of tagging text.
tagRemove (tagName, {index1. [index2]}+	Removes the tag from the specified areas but doesn't delete the tag itself.
tagDelete	Removes and delete the tag.
tagConfigure	Configure one or more properties for a tag. The tag properties are given below.
Tag Properties	
-foreground, -background, -fgstipple, -bgstipple, -font	The usual stuff. Try not to overuse these tags, or the text will look like a ransom note—bits and pieces cut from different newspapers and magazines.
-justify,	`center`, `left`, `right`.[1]
-relief, -borderwidth	Should specify both border width and background for relief to show up.
-tabs	Applies only if the first character in that line also belongs to the same tag.
-underline	Boolean option.

[1] Text processing has made it possible to right-justify any idea, even one which cannot be justified on any other grounds.
—J. Finnegan, USC.

Entry

Entry widgets are simple one-line text widgets. They do not support tags, marks, or embedded windows. The indexing syntax is consequently simpler:

number
Index into its contents, starting from 0.

`end`
End of the text.

`insert`
The position immediately after the insertion cursor.

`sel.first, sel.last`
Indicates the first and last character of a tag.

The `index` argument for all methods in Table A-7 accepts any of the styles described above.

Table A-7. Entry Widget Properties and Methods

Properties	Description
show	If false, it displays "*", not the real contents, and is used for obtaining passwords. Note that if the text is selected and pasted elsewhere, the real contents show up.
Methods	
get (index)	Gets the entire string.
insert (index, string)	Inserts a string at the index.
index (index)	Returns the numerical index.
selectionFrom (index) selectionTo (index) selection (from,to) selectionClear	To set or adjust the selection.
selectionPresent	True if there's a selection.

Listbox

Let us take a look at the indexing syntax before we examine Table A-8, which details listbox properties and methods:

number

> The index of the row, starting from 0.

`end`

> Indicates the end of the row.

`active`

> Where the location cursor is currently poised. The active location appears underlined.

`anchor`

> The anchor point of the selection.

Table A-8. Listbox Widget Properties and Methods

Properties	Description
height, width	Height in lines and width in characters. If 0, the widget resizes to accommodate all elements.
selectMode	One of `single`, `browse`, `multiple`, or `extended`.
Methods	
get (index)	Get the entire string.
insert (index, string)	Inserts a string at the index.

Table A-8. Listbox Widget Properties and Methods (continued)

Properties	Description
delete (index, [last])	Deletes at index or within range.
index (index)	Return the numerical index.
see (index)	Bring the *index*'th element within view.
selectionFrom (index) selectionTo (index) selection (from,to) selectionClear ()	Set or adjust the selection.
selectionPresent ()	True if there's a selection.
curselection()	A list of indices of the elements that have been selected.

Menus

Menu buttons support the methods shown in Table A-9. They also support the
methods of Table A-10 and delegate those calls to the underlying Menu widget.

Table A-9. MenuButton Widget Properties and Methods

Properties	Description
indicatorOn	If true, shows a small diamond to the right of the entry.
state	`normal`, `active`, or `disabled`.
Methods	
command separator radiobutton checkbutton cascade	These methods are simply delegated to the underlying menu. Please see the menu object's description in Table A-10.
menu	Return the underlying menu associated with this menu button.

Each method of the Menu widget understands the following indexing syntax:

number
> The index of the entry, starting from 0. When the tear-off option is active, the
> 0th entry is a separator automatically inserted by the menu.

`end, last`
> Indicates the last entry.

`active`
> Where the location cursor is currently poised. The active location appears
> underlined.

`none`
> Indicates that none are active. Used along with `activate()` to deactivate
> all entries.

pattern

A pattern to be matched against all entries. Currently, only exact matches are guaranteed to work.

Table A-10 shows the properties of the Menu widget and the options available for each type of entry.

Table A-10. Menu Widget Properties and Methods

Menu Widget Properties	Description
indicatorOn	If true, shows a small diamond to the right of the entry.
selectColor	The color of the indicator, if one is displayed.
tearOff	If true, the 0th entry of the menu is a separator. When you click on it, the menu "tears off" and gets a separate top-level window.
Menu Entry Properties	
Appearance:	
foreground, background, font, image, indicatorOn, label	The usual properties. Note that it is `label`, not `text`.
underline	The integer index of a character to underline.
accelerator *keysequence*	Shows a string to be displayed on the right of the label. Unlike Motif, you have to set up the key binding (typically on the top window) yourself. This option is for display only.
Action and Values:	
state	`normal`, `active`, or `disabled`.
command	For buttonlike entries, the reference of a subroutine to call.
value *var*	For radiobutton entries. Please see Table A-3.
variable *var*	Available only for checkbutton and radiobutton entries.
onvalue *val*, offvalue *val*	For checkbutton entries. Stored in the associated variable.
Methods	
command (options) separator (options) radiobutton (options) checkbutton (options) cascade (options)	Creates the corresponding type of entry item. Each entry takes its own configuration options, as illustrated above.
add (type,options)	The commands above translate to this call.
delete (index1, [index2])	Deletes entry or range of entries.
insert (index1, type, options)	Like `add`, but inserts at the requested index.
entryconfigure (index, options), entrycget (index)	Configure and retrieve menu entry properties.

Scrollbars and Scrolling

Scrollbars support the methods and properties shown in Table A-11.

Table A-11. Scrollbar Properties and Methods (in addition to Table 8-1)

Properties	Description
command	Callback is typically used to change the view in the associated widget (that is, calls that widget's **xview** or **yview**).
Methods	
set (first, last)	This is typically invoked by the associated widget to tell it about the widget's current view. Both *first* and *last* are fractions between 0 and 1. Values of 0.2 and 0.6 tell the scrollbar that the widget is currently showing the area between 20% and 60% of the document, respectively.
get	Returns the scrollbar settings as a list (first, last).

All scrollable widget types that can be scrolled (listbox, text, canvas) support the methods in Table A-12 in addition to their own (and the generic ones listed in Table A-1).

Table A-12. Scrollable Widget Properties and Methods

Properties	Description
xscrollincrement, yscrollincrement	If specified, scrolling can be done in units of these increments.
xscrollcommand, yscrollcommand	Tell widget what to do when it repositions internally. Typically, this option looks like this: `$scrollbar->configure`
Methods	
yview ('moveto', *fraction)*	**xview, yview** come in two forms. If the first argument is "moveto," then the widget is instructed to change its view in a way that *fraction* represents the topmost (or leftmost, in the case of **xview**) line or pixel.
yview('scroll', number, what) (similarly for xview)	This instructs the widget to adjust the view in the window up or down according to *number* of increments. **what** specifies whether these increments are in **units** or **pages**. If **what** is **units**, then it is in terms of the increment properties shown above.

Scale

Table A-13. Scale Methods and Properties

Properties	Description
command	Specifies a reference to a Perl subroutine, which is called when the scale's value is changed.
variable	Reference to a variable to be updated whenever the slider moves. Conversely, if you want the slider to move, you can change the variable.
width, length	Specifies the width and the length of the scale in pixels. Note that it doesn't support a property called height.
orient	Horizontal or vertical.
from, to	Real numbers.
resolution	If greater than 0, the value displayed and returned is always in even multiples of this value. Defaults to 1.
tickinterval	Spacing between numerical tick marks. If 0, no tick marks are displayed.
label, font	A label to be displayed on the top or the left of the slider (depending on orientation).
Methods	
set(value)	Same as updating the variable to the given value.

HList — Hierarchical List

This widget is part of the Tix distribution and is supported by Perl/Tk just like any other Tk widget. Table A-14 shows the properties.

Table A-14. HList Methods and Properties

Properties	Description
command	Specifies a reference to a Perl subroutine, which is called when an entry is double clicked upon.
drawbranch	If true, draws lines connecting parent and children and sibling entries.
browsecmd	Called whenever any mouse click or drag event happens over an entry.
columns	Each level of indentation is a column. Column sizes can be individually tailored.
separator	The separator character. Defaults to "."
selectmode	`single`, `browse`, `multiple`, or `extended`.
indent	Indent amount for each successive level, in pixels.

Table A-14. HList Methods and Properties (continued)

Properties	Description
Methods	
add (entrypath, option, values)	Creates a new entry. The options can be at *position*, before *path*, after *path*, and all the entry properties discussed below.
delete (option, entrypath)	Option can be `all`, `entry`, `offsprings`, `siblings`
column (col, width) column (col, 'char', nchars)	Set the width in pixels or in terms of character widths.
entryconfigure, entrycget	Set/get the entry properties discussed below.
info (option, entryPath)	Option can be `children`, `exists`, `hidden`, `next`, `prev`, `selection`, and so on.
hide, show	Hide or show an entry
Entry Properties	
'itemtype'	`text`, `imagetext`, and `widget`.
'text'	The label of that entry.
'image'	A bitmap or a pixmap. Used if itemtype is `image-text`.

Note that this is a scrollable widget, so it also supports the generic `xscrollcommand` and `yscrollcommand` properties listed in Table A-12. This also means that a simple way to create a scrolled HList box is to call `$parent->ScrlHList(options)`.

B

Syntax Summary

Thus spake the Master Ninjei:
"To the intelligent man, one word, to the fleet
horse, one flick of the whip, to the well-written
program, a single command."

—The Zen of Programming

This appendix provides a distillation of all syntax used in this book.

References

1. Scalar references:

```
$ra  = \$a;               # reference to scalar
$$ra = 2;                 # dereference scalar-ref
$ra  = \1.6;              # reference to constant scalar
```

2. Array references:

```
$rl  = \@l;               # reference to existing
$rl  = [1,2,3];           # reference to anon. scalar
push (@$rl, "a");         # Dereference
print $rl->[3]            # 4th element of array pointed to by $rl
```

3. Hash references:

```
$rh = \%h;                # reference to hash
$rh = {"laurel" => "hardy", "romeo" => "juliet"}; # ref to anon-hash
print keys (%$rh);        # Dereference
$x = $rh->{"laurel"};     # Arrow notation to extract single element
@slice = @$rh{"laurel","romeo"}; # Hash slice
```

4. Code references:

```
$rs = \&foo;              # reference to existing subroutine foo
$rs = sub {print "foo"};  # reference to anonymous subroutine
                          # (remember the semicolon at the end)
&$rs();                   # dereference: call the subroutine
```

5. Generalized dereferences. Any code inside a block yielding a reference can be dereferenced:

```
@a = @{foo()};          # dereference the array reference
                        # returned by foo()
```

6. References gotchas. All the examples below are wrong. Always use *-w* in developing and testing.

```
@foo = [1,3,4];         # Assigning an array-ref to an array
                        # Use parentheses instead.


%foo = {"foo" => "bar"}; # Assigning a hash-ref to a hash.
                        # Use parentheses instead.


$foo = \($a, @b);       # Identical to $foo = (\$a, \@b)
                        # Assiging an enumerated list to a
                        # scalar yields the last element (so,
                        # $foo gets \@b). Use [ ] if you need
                        # an array reference
```

Nested Data Structures

Each array or hash is a collection of scalars, some or all of which can be references to other structures.

7. Lists do *not* nest like this:

```
@foo = (1, 3, ("hello", 5), 5.66);
```

For nesting, make the third element a reference to an anonymous array:

```
@foo = (1, 3, ["hello", 5], 5.66);
```

8. An example of a nested data structure (a hash of array of hashes):

```
$person = {    # Anon. hash
    "name" => "John",  # '=>' is an alias for a comma
    "age"  => 23,
    "children" => [  # Anonymous array of children
                {
                    "name" => "Mike",   "age"  => 3,
                },
                {
                    "name"  => "Patty","age"    => 4
                }
            ]
};
print $person->{age}                  ; # Print John's age
print $person->{children}->[0]->{age}; # Print Mike's age
print $person->{children}[0]{age}     ; # Print Mike's age, omitting
                                      # arrows between subscripts
```

9. To pretty-print `$person` above:

```
use Data::Dumper;
Data::Dumper->Dumper($person);
# Or,
require dumpVar.pl;
main::dumpValue($person);
```

Closures

10. An anonymous subroutine that grabs lexical variables from its containing environment is a closure. Remember that it does not just take a snapshot of the value at the instant the anonymous subroutine is seen.

```
# declare an anonymous subroutine, and return a reference to it.
my $foo = 10;
$rs = sub {
        print "Foo is $foo\n"; # Grabs $foo
    };
&$rs();    # Call the closure through the reference
```

11. The closure keeps the grabbed variable's value around even when the variable goes out of scope.

```
sub init_counter {
    my $num = shift;  # lexical variable to be grabbed
    $rs = sub { print $num++," "; };
    return $rs;
}
$rs_counter = init_counter(10);  # $rs_counter is a ref-to-sub
for (1..5) {&$rs_counter()};      # Prints 10 through 14
```

Modules

12. The `package` keyword starts a new namespace (which lasts until another package declaration or until end of block). All user-defined global identifiers (variables, subroutines, filehandles) belong to this package. Lexical variables do not belong to any package.

```
package Employee; # Put in file Employee.pm
@employees = ("John", "Fred", "Mary", "Sue");
sub list_employee { print @employees; }
1;                      # Last executing statement in file must be
                        # non-zero, to indicate successful loading
```

13. To load module Employee:

```
use Employee;
#or
require Employee;
```

Specify the load path with the `-I` command-line option, PERL5LIB environment variable, or `@INC`.

14. Access foreign package's variables and subroutines with fully qualified names:

```
print @Employee::employees;
Employee::print();
```

Privacy is not enforced.

15. If a subroutine is not found in that package, a default subroutine AUTO-LOAD() is called, if present. $AUTOLOAD is set to the fully qualified name of the missing subroutine.

16. To inherit module C from modules A and B, prime C's @ISA array with the names of its superclass modules:

```
package A;
sub foo{ print "A::foo called \n";}
package C;
@ISA = ("A", "B");
C->foo();                  # Calls A::foo, because B does not
```

Objects

Salient points:

- A class is a package. There's no keyword such as **struct** or **class** to define layout of object.

- You choose object representation—object layout is not dictated by you.

- No special syntax for constructor. You choose the name of the subroutine that is going to allocate the object and return a blessed or typed reference to that object.

17. Creating an OO package—Method 1 (see also #19).

The C++ class:

```
class Employee {
    String _name; int _age; double _salary;
    create (String n, int age) : _name(n), _age(age), _salary(0) {}
    ~Employee {printf ("Ahh ... %s is dying\n", _name)}
    set_salary (double new_salary) { this->_salary = new_salary}
};
```

becomes:

```
package Employee;
sub create {                # Allocator and Initializer
    my ($pkg, $name, $age) = @_;
    # Allocate anon hash, bless it, return it.
    return (bless {name => $name, age=> $age, salary=>0}, $pkg);
}
sub DESTROY {                # destructor (like Java's finalize)
    my $obj = shift;
    print "Ahh ... ", $obj->{name}, " is dying\n";
}
```

```
sub set_salary {
    my ($obj, $new_salary) = @_;
    $obj->{salary} = $new_salary; # Remember: $obj is ref-to-hash
    return $new_salary;
}
```

18. Using object package:

```
use Employee;
$emp = Employee->new("Ada", 35);
$emp->set_salary(1000);
```

19. Creating OO package—Method 2 (see also #17). Inherit from ObjectTemplate, use the attributes method to declare attribute names, and obtain the constructor **new** and attribute accessor functions for free:

```
package Employee;
use ObjectTemplate;
@ISA = ("ObjectTemplate");
attributes("name", "age", "salary");
sub DESTROY {
    my $obj = shift;
    print "Ahh ... ", $obj->name(), " is dying\n";
}
sub set_salary {
    my ($obj, $new_salary) = @_;
    $obj->salary($new_salary);
}
```

20. Class methods:

```
Employee->print();    # 1. "Arrow notation" used for class method
new Employee ();      # 2. Class method using "Indirect notation".
```

These two class methods must expect the package name as the first parameter, followed by the rest of the arguments.

21. Instance methods. There are two ways of invoking methods on an object:

```
$emp->promote();
promote $obj;
```

Dynamic Behavior

22. Symbolic references:

```
$i = "foo";
$$i = 10;             # Sets $foo to 10
${"i"} = 10;          # Sets $foo to 10
&$i();                # Calls foo();
push (@$i, 10, 20);   # Pushes 10,20 into @foo
```

23. Run-time expression evaluation:

```
while (defined($str = <STDIN>)) {
    eval ($str);
    print "Error: $@" if $@;
}
```

This is a tiny Perl shell, which reads standard input, treats `$str` as a small program, and puts the compilation and run-time errors in `$@`.

24. Dynamic substitutions. Use the `/e` flag for the `s///` operator, to specify an expression instead of a pattern:

```
$1 = "You owe me 400+100 dollars";
$1 =~ s/(\d+)\+(\d+)/$1 + $2/e;
print $1; # prints "You own me 500 dollars"
```

25. Module and object method invocations (see also #20 and #21):

```
$modulename->foo(); # Calls foo() in the module indicated by
                    # $modulename
```

Exception Handling

26. `die` throws an exception, and `eval` traps it. Error string is found in `$@`. The following code has the possibility of two run-time errors:

```
eval {
    $c = $a / $b;                                        #1
    die "Denominator cannot be negative" if ($b < 0);   #2
};
print "Run-time error: $@";
```

`$@` can be "Illegal division by zero" at (1) or "Denominator cannot be negative" at (2).

Meta-Information

27. Call-stack information. Use `caller()` to find out who's calling this subroutine:

```
    ($package, $file, $line) = caller();
```

28. List of a package's global variables. For a package `Foo`, `%Foo::` contains the symbol table, whose keys are names of global identifiers in that package and whose values are typeglobs.

29. Find out what a reference contains. `ref($r)` returns `undef` if `$r` is an ordinary scalar, "SCALAR" if it is a reference to a scalar (similarly "ARRAY," "HASH," "CODE," and "REF") or the name of a package, if `$r` is a blessed object reference.

30. Object information:

```
$obj->isa("Foo"); # returns true if $obj inherits from Foo
$obj->can("bar"); # returns true if it supports method "foo"
```

Typeglobs

31. Typeglobs assignment aliases identifiers. In the following example, all identifiers named **a** (scalar, array, hash, subroutine, filehandle, format) are also available as **b**:

```
*a = *b ;        # Alias
$b = 10;         # Same as modifying $a
b();             # Same as calling a()
```

32. Selective aliasing:

```
*a = \$b ;       # Only $a aliased to $b
```

33. Constants:

```
*a = \10;        # Alias a typeglob to a reference to a constant
$a = 20;         # Run-time error - "Attempt to modify read-only variable"
```

Filehandles, Formats

There are no direct ways of assigning filehandles or formats, passing them as parameters to subroutines, storing them in data structures, or localizing them. Instead, use the corresponding typeglobs.

Index

Symbols

@, for dereferencing arrays, 5
\ (backslash) in static allocation, 3
{ } (braces), 12–13
    anonymous hashes, 10
[ ] (brackets), for anonymous arrays, 10
:: notation, 93
    for instance methods, 106
$ (dollar sign)
    $@ variable, 69
    dereferencing scalars, 5
-> (arrow) notation, 7–8, 14
    indirect notation versus, 109
    for instance methods, 106
< > (diamond) operator, 42
( ) for anonymous arrays, 10
%, for dereferencing hashes, 6
" (quotation marks), 72
' (single quotation mark), 72

A

absolute text widget positioning, 233
abstract syntax tree (AST), 274–275
Academy Award data (example), 32–34
accept function, 192
accessing
    object attributes, 113–114
    from other packages, 85
    privileges, persistence and, 154
    symbol table, 95–97
accessor methods, 113–114

Adaptor project, 169–187
    design notes, 173–179
    implementation of, 179–187
Adaptor::DBI module, 170, 172
    database mapping, 175
    implementation of, 184–187
    object uniqueness and, 179
Adaptor::File module, 170
    database mapping, 175–176
    implementation of, 179–184
    object uniqueness and, 179
add_prop procedure, 281
add_prop_list procedure, 281
after function, 247
alarm function, 80, 247
aliases (see typeglobs)
allocate subroutine, 111
allocating memory, 291–292, 365
anonymous
    arrays, 10, 15
    definition of, 3
    hashes, 10, 15
    subroutines
        naming, 47
        references to, 52
API, Perl, 311–313
    example of using, 313–316
Archimedean spiral (example), 232
architecture, Perl, 321–328
arrays, 17
    anonymous, 10, 15
    of arrays, 25–27

About the Author

Sriram Srinivasan ("Ram") is an expert on distributed object technologies, and develops Java middleware at WebLogic, San Francisco for fun and profit. He actively pursues his interests in programming languages, databases, transaction processing, networking, and meaningful user interfaces. Sriram has been an enthusiastic user and teacher of Perl for the last six years, and currently teaches a course on advanced Perl programming for the extension program at the University of California at Berkeley.

In his spare time, he dabbles in Indian classical music, charcoal drawing, cooking, and biking, and dreams of the day when he can say, "In his spare time, he dabbles in programming languages. . . ." He and his wife, Alka, an avowedly lifelong student, live the good life in Berkeley, California.

Colophon

The animal featured on the cover of *Advanced Perl Programming* is a black leopard. Most leopards are easily recognized by the rosette patterned spots on their coat. Black leopards, often called "black panthers," also have these spots, but they are difficult to see because of the darkness of the fur. Black leopards are born into the same litters as the more common yellowish leopards. They occur most frequently in the wet, forested areas of India and southeast Asia, where the dark color aids in camouflage and hunting.

Leopards are among the most widely distributed wild cats. Their range extends throughout most of Africa and India and into much of Asia, the Middle East, and the East Indies. Highly adaptable, leopards are able to hunt almost any animal, and can live in both very wet and arid conditions. Because they almost always share their range with bigger cats, such as lions or tigers, leopards are very cautious. After catching its prey, the leopard will carry it high up into a tree to devour it. The incredible strength of the leopard enables it to climb while carrying animals up to three times its own body weight.

Edie Freedman designed the cover of this book, using a 19th-century engraving from the Dover Pictorial Archive. The cover layout was produced with Quark XPress 3.3 using the ITC Garamond font. Whenever possible, our books use Rep-Kover™, a durable and flexible lay-flat binding. If the page count exceeds Rep-Kover's limit, perfect binding is used.

The inside layout was designed by Nancy Priest and implemented in FrameMaker 5.0 by Mike Sierra. The text and heading fonts are ITC Garamond Light and Garamond Book. The illustrations that appear in the book were created in Macromedia Freehand 5.0 by Robert Romano. This colophon was written by Clairemarie Fisher O'Leary.

More Titles from O'Reilly

Perl

Perl Resource Kit—UNIX Edition

By Larry Wall, Nate Patwardhan, Ellen Siever,
David Futato & Brian Jepson
1st Edition November 1997
1812 pages, ISBN 1-56592-370-7

The *Perl Resource Kit—UNIX Edition*
gives you the most comprehensive collection of Perl documentation and commercially enhanced software tools available
today. Developed in association with Larry
Wall, the creator of Perl, it's the definitive Perl distribution for
webmasters, programmers, and system administrators.

The *Perl Resource Kit* provides:

- Over 1800 pages of tutorial and in-depth reference
  documentation for Perl utilities and extensions, in 4 volumes.

- A CD-ROM containing the complete Perl distribution, plus
  hundreds of freeware Perl extensions and utilities—a
  complete snapshot of the Comprehensive Perl Archive
  Network (CPAN)—as well as new software written by Larry
  Wall just for the Kit.

**Essential Perl Software Tools All on One Convenient CD-
ROM**

Experienced Perl hackers know when to create their own, and
when they can find what they need on CPAN. Now all the power
of CPAN—and more—is at your fingertips. The *Perl Resource
Kit* includes:

- A complete snapshot of CPAN, with an install program for
  Solaris and Linux that ensures that all necessary modules are
  installed together. Also includes an easy-to-use search tool
  and a web-aware interface that allows you to get the latest
  version of each module.

- A new Java/Perl interface that allows programmers to write
  Java classes with Perl implementations. This new tool was
  written specially for the Kit by Larry Wall.

Experience the power of Perl modules in areas such as CGI, web
spidering, database interfaces, managing mail and USENET news,
user interfaces, security, graphics, math and statistics, and much
more.

Programming Perl, 2nd Edition

By Larry Wall, Tom Christiansen &
Randal L. Schwartz
2nd Edition September 1996
670 pages, ISBN 1-56592-149-6

Programming Perl, second edition, is the
authoritative guide to Perl version 5, the
scripting utility that has established itself
as the programming tool of choice for the
World Wide Web, UNIX system administra-
tion, and a vast range of other applications. Version 5 of Perl
includes object-oriented programming facilities. The book is
coauthored by Larry Wall, the creator of Perl.

Perl is a language for easily manipulating text, files, and processes. It provides a more concise and readable way to do many jobs
that were formerly accomplished (with difficulty) by programming with C or one of the shells. Perl is likely to be available
wherever you choose to work. And if it isn't, you can get it and
install it easily and free of charge.

This heavily revised second edition of *Programming Perl* contains a full explanation of the features in Perl version 5.003.
Contents include:

- An introduction to Perl

- Explanations of the language and its syntax

- Perl functions

- Perl library modules

- The use of references in Perl

- How to use Perl's object-oriented features

- Invocation options for Perl itself, and also for the utilities that
  come with Perl

Perl 5 Desktop Reference

By Johan Vromans
1st Edition February 1996
46 pages, ISBN 1-56592-187-9

This is the standard quick-reference guide for
the Perl programming language. It provides a
complete overview of the language, from variables to input and output, from flow control to
regular expressions, from functions to document formats—all packed into a convenient,
carry-around booklet. Updated to cover Perl version 5.003.

O'REILLY™

TO ORDER: **800-998-9938** • *order@oreilly.com* • *http://www.oreilly.com/*
OUR PRODUCTS ARE AVAILABLE AT A BOOKSTORE OR SOFTWARE STORE NEAR YOU.
FOR INFORMATION: **800-998-9938** • **707-829-0515** • *info@oreilly.com*

Perl

Learning Perl, 2nd Edition

By Randal L. Schwartz & Tom Christiansen,
Foreword by Larry Wall
2nd Edition July 1997
302 pages, ISBN 1-56592-284-0

In this update of a bestseller, two leading Perl trainers teach you to use the most universal scripting language in the age of the World Wide Web. With a foreword by Larry Wall, the creator of Perl, this smooth, carefully paced book is the "official" guide for both formal (classroom) and informal learning. It is now current for Perl version 5.004.

Learning Perl is a hands-on tutorial designed to get you writing useful Perl scripts as quickly as possible. Exercises (with complete solutions) accompany each chapter. A lengthy, new chapter in this edition introduces you to CGI programming, while touching also on the use of library modules, references, and Perl's object-oriented constructs.

Perl is a language for easily manipulating text, files, and processes. It comes standard on most UNIX platforms and is available free of charge on all other important operating systems. Perl technical support is informally available—often within minutes—from a pool of experts who monitor a USENET newsgroup *(comp.lang.perl.misc)* with tens

of thousands of readers.

Contents include:

- A quick tutorial stroll through Perl basics
- Systematic, topic-by-topic coverage of Perl's broad capabilities
- Lots of brief code examples
- Programming exercises for each topic, with fully worked-out answers
- How to execute system commands from your Perl program
- How to manage DBM databases using Perl
- An introduction to CGI programming for the Web

Advanced Perl Programming

By Sriram Srinivasan
1st Edition August 1997
434 pages, ISBN 1-56592-220-4

This book covers complex techniques for managing production-ready Perl programs and explains methods for manipulating data and objects that may have looked like magic before. It gives you necessary background for dealing with networks, databases, and GUIs, and includes a discussion of internals to help you program more efficiently and embed Perl within C or C within Perl.

Learning Perl on Win32 Systems

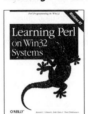

By Randal L. Schwartz, Erik Olson &
Tom Christiansen
1st Edition August 1997
306 pages, ISBN 1-56592-324-3

In this carefully paced course, leading Perl trainers and a Windows NT practitioner teach you to program in the language that promises to emerge as the scripting language of choice on NT. Based on the "llama" book, this book features tips for PC users and new, NT-specific examples, along with a foreword by Larry Wall, the creator of Perl, and Dick Hardt, the creator of Perl for Win32.

Mastering Regular Expressions

By Jeffrey E. F. Friedl
1st Edition January 1997
368 pages, ISBN 1-56592-257-3

Regular expressions, a powerful tool for manipulating text and data, are found in scripting languages, editors, programming environments, and specialized tools. In this book, author Jeffrey Friedl leads you through the steps of crafting a regular expression that gets the job done. He examines a variety of tools and uses them in an extensive array of examples, with a major focus on Perl.

O'REILLY™

TO ORDER: **800-998-9938** • **order@oreilly.com** • **http://www.oreilly.com/**
OUR PRODUCTS ARE AVAILABLE AT A BOOKSTORE OR SOFTWARE STORE NEAR YOU.
FOR INFORMATION: **800-998-9938** • **707-829-0515** • **info@oreilly.com**

Developing Web Content

WebMaster in a Nutshell, Deluxe Edition

By O'Reilly & Associates, Inc.
1st Edition September 1997
374 pages, includes CD-ROM & book
ISBN 1-56592-305-7

The Deluxe Edition of *WebMaster in a Nutshell* is a complete library for web programmers. The main resource is the Web Developer's Library, a CD-ROM, containing the electronic text of five popular O'Reilly titles: *HTML: The Definitive Guide, 2nd Edition*; *JavaScript: The Definitive Guide, 2nd Edition*; *CGI Programming on the World Wide Web*; *Programming Perl, 2nd Edition*—the classic "camel book," written by Larry Wall (the inventor of Perl) with Tom Christiansen and Randal Schwartz; and *WebMaster in a Nutshell*. The Deluxe Edition also includes a printed copy of *WebMaster in a Nutshell*.

WebMaster in a Nutshell, Deluxe Edition, makes it easy to find the information you need with all of the convenience you'd expect from the Web. You'll have access to information webmasters and programmers use most for development—complete with global searching and a master index to all five volumes—all on a single CD-ROM. It's incredibly portable. Just slip it into your laptop case as you commute or take off on your next trip andyou'll find everything at your fingertips with no books to carry.

System requirements: A web browser that supports HTML 3.2, Java, and Javascript, such as Netscape 3.0 or Internet Explorer 3.0. (The CD-ROM is readable on all UNIX and Windows platforms. However, current implementations of the Java Virtual Machine for the Mac do not support the Java search applet in the CD-ROM. A Web version of the Library is also available. See www.oreilly.com for more information.)

WebMaster in a Nutshell

By Stephen Spainhour & Valerie Quercia
1st Edition October 1996
374 pages, ISBN 1-56592-229-8

Web content providers and administrators have many sources for information, both in print and online. *WebMaster in a Nutshell* puts it all together in one slim volume for easy desktop access. This quick reference covers HTML, CGI, JavaScript, Perl, HTTP, and server configuration.

HTML: The Definitive Guide, 2nd Edition

By Chuck Musciano & Bill Kennedy
2nd Edition May 1997
552 pages, ISBN 1-56592-235-2

This complete guide is chock full of examples, sample code, and practical, hands-on advice to help you create truly effective web pages and master advanced features. Learn how to insert images and other multimedia elements, create useful links and searchable documents, use Netscape extensions, design great forms, and lots more. The second edition covers the most up-to-date version of the HTML standard (HTML version 3.2), Netscape 4.0 and Internet Explorer 3.0, plus all the common extensions.

JavaScript: The Definitive Guide, 2nd Edition

By David Flanagan
2nd Edition January 1997
664 pages, ISBN 1-56592-234-4

This second edition of the definitive reference guide to JavaScript, the HTML extension that gives web pages programming-language capabilities, covers JavaScript as it is used in Netscape 3.0 and 2.0 and in Microsoft Internet Explorer 3.0. Learn how JavaScript really works (and when it doesn't). Use JavaScript to control web browser behavior, add dynamically created text to web pages, interact with users through HTML forms, and even control and interact with Java applets and Navigator plugins. By the author of the bestselling *Java in a Nutshell*.

CGI Programming on the World Wide Web

By Shishir Gundavaram
1st Edition March 1996
450 pages, ISBN 1-56592-168-2

This book offers a comprehensive explanation of CGI and related techniques for people who hold on to the dream of providing their own information servers on the Web. It starts at the beginning, explaining the value of CGI and how it works, then moves swiftly into the subtle details of programming.

Developing Web Content *(continued)*

Information Architecture for the World Wide Web

By Louis Rosenfeld & Peter Morville
1st Edition January 1998 (est.)
200 pages (est.), ISBN 1-56592-282-4

Learn how to merge aesthetics and mechanics to design web sites that "work." This book shows how to apply principles of architecture and library science to design cohesive web sites and intranets that are easy to use, manage, and expand. Covers building complex sites, hierarchy design and organization, and techniques to make your site easier to search. For webmasters, designers, and administrators.

Learning VBScript

By Paul Lomax
1st Edition July 1997
616 pages, includes CD-ROM
ISBN 1-56592-247-6

This definitive guide shows web developers how to take full advantage of client-side scripting with the VBScript language. In addition to basic language features, it covers the Internet Explorer object model and discusses techniques for client-side scripting, like adding ActiveX controls to a web page or validating data before sending it to the server. Includes CD-ROM with over 170 code samples.

Web Client Programming with Perl

By Clinton Wong
1st Edition March 1997
228 pages, ISBN 1-56592-214-X

Web Client Programming with Perl shows you how to extend scripting skills to the Web. This book teaches you the basics of how browsers communicate with servers and how to write your own customized web clients to automate common tasks. It is intended for those who are motivated to develop software that offers a more flexible and dynamic response than a standard web browser.

Building Your Own WebSite

By Susan B. Peck & Stephen Arrants
1st Edition July 1996
514 pages, ISBN 1-56592-232-8

This is a hands-on reference for Windows® 95 and Windows NT™ users who want to host a site on the Web or on a corporate intranet. This step-by-step guide will have you creating live web pages in minutes. You'll also learn how to connect your web to information in other Windows applications, such as word processing documents and databases. The book is packed with examples and tutorials on every aspect of web management, and it includes the highly acclaimed WebSite™ 1.1 server software on CD-ROM.

Designing for the Web: Getting Started in a New Medium

By Jennifer Niederst
with Edie Freedman
1st Edition April 1996
180 pages, ISBN 1-56592-165-8

Designing for the Web gives you the basics you need to hit the ground running. Although geared toward designers, it covers information and techniques useful to anyone who wants to put graphics online. It explains how to work with HTML documents from a designer's point of view, outlines special problems with presenting information online, and walks through incorporating images into web pages, with emphasis on resolution and improving efficiency.

O'REILLY™

TO ORDER: **800-998-9938** • **order@oreilly.com** • **http://www.oreilly.com/**
OUR PRODUCTS ARE AVAILABLE AT A BOOKSTORE OR SOFTWARE STORE NEAR YOU.
FOR INFORMATION: **800-998-9938** • **707-829-0515** • **info@oreilly.com**

World Wide Web Journal *Volume 1*

Fourth International World Wide Web Conference Proceedings

*A publication of O'Reilly & Associates
and the World Wide Web Consortium (W3C)
Winter 1995/96
748 pages, ISBN 1-56592-169-0*

The *World Wide Web Journal* is a quarter-ly publication that provides timely, in-depth coverage of research developments on the World Wide Web. This issue con-tains the Conference Proceeding papers that were chosen for the 4th International World Wide Web Conference.

Key Specifications of the World Wide Web

*A publication of O'Reilly & Associates
and the World Wide Web Consortium (W3C)
Spring 1996
356 pages, ISBN 1-56592-190-9*

This issue of the *World Wide Web Journal* collects in a single volume the key specifi-cations that describe the architecture of the World Wide Web and how it works. It includes the specifications for HTML, HTTP, and URLs, plus the emerging standards for PNG, PICS, PEP, and CSS. A valuable reference for webmasters, application pro-grammers, and technical managers.

The Web After Five Years

*A publication of O'Reilly & Associates
and the World Wide Web Consortium (W3C)
Summer 1996
226 pages, ISBN 1-56592-210-7*

This issue reflects "The Web After Five Years" through an interview with Tim Berners-Lee, selections from the MIT/W3C Workshop on Web Demographics and Internet Survey Methodology, and papers from the Fifth International World Wide Web Conference. Also includes technical proposals from the W3C, lively debates on the size of the Web, the impact of advertising on caching, and ethical guidelines for using such data.

Building an Industrial Strength Web

*A publication of O'Reilly & Associates
and the World Wide Web Consortium (W3C)
Fall 1996
244 pages, ISBN 1-56592-211-5*

Issue four focuses on the infrastructure needed to create and maintain an "Industrial Strength Web," from network protocols to application design. It includes the first standard versions of core Web protocols: HTTP/1.1, Digest Authentication, State Management (Cookies), and PICS. This issue also provides guides to the specs highlighting new features, papers explaining modifications to 1.1 (sticky and compressed headers), extensi-bility, support for collaborative authoring, and using distributed objects.

O'REILLY™

TO ORDER: **800-998-9938** • *order@oreilly.com* • *http://www.oreilly.com/*
OUR PRODUCTS ARE AVAILABLE AT A BOOKSTORE OR SOFTWARE STORE NEAR YOU.
FOR INFORMATION: **800-998-9938** • **707-829-0515** • *info@oreilly.com*

World Wide Web Journal *Volume 2*

Advancing HTML: Style and Substance

*A publication of O'Reilly & Associates
and the World Wide Web Consortium (W3C)
Winter 1996/97
254 pages, ISBN 1-56592-264-6*

This issue is a guide to the specifications
and tools that buttress the user interface
to the World Wide Web: the technologies
that make the Web come alive on the
screen, on paper, in Braille, and on the
phone. It includes the HTML 3.2 spec and a corresponding user
guide, the CSS1 (cascading style sheets) spec and a corresponding user guide, a report on Amaya, an overview of GIF animation,
a look at how JavaScript can customize HTML, papers on web
accessibility, usability engineering, and multimedia design. We
also take a look behind the scenes at the members of the HTML
editorial review board, and their challenges in developing 3.2.

Scripting Languages: Automating the Web

*A publication of O'Reilly & Associates
and the World Wide Web Consortium (W3C)
Spring 1997
By Lincoln Stein, Clint Wong, Ron Petrusha,
Shishir Gundavaram, et al.
244 pages, 1-56592-265-4*

The informality, ease, and rapid development cycle of scripting languages make
them well suited to the constant change
common to most web sites. This issue of
the *World Wide Web Journal, Scripting Languages: Automating
the Web*, guides developers and users in choosing and deploying
scripting solutions such as JavaScript, Perl, VB, Python, and Win-
CGI. It also includes discussion of web database connectivity with
scripting languages, CGI programming, and an in-depth interview
with Perl developers Larry Wall and Tom Christiansen.

Web Security: A Matter of Trust

*A publication of O'Reilly & Associates
and the World Wide Web Consortium (W3C)
Summer 1997
By C. Bradford Biddle, Simson Garfinkel,
John Gilmore, Rohit Khare, Cricket Liu,
Lincoln Stein, et al.
282 pages, ISBN 1-56592-329-4*

This collection of timely, in-depth articles
frames web security as a matter of *trust*
rather than *cryptography*. It covers W3C's Digital Signature
Initiative (DSI), which breaks new ground in this area by binding
machine-readable labels to public key signatures. Other topics
include medical records privacy issues, signature legality, trust in
Internet information systems, electronic commerce, tips and
tricks for secure web programming, and an interview with
Christine Varney, FTC Commissioner and specialist in Internet-
related commerce issues.

XML: Principles, Tools, and Techniques

*A publication of O'Reilly & Associates
and the World Wide Web Consortium (W3C)
Fall 1997
By Dan Connolly (Guest Editor)
250 pages (est.), ISBN 1-56592-349-9*

XML, a landmark in the evolution of
Internet information systems, allows
authors to say what they mean, rather than
merely how to say it. The shift to XML will
unleash a diverse range of new applications, ranging from mathematical equation structures to new browser and client tools.
This issue of the *Web Journal*, by guest editor Dan Connolly, is
your first look at the technical specifications and early applications of a new data format that will rock every aspect of the Web,
including markup, linking, and exchange.

How to stay in touch with O'Reilly

1. Visit Our Award-Winning Web Site

http://www.oreilly.com/

★ "Top 100 Sites on the Web" —*PC Magazine*
★ "Top 5% Web sites" —*Point Communications*
★ "3-Star site" —*The McKinley Group*

Our web site contains a library of comprehensive product information (including book excerpts and tables of contents), downloadable software, background articles, interviews with technology leaders, links to relevant sites, book cover art, and more. File us in your Bookmarks or Hotlist!

2. Join Our Email Mailing Lists

New Product Releases

To receive automatic email with brief descriptions of all new O'Reilly products as they are released, send email to:
listmanager@list.ora.com
Put the following information in the first line of your message (*not* in the Subject field):
subscribe oreilly-news

O'Reilly Events

If you'd also like us to send information about trade show events, special promotions, and other O'Reilly events, send email to:
listmanager@list.ora.com
Put the following information in the first line of your message (*not* in the Subject field):
subscribe oreilly-events

3. Get Examples from Our Books via FTP

There are two ways to access an archive of example files from our books:

Regular FTP

- ftp to:
  ftp.oreilly.com
  (login: anonymous
  password: your email address)
- Point your web browser to:
  ftp://ftp.oreilly.com/

FTPMAIL

- Send an email message to:
  ftpmail@online.oreilly.com
  (Write "help" in the message body)

4. Contact Us via Email

order@oreilly.com
To place a book or software order online. Good for North American and international customers.

subscriptions@oreilly.com
To place an order for any of our newsletters or periodicals.

books@oreilly.com
General questions about any of our books.

software@oreilly.com
For general questions and product information about our software. Check out O'Reilly Software Online at **http://software.oreilly.com/** for software and technical support information. Registered O'Reilly software users send your questions to: **website-support@oreilly.com**

cs@oreilly.com
For answers to problems regarding your order or our products.

booktech@oreilly.com
For book content technical questions or corrections.

proposals@oreilly.com
To submit new book or software proposals to our editors and product managers.

international@oreilly.com
For information about our international distributors or translation queries. For a list of our distributors outside of North America check out:
http://www.oreilly.com/www/order/country.html

O'Reilly & Associates, Inc.
101 Morris Street, Sebastopol, CA 95472 USA
TEL   707-829-0515 or 800-998-9938
          (6am to 5pm PST)
FAX   707-829-0104

O'REILLY™

Titles from O'Reilly

Please note that upcoming titles are displayed in italic.

WEB PROGRAMMING

Apache: The Definitive Guide
Building Your Own Web Conferences
Building Your Own Website
CGI Programming for the World Wide Web
Designing for the Web
HTML: The Definitive Guide, 2nd Ed.
JavaScript: The Definitive Guide, 2nd Ed.
Learning Perl
Programming Perl, 2nd Ed.
Mastering Regular Expressions
WebMaster in a Nutshell
Web Security & Commerce
Web Client Programming with Perl
World Wide Web Journal

USING THE INTERNET

Smileys
The Future Does Not Compute
The Whole Internet User's Guide & Catalog
The Whole Internet for Win 95
Using Email Effectively
Bandits on the Information Superhighway

JAVA SERIES

Exploring Java
Java AWT Reference
Java Fundamental Classes Reference
Java in a Nutshell
Java Language Reference, 2nd Edition
Java Network Programming
Java Threads
Java Virtual Machine

SOFTWARE

WebSite™ 1.1
WebSite Professional™
Building Your Own Web Conferences
WebBoard™
PolyForm™
Statisphere™

SONGLINE GUIDES

NetActivism   NetResearch
Net Law   NetSuccess
NetLearning   NetTravel
Net Lessons

SYSTEM ADMINISTRATION

Building Internet Firewalls
Computer Crime: A Crimefighter's Handbook
Computer Security Basics
DNS and BIND, 2nd Ed.
Essential System Administration, 2nd Ed.
Getting Connected: The Internet at 56K and Up
Linux Network Administrator's Guide
Managing Internet Information Services
Managing NFS and NIS
Networking Personal Computers with TCP/IP
Practical UNIX & Internet Security, 2nd Ed.
PGP: Pretty Good Privacy
sendmail, 2nd Ed.
sendmail Desktop Reference
System Performance Tuning
TCP/IP Network Administration
termcap & terminfo
Using & Managing UUCP
Volume 8: X Window System Administrator's Guide
Web Security & Commerce

UNIX

Exploring Expect
Learning VBScript
Learning GNU Emacs, 2nd Ed.
Learning the bash Shell
Learning the Korn Shell
Learning the UNIX Operating System
Learning the vi Editor
Linux in a Nutshell
Making TeX Work
Linux Multimedia Guide
Running Linux, 2nd Ed.
SCO UNIX in a Nutshell
sed & awk, 2nd Edition
Tcl/Tk Tools
UNIX in a Nutshell: System V Edition
UNIX Power Tools
Using csh & tsch
When You Can't Find Your UNIX System Administrator
Writing GNU Emacs Extensions

WEB REVIEW STUDIO SERIES

Gif Animation Studio
Shockwave Studio

WINDOWS

Dictionary of PC Hardware and Data Communications Terms
Inside the Windows 95 Registry
Inside the Windows 95 File System
Windows Annoyances
Windows NT File System Internals
Windows NT in a Nutshell

PROGRAMMING

Advanced Oracle PL/SQL Programming
Applying RCS and SCCS
C++: The Core Language
Checking C Programs with lint
DCE Security Programming
Distributing Applications Across DCE & Windows NT
Encyclopedia of Graphics File Formats, 2nd Ed.
Guide to Writing DCE Applications
lex & yacc
Managing Projects with make
Mastering Oracle Power Objects
Oracle Design: The Definitive Guide
Oracle Performance Tuning, 2nd Ed.
Oracle PL/SQL Programming
Porting UNIX Software
POSIX Programmer's Guide
POSIX.4: Programming for the Real World
Power Programming with RPC
Practical C Programming
Practical C++ Programming
Programming Python
Programming with curses
Programming with GNU Software
Pthreads Programming
Software Portability with imake, 2nd Ed.
Understanding DCE
Understanding Japanese Information Processing
UNIX Systems Programming for SVR4

BERKELEY 4.4 SOFTWARE DISTRIBUTION

4.4BSD System Manager's Manual
4.4BSD User's Reference Manual
4.4BSD User's Supplementary Documents
4.4BSD Programmer's Reference Manual
4.4BSD Programmer's Supplementary Documents
X Programming
Vol. 0: X Protocol Reference Manual
Vol. 1: Xlib Programming Manual
Vol. 2: Xlib Reference Manual
Vol. 3M: X Window System User's Guide, Motif Edition
Vol. 4M: X Toolkit Intrinsics Programming Manual, Motif Edition
Vol. 5: X Toolkit Intrinsics Reference Manual
Vol. 6A: Motif Programming Manual
Vol. 6B: Motif Reference Manual
Vol. 6C: Motif Tools
Vol. 8 : X Window System Administrator's Guide
Programmer's Supplement for Release 6
X User Tools
The X Window System in a Nutshell

CAREER & BUSINESS

Building a Successful Software Business
The Computer User's Survival Guide
Love Your Job!
Electronic Publishing on CD-ROM

TRAVEL

Travelers' Tales: Brazil
Travelers' Tales: Food
Travelers' Tales: France
Travelers' Tales: Gutsy Women
Travelers' Tales: India
Travelers' Tales: Mexico
Travelers' Tales: Paris
Travelers' Tales: San Francisco
Travelers' Tales: Spain
Travelers' Tales: Thailand
Travelers' Tales: A Woman's World

O'REILLY™

TO ORDER: **800-998-9938** • **order@oreilly.com** • **http://www.oreilly.com/**

OUR PRODUCTS ARE AVAILABLE AT A BOOKSTORE OR SOFTWARE STORE NEAR YOU.

FOR INFORMATION: **800-998-9938** • **707-829-0515** • **info@oreilly.com**

International Distributors

UK, Europe, Middle East and Northern Africa (except France, Germany, Switzerland, & Austria)

INQUIRIES
International Thomson Publishing
Europe
Berkshire House
168-173 High Holborn
London WC1V 7AA, United Kingdom
Telephone: 44-171-497-1422
Fax: 44-171-497-1426
Email: itpint@itps.co.uk

ORDERS
International Thomson Publishing
Services, Ltd.
Cheriton House, North Way
Andover, Hampshire SP10 5BE,
United Kingdom
Telephone: 44-264-342-832
  (UK orders)
Telephone: 44-264-342-806
  (outside UK)
Fax: 44-264-364418 (UK orders)
Fax: 44-264-342761 (outside UK)
UK & Eire orders: itpuk@itps.co.uk
International orders: itpint@itps.co.uk

France

Editions Eyrolles
61 bd Saint-Germain
75240 Paris Cedex 05
France
Fax: 33-01-44-41-11-44

FRENCH LANGUAGE BOOKS
All countries except Canada
Phone: 33-01-44-41-46-16
Email: geodif@eyrolles.com

ENGLISH LANGUAGE BOOKS
Phone: 33-01-44-41-11-87
Email: distribution@eyrolles.com

Australia

WoodsLane Pty. Ltd.
7/5 Vuko Place, Warriewood NSW 2102
P.O. Box 935, Mona Vale NSW 2103
Australia
Telephone: 61-2-9970-5111
Fax: 61-2-9970-5002
Email: info@woodslane.com.au

Germany, Switzerland, and Austria

INQUIRIES
O'Reilly Verlag
Balthasarstr. 81
D-50670 Köln
Germany
Telephone: 49-221-97-31-60-0
Fax: 49-221-97-31-60-8
Email: anfragen@oreilly.de

ORDERS
International Thomson Publishing
Königswinterer Straße 418
53227 Bonn, Germany
Telephone: 49-228-97024 0
Fax: 49-228-441342
Email: order@oreilly.de

Asia (except Japan & India)

INQUIRIES
International Thomson Publishing Asia
60 Albert Street #15-01
Albert Complex
Singapore 189969
Telephone: 65-336-6411
Fax: 65-336-7411

ORDERS
Telephone: 65-336-6411
Fax: 65-334-1617
thomson@signet.com.sg

New Zealand

WoodsLane New Zealand Ltd.
21 Cooks Street (P.O. Box 575)
Wanganui, New Zealand
Telephone: 64-6-347-6543
Fax: 64-6-345-4840
Email: info@woodslane.com.au

Japan

O'Reilly Japan, Inc.
Kiyoshige Building 2F
12-Banchi, Sanei-cho
Shinjuku-ku
Tokyo 160 Japan
Telephone: 81-3-3356-5227
Fax: 81-3-3356-5261
Email: kenji@oreilly.com

India

Computer Bookshop (India) PVT. LTD.
190 Dr. D.N. Road, Fort
Bombay 400 001
India
Telephone: 91-22-207-0989
Fax: 91-22-262-3551
Email: cbsbom@giasbm01.vsnl.net.in

The Americas

O'Reilly & Associates, Inc.
101 Morris Street
Sebastopol, CA 95472 U.S.A.
Telephone: 707-829-0515
Telephone: 800-998-9938 (U.S. & Canada)
Fax: 707-829-0104
Email: order@oreilly.com

Southern Africa

International Thomson Publishing
Southern Africa
Building 18, Constantia Park
138 Sixteenth Road
P.O. Box 2459
Halfway House, 1685 South Africa
Telephone: 27-11-805-4819
Fax: 27-11-805-3648

O'REILLY WOULD LIKE TO HEAR FROM YOU

Which book did this card come from?

_____

Where did you buy this book?
- ❏ Bookstore　　　　　　❏ Computer Store
- ❏ Direct from O'Reilly　❏ Class/seminar
- ❏ Bundled with hardware/software
- ❏ Other _____

What operating system do you use?
- ❏ UNIX　　　　　❏ Macintosh
- ❏ Windows NT　❏ PC(Windows/DOS)
- ❏ Other _____

What is your job description?
- ❏ System Administrator　❏ Programmer
- ❏ Network Administrator　❏ Educator/Teacher
- ❏ Web Developer
- ❏ Other _____

❏ Please send me O'Reilly's catalog, containing
a complete listing of O'Reilly books and
software.

Name _____　Company/Organization _____

Address _____

City _____　State _____　Zip/Postal Code _____　Country _____

Telephone _____　Internet or other email address (specify network) _____

Nineteenth century wood engraving
of a bear from the O'Reilly &
Associates Nutshell Handbook®
Using & Managing UUCP.

POST CARD

BUSINESS REPLY MAIL
FIRST CLASS MAIL   PERMIT NO. 80   SEBASTOPOL, CA

Postage will be paid by addressee

O'Reilly & Associates, Inc.
101 Morris Street
Sebastopol, CA 95472-9902